The Holy Spirit

A Divine Person

The Holy Spirit

A Divine Person

Vinu V Das

Tabor Press

ISBN 978-1-997541-27-1

Chapter 1. Framing the Question: What Does "Person" Mean?

Before we can affirm that the Holy Spirit is a person rather than an impersonal force, we must first establish what "person" means in both human and divine contexts. This opening chapter sets the stage by surveying the classical and modern vocabulary, the theological stakes, and the methodological tools required to recognize personhood where it truly belongs. We begin by excavating the masks and faces of antiquity—how *persona* and *prosōpon* carried public, relational weight in Greco-Roman culture—then trace the philosophical debates over substance, relation, and self-awareness that prepared the ground for Christian reflection. From there we move into patristic corridors, medieval schools, and Reformation piazzas, showing how each era wrestled to confess God's tri-personal life without fracturing unity. Finally, we lay down criteria—intellect, will, emotion, relationship—that will guide our analysis of the Spirit's mind, heart, and actions in subsequent chapters. By the end of this chapter, readers will possess a clear, biblically rooted definition of "person" robust enough to withstand modern reductionism and sophisticated enough to encompass the Holy Spirit's unique mode of existence.

1 Linguistic and Philosophical Foundations

1.1 Persona and *Prosōpon*: Classical Etymologies

The Latin noun *persona* arose in the world of Roman theatre where a wooden or linen mask both concealed and revealed the actor's identity, allowing one performer to embody multiple roles without losing the single voice that came through the mask. From that concrete origin the word migrated into law, where a *persona* marked the standing of an individual before court and city, shaping ideas of rights and obligations in the *ius civile*. Parallel to this, the Greek term *prosōpon* moved from denoting a face to describing the public "front" of a speaker in civic debate, then broadened to cover the diplomatic face-saving arrangements of Hellenistic politics. Stoic philosophers infused *prosōpon* with metaphysical significance, asserting that every rational being must act "according to its own *prosōpon*," a seed of the later moral category of authenticity. When the Septuagint translated several Hebrew words for "face" (*panîm*) as *prosōpon*, an Old-Testament bridge was built (e.g., Num 6:25), subtly preparing Greek readers to imagine divine self-disclosure in personal terms. Early Jewish writers in Greek could therefore speak of Israel standing before the *prosōpon* of God without any hint that the word carried theatrical falseness. By the time Christian missionaries reached Rome, *persona* and *prosōpon* were waiting like empty flasks ready to be filled with Trinitarian wine. The eventual doctrinal use of *persona* retained the legal nuance of "someone with recognized agency" while shedding the theatrical sense of mere disguise. Thus, in both languages, the vocabulary for "person" began with visible faces and audible voices—fitting entry points for a theology that insists God speaks and looks upon humanity. This linguistic genealogy reminds us that Christian confession always commandeers cultural vessels, transfiguring them rather than discarding them. Understanding the masks and faces of antiquity guards modern readers from imagining that "person" imports modern individualism into the biblical text. It also warns against reducing the Spirit to an impersonal attribute, because the very words available to the first theologians carried public, relational overtones. Such etymological excavation therefore opens a path toward the conceptual work that Greco-Roman thinkers performed on these terms, a path that leads naturally into the next subsection on substance, relation, and self-awareness.

1.2 Substance, Relation, and Self-Awareness in Greco-Roman Thought

Greek metaphysics began to wrestle with the puzzle of unity and multiplicity centuries before Jesus was born, and that struggle shaped the philosophical background of the New-Testament world. Plato distinguished the unchanging realm of forms from the shifting world of appearances, setting up the question of how many discrete "ones" can share in a common essence. Aristotle answered by coining *ousia* ("substance") and *hupokeimenon* ("underlying subject"), insisting that individual beings possess both form and matter. The Stoics added a relational twist, teaching that a human's true "self" consists in rational harmony with the *logos* permeating the cosmos. Cicero imported these ideas into Latin, translating *prosōpon* as *persona* and embedding relational responsibility into Roman jurisprudence. Within this matrix, to be a "person" implied not only inward self-awareness but outward orientation toward community and law. Philosophers debated whether self-consciousness is a property of the soul alone or of the composite of soul and body, anticipating later Christian debates over the Spirit's immaterial yet personal reality. In civic life, a magistrate could possess several *personae*—one as father, another as senator—yet remain one *substantia*, an analogy later theologians would invert to speak of one divine essence subsisting in three persons. The Greco-Roman fascination with relational roles provided a conceptual sandbox where early apologists could articulate the distinction between what God is (*ousia*) and how God exists (*hypostasis*). Importantly, these thinkers never relegated personhood to raw power or impersonal energy; rather, will, speech, and mutual recognition marked the truly personal. That conviction created philosophical pressure against reducing the Holy Spirit to a mere divine force. The groundwork laid here invites us to watch how Christian bishops adapted, critiqued, and sanctified these notions during the explosive doctrinal controversies of the second and third centuries. Accordingly, we turn next to the earliest Christian discourse on personhood, where the mask, the substance, and the relation meet the crucified and risen Lord.

1.3 Modern Personalism, Dialogical Philosophy, and Relational Ontology

While patristic and medieval categories remained dominant in church dogmatics, the modern era reopened the question of *persona* under the influence of existential crises and social upheavals. Nineteenth-century idealists such as Hegel located personhood in self-conscious Spirit coming to know itself through history, sowing seeds for both Marxist and theological appropriations. In the twentieth century, Martin Buber's *I–Thou* thesis crystalized a dialogical vision in which genuine personhood arises only within reciprocal address, a framework that dovetails with Trinitarian revelation where Father, Son, and Spirit eternally say "Thou" to one another (John 17:24). Personalists like Emmanuel Mounier insisted that the person is "a spiritual being constituted as such by his relation to others," an insight later echoed in John Zizioulas's Orthodox account of being as communion. Analytic philosophers added precision by differentiating first-person indexicals ("I") from third-person descriptions, showing that personal identity involves irreducible self-reference—a point paralleling the Spirit's self-attestation in Acts 13:2 ("Set apart for *Me* Barnabas and Saul"). Contemporary neuroscience contributes data on relational brain wiring, suggesting biological resonance with biblical claims that humans image a relational God (Gen 1:26-27). Yet technological individualism threatens to fracture community, making the Spirit's role as bond of love (Rom 5:5) an urgently practical doctrine. Modern gender and disability studies further expand the horizon, arguing that true personhood cannot be measured by autonomous productivity but by capacity for communion—again resonating with the Spirit who intercedes precisely when believers are weak (Rom 8:26). These currents challenge the church to articulate a pneumatology that honors both distinct personal agency and radical relational openness. They also expose the inadequacy of any account that domesticates the Spirit into a private experience divorced from social justice. By surveying modern thought we gain fresh language for confessing the Spirit as the empowering "Thou" who meets every "I," preparing us to consider how translation and culture mediate that confession across the globe. Consequently, we proceed to examine the cross-cultural translation of personhood terminology, noting the gains and perils when ancient words travel into new linguistic homes.

1.4 Translational Challenges Across Cultures and Eras

When missionaries rendered "Holy Spirit" into Syriac, Coptic, Latin, and later Germanic tongues, they discovered that not every language boasts a ready equivalent for "person." The Syriac fathers adopted *qnoma* to mirror Greek *hypostasis*, but the term also carried connotations of concrete reality versus abstract essence, fueling Nestorian misunderstandings. Medieval Arabic translations faced the hurdle that *ruh* (spirit) already referred to a created life-force in pre-Islamic poetry, necessitating careful catechesis to maintain divine transcendence. In many Bantu languages today, the closest match for "person" denotes a visible body, forcing translators to rely on relational verbs—"the Spirit who hears and speaks"—to convey personality without corporeality. East Asian renderings encounter Confucian categories in which social role (*ren*) outweighs individual agency, requiring the church to preach that the Spirit is more than ritual harmony; He is the living Counselor (John 14:16-17). Bible societies must decide whether to capitalize pronouns for the Spirit, a typographic choice that shapes readers' intuition of personhood. Oral cultures transmit theology through story and song rather than abstract nouns, so narratives like the Spirit grieving (Eph 4:30) become vital windows into His personal nature. Translation also intersects politics: in Soviet Russia, rendering the Spirit as "Life-Giving Breath" was tolerated, whereas "Divine Person" sounded subversive against materialist ideology. Contemporary sign-language Bibles must express "Spirit" with a sign depicting invisible wind that acts intentionally, reaffirming agency without speech sounds. Each linguistic crossing reminds us that the gospel is both translatable and perilously mistranslatable. Effective mission therefore demands a nimble yet faithful doctrine of personhood that can inhabit diverse semantic fields without abandoning biblical core. Having traced the linguistic journey from masks to global idioms, we are ready to explore how early Christian teachers forged doctrinal definitions amid persecution and debate, a story that unfolds in the next major section.

2 Personhood in Early Christian Discourse

2.1 Tertullian's *Trinitas, Una Substantia*

Around AD 200 the fiery North-African lawyer Tertullian penned *Adversus Praxean*, coining the term *trinitas* while insisting on one *substantia* shared by three *personae*. Against Monarchian opponents who collapsed Father, Son, and Spirit into serial roles, he argued that a father cannot be his own son, nor can the sender be identical with the one sent (John 8:42). Tertullian's legal training surfaced as he compared the Godhead to a corporation in which multiple shareholders possess one patrimony, yet remain distinct partners. He appealed to the baptismal formula of Matthew 28:19, noting that three names under a single "authority clause" imply genuine personal plurality. His Latin breakthrough demonstrated that *persona* could name divine individuality without lapsing into tritheism. Crucially, Tertullian called the Spirit "another Advocate" (*alius Paracletus*), not a mere emanation, anchoring His personhood in the promise of John 14:16. He accused Praxeas of having "driven away the Paraclete" by denying His distinction and thus depriving believers of relational fellowship. Even so, Tertullian retained the monarchy of the Father, balancing unity and diversity with a legal metaphor of one root and three shoots. His language would echo in the Western creed for centuries, shaping Augustine and the Latin scholastics. By highlighting the Spirit's voice in the prophets (Isa 48:16) and His appointment of Paul (Acts 13:2), Tertullian undercut any impersonal

19

reading. His articulation set the stage for later Cappadocian refinement, showing that grammar must follow soteriology: believers experience Father, Son, and Spirit distinctly, therefore doctrine must confess them distinctly. The controversies he ignited would flare into larger ecumenical debates, pushing the church toward clearer terminology. That clarifying process unfolds next among the Greek-speaking theologians of Cappadocia, whose conceptual precision would prove decisive for Nicene orthodoxy.

2.2 The Cappadocians: *Hypostasis* Distinguished from *Ousia*

Basil of Caesarea, Gregory of Nyssa, and Gregory of Nazianzus confronted Arian and Pneumatomachian reductions by sharpening the difference between *ousia* (what God is) and *hypostasis* (who God is). They illustrated the distinction with the analogy of three individual humans sharing one humanity, careful to stress that divine unity is infinitely tighter than human similarity. Basil's treatise *On the Holy Spirit* argued from Scripture's doxological patterns: when the Spirit is named alongside the Father and the Son in benedictions such as 2 Corinthians 13:14, He must be co-equal in rank. Gregory of Nazianzus contended that the Spirit "proceeds" (John 15:26) rather than being created, and that procession is a personal property parallel to the Son's begetting. They coined the formula "one *ousia*, three *hypostaseis*," putting linguistic precision to pastoral use, for a God who is less than tri-personal cannot save through relational embrace. Gregory of Nyssa employed Moses' rock-struck twice (Num 20:11) as a typological argument: the Spirit is not a second-class agent but the living water issuing from Christ to quench the church's thirst (1 Cor 10:4). The Cappadocians displayed rhetorical brilliance, turning Arian proof-texts inside out and showing that verses like John 14:28 ("the Father is greater than I") refer to the Son's incarnate economy, not eternal inferiority—a strategy that equally protects the Spirit's status. They rebutted Pneumatomachians by pointing out that blasphemy against the Spirit is unforgivable (Matt 12:31-32), a gravity incompatible with treating Him as a creature. Their theological orations inspired the Council of Constantinople (381 AD) to confess the Spirit as "Lord, the giver of life." By carving conceptual space for personal properties within divine unity, the Cappadocians handed a legacy to subsequent councils. That legacy would soon crystallize in conciliar decrees, to which we now turn to trace the institutional ratification of the Spirit's personhood.

2.3 Councils of Nicaea (AD 325) and Constantinople (AD 381): Doctrinal Milestones

The Council of Nicaea initially focused on the Son's relation to the Father, declaring Him *homoousios* ("of one substance") against Arius's claim that "there was when He was not." Though the Holy Spirit received scant mention in 325, the homoousion principle implicitly safeguarded His deity because Scripture arrays Father, Son, and Spirit in a single baptismal name (Matt 28:19). Between councils, anti-Spirit factions (the Pneumatomachians) exploited Nicene silence, urging that the Spirit is a ministering angel rather than divine. Athanasius and the Cappadocians marshaled biblical evidence— Psalm 104:30, Acts 5:3-4, 1 Corinthians 12:11—showing the Spirit creates, indwells, and apportions gifts at will, acts befitting God alone. At Constantinople the creed was expanded: the Spirit is "the Lord and life-giver, who proceeds from the Father, who with the Father and the Son is worshiped and glorified, who spoke through the prophets." Each clause targeted a specific heresy: "Lord" refuted subordinationism, "life-giver" countered claims that He merely distributes created grace, "who spoke through the prophets" dismissed the notion of an impersonal force. The council's doxological motive is evident: only God may receive worship (Rev 22:9), yet Christians from earliest times baptized and blessed in the Spirit's name. The Niceno-Constantinopolitan Creed thus engraved Trinitarian personhood onto the church's liturgical heart. Its authority curbed doctrinal speculation but did not end debate; linguistic refinements would follow in the West, as scholastics probed how three divine "someones" remain one divine "something." Those medieval explorations are our next concern.

2.4 Pneumatomachian Controversy and the Defense of the Spirit's Identity

The Pneumatomachians dubbed themselves "Spirit-fighters" by their insistence that the Spirit ranks below the Son, perhaps as the first among creatures. They exploited verses like John 20:22 ("He breathed on them and said, 'Receive the Holy Spirit'"), arguing that a breath cannot be equal to the breather. Basil countered that the metaphor of breath signifies intimate procession, not ontological inferiority, just as the Son being the "radiance" of the Father's glory (Heb 1:3) entails full deity. Pneumatomachians also appealed to Proverbs 8, interpreting Wisdom as the Spirit, thereby demoting Him to created wisdom; Augustine would later redirect that passage to the pre-incarnate Word, safeguarding Trinitarian balance. The controversy pushed theologians to scrutinize every biblical text mentioning the Spirit, refining hermeneutics that still guide exegesis today. Ultimately, the movement's refusal to worship the Spirit

21

clashed with the church's unbroken liturgical instinct, forcing the conclusion that their theology contradicted doxology. The Cappadocian strategy of arguing from baptismal praxis proved decisive: believers being immersed "into" the Spirit cannot be immersing into a creature. The defeat of Pneumatomachianism secured the Spirit's status for subsequent theological development, yet questions about internal divine relations lingered, setting the stage for scholastic elaboration during the Middle Ages. That scholastic adventure forms the next major section, continuing our historical progression.

3 Medieval and Reformation Refinements

3.1 Scholastic Categories: *Suppositum*, Subsistent Relations, and Divine Simplicity

Medieval theologians inherited the creedal framework and pursued analytical precision, convinced that clarity fosters worship. Thomas Aquinas defined a divine *person* as "a subsistent relation within the divine essence," marrying Aristotelian substance metaphysics to Augustinian relational insight. The term *suppositum* distinguished an individual bearer of nature from the nature itself, enabling theologians to speak of the Spirit as a "who" not merely a "what." Thomas argued that because God is absolutely simple (*simplicissimus*), distinctions among persons cannot be parts but must be relations of origin—thus the Spirit's procession from Father and Son is His personal property. Scotus nuanced the debate, emphasizing formal distinctions that avoid real division while preserving genuine relational identity. Medieval debates on divine simplicity pushed against any hint that the Spirit is a derivative energy, for simplicity entails that the entire divine essence is present in each person, ruling out hierarchical gradations. Mystics like Bonaventure complemented scholastic rigor by portraying the Spirit as the fiery kiss between Father and Son, an image that balances relation with affective warmth (Song of Solomon 1:2 as allegory). Ecclesial practice mirrored scholastic doctrine: the Western Mass concluded with *Ite, missa est* under a Trinitarian blessing that invoked the Spirit's name, confirming His co-equal personhood. These medieval refinements equipped the church to face the linguistic and doctrinal storms of the Reformation. As humanists recovered biblical languages, the very categories of *suppositum* and subsisting relation would be tested against the fresh authority of Scripture, drawing us to the next subsection on Aquinas's lasting influence.

3.2 Aquinas on Three "Someone-nesses" in One Essence

Aquinas reasoned that intellective nature naturally produces a word (*verbum*), and will naturally spirates love (*amor*), mapping Word and Love onto Son and Spirit (John 1:1; Rom 5:5). He insisted that these internal processions are personal because they involve distinct relations of origin: the Son as "begotten," the Spirit as "breathed." The *Summa Theologiae* carefully parsed objections: if relations alone constitute personhood, do we worship relations? Aquinas replied that in God, relation and subsistence coincide without composition, preserving simplicity. His famous article declaring that the Holy Spirit proceeds "from the Father and the Son as from one principle" fortified Western Trinitarian theology. Scripturally he invoked John 20:22 (the Son breathing the Spirit) and Galatians 4:6 (Spirit of the Son), arguing that double procession safeguards the unity of divine action ad extra. Aquinas also addressed whether the Spirit has an intellectual procession like the Son; he denied this, preserving the distinction between knowledge and love. His synthesis shaped medieval catechesis, influencing art where the Spirit appears as a dove emanating from both Father and Son. Critics later accused Thomism of over-rationalizing mystery, but its precise categories helped Reformers refute anti-Trinitarian radicals. Aquinas thus stands as a hinge between medieval scholasticism and Reformation biblicism, preparing the conversation we explore in the next subsection.

3.3 Reformers on the Economic Trinity and *Sola Scriptura* Method

Martin Luther affirmed the Nicene-Constantinopolitan Creed yet shifted emphasis from speculative procession to the Spirit's role in justification by faith (Rom 1:17). He called the Spirit "the true schoolmaster of the heart," stressing personal pedagogy over metaphysical definition. John Calvin retained Western procession language but grounded it in the Spirit's internal witness (*testimonium internum*) that assures believers of Scripture's authority. The Reformers rejected medieval hierarchical mediations, insisting that the Spirit grants direct access to Christ (Eph 2:18). While they trimmed scholastic speculation, they did not dilute personhood; Calvin's *Institutes* identifies the Spirit as "the fountain of all gifts," whose sovereign distribution in 1 Corinthians 12:11 presupposes volition. Anabaptists highlighted Acts' narrative of Spirit-led community, while Lutheran and Reformed confessions preserved Trinitarian creeds verbatim. The Reformation thus democratized pneumatology, placing the personal Spirit in every believer's hands through vernacular Bibles. This shift set the stage for fresh post-Reformation scholastic consolidation, which we now survey.

3.4 Post-Reformation Protestant Scholasticism and the Reassertion of *Hypostatic* Property

Seventeenth-century theologians like Francis Turretin responded to Socinian denial of the Trinity by reasserting classical categories, coining the term "hypostatic property" to denote the distinctive marks of each divine person. They systematically listed the Spirit's properties: procession, spiration, mission, and operation of sanctification. Biblical exegesis anchored each claim: Acts 5:3-4 for deity, 1 Corinthians 2:10 for intellect, Ephesians 4:30 for emotion, and John 16:13 for volition. Turretin argued that an impersonal force cannot be "grieved," framing the text as a logical syllogism that forces personal conclusion. Protestant scholastics also defended the *filioque* as a bulwark against Unitarianism, but they showed increased willingness to dialogue with Eastern caution. Their tables and loci shaped seminarians for centuries, embedding Trinitarian orthodoxy in confessional documents like the Westminster Confession. Yet their heavy scholastic method sometimes obscured the devotional warmth of earlier mystics, paving the way for pietist critiques that emphasized experiential communion with the Spirit. That experiential turn presses us to revisit Scripture itself, which is the focus of the next major section.

4 Personhood in Scripture

4.1 Hebraic Concepts of *Nephesh* and *Ruach* as Relational Life

Hebrew anthropology never separates life from relationship; *nephesh* (soul) names a living being throbbing with desire (Gen 2:7), while *ruach* (spirit) denotes not only wind but personal breath that speaks and strives (Gen 6:3). The Old Testament ascribes to the *ruach* of God creative artistry (Ex 31:3), emotive vexation (Isa 63:10), and guiding intelligence (Neh 9:20), all hallmark traits of personhood. Psalmists cry, "Where shall I flee from your Spirit?" (Ps 139:7), implying omnipresent relational pursuit rather than impersonal energy. Prophets depict the Spirit as instructing Israel through inner whispers and external signs (Isa 30:21), culminating in the promise that He will dwell within hearts (Ezek 36:27). These Hebrew textures seed New-Testament insight by showing that God's breath acts intentionally, feels grief, and covenants with people. They also protect against reading the Testament as pure metaphor; the anthropomorphic language serves revelatory purpose, not poetic flourish. By grasping the relational density of *ruach*, we discern continuity between Israel's God and the Paraclete Jesus promises. Such continuity paves the way for examining humanity's imaging role, which we tackle in the next subsection.

4.2 *Imago Dei*: Covenant Identity and Communal Capacity

Genesis 1:26-27 grounds human dignity in the divine plurality: "Let *us* make humanity in *our* image," a proto-hint of Father, Son, and Spirit in counsel. The image entails stewardship (Gen 1:28) and relational likeness—humans speak, create, and covenant as God does. If image bearers are inherently personal, the original must be super-personal; an impersonal deity could not imprint personal identity. The New Testament intensifies this link: renewal in Christ is "according to the image of the Creator" (Col 3:10), accomplished by the Spirit's transforming work (2 Cor 3:18). Thus anthropology and pneumatology intertwine—personal Spirit re-personalizes fallen persons. Understanding the image sets theological guardrails: denying the Spirit's personhood subtly erodes human personhood, fostering reductionist ethics. With this anthropological foundation set, we explore the Greek use of *prosōpon* and *hypostasis* in Scripture.

4.3 New-Testament Usage of *Prosōpon* and *Hypostasis*

Paul employs *prosōpon* when describing Moses' veiled face and believers' unveiled gazing upon the Lord's glory (2 Cor 3:18), signaling personal encounter rather than mystical absorption. Hebrews 1:3 calls the Son the "imprint of God's *hypostasis*," proving that personal subsistence is biblical, not merely philosophical. The Spirit's speech in Acts 13:2 ("I have called them") carries a first-person pronoun, underscoring *hypostatic* self-reference. Together these usages show Scripture itself seeds the language that later councils harvest. Recognizing this continuity leads naturally to the narrative patterns of divine self-disclosure that weave Father, Son, and Spirit into a single redemptive drama.

4.4 Narrative Patterns of Divine Self-Disclosure (Father – Son – Spirit)

Biblical stories reveal tri-personal choreography: the Father sends the Son (John 3:16), the Son lives by the Spirit (Luke 4:1), and after resurrection breathes the Spirit on disciples (John 20:22). At Jesus' baptism, the Father speaks, the Spirit descends, and the Son emerges from the water (Matt 3:16-17). Pentecost completes the arc: the exalted Son pours out the Spirit promised by the Father (Acts 2:33). These narratives function like lived grammar lessons, training readers to distinguish agents without dividing essence. They also ground doctrinal reflection in concrete history, ensuring that personhood remains relational and missional. With scriptural patterns established, we now tackle the conceptual triad of essence, person, and nature to sharpen theological precision.

5 Distinguishing Essence, Person, and Nature

5.1 Classical Metaphysics versus Biblical Narrative Categories

Philosophers speak of substance and accidents, while prophets speak of covenant and story; integrating them demands careful translation. Essence (*ousia*) answers "What is God?"—infinite, immutable, holy (Mal 3:6; Rev 4:8). Person (*hypostasis*) answers "Who is God?"—Father, Son, Spirit relating eternally (John 17:24). Nature refers to attributes shareable by each person, while person refers to relations of origin unshared. Biblical narrative supplies the living data—voices, missions, covenant acts—onto which metaphysical scaffolding is fitted. Without metaphysics, narratives risk slipping into modalism; without narrative, metaphysics risks abstract speculation. Distinguishing categories prevents category errors such as treating the Spirit's gifts as His essence or confusing the Father's begetting with temporal creation. Recognizing category boundaries prepares us to guard against ancient and modern heresies, the subject of the next subsection.

5.2 Guarding Against Modalism and Tritheism

Modalism collapses persons into roles; tritheism fractures essence into three gods. Scripture resists both: Jesus prays to the Father (John 17), yet insists He and the Father are one (John 10:30). The Spirit searches the deep things of God (1 Cor 2:10) yet distributes gifts diversely (1 Cor 12:11), displaying unity and distinction. Maintaining essence–person distinction preserves monotheism while affirming relational communion. It equips pastors to refute popular analogies—ice-water-steam (modalism) or three men (tritheism)—that mislead congregations. With safeguards in place, we can appreciate the communicative interplay of divine persons, examined next.

5.3 *Communicatio Idiomatum* and the Unique Personal Properties

The communication of idioms states that actions of either nature in Christ belong to the one person of the Son; analogously, operations of the Trinity are inseparable yet appropriated to distinct persons. Creation is attributed to the Father as source, redemption to the Son as mediator, sanctification to the Spirit as perfecter, though all three cooperate (Heb 9:14). The Spirit's unique property is procession and spiration, manifest in breathing imagery (John 20:22) and wind motifs (Acts 2:2). Appreciating these personal properties prevents confusion when Scripture credits resurrection to both Father (Rom 6:4) and Spirit (Rom 8:11). Such clarity leads to practical application: believers praying for empowerment address the Spirit as willing agent, not abstract force. Having distinguished properties, we can now consider applying "person" to a non-corporeal Spirit.

5.4 Applying "Person" to the Spirit: Non-Corporeal, Yet Fully Personal

Some object that without a human body or incarnate face, the Spirit cannot be "person." Scripture refutes this by portraying angelic beings as personal without embodiment analogous to ours (Heb 1:14), and by attributing to the Spirit intellect, emotion, and volition (Rom 8:27; Eph 4:30; 1 Cor 12:11). Personhood therefore rests on relational capacity, not material structure. The Spirit's invisibility even amplifies intimacy: He dwells within believers' spirits (1 Cor 3:16) and testifies directly to conscience (Rom 9:1). Modern analogies from software or radio waves fall short unless they include self-awareness and will. The church thus confesses the Spirit as the fully personal third hypostasis who makes the Father known through the Son. This conceptual endpoint loops back to our opening etymological journey: from masks to metaphysics, the word "person" has been stretched to encompass the deepest mystery of divine life. With foundational categories secured, the book is prepared to explore the Spirit's love, fellowship, and jealous yearning in the relational dynamics of Chapter 7.

6 Personal Attributes as Criteria

6.1 Rational Intellect: Knowing, Searching, Revealing

The New Testament repeatedly affirms that the Holy Spirit possesses an active, discerning intellect. The apostle Paul declares that "the

Spirit searches everything, even the depths of God" (1 Cor 2:10), presupposing conscious inquiry. If the Spirit lacked intellect, such searching would be a mere mechanism, not a deliberate act. In Romans, Paul adds that the Spirit's intercession "searches the heart" (Rom 8:27), implying an ability to perceive hidden motives—another function of understanding rather than brute force. Moreover, Jesus promises that the Spirit of truth "will guide you into all truth" (John 16:13), which entails ongoing cognitive engagement with revelation. The Spirit's teaching office, as described in John 14:26 ("He will teach you all things"), presupposes both knowledge of divine realities and the power to communicate them. Without personal intellect, the Spirit's role in illuminating Scripture and forming godly wisdom would collapse into mere emotional suggestion. Furthermore, analogies to human teachers become incoherent if the teacher is not thinking, assessing, and selecting content. Paul's contrast between human wisdom and "spiritual wisdom" (1 Cor 2:6–7) underscores that the Spirit's knowledge transcends but does not abolish rational reflection. In Corinth, the Spirit commissions prophets and teachers (1 Cor 12:28), assigning them roles that require mental acuity and doctrinal accuracy. The Spirit's revelatory gifts are not random downloads of power but tailored insights, indicating intentionality. Recognizing the Spirit's intellect guards against viewing Him as a cosmic algorithm; instead, we see a divine mind at work. As we move from knowing to willing, we will see how the same Spirit makes decisions and directs His people with sovereign purpose.

6.2 Volitional Agency: Choosing, Sending, Distributing Gifts

Scripture ascribes clear acts of choice and direction to the Holy Spirit, demonstrating that He wills and acts in freedom. In 1 Corinthians 12:11 Paul states that the Spirit apportions spiritual gifts "to each one as He wills," using a verb of volition rather than necessity. If the Spirit were only a force, one could not speak of His "will" to distribute gifts differently; agencies choose, energies do not. Similarly, Acts 13:2 records, "the Holy Spirit said, 'Set apart for me Barnabas and Saul'," a direct imperative that presumes intention and purposes. The Spirit's mission commands appear repeatedly in the early church's narrative, as when Philip is told, "Go south to the road... that goes down from Jerusalem to Gaza" (Acts 8:29). Such redirection is not the push of an impersonal wind but the guiding word of a Person. Even forbidding speech in certain regions (Acts 16:6) reflects proactive decisions, not random obstacles. This divine agent also initiates the calling of leaders: in Acts 6:3 the apostles instruct the church to choose seven men "full of the Spirit and wisdom," indicating that the Spirit empowers particular individuals for office. In Acts 10:19 Peter hears, "Get up, go downstairs, and accompany them without hesitation," again underscoring the Spirit's commissioning role. Throughout Acts, decisions attributed to the Spirit shape the mission's geography, personnel, and timing—tasks requiring willful intention. Recognizing volitional agency prevents us from reducing the Spirit to a mere wind, a background element, or a psychological impulse. Instead, we see a sovereign Director orchestrating redemptive history. As we continue, we will turn from will to heart, exploring the Spirit's emotional life.

6.3 Affective Capacity: Loving, Rejoicing, Grieving

The divine emotions attributed to the Holy Spirit reveal His personal depth. Scripture warns, "Do not grieve the Holy Spirit of God" (Eph 4:30), equating relational sorrow with quenching His presence among believers. If grief were an impersonal force, it could neither be wounded nor lamented. In Isaiah 63:10 we read that the Israelites "rebelled, and grieved His Holy Spirit," again presenting grief as a personal reaction to disobedience. Conversely, the Spirit produces joy in Paul's shorthand for the kingdom: "righteousness and peace and joy in the Holy Spirit" (Rom 14:17). This joy is not an effect of dopamine, but a divine exuberance shared with believers. The Spirit's love is so central that Paul says, "God's love has been poured into our hearts through the Holy Spirit who has been given to us" (Rom 5:5). That phrasing implies the Spirit Himself as the agent of love, bridging divine affection and human reception. The metaphor of jealousy also appears: James reminds us, "The Spirit... longs jealously over us" (Jas 4:5), evoking the fervent zeal of a Person guarding a covenant relationship. These emotional capacities—grief, joy, love, jealousy—are distinctive of persons, not vague energies. Understanding the Spirit's affective life underscores the depth of His intimacy with the church. From feeling, we now turn to the interpersonal dimension: how the Spirit relates in speech and witness.

6.4 Relational Intentionality: Speaking, Witnessing, Interceding

Perhaps the most striking marker of personhood is communication. In Acts 8:29 the Spirit says to Philip, "Go over there and join this chariot," using direct speech to convey intention. At Pentecost, the Spirit's audible "rush of a violent wind" (Acts 2:2) accompanies the utterance of words in many tongues, pointing to a communicative purpose. Jesus promises that the Spirit "will testify about me" (John 15:26), a legal metaphor of courtroom witness that presupposes agency and accountability. The Spirit's intercession in Romans 8:26 takes the form of "groanings too deep for words," a paradoxical speech act where the Spirit itself prays within us. None of these could occur if the Spirit were a featureless force; they require the relational intentionality of a living Subject. The Spirit also identifies sins, righteousness, and judgment to the world (John 16:8), performing a prosecutorial function within the cosmic trial. In Acts 13:4 we read that "being sent out by the Holy Spirit," Paul and Barnabas embark on mission, highlighting a sending relationship: the Spirit interacts with human agents, not static matter. This communicative intentionality aligns with biblical patterns of divine self-disclosure, bridging sacramental signs and prophetic words. Recognizing the Spirit's speech prevents reduction to abstract "inspiration" and honors His ongoing dialogue with the church. Having surveyed the Spirit's mind, will, heart, and interpersonal speech, we now turn to the methodological tools that guide all healthy pneumatology.

7 Methodological Considerations for Pneumatology

7.1 Biblical-Theological Versus Systematic Approaches

Pneumatology can be pursued two primary ways: by tracing the Spirit's activity through the Bible's unfolding storyline (biblical-theological) or by organizing doctrines into topical categories (systematic). The former attends to historical context, literary genres, and progressive revelation, ensuring that the Spirit's personhood surfaces naturally in narrative, prophecy, law, wisdom, Gospel, and epistle. For example, the Spirit's creation role in Genesis (Gen 1:2) gains new depth when seen alongside Pentecost (Acts 2) and the new-creation hope in Romans 8:19–22. The systematic approach, by contrast, gathers texts under headings such as "attributes," "missions," and "gifts," facilitating comparative analysis and theological synthesis. While systematic theology helps clarify definitions (e.g., person, essence, processions), it risks abstracting the Spirit's dynamic presence into static propositions. A robust pneumatology must hold these methods in tension: narrative roots guard doctrine against decontextualization, while systematic rigor prevents anecdotal excesses. Historical theology further tempers both by showing how past communities read Scripture under the Spirit's guidance. Together, these methodologies ensure that our confession of the Spirit's personhood remains rooted in canonical witness and resistant to reduction. From here, we consider the corrective role of history itself.

7.2 The Role of Historical Theology as Hermeneutical Check

Historical theology surveys the church's reception of the Spirit's identity across time and cultures. By examining how Tertullian, the Cappadocians, Aquinas, Calvin, and modern Pentecostals have interpreted key texts, we gain perspective on interpretive biases and blind spots. For instance, the Pneumatomachian controversy in the fourth century highlighted the importance of Acts 5:3–4 to affirm the Spirit's deity, while sixteenth-century debates over justification illuminated the Spirit's role in sanctification. Pietist movements emphasized experiential communion, bringing personal devotion to the fore, whereas later liberal theologies sometimes secularized the Spirit into a moral principle. Awareness of these shifts prevents us from repeating past errors—such as modalism or impersonalism—and encourages us to recover lost emphases. Historical theology thus functions as a hermeneutical safeguard, filtering out extrabiblical innovations while retrieving forgotten insights. It reminds us that the Spirit not only inspired Scripture but also guides the ongoing interpretation of Scripture within the church. With this tool in hand, we now explore how analogical language and apophatic humility shape our discourse about the Spirit.

7.3 Analogy, Accommodation, and Apophatic Restraint in God-Talk

Because God transcends all creatures, human language can only approximate divine realities. Theologians employ analogy—speaking of God's attributes by comparison, not univocal identity—to say that the Spirit is "wise" without implying human-style cognition. Accommodation recognizes that God condescends, using human words and images (e.g., wind, dove) to reveal Himself without exhausting His essence. Yet analogy and accommodation must be balanced by apophatic restraint, acknowledging that the Spirit's personhood ultimately defies full description: "Now we see in a mirror dimly" (1 Cor 13:12). This triad of approaches prevents idolatrous literalism—taking metaphors as exact equivalents—and avoids nihilistic skepticism. In practical terms, when we call the Spirit "Teacher," we mean He instructs in ways analogous to a human teacher, yet infinitely surpasses it. Similarly, metaphors of spiration and procession capture relational process without mapping Greek philosophical categories directly onto the divine substance. Apophatic humility tempers our confidence, prompting us to pair every assertion with worship, lest we mistake our models for reality. With disciplined language in place, we can more safely navigate cross-cultural translations of personhood.

7.4 The Limits of Language and the Necessity of Doxology

Even our best analogies fall short of the Spirit's fullness, leaving gaps that only praise can fill. When scholastic precision reaches its terminus, doxology begins: we ascribe to the Spirit titles like "Lord," "Giver of Life," and "Advocate" because these reflect biblical worship patterns (Nicene-Constantinopolitan Creed). Worship both celebrates what God has revealed and acknowledges what remains beyond speech. Doxological liturgies—Sursum Corda ("Lift up your hearts"), Sanctus ("Holy, holy, holy")—embody the Spirit's presence more than definitions ever could. When theologians despair of clarity, the church counters with songs, prayers, and benedictions that place the Spirit at the center. This liturgical practice affirms that personhood cannot be contained by propositions alone but is enacted in relational adoration. In preparation for practical engagement, our final section will draw these threads together into a concise working definition.

8 Contemporary Relevance

8.1 Worship and Liturgy: Addressing the Spirit Directly

In many traditions, the Holy Spirit receives only cursory mention in the service, yet Scripture invites direct address. The New Testament records prayers "in the Holy Spirit" (Jude 20) and benedictions that invoke the Spirit's fellowship (2 Cor 13:14). Liturgies that include an epiclesis—calling down the Spirit on baptismal waters or the Eucharistic elements—embody the belief that the Spirit initiates and completes worship. Neglecting this can lead congregations to view the Spirit as passive or optional. By contrast, prayers that explicitly name the Spirit as Comforter and Guide awaken corporate expectancy for His active presence. Contemporary worship movements increasingly rediscover the value of Spirit-invocations, singing hymns like "Spirit of the Living God" or praying "Come, Holy Spirit." Such practices remind believers that worship is not merely human action but the Spirit's work within us. Integrating Spirit-focused liturgies requires catechesis: explaining why we pray "Send Your Spirit" even though He is already present. Moreover, decentralized house churches and micro-churches often practice Spirit-led gatherings without formal liturgy, illustrating that direct address transcends style. As worship renews focus on the Spirit, believers learn to discern His movements in song, silence, and sacrament. From worship we flow naturally into prayer, where relational formation takes shape.

8.2 Relational Prayer and Spiritual Formation

Prayer is the laboratory of our friendship with the Spirit. When Paul exhorts believers to "pray in the Spirit on all occasions" (Eph 6:18), he presumes an existing relational intimacy that fuels perseverance. Spiritual formation traditions—monastic lectio divina, Ignatian examen, Wesleyan bands—all rely on the Spirit's illumination to transform surface routines into deep encounters. Retreat centers, silent monasteries, and charismatic prayer houses each provide distinct environments where the Spirit forms disciples. In small-group spiritual direction, mentors listen for the Spirit's nudges in another's story, cultivating mutual support. Digital natives also experiment with breath prayers—short, Spirit-inspired phrases repeated throughout the day—to maintain awareness of His presence. As believers mature, the Spirit leads them through seasons of consolation and desolation, teaching discernment. Effective formation thus combines personal disciplines with communal practices, all animated by the Spirit's personal companionship. Having seen how the Spirit shapes prayer, we turn to the ethical outworking of that personal agency.

8.3 Ethical and Missional Implications of Personal Agency

If the Spirit is truly a Person, His presence carries moral weight. Grieving the Spirit (Eph 4:30) becomes a relational breach, not merely a failure to perform. Likewise, obeying the Spirit's "leading" in justice issues—advocating for the poor, welcoming the stranger—reflects His will for righteousness (Isa 1:17). Missionally, acknowledging the Spirit's agency compels us to depend on Him for guidance rather than resort to pragmatic strategies alone. Spiritual gifts become not tools but relationships to divine mentors: the gift of mercy models Christ's compassion, the gift of leadership embodies the Spirit's ordering wisdom. Churches that recognize the Spirit's ethical personhood prioritize holistic mission—feeding bodies, preaching justice, caring for creation—because the Spirit intercedes for creation's liberation (Rom 8:19–22). Training leaders to hear the Spirit's voice in boardrooms, classrooms, and public squares prevents secular drift. Ethical formation thus flows from acknowledging the Spirit's will and emotional investment in human flourishing. This conviction readies the way to confront popular reductions of spirituality.

8.4 Countering Impersonal "Energy" Models in Popular Spirituality

Modern New Age and self-help movements often speak of a vague "life force" or "energy field," depersonalizing what Scripture reveals as a divine Person. Reiki practitioners, chakra enthusiasts, and mindfulness coaches tap into an impersonal "power," yet offer no true fellowship or revelation. Such models can seduce Christians into believing that spirituality is about self-optimization rather than relational surrender. By contrast, the biblical Spirit invites confession, offers counsel, and reproves sin, all personal interactions absent from energy-based systems. Churches must equip believers to discern the difference: the Spirit's gifts bear fruit of love, joy, and peace (Gal 5:22–23), not mere subjective well-being. Testimonies of genuine conversion and transformation underscore that the Spirit is not a neutral force but the living God who gives new birth (John 3:5–8). Public apologetics should highlight the Spirit's personal attributes and relational commitments, offering a richer alternative to impersonal energy. As we integrate these contemporary insights, we stand ready to define "person" in a way that both honors Scripture and addresses today's challenges.

9 Toward a Working Definition

9.1 Synthesizing Historical and Biblical Insights

After surveying ancient etymologies, patristic dogmas, medieval precisions, Reformers' recoveries, and scriptural narratives, we see converging lines: personhood entails self-awareness, relational orientation, volition, and communication. Biblical texts attribute to the Spirit searching intellect (1 Cor 2:10), sovereign will (1 Cor 12:11), deep affection (Rom 5:5), and intentional speech (Acts 13:2). Historical theology affirms these traits in the church's creeds and confessions, while methodological reflection warns us against over-literalizing categories. Rather, we embrace an analogical model that holds divine simplicity alongside personal distinction. The Spirit emerges as a distinct hypostasis within the one divine ousia, eternally relating to Father and Son and dynamically engaging creation. This synthesis honors the canon's storyline and the community's worshipful confession, forging a definition both faithful to biblical testimony and robust enough to address modern reductionisms. Having brought these strands together, we now state the definition that will guide every chapter ahead.

9.2 A Relational, Communicative, Intentional Subject Distinct Within the Godhead

Our working definition reads: **The Holy Spirit is the third divine Person—fully God yet personally distinct—who eternally proceeds from the Father (and the Son), communicates the Father's will through the Son, and enters into personal relationship with believers by knowing, teaching, comforting, interceding, and empowering them for God's mission.** This definition captures the Spirit's tri-logical origin, relational communion, and active involvement in redemptive history. It stresses that the Spirit is not an impersonal attribute, a mere manifestation of God's power, or a symbolic force, but a living Person—able to think, choose, feel, speak, and love. Grounded in biblical data and ecumenical consensus, it sets clear boundaries against theological error while inviting experiential trust. This relational, communicative, intentional portrayal will frame every subsequent discussion, ensuring we never stray into abstract categories divorced from the Spirit's dynamic presence. With our terminology and definitions secured, we are now equipped to explore the Spirit's rich relational attributes in Chapter 7.

9.3 Preview: How This Definition Guides the Remainder of the Book

Armed with a precise understanding of personhood, readers can now discern the Spirit's distinct activities in each thematic focus ahead. In Chapter 7 we will explore how the Spirit's love, fellowship, and jealous yearning shape communal life. Chapter 8 will unpack His concrete ministries—teaching, guiding, advocating, interceding—and show how those flow from His personal nature. Subsequent chapters will trace Trinitarian dynamics, indwelling sanctification, gift distribution, prayer, worship, and practical living in the Spirit. Throughout, our working definition will serve as a constant hermeneutical lens, ensuring that every attribute and action we examine is rooted in the Spirit's identity as a divine Person. By maintaining this focus, the book aims not only to inform the mind but also to deepen relational trust in the Holy Spirit as our eternal Companion.

Conclusion In this foundational chapter we have traced the contours of "person" from ancient masks and legal standing through medieval abstractions to the living narrative of Scripture. We have seen how the Spirit's intellect, will, emotion, and speech mark Him as a distinct Subject within the unity of the Godhead. Methodological reflections have reminded us of the need for balanced interpretation, while contemporary applications have shown why a robust pneumatology is vital for worship, prayer, ethics, and mission today. Our working definition—calling the Spirit a relational, communicative, intentional

Person—will guide every subsequent exploration, preventing theoretical drift and inviting experiential encounter. As we move forward, each chapter will deepen this relational knowledge, inviting readers not merely to assent to doctrine but to live in conscious step with the Holy Spirit, the divine Advocate, Teacher, and Friend.

Chapter 2. Misconceptions Through the Ages: Force, Energy, or Breath?

Throughout church history the Holy Spirit has too often been reduced to an impersonal force—wind that moves when it will, a cosmic energy to be tapped, or simply "breath" without relational depth. These distortions have obscured the Spirit's true identity as the third divine Person. In this chapter we will trace how various cultures and theological movements have misunderstood and misrepresented the Spirit, and we will prepare to reclaim a biblical-Trinitarian vision that honors His personhood. By examining ancient mythologies, intertestamental texts, Greco-Roman philosophies, and early heretical controversies, we confront the roots of depersonalization and uncover the corrective path back to Scripture's living portrait.

1 Ancient Near-Eastern Backgrounds: Wind, Storm, and Cosmic Vitality

1.1 "Breath of the gods" in Mesopotamian cosmologies

Mesopotamian creation myths speak of divine beings breathing life into clay figures, suggesting that breath itself constituted the animating principle of humanity. In the *Enuma Elish*, the god Ea fashions humans from the blood of a slain god mixed with clay, then imparts consciousness via divine breath. This act established a pattern wherein mortality and vitality hinge on inhalation—an idea

Mesopotamian priests ritualized by breathing words over consecrated statues. When Israel encountered these rituals, the biblical authors repurposed the imagery: Genesis 2:7 describes Yahweh forming man from dust and "breathing into his nostrils the breath of life," but they refrained from identifying that life-breath as a distinct person. Instead, Israel's *ruach* remains Yahweh's personal Spirit (Gen 1:2), not a shared commodity among capricious deities. Despite the poetic overlap, Israel's God never splits His essence to animate multiple gods; He alone breathes life. The Psalmist exalts that "when you send forth your Spirit, they are created" (Ps 104:30), anchoring creativity in a personal divine agent rather than impersonal air. Ancient Near-Eastern sensibilities thus provided rich metaphors, yet Israel's appropriation always pointed beyond impersonal breath to the relational God who speaks and wills. Recognizing this nuance helps prevent reading Genesis as endorsing polytheistic life-force doctrines. From Mesopotamia we turn to Egypt's own breath-rituals, noting yet another variation on the theme.

1.2 Egyptian concepts of life-breath and royal animation

In ancient Egypt the Pharaoh was thought to possess divine *ka*, a life-force akin to breath that distinguished him from ordinary mortals. Priestly texts detail ceremonies in which offerings and spells ensure the Pharaoh's *ka* remains vibrant, sustaining cosmic order (*ma'at*). Temples featured hypostyle halls with columns shaped like papyrus stems, symbolizing the living breath of creation. Though this Egyptian concept shares with Israelite *ruach* the notion of breath as life, it was rooted in a hierarchical, monarchic theology rather than in covenant relationship. Hebrews sometimes lived in Egyptian contexts (Joseph, Moses), and Exodus 14:21–22 narrates the Spirit of God drying the Red Sea—an act of divine breath that defies Pharaoh's life-force potency. Unlike Egyptian priests who sought to harness the *ka*, Israelite prophets warned that misusing God's breath amounted to hubris (Isa 30:33). The Spirit's involvement in prophecy (2 Sam 23:2) further distinguishes personal agency from impersonal energy. While Egyptians ritually maintained breathing statues, Israel's *ruach* breaks into history to speak through individuals, not through mechanical invocation. Understanding Egyptian parallels thus clarifies what Israel did not mean by *ruach*—a technical life-force subject to formulaic control. As we move westward, Canaanite storm-deities add yet another layer to the ancient view of breath and wind.

1.3 Canaanite storm-deity imagery and its linguistic echoes (*ruach, pnoe*)

Canaanite religion revered Baal as the storm-god whose powerful winds and thunderclaps signaled divine victory over chaos. Ugaritic texts praise Baal's "mighty breath" that dries the sea and fells mountains. Archaeologists have unearthed ritual inscriptions invoking Baal's *pnoe* ("blowing") to deliver rain or quell drought. The Hebrew *ruach* in Genesis 1:2—"the Spirit of God was hovering over the waters"—borrows this storm-imagery vocabulary yet subverts it: instead of an alien Baal-breath, it is Yahweh's own Spirit shaping creation. Elijah's contest on Mount Carmel (1 Kgs 18) dramatizes this reversal when Yahweh sends wind, rain, and fire, showcasing His supreme storm-power over Canaanite rivals. Prophetic texts like Hosea 4:19 decry Israel's longing for the "breath" of foreign gods, warning that misplaced devotion to impersonal wind-powers brings devastation. The biblical authors use familiar storm-thunder tropes but reframe them to reveal a personal God whose breath serves covenant purposes, not capricious whims. Recognizing the Canaanite backdrop shows how easily Israel might have lapsed into animism; instead, they insisted that the divine *breath* must bear moral and relational dimensions. From Canaan's storms we turn to Israel's polemic—their deliberate contrast between God's personal Spirit and surrounding impersonal breath-powers.

1.4 Israel's appropriation and polemic against nature-deifying myths

Throughout the Old Testament, Israel consistently differentiates Yahweh's Spirit from deified nature-forces. In Isaiah 40-55 the prophet mocks idols carved from wood and metal, incapable of breath, while exalting the living God who "speaks, and the earth melts" (Isa 55:10). Ezekiel's vision of dry bones (Ezek 37:1-14) emphasizes that only Yahweh's Spirit can animate lifeless corpses into a standing army, refuting any notion that wind alone could restore life. In Psalm 104 every creature depends on God's Spirit for renewal, yet the Spirit remains sovereign, not subject to creation's cycles. Psalm 29 ascribes thunder to the voice of Yahweh, not an impersonal storm. This consistent polemic underscores that the Spirit's actions involve personal intent—delivering, judging, consoling—far beyond inert energy. When Israel entered exile, prophets emphasized the need for an inner Spirit (Ezek 36:26-27) to transform hearts, not merely external mechanics. Thus the biblical witness repurposes ancient metaphors to reveal a Spirit whose personhood transforms worldviews. Having surveyed the Ancient Near East and Israel's corrective engagement, we are prepared to examine how Second-

Temple Judaism further developed—or distorted—conceptions of Spirit.

2 Second-Temple Judaism and Inter-Testamental Literature

2.1 *Ruach* in the Dead Sea Scrolls: deterministic zeal and sectarian charisma

The Dead Sea Scrolls introduce *ruach* language that occasionally veers toward deterministic zeal, portraying the Spirit as an impersonal force animating the Qumran community's strict piety. Certain scrolls speak of a "spirit of truth" guiding the Teacher of Righteousness in doctrinal exegesis, yet this guidance often reads like mystical enthusiasm unmoored from broader Israelite worship. Community rules demand ritual purity to attract the Spirit's presence, implying that external conformity functions as a lever on cosmic energy. Simultaneously, sectarian texts describe a "Spirit of jealousy" that separates the elect from sinners, a personalization of zeal that blurs the line between divine Personhood and human fanaticism. Yet the Community's own wisdom writings still echo Ezekiel's promise (Ezek 36:27) of an inner Spirit effecting heart renewal rather than mere external performance. These tensions reveal that even devout Jews could slip into depersonalizing *ruach*, treating it as a mechanism for social cohesion. Notably, penitent Community members plead for the Spirit to remove impurity (1QS 4:14), suggesting relational dynamics—grief, shame, restoration—alongside deterministic imagery. Awareness of Qumran readings thus warns us that mysticism alone does not guarantee a personal pneumatology; only biblical critique can tether enthusiasm to covenant fidelity. We now turn to Jewish wisdom and Hellenistic philosophy for another layer of interpretation.

2.2 Wisdom of Solomon and Philo: Spirit as moralized cosmic reason

In the Wisdom of Solomon (c. 1 st cent. BC), the Spirit of God is lauded as wisdom's source, a divine intellect ordering creation in accordance with righteousness. Yet this Spirit often appears as an impersonal cosmic principle, aligning more with Platonic *nous* than with a personal envoy. Philo of Alexandria likewise equates the Jewish *ruach* with Logos, framing it as the mediating principle between transcendent God and mutable world. Philo's allegorical approach speaks of the Spirit as the "breath of life" pervading all beings, yet lacks narratives of personal speech or emotional response. His view emphasizes moralized reason—Spirit-guided virtue—over relational interaction, creating an ethical abstraction that parallels Greek Stoicism. While both writers aim to defend Jewish monotheism before Hellenistic audiences, their abstractions risk obscuring the Spirit's personal ministry revealed in Scripture. The Wisdom of Solomon even describes the Spirit as passing through generations like an undifferentiated wind (Wis 1:5), a metaphor that can devolve into cosmic flux. Philo's allegories, though creative, seldom present the Spirit praying, grieving, or speaking—actions integral to personhood. Recognizing these moralized cosmic reason models helps us appreciate the later Judeo-Christian insistence on a Spirit who engages believers in concrete dialogue. Our next stop is the apocalyptic literature that introduces angelic intermediaries, further complicating notions of Spirit.

2.3 Apocalyptic writings: angelic spirits and heavenly intermediaries

Books like 1 Enoch and 2 Baruch feature elaborate pantheons of angels—including spirits of heaven, underworld, and world-pepper—that shuttle messages between God and humanity. The "Watcher" angels in 1 Enoch (1 Enoch 7) transmit heavenly knowledge but also introduce rogue spirits that mislead, implying a plurality of spirit-beings beyond Yahweh's single Spirit. Such texts blur the boundary between God's personal Spirit and created spirit-messengers, making it challenging to maintain a unitary pneumatology. Jewish apocalypse often depicts spirits as quasi-autonomous beings inhabiting cosmic realms, sometimes even influencing weather or fate, closer to impersonal forces than to divine Personhood. Yet these writings also preserve strong monotheistic affirmations: heavenly spirits operate only by divine commission, not by independent volition. The tension between angelic intermediaries and the singular personal Spirit recurs in New Testament debates (e.g., Col 2:18; Gal 1:8). Understanding these apocalyptic imaginaries equips us to navigate Second-Temple complexity without collapsing Yahweh's Spirit into the background cast of celestial functionaries. From Jewish apocalyptic we proceed to early rabbinic discussions of prophetic cessation, where alternative conceptions of Spirit emerge.

2.4 Proto-rabbinic debates on prophetic cessation and Bat-Qol (heavenly voice)

In the early rabbinic period, a debate arose over whether prophecy had ceased after the destruction of Solomon's Temple. The concept of *Bat-Qol*—a "daughter-voice" or heavenly echo—provided a way to experience divine guidance without direct prophetic Spirit-outpouring. The *Bat-Qol* was often described as an impersonal voice that imparted guidance on legal or ritual matters, lacking the emotional warmth and relational dialogue of earlier prophetic Spirit experiences. Rabbinic sages sometimes preferred this controlled manifestation over risky prophetic impulses, effectively sidelining the personal Spirit in favor of predictable oracles. Yet Talmudic anecdotes (e.g., *Taanit* 7a) recount instances where a more robust Spirit-presence—tears, shaking, ecstatic speech—returned, suggesting that the personal Spirit could not be fully constrained. The later Pharisees affirmed that while direct prophecy ceased, the Spirit still moved in wisdom, resurrection hope, and heart transformation (Hosea 3:5). These discussions highlight the danger of constricting the Spirit to impersonal voice phenomena, demonstrating that personal communion cannot be replaced by mechanical revelation. Understanding the proto-rabbinic approach shows us why early Christians rejoiced when Jesus promised "another Counselor" (John 14:16), restoring vibrant relational Spirit-interaction. Having surveyed Second-Temple perspectives, we are equipped to consider the Greco-Roman philosophical milieu that influenced early Christian thought.

3 Early Greco-Roman Context and Philosophical Absorption

3.1 Stoic *pneuma* as animating fire and universal logos-seed

Stoics conceived *pneuma* as an all-pervading, fiery breath that binds cosmos and soul into a unified organic whole. Within this framework, *pneuma* is the "world-soul," an impersonal tension that gives coherence to matter and shapes human character via cosmic reason. Ethical discourse urged individuals to live "according to nature," aligning inner *pneuma* with universal logos. Christian thinkers like Justin Martyr encountered these ideas in Platonic schools, leading some to speak of the Spirit as analogous to Stoic *pneuma*. However, Scripture's Spirit differs: He never binds believers into impersonal cosmic conformity but invites personal relationship and moral freedom (Gal 5:1). Where Stoics saw fate, biblical authors celebrate Spirit-led contingency (Acts 16:6–10). Yet the Stoic vocabulary provided early apologists with ready terms for divine breath and logos, facilitating communication with educated Gentiles. Recognizing the Stoic influence clarifies why early Christian writers had to insist the Spirit thinks (1 Cor 2:10), feels (Eph 4:30), and chooses (1 Cor 12:11)—qualities a mere fiery tension could not possess. From Stoicism we turn to Middle Platonism's bridging role.

3.2 Middle Platonism: hierarchy of immaterial forces and daemons

Middle Platonic philosophers built on Plato's forms, positing a hierarchy of intermediary beings—daemons and angelic spirits—through which the supreme One interacts with material realms. These intermediaries function as impersonal forces or moral spirits, sometimes guiding souls toward virtue, sometimes tempting them toward vice. Philo's allegories of the Spirit as Logos carry echoes of this system, though he insists on monotheistic sovereignty. For Christians reading Philo, the challenge was distinguishing Yahweh's personal Spirit from a legion of subordinate daemons. The New Testament tightens the boundary: Ephesians 6:12 warns believers struggle not against flesh and blood but against "spiritual hosts of wickedness," highlighting a cosmic battle, yet only one Spirit is offered for guidance (Gal 5:25). Revelation's dragon and beast imagery (Rev 12–13) further dramatize the clash between impersonally diabolic spirits and the personal Spirit of God. Recognizing Platonist hierarchies helps us see why the early church canonizes only one Spirit as divine ally. From the abstract intermediaries we proceed to Gnostic emanations.

3.3 Gnostic emanations: the Spirit fragmented into syzygies and aeons

Gnostic sects reimagined divine reality as a pleroma of emanations—multiple Aeons or syzygies—emanating from an ineffable First Principle. In Valentinian systems, Sophia's fall produces a lesser spirit realm, populating the cosmos with half-divine beings. The "Holy Spirit" in some Gnostic texts becomes one among many Aeons, detached from Scripture's covenant narrative. Salvation in Gnosticism often entails awakening a spark within, a fragment of Sophia, rather than receiving a personal Spirit who indwells and intercedes. Early church fathers like Irenaeus (Against Heresies) rebutted Gnostic demotion by insisting that the Spirit's gifts, fruits, and witness (Gal 5:22–25; Rom 8:16) testify to a personal divine agent rather than an impersonal emanation. Gnostic multiplicity also risked polytheistic dualism, contrary to monotheistic confession. Recognizing Gnostic distortions clarifies why orthodox theology affirms one Spirit (Eph 4:4) united in identity with Father and Son. Having surveyed Gnostic abstractions, we move to the church's first debates over Spirit's true identity.

3.4 Christian apologetic struggle to retain transcendence and personhood

Apologists like Justin Martyr and Athenagoras sought to translate the Spirit into philosophical categories while resisting Gnostic and Stoic reductions. Justin employs Stoic logos parallels but insists the Spirit speaks through prophets (Justin, *Dialogue with Trypho*). Athenagoras argues against otherwise-worshipped idols, stating that worshipping the Spirit alone constitutes true monotheism (Athenagoras, *Embassy for the Christians*). They faced the twin perils of seeming to adopt pagan concepts or of being dismissed as irrational. Their success lay in weaving biblical narrative—Spirit hovering at creation (Gen 1:2), empowering judges (Judg 3:10), guiding apostles (Acts 13:2)—into dialogues that acknowledged cultural vocabularies yet insisted on personal agency. These apologetic efforts laid groundwork for later councils to define Spirit's personhood against impersonal and heretical alternatives. From their labors we transition to the epoch of formal patristic controversy.

4 Patristic Era Distortions and Defenses

4.1 Monarchian reductionism: Spirit as modal operation of the One God

Monarchians such as Praxeas argued that Father, Son, and Spirit are merely modes or aspects of the one God, denying distinction among persons. They cited texts like John 10:30 ("I and the Father are one") to collapse the Spirit into unconscious divine action—akin to an impersonal force emanating from God's essence when needed. Tertullian countered this modalism in *Against Praxeas*, insisting that just as the flesh in John 6:53 demands eating and drinking the Son's flesh and blood, so believers must relate to the Spirit as distinct Comforter (John 14:16). He pointed out that speaking of God's Spirit "coming" presupposes personal movement, not mere activation of divine power. Monarchianism thus prompted defenders to sharpen the language of three co-equal hypostases sharing one substance. Having turned modalism aside, the church still faced foes denying Spirit's full deity.

4.2 Pneumatomachian ("Spirit-fighters") denial of full deity

Pneumatomachians insisted the Spirit was a created being, an exalted creature rather than God. They exploited Luke 11:13 ("how much more will the heavenly Father give the Holy Spirit") to argue that only the Father gives the Spirit as gift, implying creaturely status. The Cappadocians retorted by showing that only One can grant what He alone possesses; table fellowship in early church liturgies invoked the Spirit for prayer (1 Cor 11:24–25), a form of divine worship incompatible with creaturehood. Basil's *On the Holy Spirit* marshaled Old-Testament proofs—Psalm 104:30, Isaiah 63:10—to demonstrate the Spirit's divine acts of creation and judgment. This struggle made explicit that impersonal readings of *ruach* must be rejected, for the Spirit exercises sovereign power reserved for God alone.

4.3 Montanist enthusiasm: Spirit equated with ecstatic utterance

The Montanist movement of the late second century emphasized ecstatic prophecy and new revelations, sometimes issuing women prophets as primary authorities. Critics accused Montanists of treating the Spirit as a mere wind of emotional exaltation, unaccountable and undisciplined. Tertullian's later sympathy for Montanism shows the lure of experiential immediacy, yet he still maintained the Spirit's full deity and normative apostolic witness. The church ultimately affirmed that genuine prophecy must align with apostolic teaching (1 Cor 14:29) rather than break continuity, ensuring that personal encounter with the Spirit remains within canonical bounds.

4.4 Cappadocian response—clarifying hypostatic individuality

Facing both modalism and Pneumatomachianism, the Cappadocians articulated the distinction between *ousia* (essence) and *hypostasis* (person). They insisted that the Spirit proceeds from the Father, not created by Him, thus maintaining full deity. Their eloquence laid the foundation for Constantinople I to recognize the Spirit as "Lord and giver of life." By defining personhood in terms of relations of origin and personal properties—intellect, will, emotion—they refuted impersonal reductions definitively. This doctrinal breakthrough marks the culmination of early defenses and ushers in the more refined debates of the medieval church.

5 Medieval Mysticism and Scholastic Abstractions

5.1 "Bond of love" metaphor: fruitful yet prone to relational dilution

The medieval mystics frequently described the Spirit as the "bond of love" uniting the Father and the Son, a poetic image drawn from Romans 5:5, which speaks of God's love poured into our hearts by the Holy Spirit. They saw in this bond a model for human communion, encouraging believers to cultivate inner rest in divine embrace. However, overuse of the metaphor sometimes led to privatized spirituality, where the Spirit became an impersonal "glue" rather than a dynamic Person who empathizes and converses. Mystical authors like Bernard of Clairvaux dwelt on the sweetness of this love-bond, yet produced abstract writings that readers found difficult to translate into concrete pastoral care. While the image fostered affective devotion, it risked severing the relational dynamism evident when the Spirit convicts of sin (John 16:8) or intercedes (Rom 8:26). The scholastic theologians attempted to rescue the metaphor by insisting that the bond is an active personal relation, not a static quality of God's essence. They argued that if the Spirit merely functions as a bond, He would lack a will and could not choose to distribute gifts (1 Cor 12:11). Pastors thereafter emphasized experiential testimonies— stories of grief, call, and guidance—to balance the metaphorical language. Renaissance devotional writers, in turn, linked the bond image to the bridal mysticism of Song of Solomon, imbuing it with erotic overtones that sometimes distracted from the Spirit's broader ministries. Nonetheless, the bond metaphor persisted because it sprang from the biblical theme of unity in love (Eph 4:3–4). Modern theologians reclaim it by emphasizing its relational depth: the Spirit is both the bond and the personal Agent who animates that bond. This reformulation sets the stage for examining how scholastic habitus and grace further abstracted the Spirit's personal ministry.

5.2 Scholastic *habitus* and grace: Spirit flattened into created quality

Medieval scholastics like Thomas Aquinas developed the concept of *habitus*—a stable disposition within the soul—to explain sanctification. They categorized grace as a created habit, an infused quality enabling moral virtue, and often located the Spirit within this framework. Consequently, the Spirit's work of holiness risked being viewed as an impersonal force that "inheres" in the soul like a habitus, rather than as a Person who wills, guides, and empathizes. When Aquinas spoke of sanctifying grace as "the habitual gift, by which God dwells in us," he meant the Spirit's presence, but his technical vocabulary made grace sound more like a static attribute than an active Advocate (John 14:16). Critics noted that if grace is merely a habitus, it cannot intercede within us or groan beyond words (Rom

8:26). Pastoral manuals therefore incorporated both doctrinal precision and devotional narrative, reminding believers that the Spirit is neither a mere inner power nor an abstract quality, but the living Sanctifier who convicts, consoles, and transforms. By the late Middle Ages, mystics like Meister Eckhart reasserted the Spirit's immediacy, yet often slipped into language that sounded like pantheistic indwelling. The Council of Trent's canons on justification responded by emphasizing that sanctifying grace is a gift from the personal Spirit, preserving relational agency. This corrective paved the way for Reformation debates over Spirit-driven justification and sanctification.

5.3 Popular piety: dove, flame, and uncritical symbol-only devotion

In medieval art and devotion the Spirit often appears as a dove descending from heaven or as tongues of flame above believers' heads. These symbols, drawn from Matthew 3:16 and Acts 2:3, distilled complex pneumatology into accessible iconography. While they powerfully communicated divine presence, they also fostered a devotional piety that appreciated symbol without probing personal agency. Churchgoers could gaze upon a stained-glass dove and experience comfort without necessarily engaging the Spirit in prayer or discernment. Preachers sometimes exploited these images to evoke emotion, yet offered little teaching on the Spirit's intellect, will, or relational capacity. Lay brotherhoods introduced novenas invoking the seven gifts of the Spirit (Isa 11:2), but often without clarifying how those gifts arise from personal interaction rather than from impersonal empowerment. The Brethren of the Common Life sought to recover a more personal devotion through communal prayer and scriptural meditation, emphasizing that the Spirit "prays with sighs too deep for words" (Rom 8:26). Nevertheless, popular symbols retained currency because symbols shape the imagination more quickly than doctrines. Contemporary worship planners learn from this history: symbols must be paired with explanation and invitation to dialogue, lest congregations relegate the Spirit to mere decoration. From symbol abuse we transition to exploring how medieval dialogue with Islamic and Jewish thought further complicated conceptions of divine breath.

5.4 Islamic and Jewish medieval dialog partners on divine breath

Medieval Christian scholars engaged with Islamic theologians who described God's breath (*nafas*) as the origin of angels, life, and cosmic order. Muslim philosophers like Avicenna spoke of a "first intellect" emanating spirit for creation, while Jewish thinkers such as

Maimonides emphasized divine simplicity, denying any real multiplicity in divine activity. Christian interlocutors found points of contact—both affirmed that breath conveys life—but also stark divergences. Islamic insistence on God's absolute unity resisted any internal relations, pushing medieval Christians to defend the Spirit's procession without implying composite deity. Jewish debates over the Bat-Qol (the Heavenly Voice) prompted Christians to specify that only one Spirit, personally, speaks (Acts 13:2). Scholastic disputations at universities required logicians to articulate why the Spirit's procession from the Father and the Son does not divide divine essence. These cross-confessional dialogues enriched Christian theology by forcing finer distinctions, yet also risked importing adversarial categories that flattened relational personhood into metaphysical necessity. The corrective lay in returning to biblical narrative: no dialogue partner challenges the Spirit's personal speech recorded in Acts like the Qumran sect or Epicureans did. This resolution readied the church to face the seismic shifts of the Reformation, to which we now turn.

6 Reformation to Enlightenment: From Presence to Principle

6.1 Radical Reformation and inner-light individualism

The Radical Reformers—Anabaptists, Quakers, and others—emphasized the "inner light," a direct illumination of the Spirit within each believer. They challenged state-church hierarchies by asserting that no external institution could mediate the Spirit's counsel. While this restored personal immediacy, it sometimes led to extreme individualism, neglecting the Spirit's communal and doctrinal dimensions. George Fox of the Quakers famously declared that the Spirit speaks "in our hearts," a comforting but vague assertion that sometimes prioritized subjective impressions over scriptural norms (2 Tim 3:16–17). Without accountability, inner-light movements risked multiplicity of spirits, echoing Gnostic fragmentation (1 John 4:1–3). Yet their insistence on personal access pressured the Magisterial Reformers to clarify that the Spirit teaches in harmony with Scripture, not in isolation from it (1 John 2:27). The Radical Reformers also pioneered democratic meetings where any moved by the Spirit could speak, foreshadowing modern charismatic gatherings. Their legacy underscores the balance needed: upholding personal encounter while safeguarding communal discernment. As we move to Magisterial Protestantism, we see how the Spirit's presence was reframed as doctrinal principle.

6.2 Continental scholastic Protestantism: forensic Spirit and neglect of communion

Lutheran and Reformed scholastics retained much medieval metaphysics but recast the Spirit's work primarily in forensic terms—imparting justification, applying Christ's merit, and ratifying redemption. They emphasized the Spirit's objective operations in baptizing and convincing sinners (Gal 3:14), yet sometimes paid scant attention to His ongoing relational ministries such as guidance and intercession. The Heidelberg Catechism speaks eloquently of the Spirit's work in renewing hearts, but academic theology often reduced the Spirit to the bond of union between Christ and believers. Schools debated the Spirit's procession mainly to defend the filioque clause, rather than to explore His active presence in sanctification. Pastoral care sometimes suffered as congregants were assured of justification but lacked teaching on prayer in the Spirit (Eph 6:18). Pietism arose in part to recover experiential communion, yet retained the scholastic stress on doctrine. This emphasis on principle over presence mirrored Enlightenment trends, where rational justification overshadowed relational reality. Our next subsection examines how Cartesian dualism further abstracted the Spirit's work.

6.3 Cartesian dualism and the Spirit as explanatory "gap" for mind–body questions

René Descartes' sharp division between res cogitans (thinking substance) and res extensa (extended substance) left little conceptual space for a Spirit who bridges body and soul. Cartesian philosophy often treated the Spirit as the explanatory "ghost in the machine," invoked to account for human consciousness but lacking a robust ontological status of its own. In theological circles, some equated the Spirit with the human mind's rational faculties, implying that divine Spirit and human reason operate on the same plane. This led to a subtle erosion of the Spirit's personal transcendence; He became a theological placeholder for phenomena not yet understood by neurophysiology. Pastors and theologians responded by reaffirming that the Spirit indwells believers' "spirit" (1 Cor 2:11), not merely their intellect, preserving the relational dimension absent from dualist abstractions. Subsequent thinkers like Malebranche and Leibniz sought to integrate Spirit into pre-established harmony, yet often at the cost of personal immediacy. The Cartesian legacy thus reminds us that philosophy can both illuminate and constrict pneumatology. As Enlightenment rationalism gave way to deistic restraint, the Spirit's public role was further diminished.

6.4 Deism and rationalist dismissal of ongoing spiritual activity

Deists of the eighteenth century accepted a Creator but denied ongoing divine intervention, relegating the Spirit to the act of creation alone. Figures like Voltaire and Jefferson described God's breath as a one-time infusion, a mechanism for cosmic order, not an enduring personal Presence. In such frameworks, prayer became wishful thinking, and the Spirit's intercession (Rom 8:26) sounded superstitious. Churches influenced by deism struggled to preach the Spirit's ministries of guidance, empowerment, and consolation, focusing instead on moral philosophy and natural religion. The Great Awakenings arose partly in reaction, reviving preaching on the necessity of the Spirit's new-birth work (John 3:8) and rekindling experiential faith. Evangelicals insisted that without the Spirit's ongoing presence, the church would become a mere cultural institution. This back-and-forth between deistic abstraction and revivalist passion foreshadows modern tensions between secular spirituality and charismatic renewal, the focus of the next section.

7 Modern Charismatic, Cessationist, and Pentecostal Extremes

7.1 Revivalism's "power surge" motif—Spirit reduced to emotional electricity

Nineteenth- and early twentieth-century revivalists often described the Spirit's coming as a "power surge," likening revival to an electrical charge that energizes services. While this metaphor captured the suddenness of spiritual outpourings, it also risked reducing the Spirit to impersonal voltage. Participants spoke of "getting charged up," implying passivity in content reception and neglecting relational engagement with the Spirit. Critics noted that after the surge, some congregations experienced moral lassitude, as if the emotional high had replaced enduring discipleship. Moreover, the power-surge language obscured the Spirit's teaching ministry (John 14:26) and His ongoing conviction of sin (John 16:8). Contemporary renewal movements have sought to correct this by emphasizing the Spirit's fruitfulness (Gal 5:22–23) rather than merely His power. They teach that true revival bears lasting transformation, not just emotional intensity. Recognizing the limits of the power-surge metaphor readies us to consider the reactionary rise of cessationism.

7.2 Cessationist reaction—Spirit confined to canonical inspiration history

Cessationists argue that the Spirit's miraculous gifts ceased with the apostolic age, interpreting "gifts" as foundational signs (Eph 2:20) now obsolete. This position often stems from a desire to protect biblical authority and avoid excess, yet it can unintentionally depersonalize the Spirit by confining Him to past events. If the Spirit no longer heals, speaks prophetically, or empowers for mission, His identity as a dynamic Advocate is diminished. Cessationists counter that the Spirit still regenerates and sanctifies, but critics point out that this view sometimes neglects Romans 8's promise of the Spirit's intercession and guidance. The debate highlights how doctrinal reaction can distort the Spirit's personhood by over-focusing on one domain of His work. Balanced theology affirms both the normative sufficiency of Scripture (2 Tim 3:16) and the ongoing relational ministries of the Spirit, as evidenced in contemporary testimonies of guidance and conviction. This balance paves the way for understanding Pentecostal extremes.

7.3 Early Pentecostal over-identification with glossolalia as sole evidence

Pentecostal pioneers in Azusa Street and beyond emphasized speaking in tongues (Acts 2:4) as the definitive sign of Spirit baptism. While this focus recovered a biblical practice, some leaders taught glossolalia as the exclusive evidence of Spirit filling, marginalizing other ministries such as teaching, guidance, and intercession. Church governance sometimes became contingent on public utterance, pressuring members to seek the gift for status rather than relational growth. Academic theologians criticized this approach for reducing personhood to performance. Nevertheless, early Pentecostalism also rediscovered the Spirit's global mission focus, racial integration under one Spirit (Acts 10:34–35), and the value of lay empowerment. Later charismatic movements have broadened the understanding of Spirit baptism—recognizing multiple evidences and emphasizing the Spirit's ongoing guidance and comfort. Learning from Pentecostal history reminds us that no single gift exhausts the Spirit's personhood.

7.4 Neo-charismatic marketing of "anointing" as transferable commodity

In late twentieth-century neo-charismatic circles, conferences and media ministries began marketing the "anointing" as a transferable commodity, sometimes purportedly moved by laying on of hands or by sending oil by mail. Promotional language touted "reception of power" as if it were a product to be purchased or shipped, a stark reduction of the Spirit's personal will. Critics decried the transactional tone—"give your $50, receive anointing for $500"—as commodification of the divine. Such practices often overlooked Jesus' warning against public displays for personal gain (Matt 6:1) and the Spirit's modest, relational approach. Churches responded by developing accountability standards for healing ministries and clarifying that spiritual empowerment cannot be brokered as a commercial transaction. Teaching returned to emphasizing prayerful dependence (Acts 4:31) and the Spirit's sovereign distribution of gifts "as He wills" (1 Cor 12:11). This corrective underscores that the Spirit's personhood cannot be harnessed by marketing strategies, leading us naturally to survey popular New Age portrayals of impersonal energy.

8 Contemporary Culture: New Age Energies and Secular Psychologizing

8.1 Reiki, chakra, and "universal spirit energy" syncretisms

Reiki and chakra traditions present a spiritual energy that practitioners learn to channel, balance, and manipulate for healing and empowerment. This energy is often described as impersonal, flowing through meridians or aura fields, with little or no reference to a conscious Actor. Christian participants sometimes adopt these practices seeking wellness, only to discover that they bypass prayer, repentance, and relational surrender to the triune God. Unlike the biblical Spirit who convicts of sin (John 16:8) and intercedes (Rom 8:26), Reiki energy remains indifferent to moral categories. Pastors have responded by teaching that true healing comes from "the God of peace … sanctifying you wholly" (1 Thess 5:23), not from an ambiguous force. They also encourage discernment: distinguishing "spiritual gifts" that bear the fruit of holiness (Gal 5:22–23) from impersonal life-force techniques. This contrast readies believers to resist secular psychologizing, which we examine next.

8.2 Self-help literature: Spirit reframed as inner potential and mindfulness boost

The self-help industry frequently co-opts spiritual language—"find your inner power," "awaken your spirit"—to promote techniques like positive affirmation, visualization, and mindfulness. These approaches cast the Spirit as a latent potential within the self, accessible through disciplined practice, and often detach spiritual growth from repentance and divine initiative. By contrast, biblical pneumatology begins with human inability (Rom 8:7) and relies on the Spirit's gracious breaking-in, not on self-actualization. Churches have developed discipleship pathways that integrate biblical meditation, prayer, and community—practices that ground spiritual formation in God's revealed Word (Ps 119:105) rather than psychological frameworks. Teaching that "apart from me you can do nothing" (John 15:5) counters the self-help emphasis on autonomous progress. This corrective informs how we engage cultural tropes in media, which we analyze in the next subsection.

8.3 Hollywood and gaming tropes: ethereal force fields and magic streams

Popular films and video games depict spiritual energy as color-coded force fields, magic streams, or mystical auras—the Force in *Star Wars*, Ki in anime, mana in fantasy RPGs. These portrayals shape cultural imaginations of spirituality as amoral power to be harnessed or battled. Such tropes risk predisposing viewers to think of the Spirit as a neutral "force" for good or evil, rather than as a Person who chooses to empower righteousness (John 16:13) and convicts of evil (John 16:8). Christian media educators counter by producing films and games that foreground the Spirit's personhood, embedding narrative moments where characters dialogue with a loving Counselor rather than channeling an abstract power. They also host workshops showing how to discern narrative influences on spiritual perception, urging believers to test every force by the fruit it bears (Gal 5:22–23). These efforts demonstrate that pop culture's force-based images must be reinterpreted through Scripture's personal pneumatology. Having surveyed media, we conclude by examining the commodification of breath-work in wellness industries.

8.4 Wellness industry: essential oils, breathwork, and the commodification of *ruach*

Contemporary wellness trends market essential oils, breathwork retreats, and biohacking gadgets as means to optimize "life force." Aromatherapy labels claim oils carry vibrational frequencies, while breathwork coaches promise altered states akin to spiritual experiences—all framed as impersonal energies. Christians sometimes adopt these modalities for stress relief, yet risk neglecting the Spirit's relational intercession (Rom 8:26) and His role as Comforter (John 14:16). Pastors and spiritual directors now equip congregants to differentiate between self-induced altered consciousness and Spirit-led transformation. They teach breath prayers—short Scriptural phrases recited with breath—as a Christian alternative, grounding breath in the personal Spirit's presence (Acts 2:2). The wellness industry's commodification of breath challenges the church to reclaim *ruach* as a relational reality, not a retail product. This sets the stage for diagnosing global syncretisms and charting diagnostic criteria in the chapters to follow.

9 Global South Syncretisms and Post-Colonial Challenges

9.1 African Spirit traditions and ancestor veneration conflations

Across sub-Saharan Africa, indigenous religions often conceive of spirits as ancestral intermediaries, with rituals invoking the departed as ongoing guides. These practices frequently blend with Christian vocabulary, leading some communities to pray for the "Holy Ancestor" or to seek blessings from forebears alongside the Holy Spirit. Such syncretism risks portraying the Spirit as merely another spiritual force among many, rather than the uniquely divine Paraclete promised by Christ (John 14:16). Yet African theologians have crafted powerful contextual theologies, demonstrating how biblical images of the Spirit as "life-giver" (Rev 11:11) can supplant notions of ancestral power. They emphasize that unlike ancestors, the Holy Spirit lives eternally, transcends human lineage, and cannot be bribed or coerced by ritual. Biblical teaching shows that the Spirit convicts of sin (John 16:8) and draws people to repentance, whereas ancestral spirits may enforce moral codes without offering forgiveness. African liturgies often involve drumming, dance, and symbolic pouring of libations; contextualized worship leaders now harness these forms to celebrate Pentecost's fire (Acts 2:3) while preaching against any invocation of deceased humans. Seminaries in Nairobi and Lagos train pastors to discern cultural resonance from theological distortion, urging congregants to replace ancestor-centrism with Christ-centered pneumatology. By affirming the Spirit's personal agency, they recover the biblical pattern of direct communion with God, not mediated by created spirits. As African churches reclaim their heritage, they model how to untangle syncretism elsewhere. From Africa we turn to how Latin American folk Catholicism negotiates indigenous and Christian spirit-concepts.

9.2 Latin American folk Catholicism: Spirit symbols blended with indigenous deities

In parts of Latin America, Christian devotion to the Holy Spirit coexists with indigenous beliefs in nature deities—mountain spirits, rain gods, and earth mothers—leading to hybrid festivals where Pentecost is celebrated alongside Pachamama offerings. Images of the Spirit as a dove may stand beside statues of local gods, blurring the boundaries between divine Personhood and impersonal earth-powers. Folk rituals sometimes ask the Spirit for agricultural fertility using traditional dances originally directed at rain-spirits, suggesting that the Spirit controls seasons like an earth-force rather than exercises personal discretion. Contextual theologians protest that Scripture locates the Spirit's power not in creation's cycles but in new-creation hearts (2 Cor 5:17). They teach that only the triune God renews souls from within (Ezek 36:26) rather than merely ensuring external abundance. Liberation theologians further emphasize that the Spirit's preferential option for the poor (Luke 4:18) differs fundamentally from indigenous spirit-veneration, which often serves hierarchical elites. Pastoral training centers now integrate inculturation principles that honor native music and dance while reinterpreting them as celebrations of Christ's resurrection power (Rom 8:11). By decentering earth-deities and recentring the Spirit's personal witness, Latin American churches overcome folk syncretism. These insights resonate with analogous challenges in Asian contexts, as we will see next.

9.3 Asian contexts: Spirit paralleled with *qi*, *prana*, and animistic forces

In East and South Asia, life-energy concepts like Chinese *qi*, Indian *prana*, and Japanese *ki* permeate health systems, martial arts, and meditation traditions. Practitioners often conceive these energies as impersonal currents to be balanced through breath control, acupuncture, or yoga, rarely attributing agency or relationality. Christian converts may thus assume that the Holy Spirit functions similarly—as an energy to be channeled for well-being—while Scripture portrays Him as a Person who can be grieved (Eph 4:30) and who chooses to anoint (Luke 4:18). Asian theologians like Kosuke Koyama have addressed this by contrasting *qi*'s impersonal flow with the Spirit's intentional guidance into truth (John 16:13). They maintain that whereas *qi* cannot intercede or reveal God's will, the Holy Spirit prays within believers (Rom 8:26) and teaches all things (1 John 2:27). Local churches incorporate Asian artistic forms—calligraphy, incense, and Tai Chi movements—reframing them as embodied prayers to the living Advocate rather than as energy manipulation. Seminaries encourage contextual Bible studies that compare Genesis breath-metaphors with Hebrew relational *ruach*, preventing conflation. By reaffirming personal agency, Asian Christians demonstrate that spiritual health ultimately rests on communion with a Person, not mastery of an impersonal force. This global survey of syncretism now leads us to formulate diagnostic criteria for spotting depersonalization.

9.4 Missiological strategies for disentangling personhood from impersonal powers

Mission agencies have developed protocols to detect syncretism, such as tracking local metaphors for spirit, analyzing ritual elements that imply impersonal control, and interviewing believers about how they experience divine guidance. Field teams use approaches like "shared discovery Bible studies," prompting participants to compare their traditional practices with explicit biblical texts—e.g., contrasting ancestral invocations with the Spirit's promise of adoption (Rom 8:15). Training modules teach "spiritual mapping" of local cosmologies, enabling missionaries to identify which components derive from indigenous energy-concepts and which align with personal pneumatology. Indigenous pastors are equipped to repurpose native arts—dances, chants, carvings—in ways that affirm the Spirit's relational leadership rather than animate mystical forces. Academic publishing in missiology now features case studies from Africa, Latin America, and Asia, documenting how churches reoriented syncretic rituals toward biblical patterns of personal communion. These strategic efforts illustrate that diagnosing impersonal reductions requires both cultural sensitivity and doctrinal clarity. Having equipped readers with global examples and initial detection tools, we next turn to articulate precise diagnostic criteria.

10 Diagnostic Criteria: How to Recognize an Impersonal Reduction

10.1 Absence of intentional speech and relational address

An impersonal reduction becomes evident when spiritual experiences lack direct communication with a conscious Agent. For instance, if prayer or worship emphasizes "tapping into universal energy" without any expectation of the Spirit responding personally, this signals a shift from biblical patterns where the Spirit speaks (Acts 8:29) and witnesses (John 15:26). Diagnostic listening attends to whether individuals report hearing a distinct voice, receiving counsel, or sensing relational affection—markers of personhood—versus experiencing only vague sensations of power. Congregational surveys can include questions such as, "Do you expect the Spirit to answer your prayers in specific words or images?" If most answer negatively, this suggests an impersonal model. Leaders should also note whether confession and repentance are guided by convictions attributed to the Spirit (John 16:8) or merely by communal norms. Discernment workshops teach participants to distinguish between internal promptings they believe originate from the Spirit and generic emotional reactions. By focusing on the presence or absence of intentional dialogic elements, churches can identify areas needing corrective teaching. With speech as a diagnostic lens established, we turn to functionalism.

10.2 Functionalism: Spirit as mere mechanism for miracles or morality

Reducing the Spirit to a means of achieving outcomes—healing, prosperity, moral uplift—treats Him as a divine vending machine rather than a Person with intrinsic worth. Diagnostic attention reveals this when prayers center on requests like "Activate my destiny energy" or "Release your power for my success," with little emphasis on seeking the Spirit's companionship or character formation. A church climate focused exclusively on manifest gifts (healings, prophecies) while neglecting fruit of the Spirit (Gal 5:22–23) indicates functionalism. Leaders can audit sermon content: is the Spirit primarily presented as a tool or as a teacher and Advocate? Small-group discussions might reveal whether members relate to the Spirit mainly in crisis moments or also in mundane companionship—another sign of functional reduction. Developing teaching series on the Spirit's ongoing relational ministries helps recalibrate expectations. Having examined functionalism, we next consider reliance on energetic metaphors.

10.3 Energetic metaphors without volitional agency

When discourse about the Spirit relies heavily on metaphors of electricity, vibrations, frequencies, or cosmic winds—without corresponding language about willful choice—the risk of depersonalization is high. Diagnostic content analysis of worship songs, teaching materials, and marketing language can quantify the frequency of such metaphors. If metaphors outnumber references to the Spirit's will ("He wills," "He chooses," "He directs"), a corrective emphasis on volitional texts (1 Cor 12:11; Acts 16:6–7) is needed. Workshops can encourage alternative imagery—e.g., "The Spirit who chooses to dwell with you"—to counterbalance impersonal tropes. Additionally, prayer guides should include petitions acknowledging the Spirit's personal directives ("Speak, Lord, your servant is listening," 1 Sam 3:9) rather than generic energy invocations. With energetic metaphor detection in place, we proceed to examine the loss of Trinitarian context.

10.4 Loss of Trinitarian context—Spirit detached from Father and Son

A final diagnostic marker is when teaching or practice mentions the Spirit apart from the Father and the Son, severing the biblical pattern of mutual relations (Matt 28:19). If sermons celebrate the Spirit's power but omit His procession from the Father or His sending by the Son (John 15:26; 16:7), congregants may unconsciously adopt a sub-biblical pneumatology. Diagnostic tools include reviewing liturgical elements—are doxologies invoking "Father, Son, and Holy Spirit" regularly used? Do baptismal services contextualize Spirit-impartation within the triune name? Do educational materials explain the Spirit's relational origin? Identifying gaps in Trinitarian framing prompts curriculum development that weaves Father-Son-Spirit narratives through Bible exposition. By maintaining the Spirit's place within the triune life, communities preserve relational depth and avoid isolating Him as a standalone force. Having outlined clear criteria for detecting impersonal reductions, we now consider the importance of correcting these distortions.

11 Bridging to the Remedy: Importance of Correcting the Distortions

11.1 Worship implications: from instrumentality to adoration

When the Spirit is perceived as impersonal, worship often shifts to a transactional model—"I give praise so I receive power"—rather than a posture of humble awe before a personal God. Corrective teaching reintroduces Spirit-focused doxologies such as "Come, Holy Spirit, fill the hearts of your faithful" (ancient hymn), redirecting hearts from utilitarian outcomes to genuine adoration. Worship planners incorporate moments of silence and invitation, allowing space for the Spirit to speak personally rather than merely powering up the service.

Testimonies emphasize relational encounters—stories of listeners sensing a voice or conviction—rather than solely recounting miracles. By modeling heartfelt adoration, congregations relearn how to lift their eyes to the Spirit's face. As worship reorients, it prepares believers for relational recovery in everyday life.

11.2 Doctrinal health: guarding against modalism, animism, and utilitarianism

Ensuring doctrinal integrity safeguards the church from reducing the Spirit to a mode of God, a local power, or a mere tool. Systematic instruction on the distinctions among essence, person, and operation—rooted in Chapters 1 and 2—equips leaders to refute modalism and animism effectively. Seminars analyze case studies where impersonalism led to ethical compromise or spiritual abuse, highlighting the necessity of affirming the Spirit's personal will and moral agency. Accountability groups monitor teaching materials and practices, ensuring alignment with the book's working definition of the Spirit as a relational, communicative, intentional Subject. With doctrinal health secured, churches can more confidently welcome the Spirit into all spheres of life.

11.3 Spiritual formation: cultivating communion rather than consumption

Recovering the Spirit's personhood transforms spiritual formation from a self-help venture into a journey of friendship. Discipleship programs shift focus from skill acquisition—"How to get more anointing"—to relational practices—"How to listen for the Spirit's voice." Mentoring relationships emphasize mutual listening, confession of missteps in hearing, and affirmation of genuine encounters. Retreats invite participants to rest in the Spirit's presence, experiencing His comfort rather than seeking his power. Spiritual formation thus becomes an apprenticeship in communion, cultivating trust rather than a checklist of experiences.

Conclusion The world's impulse to reduce the Spirit to wind, power, or mere breath arises from deep-seated cultural and philosophical predispositions that span millennia. From Mesopotamian life-breath myths to Greek Stoic *pneuma* and Patristic modalism, each distortion reflects a failure to recognize the Spirit's personal mind, will, and heart. Yet Israel's prophetic polemics, intertestamental critiques, Greco-Roman apologetics, and Cappadocian clarifications together rescue the Spirit's true identity as the living Advocate. Having dismantled misconceptions, we stand poised to embark on Chapter 3's examination of how the Old Testament anticipates the Spirit's personal activities, preparing the way for fuller revelation in the New Testament.

Chapter 3 – Old-Testament Foundations: Personal Activities Anticipated

The Old Testament lays the groundwork for understanding the Holy Spirit not as an abstract force but as a dynamic agent whose personal activities anticipate the fuller revelation of the Paraclete in the New Testament. Across the Torah, the Prophets, and the Writings, the Spirit emerges in creation accounts, prophetic oracles, and covenantal promises—engaging in actions that presuppose intellect, will, emotion, and relationship. By examining these foundational texts, we trace a living thread: the Spirit hovers over primeval waters, empowers deliverers, speaks through prophetic messengers, and moves with tender sensitivity toward God's people. This chapter uncovers these foretaste encounters, revealing that the living God has always operated through a personal Spirit, preparing Israel—and ultimately the church—for the outpouring of divine fellowship at Pentecost.

1 The Spirit Creating, Ordering, and Beautifying the Cosmos

1.1 Hovering over primordial chaos (Gen 1:2)

In the initial verses of Genesis, the Spirit of God is depicted as "hovering" over the formless void, using a verb that evokes bird-like care and protective intention. This image portrays the Spirit not as a mere wind but as a vigilant Presence, surveying chaos with deliberate purpose. The Hebrew term *rachaph* suggests gentle motion—akin to a mother bird brooding over her eggs—underscoring relational tenderness even at creation's outset. Unlike ancient Near-Eastern myths where divine breath is capricious or violent, Israel's narrative emphasizes the Spirit's orderly approach to forming a habitable world. The Spirit's agency here implies plan and design: He does not merely stir atoms, but prepares a realm for life and covenant. By the close of Genesis 1, each act of separation and naming reflects Spirit-guided intention, laying the groundwork for relational partnership between Creator and creature. Later Jewish interpreters saw this hovering as the Spirit's ongoing sustenance of creation, a continuous act of personal involvement rather than a one-off mechanical spark. The New Testament echoes this creative Spirit in passages like Hebrews 11:3, affirming that the worlds were framed "by the word of God, so that things which are seen were not made of things which are visible," a process in which the Spirit is co-agent. Thus the Spirit's hovering prefigures His later indwelling—moving from cosmic architect to intimate renewer of hearts (Ezek 36:27). This creative care transitions seamlessly into the Spirit's role as sustainer of life at every level.

1.2 Sustaining every living creature (Ps 104:29–30; Job 33:4)

Psalm 104 beautifully describes the Spirit as the continual source of life: God's breath revives the earth whenever He draws back His Spirit, it dies and returns to dust. The psalmist's confidence in a recurring Spirit-breath reveals a belief in personal divine oversight of ecological cycles. Job's declaration that, "the Spirit of God has made me, and the breath of the Almighty gives me life," ties individual human vitality to the same personal breath sustaining all creatures. These poetic texts resist impersonal reduction by attributing life's renewal to the Spirit's deliberate outpouring. They also introduce the idea that the Spirit's withdrawal results in decay, a relational separation rather than a mechanistic process. In reflecting on these verses, later Jewish sages taught that every heartbeat depends on the Spirit's presence, forging a theology in which human mortality and dependence echo covenantal dependence. Early Christians extended these insights, reading such passages Christologically— linking the Spirit's life-giving work to the resurrection power at Pentecost. By situating personal sustenance within a cosmic framework, the Spirit emerges as a relational source of continual renewal, preparing us to witness His specific empowerment of chosen leaders.

1.3 Inspiring artistry for the tabernacle (Ex 31:1–5; 35:30–35)

The construction of the tabernacle in Exodus underscores the Spirit's role as inspirer of human creativity. Bezalel is described as filled "with the Spirit of God, with ability, with intelligence, with knowledge, and with all craftsmanship." The narrative lists metalworking, weaving, carving, and design as gifts imparted by the Spirit—activities that require cognitive intent and aesthetic discernment. This divine-empowered artistry signals that the Spirit values beauty and order, reflecting His personal delight in craftsmanship. Moreover, the Spirit's endowment of skills reinforces relational partnership: God does not command and abandon; He equips and dwells among His people through their handiwork. The recounting of Bezalel's skills alongside Oholiab's in Exodus 35:34–35 further shows the Spirit's distributive will, personalizing the allocation of talents. The tabernacle itself becomes a living symbol of Spirit-enabled communion—God's dwelling shaped by human hands under divine direction. Later temple expansions and artistic patronage in Solomon's reign echo this Spirit-anointed tradition, linking sacred architecture to personal Spirit-giving. Recognizing this creative equipping deepens our understanding of spiritual gifts and transitions us into exploring how the Spirit empowers leaders for deliverance.

1.4 Granting architectural insight for the temple (1 Chr 28:12; 29:19)

King David's charge to Solomon includes a Spirit-given blueprint: "the Spirit of the LORD spoke by me, and His word was on my tongue, and He said, 'Behold, Solomon your son...build a house for My name.'" The Spirit's communication is both verbal and visionary, equipping David with technical plans for the temple. The chronicler emphasizes that these instructions were not David's own invention but direct transmissions from the Spirit, underscoring personal relational address and authoritative mandate. The architectural vision encompasses dimensions, materials, and ritual functions, reflecting the Spirit's comprehensive care for both form and function. This divine guidance contrasts with secular commissions, where architects rely on human expertise absent personal mandate from God. David's stirring narrative anticipates the Spirit's role in guiding the church's mission blueprints in the New Testament. The temple's eventual completion under Solomon stands as a testament to Spirit-led collaboration between divine initiative and human execution. From cultic design we move into the realm of personified wisdom, which further reveals the Spirit's creative character in symbolic form.

1.5 Personified Wisdom as the Spirit's creative analogue (Prov 8; Isa 11:2)

Proverbs 8 and Isaiah 11:2 personify divine Wisdom and the Spirit interchangeably, portraying Wisdom calling from the heights at creation's dawn and the Spirit resting upon the Messiah with understanding and counsel. In Proverbs 8, Wisdom speaks in the first person—"I was there when He founded the earth"—blurring the lines between Wisdom and the Spirit of Genesis 1:2. This personification underscores that creative activity involves intentional speech and relational delight. Isaiah 11:2's seven-fold Spirit—wisdom, understanding, counsel, might, knowledge, fear of the LORD—portrays creative and judicial capacities as facets of Spirit-endowment. These passages illustrate that the Spirit's creative work extends beyond physical formation into moral and intellectual realms. The interpretive tradition in Jewish and Christian exegesis reads these texts as anticipatory images of the Spirit's full economy in the Messiah, who inaugurates new creation. By connecting personified Wisdom to the Spirit's anointing, the Old Testament foreshadows the Spirit's empowerment of Christ's ministry in the Gospels. This theological thread prepares us to explore the Spirit's direct engagement in Israel's story of deliverance and leadership.

2 Empowering Judges, Kings, and Administrators

2.1 Charismatic deliverers—Othniel, Gideon, Jephthah, Samson (Judg 3:10; 6:34; 11:29; 15:14)

The Book of Judges repeatedly notes that "the Spirit of the LORD came upon" leaders, equipping them for deliverance. In Judges 3:10, Othniel's Spirit-anointing enables military victory, demonstrating that success depends on divine empowerment, not mere human strategy. Gideon's narrative (Judg 6:34) shows the Spirit as transformative power, changing him from hesitant farmer to fearless commander. Jephthah (Judg 11:29) likewise receives the Spirit to rally troops, indicating that personal courage is a divine gift. Samson's exploits (Judg 15:14) portray the Spirit as manifested strength, not an impersonal force but the Spirit acting "mightily" within a person. Each account underscores personal agency: the Spirit chooses specific individuals, indwells them temporarily, and then withdraws—evident when Samson's strength departs with the Spirit (Judg 16:20). These stories combat reductionism: the Spirit's coming is neither random wind nor mystical atmosphere but a deliberate inhabitation for mission. Moreover, the moral ambivalence of certain judges warns that Spirit's presence does not guarantee perfect character, signaling that personal agency must align with covenant faithfulness. From judges we transition to monarchy.

2.2 Transition to monarchy—Saul's transformation and David's anointing (1 Sam 10:6–10; 16:13)

Saul's early reign receives Spirit-empowerment marked by prophetic ecstasy (1 Sam 10:6–10), yet his later disobedience leads to Spirit's departure (1 Sam 16:14), illustrating the relational dimension of personal agency: the Spirit stays when the king walks in God's ways. David's anointing by Samuel (1 Sam 16:13) brings the Spirit upon him "from that day forward," indicating a permanent indwelling rather than episodic filling. Yet even David's Spirit-led status involves his response—he composes psalms of gratitude (Ps 51) and seeks God's presence continually. The contrast between Saul and David underscores that Spirit-anointing is not mechanical; it interacts with human obedience and faith. David's Spirit-enabled leadership further establishes that God's personal Spirit accompanies both prophetic speech and royal governance. This extends into wisdom literature and administrative guidance, which we explore next.

2.3 Administrative discernment for Joseph and Daniel (Gen 41:38; Dan 4:8; 5:14)

Joseph's appointment as Pharaoh's second-in-command (Gen 41:38) occurs after his dream-interpretation unveils divine wisdom, a Spirit-driven insight that surpasses Egyptian magicians. The text credits Pharaoh's recognition of "the Spirit of God" in Joseph's discernment—a personal stamp of authenticity. Similarly, Daniel's superb counsel under Nebuchadnezzar (Dan 4:8) and Belshazzar (Dan 5:14) arises from divine revelations imparted through dreams and visions. Daniel attributes these insights to the Spirit's direct communication, not to personal genius alone. His refusal of royal honors (Dan 6) further testifies to the Spirit's moral empowerment, sustaining integrity against coercion. These narratives emphasize the Spirit's personal provision of administrative wisdom necessary for just governance. By humanizing empire through Spirit-inspired counselors, Scripture reveals that divine Personhood intersects public duty. This leads naturally into the theme of Spirit's departure and its costs.

2.4 Departure of the Spirit and the cost of apostasy (Judg 16:20; 1 Sam 16:14)

The withdrawal of the Spirit from leaders illustrates relational consequences: when Saul disobeys, "an evil spirit from the LORD" troubles him until David's harp restores calm (1 Sam 16:14–23), a dramatic depiction of Spirit-presence and absence. Samson's betrayal by Delilah results in the Spirit's departure, leading to his capture and blindness (Judg 16:20–21). These accounts reveal that the Spirit's personal agency can be lost, not through divine caprice but through covenant breach. The consequences—military failure, moral collapse, subjugation—underscore that life apart from the Spirit is impoverishment, not just lack of power. They also prefigure New-Testament warnings about grieving the Spirit (Eph 4:30) and quenching Him (1 Th 5:19). Recognizing the Spirit's relational departure prepares us to hear His prophetic speech, which we examine in the next section.

3 Speaking Through the Prophets

3.1 "Thus says YHWH" by the Spirit's mouth (2 Sam 23:2; Mic 3:8)

Prophets consistently preface oracles with "Thus says the LORD," framing their speech as direct Spirit-mediated communication. In 2 Samuel 23:2 David testifies that "the Spirit of the LORD spoke by me," highlighting that prophetic words are not human inventions but personal messages delivered by the Spirit. Micah (Mic 3:8) declares that he is "full of power, with the Spirit of the LORD," equating prophecy with Spirit-filling rather than mere rhetorical skill. The intentionality of prophetic speech underscores the Spirit's role as communicator, addressing specific historical contexts and moral crises. Unlike visions or symbolic acts, prophecy involves deliberate articulation of divine will, presuming a personal speaker. Prophetic speech also carries ethical force: the Spirit reproves injustice (Isa 1:16–17) and comforts the brokenhearted (Isa 61:1), roles incompatible with impersonal energy. By entrusting His words to messengers, the Spirit engages in covenant dialogue worthy of personal encounter. These prophetic ministries pave the way for the New-Testament Spirit who speaks directly to the church.

3.2 The Servant's anointing for proclamation (Isa 42:1; 61:1)

Isaiah's Servant Songs begin with the Spirit's anointing: "Behold My servant, whom I uphold… I have put My Spirit upon him" (Isa 42:1). The same Spirit-anointing empowers the Servant to bring justice to nations, signaling a mission that transcends Israel's borders. In Isaiah 61:1 the Servant proclaims good news to the poor and liberty to captives "by the Spirit of the LORD," linking proclamation to personal empowerment. These texts anticipate the Messiah's public ministry, which Jesus affirms in Luke 4:18–19. The prophetic pattern shows that proclamation is not a general dispensation of energy but a targeted commissioning by a Person. The Servant's obedient speech flows from the Spirit's intentional equipping, modeling how divine Personhood engages world transformation. This prophetic anointing introduces a New-Testament dynamic that will be fully realized at Pentecost.

3.3 Covenant prosecutions and comfort oracles (Neh 9:30; Hag 2:4–5)

Nehemiah's recounting of Israel's history notes that despite repeated idolatry, "Many years You bore with them and warned them by Your Spirit through Your prophets" (Neh 9:30), portraying Spirit-led warnings as relational patience rather than impersonal churn. Haggai contrasts remnant apathy with divine initiative: "I am with you, declares the LORD" (Hag 2:4), a phrase reminiscent of Spirit-breathed assurance. The interplay of prosecution—warning of judgment—and comfort—promise of presence—reveals the Spirit's nuanced, personal ministry. He counsels, convicts, and consoles in response to covenant fidelity or failure. This dual role underscores that the Spirit is neither harsh executioner nor impersonal balm but a Person attuned to Israel's communal heart. Such texts prepare us for the Spirit's similar interplay of judgment and comfort in the New Testament.

3.4 Grieving and resisting the Spirit (Isa 63:10; Zech 7:12)

Isaiah's lament over Israel's rebellion—"They rebelled and grieved His Holy Spirit; therefore He turned to be their enemy" (Isa 63:10)—attributes emotional hurt to the Spirit, a hallmark of personal depth. Zechariah recounts prophets whose messages were ignored: "They made their hearts like flint and would not hear the law or the words that the LORD of hosts had sent by his Spirit" (Zech 7:12), depicting active resistance. Both passages treat the Spirit as a speaker whose words can be spurned, causing relational rupture rather than neutral malfunction. Grieving the Spirit carries consequences—loss of divine favor and protective presence—underscoring the Spirit's stake in covenant fidelity. These Old-Testament admonitions resonate with Paul's warning not to grieve the Spirit (Eph 4:30), revealing continuity in divine-personal response to human disobedience. Recognizing the Spirit's vulnerability to grief sets the stage for appreciating His compassion, which we explore next.

4 Expressing Emotion and Relational Sensitivity

4.1 Jealous love and shepherd-like compassion (Isa 63:11–14)

Isaiah recalls how God's Spirit guided Israel like a flock, yet when the people rebelled, He "remembered the days of old, ... the day when you came out of the land of Egypt" (Isa 63:11). The text combines shepherd imagery with a sense of divine jealousy, reflecting covenant zeal (Ex 34:14). The Spirit's jealousy is not petulant but protective—intended to guard exclusive devotion to Yahweh. This relational sensitivity surfaces in God's lament over waywardness and His yearning for restoration. The Spirit's compassion as shepherd contrasts with Canaanite deities' indifference to moral fidelity. By presenting the Spirit's emotional involvement at the national level, the text invites Israel to repentance through personal narrative. The psalmist similarly prays for a "steadfast spirit" (Ps 51:12), indicating awareness of Spirit's compassionate response to broken contrition. This interplay of jealousy and care reveals the Spirit's complex personal character, priming us to consider His consoling presence in exile.

4.2 Consolation amid national trauma (Hag 2:5; Zech 4:6)

In the post-exilic period, Haggai and Zechariah address shattered hopes: "Who is left among you who saw this house in its former glory? How do you feel now?" (Hag 2:3). The Spirit's comfort arrives as a renewed promise—"I am with you" (Hag 2:4) and "Not by might, nor by power, but by my Spirit, says the LORD of hosts" (Zech 4:6). These assurances soothe communal shame and fatigue, underscoring the Spirit's role as personal Comforter. Unlike impersonal energies that offer generic uplift, the Spirit's consolation is specific to covenant identity and future hope. The returnees learn that rebuilding God's house depends not on political alliances or military strength but on the Spirit's personal empowerment. This relational solace empowers ordinary people to participate in sacred reconstruction, foreshadowing the Spirit's empowering role in the church. Having surveyed consolation, we turn to the Spirit's righteous indignation.

4.3 Anger at covenant breach (Ps 106:33; Isa 63:10)

Psalm 106 catalogs Israel's persistent rebellion and states, "Therefore He gave them over to the power of the sword... He was filled with fury" (Ps 106:33), attributing anger to the Spirit's personal response to covenant breach. Isaiah's earlier note that Israel "grieved" the Spirit (Isa 63:10) pairs sorrow with anger, both emotional reactions that presuppose personal engagement. The Spirit's anger is not capricious wrath but measured judgment intended to awaken repentance. These texts affirm that the Spirit experiences righteous indignation against injustice and idolatry—a personal attribute incompatible with impersonal breath. They also highlight that the Spirit's emotional life serves covenant fidelity, not merely punitive function. The interplay of grief and anger points forward to the New-Testament Spirit who convicts the world of sin and righteousness (John 16:8). Recognizing divine anger sets the stage for embracing His restorative work, which we examine next.

4.4 Joy in eschatological flourishing (Isa 32:15–18; 44:3–4)

Prophetic visions of future blessing celebrate the Spirit as bringer of joy and abundance. Isaiah promises that "the Spirit will be poured upon us from on high, and our wilderness will become a fruitful field" (Isa 32:15–16), linking personal celebration with communal transformation. In the same prophetic stream, the Lord declares, "I will pour my Spirit on your offspring, and my blessing on your descendants" (Isa 44:3), a promise metonymically associated with gladness and flourishing. This eschatological joy highlights the Spirit's delight in covenant renewal, contrasting sharply with His earlier grief and anger. The prophetic joy is communal—transforming landscapes, social structures, and interpersonal relationships—underscoring the Spirit's broad emotional compass. These anticipatory glimpses of joy prepare Israel for the Messianic age, where the Spirit's personal ministries culminate in resurrection life. By portraying the Spirit as both Judge and Joy-Giver, the Old Testament crafts a holistic portrait of divine emotion that finds its consummation in Christ's victory and Pentecost's jubilee.

5 Teacher of Wisdom and Moral Insight

5.1 Outpouring of wisdom for righteous living (Prov 1:23; 2:6; 9:10)

The book of Proverbs identifies wisdom itself as a divine gift accessible through the Spirit, promising "If you turn at my reproof, behold, I will pour out my spirit to you" (Prov 1:23). This promise equates the Spirit's outpouring with the granting of moral insight, implying conscious bestowal rather than impersonal diffusion. Solomon's assertion that "the LORD gives wisdom; from his mouth come knowledge and understanding" (Prov 2:6) personalizes the Spirit's pedagogical ministry, since knowledge and understanding are the fruit of intentional instruction. The fear of the LORD is described as the "beginning of wisdom" (Prov 9:10), yet it is the Spirit who awakens that reverential posture. Ancient Israelite teachers knew that the Spirit's schooling did not result from mere human ethics but from divine intervention in the human mind. Rabbinic tradition expanded these texts by linking scriptural study with Spirit illumination, insisting that Torah learning requires Spirit-led discernment to avoid misinterpretation. The pattern of Spirit-imbued wisdom continues in the New Testament, where Paul speaks of the "mind of Christ" given by the Spirit (1 Cor 2:16). This continuity underscores that moral insight has always been a relational gift from God's personal Spirit, not a byproduct of philosophical reasoning alone. Recognizing the Spirit's role here prepares us to appreciate His specific empowering of individuals outside Israel's wisdom schools.

5.2 Inspiration of Job's youthful counsellor (Job 32:8)

Job's anguished laments give way to the appearance of Elihu, who declares, "But it is the spirit in man, the breath of the Almighty, that makes him understand" (Job 32:8). Elihu positions himself as a vessel for divine insight, attributing his capacity to counsel Job to the Spirit's indwelling operation. Unlike the earlier friends, Elihu claims his words are inspired rather than self-generated, marking a shift towards a more explicit pneumatology. His speeches underscore that even unmarried youth may serve as Spirit-empowered advisors when elders have failed, democratizing spiritual authority. Job's story thus anticipates New-Testament experiences where God raises up unlikely persons through Spirit endowment (e.g., 1 Cor 12:7–11). The emphasis on "breath of the Almighty" intertwines physical life with intellectual illumination, personalizing the Spirit's cognitive ministry. Because Job is already righteous, Elihu's correction highlights the Spirit's commitment to truth over human status. His example illustrates the Spirit's willingness to speak through unexpected

70

channels to guide those in distress. By attributing understanding to God's Spirit, Job 32 bridges the gap between cosmic breath metaphors and the personal Teacher later promised by Jesus (John 14:26). This narrative moves us from wisdom texts into reflections on the Scripture itself as Spirit-shaped revelation.

5.3 Ecclesiastes' closing affirmation of God-breathed words (Eccl 12:11)

Ecclesiastes concludes by declaring, "The words of the wise are like goads, and like nails firmly fixed are the collected sayings; they are given by one Shepherd" (Eccl 12:11), a stanza traditionally understood to evoke Spirit-breathed Scripture. The metaphor of a shepherd suggests the Spirit's personal guidance, rather than mere conceptual impetus. As the teacher of wisdom speaks, listeners experience convictions that penetrate their hearts as a shepherd's crook directs a flock. The collection of sayings, "like nails," implies permanence—an indication that the Spirit's influence endures beyond ephemeral enlightenment. Ecclesiastes frames these words as given by a singular divine Shepherd, pointing to the Spirit's unified role across diverse teachers. This understanding underscores the Spirit's authorship of Scripture, a theme Paul later reaffirms when he equates Scripture with "God-breathed" writings (2 Tim 3:16). By recognizing the Spirit's personal involvement in shaping wisdom literature, we affirm that biblical texts are more than moral maxims: they are relational communications from the Spirit-Speaker. This realization transitions us into examining how post-exilic communities renewed their commitment through Spirit-shaped readings.

5.4 Post-exilic sages and the Spirit's role in shaping Scripture (Neh 9:20; Zech 7:12)

In the post-exilic period, Nehemiah lauds God's faithfulness: "You gave your good Spirit to instruct them" (Neh 9:20), identifying the Spirit as the tutor of returning exiles. This teaching ministry ensured that the Torah regained primacy after years of displacement, emphasizing relational re-education rather than simple political reform. Zechariah laments that Israel "refused to heed the voice of the Lord," noting that it was the Lord who "sent by his Spirit through the former prophets" (Zech 7:12), attributing prophetic warnings to personal Spirit operation. These texts highlight the Spirit's continuity across generations, preserving covenant identity through inspired instruction. Jewish scribes and sages who compiled canonical texts undoubtedly saw their work as guided by the Spirit, a conviction that ensures the integrity of Old-Testament Scripture. By framing post-exilic reforms as Spirit-enabled instruction, these books emphasize that communal restoration depended on personal divine teaching, not just human ingenuity. The Spirit's role in shaping Torah reading and prophetic reinterpretation prepared Judaism for the radical reinterpretations found in the New Testament. Having surveyed wisdom and teaching, we now turn to the Spirit's promises of interior transformation.

6 Indwelling and Heart-Renewal Promises

6.1 New-heart, new-spirit motif (Ezek 36:25–27)

Ezekiel prophesies a radical covenant renewal: "I will give you a new heart, and a new spirit I will put within you" (Ezek 36:26). This promise locates transformation within the individual's inner person, presupposing the Spirit as a personal agent effecting radical change. The text contrasts external Law-given tablets with Spirit-written hearts, indicating relational intimacy rather than external compulsion. The Spirit's role here involves moral reconstitution, enabling obedience from the heart, not merely modifying behavior. Ezekiel emphasizes that this Spirit-driven renewal ensures lasting loyalty: the Spirit "will put his Spirit within you, and I will cause you to walk in my statutes" (Ezek 36:27). This relational act of indwelling marks a significant development from earlier Spirit-visits: now the Spirit becomes the permanent resident of the believer's inner being. The promise also foreshadows the New-Covenant Spirit baptism described by Jesus (John 7:38–39). Further, Ezekiel's vision underlines that transformation is communal: Israel as a corporate body receives a shared Spirit, uniting diverse individuals in covenant identity. Understanding this promise helps us see the Spirit's personal role in sanctification, leading into visions of corporate resurrection.

6.2 Corporate resurrection in the valley of bones (Ezek 37:1–14)

Ezekiel's vision of dry bones proclaims that "you shall live," as the Spirit enters the corpses, demonstrating personal agency in raising a lifeless community (Ezek 37:6). The narrative emphasizes the Spirit's breath bringing animation, not as a metaphor for national revival alone but as a literal depiction of the Spirit as life-Giver. The communal nature of the bones underscores that the Spirit's indwelling extends beyond individuals to corporate identity. The personal pronoun "I" recurs—"I will put my Spirit within you" (Ezek 37:14)—revealing the Spirit as a distinct subject performing the miracle. This prophetic drama foreshadows Pentecost's communal outpouring (Acts 2:1–4), where the Spirit's presence unites many into one body (1 Cor 12:13). Ezekiel's valley also highlights the Spirit's power over death, a personal victory that Christians later see in Christ's resurrection and the gift of eternal life. The vision bridges Israel's physical restoration with spiritual renewal, stressing the Spirit's holistic personal ministry. From resurrection promise we move to universal outpouring in prophetic Joel.

6.3 Universal and inclusive outpouring (Joel 2:28–29)

Joel announces an unprecedented event: "I will pour out my Spirit on all flesh" (Joel 2:28), dissolving the boundaries that previously limited prophetic speech to a select few. This inclusive promise underscores the Spirit's personal decision to democratize revelation, empowering sons, daughters, old and young alike. The Spirit's poured-out action metaphor evokes wine flowing from a jug, yet the passage insists on Personhood—"your sons and daughters shall prophesy" and "your old men shall dream dreams"—indicating relational inspiration rather than impersonal overspill. Peter's Pentecost sermon explicitly applies Joel's promise to the church (Acts 2:16–18), confirming the Spirit's personal fulfillment of the prophecy. Moreover, Joel's close link between Spirit outpouring and cosmic signs (Joel 2:30–31) underscores the personal scope of the Spirit's mission to renew all creation. The promise's universal language prepares the way for a global church, commissioned under the Spirit's authority. By grounding inclusion in personal outpouring, Joel transitions us to texts that identify the Spirit as the distinguishing hallmark of the eschatological people.

6.4 Spirit as the distinguishing mark of the end-time people (Isa 32:15; 44:3; Zech 12:10)

Isaiah foretells that when the Spirit is "poured out on us from on high," justice and righteousness will flourish, distinguishing God's people by their transformed ethics (Isa 32:15). Later, Isaiah repeats, "I will pour my Spirit on your offspring" (Isa 44:3), associating the Spirit's personal presence with generational blessing. Zechariah deepens this theme: "they will look on me whom they have pierced, and they shall mourn... and I will pour out on the house of David and the inhabitants of Jerusalem a spirit of grace and pleas for mercy" (Zech 12:10). This Spirit-prompted mourning and repentance delineates Israel's restored identity in the eschaton. The personal outpouring functions both as spiritual marker and moral catalyst, proving that covenant renewal hinges on personal Spirit-interaction. These passages set the theological horizon for the Messianic age, emphasizing that the Spirit's personal operations will characterize the end-time community. Having seen the Spirit's indwelling promises, we proceed to anticipate the Messiah's unique anointing.

7 The Spirit and the Coming Messiah

7.1 The Branch of Jesse endowed with a seven-fold Spirit (Isa 11:1–5)

Isaiah 11:1–5 portrays the coming Davidic Branch as endowed with the Spirit "of wisdom and understanding, the Spirit of counsel and might, the Spirit of knowledge and the fear of the LORD." This seven-fold classification personalizes the Spirit's manifold gifts, each reflecting deliberate choice. Wisdom and understanding speak to intellect; counsel and might to relational guidance and sovereign power; knowledge and fear of the LORD to moral sensibility and reverential devotion. The parallel of the Spirit resting on the Messiah as a garment (Isa 11:2) conveys intimacy and constant presence. In messianic expectation, this Spirit-anointing assures that the Servant will administer justice (Isa 11:4) with compassionate rulership— qualities beyond human potential. Early Christians recognized Christ's life as the fulfillment of this passage (Luke 4:18; Acts 10:38), affirming the Spirit's personal role in equipping Jesus for ministry. The seven-fold Spirit motif thus establishes a template for understanding Spirit-enabled mission, bridging Old-Testament promise and New-Testament realization.

7.2 Servant Songs—Spirit-guided justice for the nations (Isa 42:1–4; 61:1–3)

The Servant Songs of Isaiah present the Messiah as one upon whom the Spirit rests to enact justice and bring hope. In Isaiah 42:1–4, the Spirit's personal empowerment enables gentle yet unstoppable mission, softly breaking oppression and illuminating darkness without loud fanfare. The promised "gentle" Servant uses Spirit-bestowed authority to establish righteousness among nations. Isaiah 61:1–3 echoes Joel's promise, but here the Servant proclaims "good news to the poor" "in the power of the Spirit," linking prophecy with tangible acts of mercy. The text emphasizes that the Spirit's election of the Servant includes comforting the brokenhearted and binding up wounds, a ministry requiring both emotional intelligence and sovereign capability. These passages reveal that the Spirit's personal collusion with the Servant extends beyond Israel to the ends of the earth—a foreshadowing of the church's universal mission. Luke's Gospel directly ties Jesus' inaugural sermon to Isaiah 61 (Luke 4:18–19), demonstrating the continuity of personal Spirit anointing. The Servant Songs thus function as theological scaffolding for understanding the Spirit's role in Christ's redemptive work.

7.3 Priest-king in Zechariah's night visions (Zech 4:6; 6:12–13)

Zechariah's visions portray a dual priest-king figure, Zerubbabel, empowered by Spirit, building the temple "not by might, nor by power, but by my Spirit" (Zech 4:6). The emphasis on the Spirit's personal power underscores that temple rebuilding is a divine initiative, not a human endeavor. Later, Zechariah presents the Branch as "a priest upon his throne" (Zech 6:13), a unity of redemptive roles empowered by the same Spirit. This Messianic figure embodies both intercession and governance, made possible only through personal Spirit-anointing. The interweaving of priesthood and kingship illustrates that the Spirit's Personal ministry encompasses worship, judgment, and leadership. Post-exilic communities drew courage from these promises, viewing Spirit-guided leadership as necessary for national restoration. Early church Fathers saw in these words a pointer to Christ's royal priesthood and the Spirit's enabling of His intercessory work (Heb 7:25). The priest-king motif thus deepens our appreciation of the Spirit's personal investment in messianic mission.

7.4 Davidic covenant fulfilled by a Spirit-anointed heir (Ps 89:20; 132:17–18)

The Davidic Psalms affirm that God has found David, "my servant, with whom my soul is pleased; I have put my Spirit upon him" (Ps 89:20), emphasizing divine delight and Spirit-endowment as inseparable in covenant monarchy. Psalm 132:17–18 extends the promise: "There will I make the horn of David flourish; I have prepared a lamp for my anointed," suggesting ongoing Spirit-facilitated prominence for David's lineage. These royal prayers underscore that the Spirit's personal indwelling secures the covenant's continuity. Jewish tradition linked these texts to the awaited Messiah, while Christians saw their fulfillment in Jesus Christ, sealed by the Spirit at baptism (Mark 1:10). The combination of covenant faithfulness, divine pleasure, and Spirit-anointing illustrates how personal Spirit presence validates messianic authority. This leads naturally into how Israel's worship life integrates personal Spirit encounter.

8 Personal Presence in Israel's Worship

8.1 Omnipresent yet intimate—"Where can I flee?" (Ps 139:7–10)

Psalm 139's rhetorical question "Where shall I go from your Spirit? Or where shall I flee from your presence?" (Ps 139:7) portrays the Spirit as an inescapable yet personal presence. The psalmist affirms that whether ascending to heaven or descending to Sheol, the Spirit's companionship persists, a theological assertion of personal omnipresence. The imagery of God's hand leading and holding the psalmist (Ps 139:10) underscores intimacy: the Spirit is not a distant force but the close Friend who guides every step. This dual reality—cosmic reach and pastoral closeness—lays groundwork for later New-Testament promises of Spirit abiding (John 14:16). Jewish liturgical traditions leveraged Psalm 139 in prayers of refuge, teaching congregants to seek the Spirit's nearness in both joy and despair. Recognizing personal omnipresence prepares worshipers to welcome the Spirit's indwelling in house, temple, and heart. This intimate presence transitions us to texts on moral renewal in worship contexts.

8.2 Moral renewal and steadfast spirit (Ps 51:10–12)

In David's penitential psalm, he pleads, "Create in me a clean heart, O God, and renew a right spirit within me" (Ps 51:10). The juxtaposition of heart and spirit points to the Spirit's role in moral transformation, not as a static attribute but as a renewing Person. David acknowledges that mere ritual cleansing cannot suffice; only the Spirit's personal action can restore vitality and steadfastness. The plea for the Spirit to "not cast me away" (Ps 51:11) highlights relational fear of estrangement, indicating the Spirit's personal engagement with the worshiper's conscience. The psalmist's subsequent vow to teach transgressors the way of God (Ps 51:13) testifies to the Spirit-enabled commitment to communal renewal. Jews incorporated this psalm in Yom Kippur liturgies, emphasizing that moral restoration arises from Spirit-mediated contrition. This moral renewal within worship circles our focus on Spirit-guided praise and prophecy.

8.3 Prophetic praise and communal guidance (2 Chr 20:14–18; Ps 78:70–72)

When Jehoshaphat faced a confederation of enemies, the Spirit came upon Jahaziel who proclaimed, "Do not be afraid… the battle is not yours but God's" (2 Chr 20:15). This Spirit-utterance led the congregation in praise and trust, producing a miraculous deliverance. The scenario underscores that Spirit-inspired speech can guide communal worship and strategy. Psalm 78:70–72 recounts how God chose David "with his heart and skillful hands, he shepherded them with integrity of heart"—implying that Spirit-given praise and leadership function hand-in-hand. The Spirit's personal guidance in worship contexts affirms that liturgy is not mere ritual but living dialogue with God's Spirit. Such episodes anticipate the New-Testament pattern of Spirit-led praise gatherings (Acts 2:46–47). Understanding prophetic praise's Spirit origin equips communities to expect personal guidance in their corporate worship. This leads to celebrating creation's own songs of Spirit-powered life.

8.4 Creation hymns celebrating the Spirit's life-giving breath (Ps 33:6; 104:30)

Psalms 33:6 proclaims, "By the word of the LORD the heavens were made, and by the breath of his mouth all their host," while Psalm 104:30 declares, "When you send forth your Spirit, they are created, and you renew the face of the ground." These creation hymns explicitly link the Spirit's personal breath with ongoing creative renewal. Worshipers singing these texts recognize that every new day's vitality depends on the Spirit's conscious decision to breathe life. The pairing of word and breath underscores the Spirit's integrated ministries of revelation and sustenance. Ancient temple choirs would intone these verses to remind congregants of God's personal involvement in cosmic and ecological rhythms. By celebrating the Spirit's life-giving breath, Israelite worshipers embraced a personal encounter with the Spirit as the source of all blessing. This cosmic worship motif bridges the natural world and sacred assembly, preparing us for the canonical trajectory toward the New Covenant.

9 Canonical Trajectory Toward the New Covenant

9.1 Thread of personal agency running through Torah, Prophets, Writings

From Genesis's Spirit hovering (Gen 1:2), through prophetic oracles, to wisdom literature's Spirit-enlightenment, the Old Testament consistently portrays the Spirit as a personal agent. This canonical thread ensures that the Spirit's attributes—intellect, will, emotion, relationship—are woven throughout Israel's entire narrative, not confined to isolated texts. Each genre emphasizes different aspects: creative care in the Torah, prophetic speech in the Prophets, moral teaching in Writings. Yet all genres affirm a Spirit-Person who interacts with humanity. Recognizing this continuity fortifies our interpretation of New-Testament promises, confirming that the Spirit's personhood is not a late innovation but rooted in the Hebrew canon. Having traced these strands, we see how the Old Testament prepares for the New Covenant's full realization of Spirit-filled life.

9.2 Typological anticipation of Pentecost and the universal church

Joel's universal outpouring (Joel 2:28) and Ezekiel's valley-of-bones (Ezek 37) serve as living types that find fulfillment at Pentecost (Acts 2). The Church Fathers and Reformers recognized these typologies, reading the Old Testament backwards into the New. The Spirit's personal activities among Israel anticipate the Spirit's global mission to Jew and Gentile alike. Typology here does not erase historical particularity but enlarges it into covenantal promise. By seeing these Old-Testament events as shadows, Christians discern the Spirit's personal outpouring as inaugurating the universal, multiethnic church. This typological reading underscores that the Spirit's personhood transcends national boundaries, a grace extended to "all flesh."

9.3 Foreshadowing of Trinitarian revelation—Father sends, Spirit works, Messiah receives

Old-Testament narratives exhibit a triadic pattern: the Father's sovereignty, the Messiah's mission, and the Spirit's empowering presence. In Genesis 1, the Spirit proceeds from God; in Isaiah 11, the Spirit rests on the Branch; in Zechariah, the Spirit anoints the priest-king. Though not yet formally articulated in creeds, these patterns foreshadow the Trinitarian economy later clarified in the New Testament. Worship, prophecy, and covenant enactments all involve three Persons at work. The Spirit's personal agency in Old-Testament history thus prepares the interpretive horizon for the distinct persons of the Trinity. Recognizing this triadic foreshadow helps readers appreciate the fullness of Father-Son-Spirit relations revealed in John's Gospel.

Conclusion Our survey of the Old Testament reveals a Spirit who acts with intentionality, relational depth, and emotional complexity— hovering over chaos, empowering leaders, speaking through prophets, and responding to covenant faithfulness with both judgment and joy. Far from the impersonal "wind" of ancient myth, the Spirit engages Israel's history in personal ways that foreshadow His fuller self-revelation in Christ and the early church. These canonical anticipations equip us to recognize the same personal dynamics at work when the Spirit descends at Pentecost and guides the global mission of God. As we move into the New Testament narrative, we carry forward the conviction that behind every redemptive act stands a living divine Person—our Advocate, Teacher, and Friend.

Chapter 4. The Paraklētos in John's Gospel: Personal Advocate Revealed

In John's Gospel, the promise of the *Paraklētos* marks a watershed: Jesus does not leave His followers alone but ensures that a distinct divine Person—the Advocate—will continue His work. Unlike earlier anticipations, John names, describes, and situates the Spirit's personhood within the intimate Farewell Discourse, unveiling facets of His character, mission, and relational dynamics. This chapter unpacks that discourse against its covenantal backdrop, explores the rich semantic field of *paraklētos*, and traces how Jesus distinguishes His own ministry from that of the coming Advocate. Through careful exegesis of key Johannine texts, we will see how the Spirit embodies continuity with Jesus while exercising unique personal agency—indwelling believers, teaching the church, testifying in cosmic judgment, and guiding into all truth. As we move through the Farewell Discourse's literary setting, lexical nuances, and theological implications, we prepare to witness the Spirit's unfolding revelation, from the cruciform promise to the Pentecostal reality.

1 Literary and Historical Setting

1.1 The Farewell Discourse as Covenant-Renewal Scene

Jesus' words in John 13–17 function as the climax of covenant narrative, recasting the Sinai covenant's relational texture for the new community. He gathers His disciples around a final meal, echoing Israel's Passover, yet reorients its symbolism toward Himself as the true Lamb and toward the Spirit as the sustaining presence. The discourse's structure resembles ancient covenant renewal ceremonies: preamble, historical prologue, stipulations, blessings, and epilogue. Verses such as "If you love me, you will keep my commandments" (John 14:15) serve as stipulations, while promises of peace and the Spirit read like blessings. This deliberate framing signals that the Son inaugurates a new covenantal order, one sustained by the Advocate rather than temple rites. The personal tone—"I will not leave you as orphans" (John 14:18)—intimates emotional intimacy, preparing disciples for a relational bond with the Spirit that surpasses physical proximity to Jesus. Historically, the Farewell Discourse emerges in a post-Temple context, when Jewish worshipers grappled with loss; Jesus' promise of the Spirit anticipates a worship unbound by geography. The rhetorical urgency and repeated "truly, truly" tags underscore the discourse's normative weight for the believing community. Recognizing this covenantal renewal setting equips readers to hear the Spirit's inaugural words not as abstractions but as the linchpin of Jesus' final will and testament. As we turn to the disciples' emotional landscape, we see why a Helper is so desperately needed.

1.2 Grief, Consolation, and the Need for Another Helper

The Gospel repeatedly emphasizes the disciples' sorrow at Jesus' departure—"Now I am going to Him who sent me, yet none of you asks me, 'Where are you going?'" (John 16:5). Their grief arises from impending loss of tangible guidance, community cohesion, and prophetic certainty. Into this vacuum Jesus introduces the Spirit as *allos*, another Helper "of the same kind," signaling both continuity and distinction. Consolation becomes a central pastoral theme: Jesus assures them that the Spirit will bring "peace" (John 14:27) unlike the fragile peace the world offers. The deep emotion of the discourse— tears, longing, confusion—exposes human dependency on embodied presence, setting the stage for the Spirit's indwelling solution. In the post-Temple era, sorrow over cultic displacement amplifies the need for a non-geographic Helper. John's community, facing dispersion and persecution, would have heard fresh comfort in the promise of a Helper who remains within rather than beside believers. This contrast between grief and consolation highlights the Spirit's unique ministry: He does not merely replace Jesus' physical form but fulfills the

81

disciples' relational needs more profoundly. Having sensed their sorrow, we now ask: who exactly is this Advocate in linguistic and cultural terms?

1.3 Johannine Audience and Post-Temple Context

John wrote with an audience likely spanning Jewish and Gentile Christians, many of whom had witnessed the Temple's destruction in 70 AD. Their identity crises—Is Christianity distinct from Judaism? How do we worship without a central Temple?—resonated deeply with Jesus' paradigm shift toward Spirit-led presence. The Gospel's heavy use of temple imagery (e.g., Jesus predicting its destruction in John 2:19–21) prepares readers to receive a new locus of divine presence: the believer's body as Spirit-temple (1 Cor 6:19). Johannine communities in Asia Minor faced social ostracism and theological fragmentation; the promise of a Helper who convicts, unifies, and empowers would have been profoundly stabilizing. Moreover, secessionist movements within early Christianity disputed the Spirit's authenticity; John's clear testimony—"the Spirit of truth… whom the world cannot receive" (John 14:17)—serves as corrective. Understanding this context helps us appreciate why John emphasizes both the Spirit's intimacy (indwelling) and transcendence (world's inability to receive Him). As we move into lexical analysis, this background reminds us that *paraklētos* offered hope to readers living in the shadow of Temple loss and doctrinal confusion.

2 Lexical Portrait: Paraklētos in Greco-Roman and Jewish Usage

2.1 Legal Advocate versus Intimate Comforter—semantic spectrum

The Greek term *paraklētos* combines *para* ("beside") with *kaleō* ("to call"), yielding "one called alongside" for support. In Greco-Roman courts, a *paraklētos* was a legal advocate, pleading another's case before a magistrate—a role requiring rhetorical skill, moral authority, and personal presence. Jewish hearers familiar with the Septuagint would also know *paraklēsis* as consolation offered to mourners (Isa 40:1), carrying tender emotional support. John's readers thus perceived the Spirit simultaneously as courtroom defender and sympathetic companion. This semantic breadth resists reduction to mere energy: a force cannot plead, and an emotion cannot argue persuasively. The dual imagery shapes our understanding of the

Advocate's ministries—He both defends believers in cosmic judgment (John 16:8–11) and comforts them in personal grief (John 14:18–19). Early Christian apologists leveraged this lexical spectrum to illustrate how the Spirit's advocacy addresses both legal standing before God and experiential consolation. Recognizing these nuances primes us to trace how the Spirit engages in courtroom testimony alongside apostolic eyewitnesses.

2.2 Septuagintal antecedents of paraklēsis and consolation

In the Septuagint, *paraklēsis* appears in prophetic texts offering comfort: "Comfort, comfort my people, says your God" (Isa 40:1). The verb *parakaleō* also describes God's exhortation to return from exile (Jer 13:11), blending encouragement with moral summons. Such uses reveal that consolation in Jewish Scripture is never sentimental but covenantal, calling Israel back to fidelity. The Spirit's role as *paraklētos* thus inherits both the comforter's warmth and the convictor's urgency. In Nehemiah 9:30, the Spirit's warnings to Israel are described as a form of exhortation—another facet of *parakaleō*. These LXX precedents frame the Spirit's ministry as deeply involved in Israel's moral renewal, anticipating the New-Testament Advocate's convicting work (John 16:8). Understanding the LXX context illuminates why John's Jewish-Christian audience would perceive the Spirit not as impersonal wind but as a personal Comforter whose first language is Hebrew-infused consolation. This leads us naturally to explore Graeco-Roman courtroom imagery.

2.3 Hellenistic courtroom imagery and forensic resonance

Legal advocacy in Hellenistic cities involved professionals who took up the defense of those lacking rhetorical training, often speaking extemporaneously and forging personal bonds with judges and juries. Public records show that *paraklētai* argued cases of debt, land disputes, and citizenship, forging social trust alongside legal strategy. The judge's decision hinged not merely on facts but on the advocate's character and persuasive presence. For early Christians, understanding this milieu meant perceiving the Spirit as one who not only pleads their defense against cosmic accusations (Rom 8:33–34) but does so with personal integrity. Paul's later language—"Christ Jesus... who also makes intercession for us" (Rom 8:34)—draws on the same imagery. By situating *paraklētos* within Hellenistic law courts, we grasp that advocacy entails volitional choice, rhetorical facility, and relational proximity—qualities incompatible with impersonal explanations. This forensic background sets the stage for

Jesus' promise of "another Paraclete" who will continue His legal and pastoral ministries.

3 "Another Paraklētos": Continuity and Distinction from Jesus (John 14:16–17)

3.1 "Another of the same kind" (*allos*)—functional succession

Jesus uses the term *allos*—"another of the same kind"—to describe the coming Spirit, signaling both similarity and distinction. *Heteros* would imply a different type; *allos* conveys one who functions equivalently. Disciples observing Jesus' teaching, healings, and prophetic insight would expect a replacement able to mirror these ministries. The Spirit thus assumes roles Jesus performs—teaching, bearing witness, guiding—yet does so in a unique mode: indwelling rather than incarnate. The choice of *allos* also highlights the personal continuity of care: the Advocate shares the Son's compassionate heart, ensuring that believers continue to receive personalized guidance. At the same time, the distinction prevents conflation: the Spirit is not a reincarnated Jesus but another Person executing complementary tasks. This delicate balance of continuity and distinction is central to Trinitarian theology. Recognizing the import of *allos* prepares readers to explore the Spirit's abiding presence.

3.2 Abiding *meta* and *en* believers—permanent indwelling

John employs two prepositions—*meta* ("with") and *en* ("in")—to describe the Spirit's abiding presence (John 14:17). *Meta* emphasizes relational accompaniment: the Spirit remains beside believers as a constant companion. *En* signals internal indwelling: the Spirit enters the believer's inner life, shaping thoughts and affections. This dual language surpasses Old-Testament episodic fillings; it introduces a permanent residency model, a personal interiority accessible at any moment. The term *abide* (menō) echoes Jesus' own abiding in the Father (John 14:10), suggesting that Spirit-indwelt believers participate in the same interpenetration that characterizes the Trinity. Abiding also implies mutual dwelling: as Jesus abides in believers (John 15:4), so they abide in Him through the Spirit, forging a triadic relational network. The permanence of indwelling ensures that the Spirit's personal advocacy and teaching ministries are ever-present, a critical assurance for persecutions and trials. Understanding *meta* and *en* readies us to appreciate the love-obedience matrix where this communion unfolds.

3.3 Spirit of Truth contrasted with the world's inability to perceive

Jesus calls the Spirit the "Spirit of truth," highlighting His role in disclosing divine reality (John 14:17). This title contrasts with the "spirit of error" that blinds the world (1 John 4:6), underscoring that truth-telling is personal testimony, not abstract fact delivery. The world's inability to receive the Spirit—"it neither sees him nor knows him"—emphasizes that personal receptivity requires relational openness, not intellectual assent alone. The Spirit's truth ministry entails discerning the world's patterns, convicting of sin, and guiding into righteousness (John 16:8–11). Such functions presuppose personal volition and active engagement with human hearts, rather than passive diffusion of objective data. The dichotomy between those "who do what is evil" (John 3:19) and Spirit-receptive believers highlights the Person's intentional outreach. Recognizing the Spirit as Truth-person clarifies why His ministry must be discerned through relational criteria—a theme we will see echoed in His teaching and reminding work.

4 Indwelling Presence: "I Will Not Leave You Orphans" (John 14:18–23)

4.1 Mutual indwelling of Father, Son, and Spirit in disciples

Jesus' promise, "I will not leave you as orphans; I will come to you," unfolds into a mutual indwelling framework: the Father's love is given "in my name" by the Spirit, and the Son makes His home in believers who keep His word (John 14:23). This triadic reciprocity mirrors the intra-Trinitarian perichoresis—one Person's love and presence extended through the others into the disciple's heart. The Spirit's role is pivotal: as the personal conduit of divine presence, He mediates both the Father's and the Son's indwelling. Such relational intimacy presupposes a Person who can transfer presence, maintain relational identity, and preserve mutual indwelling without confusion. The communal impact is profound: each believer becomes a dwelling place for the triune God, fostering unity among disparate individuals. This mutual indwelling also safeguards personal distinctiveness, for the Spirit bears witness to the Son in the same hearts. Understanding this dynamic prepares us to explore the love-obedience matrix that actualizes such presence.

4.2 Love-obedience matrix as the sphere of divine disclosure

Jesus insists that loving Him and keeping His commandments constitutes the sphere in which the Spirit's personal presence flourishes (John 14:15, 21). Love here is not mere affection but covenantal fidelity, an active commitment animated by the Spirit's transformative work. Obedience is not legalistic compliance but relational responsiveness, enabled by Spirit-empowerment. In this love-obedience matrix, the Spirit discloses deeper knowledge of the Father's character and the Son's mission (John 14:21–23). Personal transformation thus becomes the litmus test for genuine indwelling: only those who love Jesus experience the Advocate's presence in fullness. This ethical dimension underscores that personal presence is not automatic but conditioned on relational openness, a synergy unique to a Person with will and discernment. Recognizing the matrix's contours readies us to perceive how personal communion replaces physical sight of Jesus.

4.3 Personal communion replacing physical sight of Jesus

Jesus comforts His disciples with the promise that whereas they have seen Him physically, they will know the Father and the Son through the Spirit's personal presence (John 14:19–20). This shift from visible proximity to indwelling communion underscores the Spirit's role as relational mediator. Physical sight, tied to space and time, yields to spiritual perception, accessible across distances and ages. The Spirit enables believers to "see" Jesus in inner experience—through guidance, remembrance of His words, and manifestation of His character (John 16:14). This intimate communion transforms the nature of discipleship: it becomes an ongoing conversation with a divine Person rather than retrospective memory of a historical figure. The promise anticipates the church's sacramental and communal life, where the Spirit continually unveils Christ's presence. Understanding this transformative replacement of physical sight with personal communion prepares us to appreciate the Spirit's teaching and reminding ministries.

5 Teaching and Reminding Ministry (John 14:26)

5.1 Recall of Jesus' words—canonical foundation for Gospel composition

Jesus promises that the Spirit "will remind you of all that I have said to you," indicating an active ministry of memory rather than passive recollection. This promise assumes that the disciples will forget or misremember, revealing their human limitations. The Spirit's role is not merely to jog their minds but to bring Jesus' exact words and their intended meaning back into focus, ensuring doctrinal fidelity. In the early church, this ministry underwrote the composition of the Gospel itself: the Spirit guided eyewitnesses and authors such as John in selecting, arranging, and preserving Jesus' teachings (cf. Luke 1:4; 2 Tim 3:16). As letters circulated, congregations read them "in the hearing of the Spirit" (1 Cor 14:2), trusting that the Spirit would authenticate the apostolic message. This dynamic preserved the unity of Gospel proclamation across diverse communities, preventing inventiveness or doctrinal drift. In practical terms, Spirit-led remembrance empowered preachers to apply Jesus' parables, discourse, and commands to new circumstances—whether encountering persecution, internal division, or moral dilemmas. The Spirit's accuracy in recalling Jesus' words also testifies to His intimate knowledge of the Son's mind (1 Cor 2:11), affirming personal continuity between the incarnate ministry and the church's teaching. This precision contrasts sharply with vague spiritual impressions, insisting that genuine Spirit activity is tethered to Jesus' revealed word. As communities reflected on these words, the Spirit illumined deeper layers of meaning, moving us into progressive illumination.

5.2 Progressive illumination without doctrinal novelty

Beyond simple recollection, the Spirit "will teach you all things" but "will not speak on his own authority" (John 16:13). This coupling indicates that the Spirit's teaching ministry is both revelatory and subordinate to Jesus' self-disclosure. The Spirit gradually unfolds implications and applications of Jesus' life and death, guiding the church into contexts unforeseen by the disciples—such as Gentile inclusion (Acts 10) and the shape of ecclesial ministry (1 Cor 12). Yet this illumination never contradicts the apostolic witness: the Spirit protects doctrinal continuity, preventing novelty that undermines the Gospel's core. Historical controversies—Gnostic claims to secret wisdom or Montanist pronouncements of new prophetic revelations— were refuted by reaffirming that true Spirit-inspired teaching always aligns with the apostolic deposit (2 Pet 1:21). Within local gatherings, the Spirit prompted further questions, communal discernment, and application-oriented insights, fostering spiritual maturity (Eph 4:11– 16). This progressive illumination equipped believers to navigate cultural shifts, ethical challenges, and theological debates without losing foundational truths. By demonstrating both dynamism and restraint, the Spirit shows Himself as a personal Teacher—willing to reveal more yet unwilling to deviate from the Christ-centered Gospel.

As we see Him teaching, we also hear Him echoing Old-Testament wisdom traditions.

5.3 Pedagogical parallels with Old-Testament Wisdom traditions

John's depiction of the Spirit as *didaskalos* ("teacher") resonates with Old-Testament images of Wisdom personified, whose voice calls to learners (Prov 1–9). Just as Wisdom guided Israel in moral and practical decisions, the Spirit illumines the path of discipleship (Prov 2:10–11). The Spirit's teaching integrates head and heart, echoing Psalm 119's depiction of Torah as life-giving instruction—"your word is a lamp to my feet and a light to my path" (Ps 119:105)—but now internalized through personal indwelling. In Deuteronomy, Moses commands the Spirit to instill God's statutes in children's hearts (Deut 6:6); in John, this promise finds fulfillment as the Spirit etches Christ's words into believers' lives. The didactic functions of prophecy and instruction in the prophets (Isa 30:21; Jer 31:33) anticipate the New-Testament Spirit's ministry of teaching and remembrance. These parallels highlight continuity: the Spirit who taught Israel externally now teaches the church internally, reinforcing personal agency across covenants. Recognizing these wisdom intersections primes us for exploring the Spirit's courtroom-type witness in John 15.

6 Witness in the Cosmic Trial (John 15:26–27)

6.1 Spirit's courtroom testimony alongside apostolic eye-witness

Jesus describes the Spirit as one who "will testify about me" in concert with the disciples' witness (John 15:26–27). The courtroom metaphor evokes a public trial in which multiple witnesses confirm the truth of Jesus' identity and mission. In the Roman and Jewish judicial systems, corroboration by more than one witness ensured legal credibility (Deut 19:15). The Spirit's testimony thus functions as divine attestation, validating the apostles' testimonies against accusations by religious authorities and cosmic adversaries. Unlike mere human witnesses, the Spirit's testimony is omniscient and infallible, exposing hidden truths and countering counterfeit claims. This assures the church that its mission rests on a transcendent foundation, not mere human eloquence. The Spirit's testimony transcends temporal limitations, persisting through successive generations and across cultural boundaries. By placing the Spirit on the stand, John emphasizes personal agency: the Spirit chooses to speak, confront, and vindicate. This forensic role transitions naturally into the themes of opposition and vindication.

6.2 World hatred, persecution, and vindication themes

Jesus warns that "the world will hate you," echoing His own experience, yet assures disciples that the Spirit will empower their testimony (John 15:18–21; 16:1–3). This hatred stems from the world's hostility to truth—a truth the Spirit proclaims without compromise. Persecution becomes the arena of witness, where the Spirit's courtroom role intensifies: He grants courage, clarity of speech (Luke 12:11–12), and boldness to face legal and social sanctions. The Spirit's vindication theme surfaces as He confirms believers' integrity through miraculous signs, communal solidarity, and ultimate eschatological approval (Rev 6:9–11). Early Christian martyrs testified to this vindication, singing hymns under Roman persecution. The Spirit's judicial ministry thus encompasses both present empowerment and future vindication, ensuring that hatred cannot extinguish divine purposes. This comprehensive advocacy readies us to consider how the Spirit convicts the world.

6.3 Missionary horizon—Spirit-empowered proclamation to the nations

The Spirit's testimony is not confined to Jerusalem's courts but extends to "the ends of the earth" (Acts 1:8). "You will bear witness… to the end" (John 15:27) foreshadows the global mission empowered by the Spirit, who equips apostles for cross-cultural communication, languages, and contextual proclamation (Acts 2:4; 10:44–48). Missionary journeys—Paul in Asia Minor, Peter in Caesarea— demonstrate how the Spirit directs travel, opens doors, and authenticates message through signs (Rom 15:18–19). The Spirit's personal guidance ensures that proclamation remains faithful and relevant, preventing syncretistic dilution. His witness to Christ transcends ethnic and linguistic barriers, uniting diverse peoples under one testimony. By positioning the Spirit at the heart of mission, John aligns courtroom advocacy with global evangelism, showing that the Spirit's personal ministry launches and sustains the church's outward movement. Having seen His witness, we next examine His convicting work.

7 Convicting the World (John 16:8–11)

7.1 Sin exposed: unbelief as relational rupture

Jesus foretells that the Spirit "will convict the world concerning sin, because they do not believe in me" (John 16:8). This conviction is not an abstract moralizing but a relational diagnosis: unbelief constitutes a breach in fellowship with God. The Spirit's personal ministry here involves discerning hearts (1 Cor 2:10), shining a light on hidden unbelief, and prompting awareness of alienation from the Father. The term *convict* (Greek *elego*) implies personal confrontation, akin to a defender exposing inconsistencies in testimony. This interpersonal exposure awakens souls to their need for repentance, as in Saul's Damascus encounter (Acts 9:4–6). Recognizing unbelief as sin reframes evangelism: the Spirit's convicting work precedes saving faith, ensuring that conversion is relational restoration rather than mere behavior modification. This foundational conviction leads to the revelation of righteousness.

7.2 Righteousness revealed: vindication of the ascended Son

Following conviction of sin, the Spirit "will convict the world concerning righteousness, because I go to the Father, and you will see me no more" (John 16:10). Here *righteousness* denotes the vindication of Christ's person and work—His resurrection and ascension demonstrate divine approval (Rom 1:4). The Spirit's personal task is to make this righteousness known, persuading individuals that Jesus' life, death, and exaltation inaugurate a new standard of divine acceptance. The disciples themselves received this conviction at Pentecost (Acts 2:14–36), proclaiming Jesus as both Lord and Christ. The Spirit's unveiling of Christ's righteousness transforms disciples' identities, aligning them with the ascended Son. This personal testimony's power is seen in changed lives and communities, as believers embody the righteousness the Spirit reveals. From righteousness, the Spirit moves to judgment.

7.3 Judgment pronounced: defeat of the ruler of this world

Lastly, the Spirit "will convict the world concerning judgment, because the ruler of this world is judged" (John 16:11). This judgment refers to Satan's decisive defeat through Christ's cross and resurrection (Col 2:15), a verdict the Spirit proclaims with authority. The Spirit's personal ministry here involves exposing evil's dominion and announcing its downfall, empowering believers to live in freedom (Luke 10:18–19). This cosmic judgment reassures the church that opposition has been disarmed, even as persecution continues. The Spirit accompanies each believer's stand against the powers, reminding them that ultimate victory belongs to Christ and His witnesses. By completing the triad of convicting sin, unveiling righteousness, and declaring judgment, the Spirit fulfills the courtroom metaphor introduced in John 15. Having seen His judicial ministries, we now turn to His guiding work.

8 Guiding into All Truth (John 16:12–15)

8.1 "He will speak … He will declare"—verbal inspiration and prophecy

Jesus says, "He will not speak on his own authority, but whatever he hears he will speak" (John 16:13), emphasizing the Spirit's fidelity to the Son's revelation. This double *speaking* motif—first, *lalei* ("will speak"), then *anaggellei* ("will declare")—suggests both immediate utterance and formal proclamation, akin to prophetic announcement. The Spirit's verbal inspiration extends prophecy into the church's life, equipping believers for mission and discernment. Early Christian communities expected the Spirit to reveal God's will in corporate gatherings (1 Cor 14:24–25) and to direct apostolic letters. This guidance balances spontaneity with continuity: the Spirit brings fresh light while maintaining doctrinal coherence. Recognizing the Spirit's verbal ministry situates prophecy as an ongoing, personal dialogue between God and the church, not a closed canon of the past. As the Spirit speaks, He also points ahead to things to come.

8.2 Things to come: eschatological orientation of Spirit guidance

Jesus adds that the Spirit "will declare to you the things that are to come" (John 16:13), indicating a prophetic unveiling of future realities. This orientation prepares believers for unfolding redemptive events— Pentecost, the church's expansion, Christ's return—ensuring that faith remains future-directed. The Spirit's guidance into eschatological truths enables the church to persevere amid trials, hunger for consummation, and anticipate divine restoration. In Acts, the Spirit propels the missionary trajectory (Acts 16:6–10) and warns of upcoming hardships (Acts 20:23). Revelation's vivid visions (Rev 1:10; 4:1) derive their authority from the Spirit's foresight, confirming the Spirit-person's role as apocalyptic interpreter. Eschatological guidance thus intertwines personal encouragement with cosmic scope. From future revelations we move to the Spirit's doxological focus.

8.3 Doxological focus—Spirit glorifies the Son and, through Him, the Father

Finally, Jesus declares, "He will take what is mine and declare it to you… the Spirit will glorify me, for he will take what is mine and declare it to you" (John 16:14). The term *glorify* (*doxazō*) speaks of magnifying worth and leading worship. The Spirit's personal ministry is thus not self-promotional but Christocentric and, by extension, Fatherward. By revealing Jesus' exaltation, the Spirit channels glory from Son to Father, sustaining the Trinitarian economy of praise. This doxological function shapes the heart of Christian worship, centering it on Christ's person and work rather than on human emotional experiences. Spirit-led doxology unites truth, love, and future hope into acts of worship that reflect the personal relations within the Godhead. Having surveyed teaching, witnessing, convicting, and guiding, we are now poised to examine textual markers of the Spirit's personhood.

9 Grammatical Markers of Personhood

9.1 Masculine pronoun *ekeinos* governing neuter *pneuma*

John's careful use of the masculine pronoun *ekeinos* ("he") to refer to the neuter noun *pneuma* ("spirit") signals intentional personhood. Greek typically defaults to neuter pronouns for neuter nouns, yet John insists on *ekeinos*, aligning the Spirit with personal referents like Jesus (John 1:29). This grammatical choice underscores that the Spirit is not an impersonal entity but a "he" who thinks, wills, and loves. Early Greek-speaking believers would have noticed this nuance, distinguishing the Spirit from abstract qualities. The Johannine community, accustomed to fine literary detail, would hear *ekeinos* as a mark of ontological distinction—a Person in God's economy. Patristic commentators, such as Theophilus of Antioch, cited this usage to support the Spirit's deity and personality. This pronoun usage also shapes how subsequent Trinitarian formulas are crafted, ensuring that all three Persons are linguistically coherent. The *ekeinos* choice ties into patterns of personal address—believers pray "Come, Spirit" (Rev 22:17)—rather than invoking an "it." Recognizing this grammatical marker prepares us to see further syntactical emphases in Jesus' promises.

9.2 Change of verb gender in 14:26 and 16:13–14—stylistic emphases

In John 14:26 and 16:13–14, John strategically shifts verb forms to reflect the Spirit's agency. In 14:26, the reminding function uses a masculine participle (*ho mnasqhēsōn*), aligning with *ekeinos* to emphasize personal action. By contrast, the verb "take" (*lambanēsei*) in 16:14 appears in the neuter, highlighting the content of revelation rather than the Actor. These shifts are not random but draw readers' attention to moments of relational intimacy (reminding) versus doctrinal transmission (taking). In Greek rhetoric, such verb gender alternations create subtle emphases, a technique John uses elsewhere when highlighting the Word's personhood (John 1:1, "ho logos ēn pros ton Theon"). The interplay between masculine and neuter forms underscores that while the Spirit's personhood is primary, His functions—revealing Christ's words—are content-focused. Early exegetes like Cyril of Alexandria remarked on these stylistic nuances to defend the Spirit's personal activity against logoi or impersonal interpretations. This grammatical artistry thus reinforces theological points: the Spirit is both Person and messenger. Understanding these subtleties readies us to explore how these personal and functional distinctions map onto broader Trinitarian relations.

9.3 Implications for Trinitarian syntax and theology

John's grammatical precision provides fodder for early Trinitarian formulations. By using masculine pronouns and carefully gendered verbs, John models how to speak of three distinct Persons without lapsing into modalism or tritheism. The syntactical pattern—Father sends Son, Son sends Spirit (*pempo*)—establishes a sequential order of missions while preserving ontological equality. This linguistic choreography anticipates later creedal language—"who proceeds from the Father" (Nicene Creed)—by showing how grammatical markers can safeguard doctrinal clarity. Augustine and the Latin Fathers drew on Johannine syntax to argue for the Spirit's distinct hypostasis within the one divine essence (*una substantia*). Modern theologians likewise note that grammar shapes doctrine: misreading these markers can lead to depersonalized pneumatology or subordinationism. Recognizing the Spirit's personhood at the level of syntax thus becomes a hermeneutical principle for interpreting all triadic passages. As we move from grammatical proof-texts to narrative evidence outside the Farewell Discourse, these linguistic insights remain our guide.

10 Johannine Spirit Passages Outside the Farewell Discourse

10.1 Baptismal descent and abiding on Jesus (John 1:32–34)

In John 1:32–34, John the Baptist testifies that he saw the Spirit descend "like a dove" from heaven and remain ("menei") on Jesus. The Spirit's descent is personal and visible, a theophanic sign marking Jesus as the Chosen One. The verb *menei* mirrors the abiding motif of the Farewell Discourse, yet here it attaches specifically to Jesus, confirming His divine sonship. Observers witness a relational indwelling: the Spirit stays with Jesus throughout His ministry, a continuous personal presence rather than a temporary empowerment. The image of the dove conveys gentleness and peace, preluding the Spirit's role as Comforter. This baptismal event sets a precedent for believers' own Spirit baptisms (Acts 2:4), establishing a pattern of visible descent followed by abiding companionship. The early church linked this first anointing to the church's initiation, interpreting believers' baptisms as participation in Jesus' Spirit-anointing. The narrative thus broadens our understanding of the Spirit's personal presence beyond the Upper Room.

10.2 New-birth dialogue with Nicodemus (John 3:5–8)

Jesus' conversation with Nicodemus introduces the necessity of being "born of water and Spirit" (John 3:5). The Greek *pneumatos* clearly refers to the personal *Pneuma*, not abstract wind. Jesus contrasts fleshly water birth with Spirit-born life, emphasizing the Spirit's personal agency in regeneration—"You must be born again" implies a direct act of the Spirit within the individual. The ensuing statement—"The wind blows where it wishes"—employs the wordplay between *pneuma* (Spirit) and *pneuma* (wind), but Jesus immediately refocuses on the Spirit's intentional movement: believers experience new life not by chance breeze but by Spirit's personal will. Nicodemus's confusion highlights the difficulty of grasping the Spirit's invisible but efficacious Personhood. Jesus' corrective underlines that spiritual rebirth is a relational event initiated by the Spirit, who chooses time and subject. This intimate regeneration anticipates the indwelling community identity discussed later.

10.3 Living water promise at Tabernacles (John 7:37–39)

On the final day of the Feast of Tabernacles, Jesus invites those thirsty to drink, promising they will receive "streams of living water" (John 7:38). John clarifies that this refers to the Spirit "not yet given" because Jesus was not yet glorified (7:39). The living water metaphor resonates with Ezekiel 47's river flowing from the temple, yet John recasts it as Spirit-outpouring into hearts rather than geographic phenomena. The streams suggest ongoing personal refreshment, a dynamic ministry rather than static possession. The context of Tabernacles—the festival commemorating wilderness water miracles—underscores the Spirit's role in fulfilling Israel's historical thirst. Jesus' promise thus transforms cultic ritual into personal spiritual reality, marking the Spirit's imminent arrival as both gift and empowerment. This passage anticipates the Spirit's communal works in the church and transitions us toward post-resurrection inbreathing.

10.4 Resurrection commissioning and symbolic inbreathing (John 20:22)

In John 20:22, the risen Jesus breathes on the disciples and says, "Receive the Holy Spirit." This symbolic action parallels Genesis 2:7's divine breath creating humanity, now signifying new creation for the church. The inbreathing conveys personal intimacy: Jesus imparts the Spirit directly, not through visible signs like wind or tongues. This gesture inaugurates the disciples into post-resurrection mission, equipping them with the Advocate before Pentecost. The personal impartation underscores that the Spirit's presence arises from Christ's own breath, highlighting relational continuity. The disciples' reception of the Spirit prepares them for authoritative proclamation of forgiveness (John 20:23), indicating judicial empowerment. This narrative motif bridges Old-Testament inbreathings with New-Testament Spirit-empowerment, reinforcing the Spirit's role as personal life-giver and commission-giver. From these varied Johannine contexts we proceed to examine how the Spirit's sending unfolds trinitarian dynamics.

11 Trinitarian Dynamics in the Sending of the Paraklētos

11.1 "Whom the Father will send in My name" (mission from the Father)

Jesus repeatedly affirms that the Advocate is sent by the Father "in my name" (John 14:26), emphasizing that the Spirit's mission originates with the Father and is authorized by the Son's identity. Sending *in name* connotes artistic representation and delegated authority: the Spirit carries the Son's authority into the world, ensuring continuity of Christ's presence. This trinitarian sending mirrors the Father's sending of the Son (John 3:16) and forms a pattern for divine missions: Father initiates, Son embodies, Spirit sustains. The Spirit's relational origin in the Father secures His deity, refuting any creaturely reduction. Early liturgical prayers—"Come, Holy Spirit, sent by the Father"—echo this model, embedding trinitarian theology into corporate worship. Understanding this dimension underscores the Spirit's personal distinctiveness within the Godhead's sending economy.

11.2 "Whom I will send to you from the Father" (mission from the Son)

Jesus also declares, "I will send him to you" (John 15:26; 16:7), affirming His own role in the Spirit's mission. This sending *from* the Father by the Son reflects eternal relations—just as the Son proceeds from the Father, so the Spirit proceeds from the Father and is sent by the Son. The preposition *anhōthen* ("from above" or "again") in John 3:31 further connects Christ's heavenly origin to the Spirit's descending mission. By involving both Father and Son in the Spirit's sending, John weaves a triadic tapestry of personal relationships. This interpenetration of missions safeguards unity: the Spirit never acts independently but always in harmony with the Father's will and the Son's commission. Corporate formulas such as "In the name of the Father, and of the Son, and of the Holy Spirit" thus find their biblical warrant. Recognizing this dual sending clarifies how the Spirit's personal ministries serve the wider divine economy rather than individual preference.

11.3 Eternal procession and temporal mission—Filioque dialogue

John's language anticipates later theological debates over the Spirit's procession—*ek tou Patros* in Eastern tradition or "and the Son" (*Filioque*) in the Western Creed. The dual sending statements in the Farewell Discourse underscore both eternal relations (procession as personal property) and temporal missions (sending as economic action). The Spirit's personal link to both Father and Son allows for a nuanced filioque understanding: procession grounds mission without confounding essence. John's text thus becomes a locus classicus for exploring how temporal sending reflects eternal procession, a dynamic that sustains the church's doctrinal integrity. The Spirit's personal procession ensures that He shares in the Father-Son communion, while His mission extends that communion into the world. This synthesis readies us to consider the implications of the Paraklētos promise for discipleship and ecclesiology.

12 Implications for Johannine Discipleship and Ecclesiology

12.1 Obedience, love, and experiential knowledge of God

John ties the Spirit's presence to the believer's obedience and love: "If anyone loves me, he will keep my word, and my Father will love him... and we will come to him and make our home with him" (John 14:23). The Spirit actualizes this promise by enabling both the capacity to obey and the experiential knowledge of God's love. Discipleship thus becomes an embodied relationship with a Person who empowers moral fidelity and intimate knowing. This experiential knowledge transcends propositional assent, transforming identity through union with the triune God. Small-group pilgrimages and personal spiritual disciplines in Johannine communities would have emphasized Spirit-facilitated behaviors—service, confession, mutual love—over mere ritual compliance. The Spirit-person's presence turns obedience into joyful participation in divine life, a hallmark of authentic Christian formation.

12.2 Community identity shaped by indwelling Spirit rather than Temple cult

In John's community, the Spirit replaces the Temple as the locus of divine presence, forging new communal identity. Baptism into the Spirit (1 Cor 12:13) unites Jew and Gentile, slave and free, male and female, dissolving ethnocentric and socio-cultural barriers (Gal 3:28). Spirit-indwelt believers become living stones in a spiritual house (1 Pet 2:5), a communion not limited by geography or ethnicity. The Spirit's presence thus defines the church as the new Temple—a global, egalitarian body animated by a personal Advocate. Liturgical practice shifts from sacrifice at an altar to Spirit-led assemblies marked by prophetic speech (1 Cor 14), sacramental remembrance (John 6:53–58), and mutual edification. This ecclesiology undergirds later creeds that call the church the "Temple of the Holy Spirit," highlighting the Spirit-person's shaping of communal life.

12.3 Assurance in persecution—presence of the Advocate in every age

John's promise of the Spirit as Helper offers assurance to disciples facing hostility: "The world cannot hate you, but it hates me... because you are not of the world" (John 15:18–19). The Spirit's indwelling presence provides steadfast companionship, courage, and prophetic clarity in trials. Early Christians drew hope from the Advocate's promised presence, writing letters from prison (e.g., 2 Tim) and singing hymns in catacombs. Martyrdom narratives repeatedly invoke the Spirit's strengthening assurance (Acts 7:55–60). This personal solidarity across generations assures believers that the Advocate remains faithful even when visible leaders fall. The Spirit's ongoing advocacy before the Father grants legal and relational security for the persecuted church. This enduring presence prepares us to trace the Spirit's promised work in Acts.

13 Bridge to Acts: From Upper-Room Promise to Pentecostal Reality

13.1 Narrative continuity—same personal Spirit, expanded arena

The transition from John's Gospel to Acts preserves the same Advocate-person, now moving from intimate farewell to public outpouring. Acts 1:4–5 echoes John's promise of Spirit baptism, while Acts 2:1–4 fulfills it with wind, fire, and tongues. The Spirit's personal identity remains consistent: He speaks, convicts, guides, and empowers the early church. The arena expands from the inner circle of twelve to a global mission, yet the Spirit's personal ministries— teaching, witnessing, convicting, guiding—retain their character. This narrative continuity assures readers that the Paraklētos promise is not symbolic but historically enacted.

13.2 Apostolic memory and Spirit-breathed proclamation

The apostles recall Jesus' Farewell words as they preach on Pentecost (Acts 2:14–36), attributing their boldness and accuracy to the Spirit's inspiration. Peter's speech mirrors Johannine themes— conviction of sin, revelation of Christ's righteousness, declaration of judgment—demonstrating the Spirit's personal work in public testimony. As the message spreads, congregations around the Mediterranean receive Spirit baptism, confirming the Spirit's personal ministry across cultures. This apostolic memory, preserved in Luke's narrative, underscores the Spirit's role in authorizing and authenticating the church's foundational proclamation.

Conclusion The Farewell Discourse in John's Gospel unveils the *Paraklētos* as the personal Advocate who embodies and extends Christ's own mission. Against the covenantal backdrop, John crafts a rich semantic tapestry—legal advocacy, intimate consolation, and forensic truth-telling—to describe a Spirit who indwells, teaches, convicts, and empowers. By distinguishing *allos* from *heteros*, emphasizing abiding *meta* and *en*, and situating the Spirit within the triadic perichoresis of Father and Son, John reveals a relational architecture poised to sustain the church in every era. As we have seen, the Spirit's personhood unfolds in mutual indwelling, love-conditioned disclosure, and the transformative replacement of physical sight with interior communion. These insights pave the way for exploring the Spirit's concrete ministries in Acts and Paul's letters, where the promised Advocate springs to life in the missionary church.

Chapter 5. Acts of the Apostles: The Spirit Directs a Mission

The Book of Acts unfolds the dynamic outworking of Jesus' promise that the Holy Spirit would guide, empower, and validate the church's mission. From the Upper Room's expectant waiting to the farthest reaches of the Roman Empire, Luke portrays the Spirit not as impersonal power but as a personal guide, commissioning leaders, equipping communities, convicting hearts, and orchestrating divine strategy. In this chapter, we will trace the Spirit's concrete actions—how He directs election, inspires proclamation, brings unity amid conflict, and upholds holiness within the nascent church—demonstrating that mission is fundamentally a Spirit-driven enterprise. By examining key narratives and theological patterns, we will see that the Apostle's journeys, communal structures, and global expansion all bear the hallmark of the Paraclete's personal agency, fulfilling Jesus' farewell promise in vibrant history.

1 From Promise to Presence: Narrative Bridge (Acts 1:1–14)

1.1 Forty-day instruction "through the Holy Spirit"—continuity with the risen Jesus

In the forty days between resurrection and ascension, Luke records that Jesus "presented himself alive by many proofs, appearing to them during forty days and speaking about the kingdom of God" (Acts 1:3). This instruction occurs "through the Holy Spirit," highlighting that Christ's post-resurrection teaching is mediated by the Spirit rather than by His former physical presence. Such a phrase signals continuity: the disciples' learning now proceeds via the Spirit, foreshadowing the Spirit's future teaching ministry in the church. Jesus does not simply impart information; He inaugurates a new mode of revelation whereby the Spirit will echo His words and illuminate their meaning. This period shapes the Apostles for Spirit-enabled mission, reinforcing that all foundational instruction for the church comes by Spirit inspiration. The Spirit-mediated teaching also underscores that the resurrected Jesus remains present and active, now abiding in the community through His Spirit. When Jesus affirms that repentance and forgiveness will be preached "in his name to all nations" (Acts 1:8), the disciples grasp that the Spirit will authenticate and empower this proclamation. The forty-day window thus builds a seamless narrative bridge: Jesus uses Spirit agency to train His followers for the worldwide advance they will soon undertake. Anticipation builds as the Paraklētos draws near, preparing the stage for corporate waiting.

1.2 Apostolic waiting and unified prayer in the upper room

Following Jesus' ascension, the eleven disciples return to Jerusalem and "devoted themselves to prayer" along with "the women and Mary the mother of Jesus, and his brothers" (Acts 1:14). This upper-room gathering is more than spiritual pietism; it is an apostolic convergence of prayerful expectancy, corporate discernment, and relational solidarity. The group prays for the Spirit's promised empowerment, modeling the "unceasing prayer" (1 Th 5:17) that sustains missional exertion. Their unity in prayer underscores that Spirit-directed ministry arises from communal dependence rather than individual charisma. The context of prayer also provides the framework for discernment: decisions about leadership, timing, and mission emerge from the Spirit's prompting within the fellowship. This contrast with impulsive activism highlights that genuine mission begins in the sanctuary of collective prayer. Luke's emphasis on prayer in the Spirit foreshadows later patterns where the Spirit speaks during corporate fasting (Acts 13:2) and guides councils (Acts 15:28). The upper room becomes the incubator where the Spirit's presence is awaited, reminding readers that mission must spring from Spirit-enabled communion. As the community prays, the narrative turns to the Spirit's first act of guiding apostolic leadership.

1.3 Spirit-guided replacement of Judas by the lot, foreshadowing future guidance

With the group gathered in prayer, Peter stands among the believers to address the vacancy left by Judas Iscariot's betrayal and death. Citing Scripture (Ps 69:25; 109:8), Peter proposes that the replacement must be one who accompanied them from baptism through resurrection (Acts 1:20–22). The apostles cast lots to choose between Joseph called Barsabbas and Matthias, and the lot falls on Matthias (Acts 1:26). While the method may seem quaint, it reflects a Spirit-guided process: lot-casting in Jewish practice often served as a means of discerning divine will when accompanied by prayer (Prov 16:33). Importantly, the community's prayerful posture ensures that the casting of lots is not random chance but a ritual seeking the Spirit's personal direction. This early instance foreshadows more explicit Spirit directives, such as "Do not go into Bithynia" (Acts 16:6) or "Set apart Barnabas and Saul" (Acts 13:2). The replacement of Judas thus prefigures the Spirit's ongoing guidance in selecting leaders, sending missionaries, and governing the church. As this foundational episode concludes, the Spirit's promised presence is now poised to descend, initiating the community's public mission.

2 Pentecost—Birth of a Spirit-Formed Community (Acts 2:1–47)

2.1 Audible, visible descent: wind, fire, and multilingual praise

On the Feast of Weeks, the gathered disciples experience a sudden, audible sound "like a mighty rushing wind" filling the house (Acts 2:2). This audible manifestation parallels Genesis's creation breath (Gen 1:2), signaling new creation in the community. Simultaneously, tongues of fire appear and rest on each participant (Acts 2:3), evoking purification and empowerment. Then the disciples begin speaking in other languages as the Spirit enables (Acts 2:4), reversing Babel's confusion (Gen 11) and symbolizing the Spirit's intention to reach all nations. The visible and audible signs confirm to bystanders that God is initiating a new covenant community—one bound by Spirit rather than by ethnicity or language. This dramatic descent underscores the personal dimension: the Spirit arrives to abide within, not just to energize from without. The communal effect is immediate—each member is included in the indwelling presence—creating a Spirit-formed unity that transcends social divisions. As the crowd marvels, Peter stands to interpret, unveiling the meaning of the signs.

2.2 Peter's Spirit-inspired interpretation of Joel and David

Filled with the Spirit's boldness (Acts 2:14), Peter addresses the astonished crowd, explaining that the phenomenon fulfills Joel's prophecy: "I will pour out my Spirit on all flesh" (Joel 2:28; Acts 2:17–21). He then connects the Spirit's outpouring to David's words about the resurrection and exaltation of Christ (Ps 16:8–11; Acts 2:25–31). This exegesis exemplifies the Spirit's role in teaching and revealing Scripture's deeper redemptive patterns, bridging prophecy and fulfillment. Peter's speech demonstrates the Spirit's personal guidance in selecting texts, constructing arguments, and applying them to Jesus' death and resurrection. The Spirit's interpretive ministry ensures that the church's foundational proclamation is not mere opinion but divinely authorized truth. As listeners respond with "What shall we do?" (Acts 2:37), Peter issues Spirit-driven pastoral directions, blending forensic declaration with relational invitation. This Spirit-inspired sermon sets the pattern for all apostolic witness.

2.3 Repentance, baptism, and Spirit gift—promise for successive generations

Moved by Peter's message, the crowd asks for guidance and receives three imperatives: repent, be baptized in the name of Jesus Christ, and receive the gift of the Holy Spirit (Acts 2:38). Peter promises that this gift is for them and their children and for all whom the Lord will call in future generations (Acts 2:39), framing Spirit reception as a perpetual covenant sign. Repentance marks a relational turn toward God, baptism signifies union with Christ in death and resurrection (Rom 6:4), and the Spirit gift ensures indwelling accompaniment. This triad becomes normative for Christian initiation: each believer participates in the same Spirit-baptism that launched the church. The communal dimension is equally vital: the initial 3,000 are added to the fellowship, signifying that Spirit-gift is both personal possession and corporate formation. As the chapter closes, the Spirit's presence shapes a community defined by new life and mission.

2.4 New communal ethos: teaching, table-fellowship, prayers, and awe

The text describes the early believers as devoted to apostles' teaching, fellowship, breaking of bread, and prayers (Acts 2:42). This fourfold rhythm—*didaskalia, koinōnia, klēsis tou artou, proseuchē*—reflects the Spirit's shaping of communal identity. Apostolic teaching, under Spirit inspiration, anchors the community in Christ's revelation. Fellowship arises from Spirit-wrought unity, breaking down barriers as "no one said that any of his possessions was his own" (Acts 4:32). Table-fellowship (often Eucharistic) embodies the incarnational presence of Christ mediated by the Spirit. Prayer, both private and corporate, remains open to Spirit guidance, anticipating further directives. An atmosphere of awe permeates gatherings (Acts 2:43), a spiritual "fear" that respects the Holy Spirit's personal holiness. This ethos prepares the church for the trials and expansions to come, setting the pattern for Spirit-driven community life. As conflicts emerge, the Spirit's boldness empowers public witness.

3 Courage and Signs: Public Witness under Spirit Boldness (Acts 3–4)

3.1 Lame man healed—Spirit-empowered continuation of Jesus' works

Peter and John, "filled with the Holy Spirit," approach the temple gate and heal a man lame from birth (Acts 3:1–6). Peter's declaration, "In the name of Jesus Christ of Nazareth, rise and walk," reflects Spirit-enabled authority, echoing Jesus' own healing ministry. The man's leap into the temple courts incites amazement and draws a crowd, creating an opportunity for Spirit-driven proclamation. This healing underlines continuity: the same divine power that raised Jesus operates through the church's leaders, demonstrating the Spirit's personal endorsement. The narrative affirms that miraculous signs are not mere spectacles but serve the Spirit's purpose of authenticating the gospel and inviting repentance. The visible outcome of personal Spirit action bridges the gap between Word and demonstration, setting the stage for confrontation with religious authorities.

3.2 Sanhedrin confrontation—Spirit fills Peter for fearless speech

When arrested and brought before the Sanhedrin, Peter stands "filled with the Holy Spirit" and delivers a fearless defense (Acts 4:8). Without prescribed rhetoric, he proclaims Jesus' resurrection and condemns his audience's rejection of the Messiah (Acts 4:10–12). The Spirit's filling here enhances courage, clarity, and theological precision; Peter's speech outflanks the priests' expectations of fearful compliance. The council, astonished by the apostles' boldness despite their lack of formal education, recognizes a supernatural underpinning (Acts 4:13). The Spirit's personal empowerment thus becomes both apologetic proof and pastoral encouragement: the church learns that opposition only amplifies Spirit-given witness. This event prompts the community to revise its prayer strategy the next day.

3.3 Corporate prayer meeting—earthquake and renewed boldness

Facing renewed threats, the believers gather in prayer, invoking Psalm 2's promise: "Why do the nations rage?" (Acts 4:24–26). Their petition asks for boldness to continue proclaiming Jesus' name and for signs of healing (Acts 4:29–30). In response, "the place in which they were gathered was shaken" (Acts 4:31), a tangible affirmation of the Spirit's presence and endorsement. The group is filled with the Spirit again, and they speak God's word with boldness. This divine shake-up cements corporate confidence that the Spirit actively supports their mission. By linking prayer, Spirit filling, and public proclamation, Luke illustrates a cyclical pattern: Spirit-inspired boldness leads to witness, opposition leads to prayer, prayer leads to renewed filling, and the cycle fuels mission momentum. As the community worships in "fear," their unity and witness prepare them for protecting purity in the Spirit.

4 Guarding Purity: Spirit as Judge of Deceit (Acts 5:1–11)

4.1 Ananias and Sapphira's conspiracy—lying "to the Holy Spirit"

Ananias and Sapphira sell property and claim to donate the full proceeds while secretly withholding part of the funds (Acts 5:1–3). Peter confronts Ananias: "Why has Satan filled your heart to lie to the Holy Spirit and to keep back for yourself part of the proceeds?" (Acts 5:3). This direct accusation highlights the Spirit's personal reality: the couple's deceit is a relational offense against a Person, not an abstract miscalculation. Their sin involves not merely lying to Peter or the church but to the Spirit who sanctifies and empowers communal witness. Sapphira's subsequent attempt to corroborate her husband's lie and her resulting death (Acts 5:8–10) further reinforce the Spirit's judicial authority. The story warns that the Spirit exercises personal holiness, capable of sorrow and righteous judgment. This dramatic episode underscores that upholding moral integrity is integral to Spirit-driven mission. As fear spreads through the young community, the narrative pivots to administrative structures for preserving Spirit purity.

4.2 Immediate discernment and prophetic exposure through Peter

Peter's instantaneous recognition of Ananias's sin demonstrates Spirit-enabled discernment, akin to prophetic insight in the Old Testament (1 Sam 16:1–13). He speaks as the Spirit's mouthpiece, declaring that Ananias has not lied to human beings but to God's Spirit. This prophetic exposure bypasses any human forensic process, underscoring the Spirit's direct judicial role. Sapphira's equal condemnation confirms that Peter's word reflects the Spirit's personal decree. The Spirit's immediate action affirms both His omniscience and His authority to enact consequences without intermediate agencies. This moment informs later Christian ethics: sin in the assembly is a direct affront to the Spirit, requiring repentance and communal accountability. Recognizing the Spirit's personal exposure of deceit prepares leaders to implement structures for Spirit-led delegation.

4.3 Holy fear spreads, reinforcing the Spirit's personal holiness

Following Ananias and Sapphira's deaths, "great fear came upon the whole church and upon all who heard of these things" (Acts 5:11). This fear is not terror of human reprisal but reverential awe before the Spirit's personal holiness and justice. Houses open for healing, and signs and wonders accompany the apostles, yet no one dares to join them falsely. The pervasive sense of fear functions as a protective communal ethos, ensuring sincerity in worship and mission. This phenomenon illustrates that the Spirit's personal presence carries ethical gravity, shaping both external operations and internal dispositions. The balance of power and humility established here allows the church to grow (Acts 5:14) without succumbing to superficial expansion. As the community thrives under Spirit purity, they turn next to wise administrative appointments for equitable service.

5 Administrative Insight: Choosing Servant-Leaders (Acts 6:1–7)

5.1 Crisis of neglected widows and communal murmuring

As the church grew, a tension arose: Hellenistic Jewish widows felt overlooked in the daily distribution of food while Hebraic widows were cared for (Acts 6:1). This disparity sparked murmuring among the Hellenists, threatening the unity essential for Spirit-directed mission. The murmurs reflect not merely logistical objections but a deeper anxiety: if temporal needs go unmet, the community's witness to Christ's compassion will be undermined. Luke's inclusion of this conflict underscores the Spirit's concern for holistic well-being—material equity as vital as spiritual proclamation. The apostles, perceiving that the Spirit's work in prayer and the ministry of the word should not be hindered, propose a structural solution rather than unilateral power-moves. Their response models Spirit-led leadership: listening to community concerns, diagnosing root causes, and devising inclusive strategies. The crisis thus becomes an opportunity to demonstrate that the Spirit's personal oversight extends to administrative details. This episode anticipates later biblical calls for wise stewardship (1 Cor 4:2) and reminds us that the Spirit values both Word ministry and social justice. The resolution of this murmuring crisis sets the stage for defining criteria for Spirit-filled service.

5.2 Criteria of "full of the Spirit and wisdom" for the Seven

In response to the crisis, the apostles instruct the community to select seven men "of good repute, full of the Spirit and of wisdom" (Acts 6:3). These dual criteria—Spirit-fullness and wisdom—underscore that leadership in the church requires both personal communion with the Spirit and the practical discernment to manage resources fairly. Good repute highlights character integrity, ensuring that those tasked with care enjoy the trust of the whole fellowship. Being "full of the Spirit" affirms that administrative functions, like preaching or healing, cannot be performed in a purely secular mode but require the same personal indwelling that empowers other ministries. Wisdom, rooted in God's own nature (James 3:17), enables servant-leaders to navigate complex cultural and interpersonal dynamics. The combination ensures that the Seven will represent the Spirit-person's priorities: compassion blended with discernment. Early Christian communities would have recognized these markers as essential for preventing abuses and maintaining unity. The selection process thus embodies

Spirit-guided democratization: authority distributed without hierarchical monopolies. These criteria transition naturally into how prayer and discernment function together.

5.3 Harmonizing prayer, discernment, and delegation

The apostles instruct the disciples to "look out among you seven men...whom we may appoint over this business," then pray and lay hands on them (Acts 6:3–6). This sequence—selection, prayer, laying on of hands—harmonizes communal discernment with apostolic authorization. Prayer invokes the Spirit's personal affirmation, while laying on of hands symbolizes transmission of blessing and responsibility. Delegation in this Spirit-empowered context never reduces ministry to bureaucratic task lists; it becomes an extension of Christ's shepherding care through chosen individuals. The result is two simultaneous streams of service: apostles continue in prayer and the word, while the Seven ensure equitable care. This division of labor reflects the Spirit's personal orchestration, preventing role-confusion and burnout. The seamless integration of spiritual and practical leadership anticipates Paul's later discussion of spiritual gifts and offices (Rom 12; 1 Cor 12). By delegating wisely under Spirit guidance, the early church preserves its missional vitality and communal health. Having structured leadership for internal needs, the church soon faces external opposition spurring martyrdom and mission.

6 Spirit-Filled Martyrdom and Missionary Spark (Acts 6:8 – 8:4)

6.1 Stephen—"full of the Holy Spirit," sees the exalted Son

Stephen, one of the Seven, is described as "a man full of God's grace and power" who "did great wonders and signs among the people" (Acts 6:8). More significantly, during his debate with the synagogue leaders, Stephen's face shines "like the face of an angel" (Acts 6:15), and at his moment of death, he sees "the heavens opened and the Son of Man standing at the right hand of God" (Acts 7:56). This vision underscores the Spirit's personal revelation, granting Stephen heavenly sight to confirm Christ's exaltation. The Spirit enables Stephen to endure martyrdom with Christ-like compassion, praying for his persecutors (Acts 7:60). His death catalyzes the church's first large-scale persecution, illustrating that Spirit-filled witness may lead to sacrificial death yet also to deeper unity. Stephen's example models how personal Spirit anointing sustains believers in the face of hostility and points to the ultimate vindication in Christ's presence. From Stephen's martyrdom, the narrative shifts to how suffering disperses the church.

6.2 Persuasive speech, prophetic indictment, and heavenly vision

Stephen's speech before the Sanhedrin mirrors prophetic indictments in the Old Testament, showcasing the Spirit's role in equipping bold rhetoric and piercing theological argument. He reviews Israel's history, accuses the Jewish leaders of resisting the Holy Spirit, and proclaims Jesus as the righteous stone they have rejected (Acts 7:51–53). The Spirit's personal empowerment allows Stephen to speak with prophetic clarity, binding past covenant unfaithfulness to present accountability. His final vision of the Son of Man underscores the Spirit's personal testimony to Jesus' exalted status. As the crowd stones him, Stephen's unwavering focus on Christ demonstrates the Spirit's sustaining presence in persecution. This confluence of speech, prophetic indictment, and vision reveals the Spirit-person's multi-faceted engagement with both speaker and audience. Stephen's example transitions to the broader church's dispersion under persecution.

6.3 Persecution disperses believers, turning tragedy into missionary momentum

Following Stephen's martyrdom, "a great persecution arose against the church in Jerusalem, and they were all scattered throughout the countryside of Judea and Samaria" (Acts 8:1). Far from halting the gospel, this Spirit-orchestrated scattering propels Christianity beyond its Jewish stronghold. Believers carry the message to new towns, catalyzing fresh preaching opportunities that might not have arisen otherwise. Philip's ministry in Samaria (Acts 8:5) and the Samaritan reception demonstrate that the Spirit intentionally overcomes historical enmities, uniting Jews and Samaritans under Christ. The pervasiveness of persecution—Saul ravaging the church (Acts 8:3)—intensifies urgency and authenticity in witness. The Spirit turns human tragedy into missionary momentum, showing that divine strategy often employs apparent setbacks to accomplish expansion. From scattering, the Spirit leads individual evangelists to targeted missions beyond familiar territories.

7 Guiding Evangelists beyond Jerusalem (Acts 8:5–40)

7.1 Samaria's reception—Spirit confirms Philip's preaching through signs

In Samaria, Philip proclaims Christ, and the people heed his message, experiencing unclean spirits cast out and paralytics healed (Acts 8:6–7). The Spirit's confirmation through visible signs authenticates Philip's mission among a people historically estranged from Jerusalem's worship. The rapid conversion of many Samaritans into the faith demonstrates the Spirit's power to transcend ethnic and religious boundaries. This event fulfills Jesus' mandate to be witnesses "in Samaria" (Acts 1:8) and highlights that Spirit-guided evangelism requires both faithful preaching and expectant anticipation of divine confirmation. The Samaritans' joy at deliverance illustrates the Spirit's personal ministry of healing and inclusion. Recognizing Samaria's reception as Spirit-empowered prepares us to see how apostolic oversight ensures proper Spirit reception.

7.2 Apostolic visit: Spirit falls, healing centuries-old schism

News of Samaritan conversions reaches the Jerusalem church, prompting Peter and John to travel and pray for the new believers to receive the Holy Spirit (Acts 8:14–17). Although they have believed and been baptized in Jesus' name, only after apostolic laying on of hands and prayer does the Spirit fall upon them. This two-stage reception—faith and Spirit with apostolic commissioning—highlights the Spirit's personal decision to dwell and the community's role in facilitating genuine indwelling. The healing of the Jew-Samaritan schism demonstrates the Spirit's reconciling agency, mending historical divisions through personal presence. The Samaritans' reception of the Spirit marks the first Gentile-adjacent group to receive the Advocate, paving the way for broader inclusion. This apostolic affirmation transitions to individual Spirit-guided taskings.

7.3 Angelic command and Spirit directive—road to Gaza encounter

An angel of the Lord instructs Philip to "rise and go toward the south to the road that goes down from Jerusalem to Gaza" (Acts 8:26). Shortly thereafter, the Spirit tells Philip, "Go over and join this chariot" (Acts 8:29). This twofold guidance—angelic and Spirit—demonstrates the Spirit's personal capacity to direct missionaries in real time, complementing external visions. The precise coordination of angelic and Spirit directives underscores that multiple divine agents work in harmony to accomplish mission. Philip's obedience leads to the transformative encounter with the Ethiopian eunuch, highlighting the Spirit's personal initiative in cross-cultural evangelism. The narrative shows that Spirit guidance may bypass human expectations and logistical plans, calling ministers into unexpected contexts. From this directive, Philip moves into a personal, one-on-one evangelistic moment.

7.4 Ethiopian official baptized, continues rejoicing under Spirit guidance

Philip finds the Ethiopian eunuch reading Isaiah and, prompted by the Spirit, interprets the passage to him, proclaiming Jesus (Acts 8:35). At the eunuch's request, Philip baptizes him in the desert (Acts 8:38), a personal act of obedience to Spirit-given opportunity. Immediately after, the Spirit snatches Philip away (Acts 8:39), leaving the eunuch rejoicing on his way. This narrative illustrates the Spirit's personal mentorship: guiding Philip in exegesis, leading to baptism, and orchestrating departure. The eunuch's rejoicing "on his way" model's personal faith journeys informed by Spirit revelation. His continued witness in Ethiopia, though not detailed in Acts, exemplifies how the Spirit's personal guidance extends through cultural networks. Having seen Philip's obedience, we next consider the Spirit's transformative work in Saul's conversion.

8 Transforming Enemies into Instruments (Acts 9:1–31)

8.1 Saul's Damascus encounter—Spirit-commissioned witness to Gentiles

Saul, breathing threats against the church, confronts the risen Lord on the road to Damascus and is struck blind (Acts 9:3–5). The voice identifies itself as Jesus ("I am Jesus, whom you are persecuting"), and Saul's conversion is sealed by three days of fasting. Though the Spirit is not yet explicitly mentioned, the post-resurrection Son's revelation carries the Spirit's authority, commissioning Saul for mission. Jesus predicts that Saul will be told how much he must suffer, demonstrating that Spirit-enabled mission may involve personal cost. The narrative foreshadows Saul's future Spirit baptism and Gentile calling. By choosing Israel's most zealous persecutor, the Spirit-person demonstrates redemptive transformation, turning an enemy into an apostle. Saul's Damascus encounter thus becomes a template for the Spirit's personal power to overhaul identity and purpose, leading directly into Ananias' role.

8.2 Ananias, prompted by the Lord, ministers healing and Spirit filling

The Lord appears in a vision to Ananias, instructing him to go lay hands on Saul for restoration and Spirit reception (Acts 9:10–12, 17). Despite fearing Saul's reputation, Ananias obeys, demonstrating personal trust in Spirit direction. Ananias addresses Saul as "Brother Saul," signifying immediate relational reclassification from enemy to fellow believer. His laying on of hands results in Saul's sight restored and filling with the Holy Spirit, enabling immediate proclamation of Jesus as Son of God (Acts 9:17–18). This personal encounter illustrates the Spirit's relational prompting—Ananias is commissioned as a Spirit-enabled intercessor and instigator of transformation. The sequence highlights that Spirit operations often occur through human instruments, underscoring interpersonal cooperation. Having seen Saul's filling, we turn to his first preaching in Damascus.

8.3 Early preaching in synagogues—boldness rooted in fresh indwelling

Saul immediately begins proclaiming Jesus in the synagogues, astounding listeners who know him as a persecutor (Acts 9:20–22). His boldness and clarity demonstrate the Spirit's personal empowerment: Saul proclaims the gospel "confidently," undeterred by threats. His transformation serves as powerful apologetic evidence of the Spirit's life-changing presence. Authorities plot against him, forcing Saul to escape by being lowered in a basket (Acts 9:23–25). Yet Saul's Spirit-driven zeal leads him to Jerusalem, where his initial reception by the disciples is cautious until Barnabas introduces him (Acts 9:27). Saul's case shows that Spirit baptism yields both personal boldness and communal discernment processes, ensuring that Spirit-filled ministry is recognized and integrated. His Damascus preaching thus exemplifies how fresh indwelling fuels mission continuity.

9 Crossing Ethnic Frontiers: Caesarea Breakthrough (Acts 10:1 – 11:18)

9.1 Angelic vision to Cornelius; concurrent Spirit-initiated trance for Peter

Cornelius, a God-fearing centurion in Caesarea, receives an angelic visitation instructing him to send for Peter in Joppa (Acts 10:1–6). Simultaneously, Peter is caught up in a trance while praying on the rooftop, seeing a sheet descending with unclean animals (Acts 10:9–16). The Spirit prompts Peter to remain receptive, telling him three times, "What God has made clean, do not call common." This double vision—angelic command and Spirit-led correction—demonstrates the Spirit's personal coordination across geography. Cornelius's household, awaiting Peter's arrival, represents Gentiles longing for divine insight. The Spirit breaks cultural taboos before Peter's rational mind can adjust, highlighting personal agency that overrides ethnic prejudice. Luke's narrative stresses that both visions occur "about the same hour" (Acts 10:30), underscoring divine orchestration. Peter's trance is not a passive hallucination but a Spirit-induced revelatory encounter, reshaping his understanding of kosher boundaries. Cornelius's angelic message and Peter's Spirit-filled vision converge to lower the wall between Jew and Gentile, foreshadowing the Spirit's universal outreach.

9.2 "Doubting nothing"—Spirit instructs Peter to accompany envoys

Upon returning with Cornelius's messengers, Peter declares, "I truly understand that God shows no partiality, but in every nation anyone who fears him and does what is right is acceptable to him" (Acts 10:34–35). The Spirit's prompting emboldens Peter to overcome Jewish ceremonial scruples and embrace hospitality. Peter's phrase "doubting nothing" signals full assurance conveyed by Spirit conviction rather than human persuasion. The Spirit's prior vision equips Peter with immediate confidence to preach without apology. This Spirit-sanctioned hospitality challenges the Jerusalem church's prevailing norms and anticipates future debates on Gentile inclusion. The Spirit's personal guidance thus reshapes ecclesial boundaries, aligning mission with divine impartiality. As Peter journeys with the envoys, he models obedience to Spirit direction in real time. The result is not only spatial expansion but also an epistemic shift: understanding that Spirit baptism transcends ethnic markers.

9.3 Sermon interrupted—Spirit falls, validating Gentile inclusion

Peter begins to speak about Jesus' death and resurrection when "the Holy Spirit fell on all who heard the word" (Acts 10:44). Even before baptism, the Gentile listeners receive the same personal Spirit outpouring experienced at Pentecost, complete with speaking in tongues and magnifying God (Acts 10:46). This Spirit-fall interrupts Peter's sermon to demonstrate that divine acceptance precedes and undergirds Christian initiation. The phenomenon serves as incontrovertible proof to Jewish observers that God Himself has extended the covenant promise beyond Israel. The Spirit's personal agency in choosing the timing and recipients here validates policy shifts the apostles might otherwise debate. Luke notes Peter's astonishment—he asks, "Can anyone withhold water for baptizing these people?"—underscoring that Spirit activity compels sacramental action. The outpouring among Gentiles thus both confirms their belonging and fulfills Joel's prophecy regarding Spirit on "all flesh" (Acts 2:17). Understanding this divine interruption sets the stage for the Jerusalem council's deliberations.

9.4 Jerusalem debate resolved: "God gave the same gift to them as to us"

News of the Caesarea outpouring reaches Jerusalem, igniting debate among believers whether Gentile converts must be circumcised or follow the Law of Moses (Acts 11:1–3). Peter recounts his vision, Cornelius's household, and the Spirit's descent in their hearing, culminating in his declaration: "If then God gave the same gift to them as he gave to us when we believed in the Lord Jesus Christ, who was I that I could stand in God's way?" (Acts 11:17). The Spirit's personal gift functions as the decisive argument, transcending Scripture quotations or cultural traditions. The debate's resolution rests on recognizing the Spirit's sovereign agency: God's initiative defines the church's boundaries. The council's acceptance of Peter's report underscores that Spirit-driven reality shapes ecclesial policy. This decision prepares the Antioch church to become a hub for diverse discipleship, demonstrating that the Spirit's personal outreach mandates structural adaptation.

10 Antioch Hub and Missionary Commission (Acts 11:19–30; 13:1–4)

10.1 Multicultural discipleship incubator—Barnabas discerns grace of the Spirit

In the wake of persecution-driven dispersion, believers from Jerusalem preach in Antioch, leading to a growing, ethnically mixed church (Acts 11:19–21). Barnabas is sent from Jerusalem to encourage and validate this work, arriving to witness a community flourishing under the Spirit's grace. He sees "the grace of God" at work among Gentiles, a recognition reflecting Spirit-enabled discernment. Barnabas's name, meaning "son of encouragement," aligns with his role as Spirit-motivated mentor. His presence brings apostolic endorsement, fostering unity and doctrinal soundness. Barnabas then travels to Tarsus to recruit Saul, bringing him to Antioch to teach the believers for a year (Acts 11:25–26). This extended teaching ministry under Spirit anointing underscores the importance of doctrinal formation in a multicultural context. The Antioch church thus becomes the first to be called "Christians," marking the Spirit's personal influence in forging new identity. With discipleship solidified, the scene is set for practical compassion.

10.2 Prophetic famine relief—Spirit fosters practical compassion

Agabus, a prophet from Judea, arrives in Antioch and, moved by the Spirit, predicts a coming famine that will afflict the broader Roman world (Acts 11:27–28). The Spirit's personal disclosure triggers a tangible response: each believer, according to his ability, sends relief to the elders in Judea via Barnabas and Saul. This coordinated effort demonstrates that the Spirit's guidance extends beyond theological insight to practical acts of mercy. The famine relief serves as a prophetic fulfillment and a concrete expression of the Spirit's compassion, uniting disparate communities. Luke commends this initiative as "a good and wholesome work" (Acts 11:29), showing that Spirit-led mission encompasses both spiritual proclamation and social care. The Antioch church's response under Spirit prompting sets a precedent for integrative mission strategies in Gentile contexts. With communal compassion enacted, the church next turns to corporate worship and commissioning.

10.3 Worship and fasting: Spirit speaks, "Set apart Barnabas and Saul"

During a period of fasting and prayer, the Holy Spirit speaks to the Antioch church, saying, "Set apart for me Barnabas and Saul for the work to which I have called them" (Acts 13:2). This direct utterance in a worship assembly underscores the Spirit's personal role in appointing apostolic teams. Fasting and prayer create a receptive environment for Spirit speech, demonstrating that divine direction often arises within embodied liturgical contexts. The congregational act of laying hands on Barnabas and Saul formalizes the Spirit's commission, blending human recognition with divine empowerment. This sending event mirrors Jesus' commissioning of the disciples

(Luke 24:49), now applied to the church at large. By speaking personally and specifying persons, the Spirit affirms that missionary vocation is not self-chosen but divinely apportioned. The methodology—fasting, prayer, Spirit speech, laying on hands—becomes a liturgical blueprint for commissioning ministries. As Barnabas and Saul depart, the Spirit's strategic role in geographical expansion becomes evident.

10.4 First journey launched "by the Holy Spirit," redefining apostolic geography

Luke notes that Barnabas and Saul were "sent out by the Holy Spirit" (Acts 13:4), reiterating the Spirit's personal initiative in missionary dispatch. The pair travels to Seleucia, then Salamis, and across Cyprus, following Spirit-guided itineraries rather than predetermined routes. At Paphos, the Spirit arranges confrontation with a sorcerer who seeks to oppose them, leading to the proconsul's conversion (Acts 13:6–12). The Spirit's personal oversight thus includes strategic opposition to highlight the power of the gospel. From Cyprus, the team moves to Perga and Pisidian Antioch, where Paul's sermon sparks both reception and rejection. The Spirit's narrative strategy uses mixed responses to propel the mission forward, encouraging believers to turn to Gentiles when Jews oppose (Acts 13:46). This adaptive, Spirit-led approach redefines apostolic geography, emphasizing relational responsiveness over static territorial claims. Understanding this Spirit direction prepares us for the subsequent redirections that lead toward Europe.

11 Strategic Redirection and Europe's Open Door (Acts 15:36 – 16:40)

11.1 Phrygia-Galatia blockade: Spirit forbids preaching in Asia

On their second missionary journey, Paul and Barnabas attempt to revisit Asia, but "the Holy Spirit prevented them" (Acts 16:6). This prohibition, delivered through inner conviction rather than external signs, highlights the Spirit's personal capacity to set and impose boundaries. The Spirit's negative guidance preserves resources and prevents missionary burnout, demonstrating that restraint is as vital as commissioning. The Christians' submission to Spirit direction, rather than insisting on preconceived plans, reflects deep relational trust. The prohibition in Asia also foreshadows the Spirit's broader strategy: opening doors elsewhere vastly more receptive. This initial redirection prepares the ground for the Spirit's positive call toward Europe.

11.2 Bithynia closed; vision of the Macedonian man—Spirit's positive guidance

Encountering another geographical impasse in Bithynia, the team receives a vision during the night: a man pleading, "Come over to Macedonia and help us" (Acts 16:9). The Spirit interprets the vision personally through Paul's discernment, confirming a call into Europe. This Spirit-guided vision underscores that guidance often combines negative constraints with positive invitations. The Macedonia call inaugurates the first European mission, shifting the gospel frontiers from Asia Minor to the Greek world. Philippi becomes the focal point, where the Spirit's call results in Lydia's conversion and the establishment of a European church. The Spirit's personal guidance thus challenges and transcends ethnic confines, testifying to God's universal mission strategy.

11.3 Lydia's heart opened, jailer's household saved—Spirit births the Philippian church

At Philippi, Paul's preaching leads to Lydia, a dealer in purple cloth, whose heart the Lord opens to receive the word (Acts 16:14). The Spirit's action in opening hearts contrasts with resistances encountered elsewhere, reflecting personal initiative in salvation. After the miraculous jail delivery, the Philippian jailer and his entire household believe and are baptized (Acts 16:30–34), forming the nucleus of the first European church. Each conversion narrative underscores the Spirit's personal work in both sovereign openings of hearts and communal baptisms. The Philippian church's birth marks a significant milestone: the gospel's entrance into Europe under Spirit orchestration. This local community becomes a strategic base for further missionary and epistolary developments. As we observe the Spirit guiding mission expansion, we move next into how the early church exercised conciliar discernment under Spirit guidance.

12 Conciliar Discernment: "It Seemed Good to the Holy Spirit and to Us" (Acts 15:1–35)

12.1 Circumcision controversy threatens Gentile mission

As Gentile conversions multiply, certain believers insist that Gentiles must be circumcised according to Moses (Acts 15:1). This

117

requirement, though rooted in Mosaic covenant, threatens to reimpose Jewish law on all, jeopardizing the gospel's accessibility and unity. The dispute escalates, leading Paul and Barnabas to travel to Jerusalem for conciliar deliberation. The tension exemplifies how theological and cultural collisions can fracture Spirit-led expansions. Recognizing the Spirit's role in preserving mission integrity, the church assembles its leaders to seek divine guidance rather than impose unilateral cultural norms. This controversy highlights that Spirit-directed mission requires ongoing doctrinal discernment at the highest communal levels.

12.2 Testimonies of signs and wonders under Spirit direction

During the Jerusalem council, Peter stands and recounts how God "made no distinction between us and them, having cleansed their hearts by faith" and how the Spirit fell upon the Gentiles as on the Jews (Acts 15:8–9). James follows, referencing Amos 9:11–12 and noting that God's purpose is to restore David's fallen tent, which includes Gentiles under the gospel's blessing. Barnabas and Paul then relate their experiences of the Spirit's empowering signs among Gentiles. These testimonies of Spirit-driven signs and wonders provide empirical evidence that confirms the council's theological deliberations. The Spirit's personal agency thus becomes the decisive criterion in conciliar decisions: if the Spirit has validated Gentiles through gifts and transformation, then no human tradition can invalidate that work. This reliance on Spirit-inspired testimony reinforces communal confidence in decisions that shape mission boundaries.

12.3 Crafted decree—Spirit-sanctioned compromise safeguarding unity

The council concludes with a letter stating it "seemed good to the Holy Spirit and to us" to impose only minimal requirements—abstaining from certain food, sexual immorality, and idolatrous practices—on Gentile believers (Acts 15:28–29). This phrasing places the Spirit as co-author of the decree, integrating divine authority with communal discernment. The letter's careful balance preserves Jewish consciences while welcoming Gentiles without cultural imposition. This Spirit-sanctioned compromise models conciliar governance under the Advocate's personal guidance, ensuring that doctrinal decisions serve mission rather than control. The letter is then delivered by chosen leaders, accompanied by Paul and Barnabas, demonstrating the Spirit's personal endorsement of the decree through apostolic agency. This Spirit-led compromise safeguards unity and paves the way for further mission expansion.

13 Prophetic Warnings and Apostolic Resolve (Acts 18–21)

13.1 Corinth encouragement—Spirit assures Paul amid opposition

Paul, after establishing a church in Corinth, faces persistent hostility from both Jewish and pagan opponents (Acts 18:5–6). In response, the Lord appears to Paul in a night vision, saying, "Do not be afraid, but go on speaking and do not be silent, for I am with you" (Acts 18:9–10). This personal reassurance from the risen Christ, mediated by the Spirit, renews Paul's courage and dedication to evangelism. The Spirit's presence transforms Paul's outlook: he recognizes that opposition does not signify divine disfavor but a testing ground for deeper faithfulness. Paul spends eighteen months teaching in Corinth (Acts 18:11), while continuing tentmaking to support himself, demonstrating the Spirit's empowerment for both proclamation and practical labor. The church's growth amidst persecution reflects the Spirit's guarantee of divine accompaniment. Paul's pattern—receiving Spirit-fostered visions and continuing steadfastly—becomes a template for persecuted missionaries. The Spirit's personal assurance enables Paul to view threats as opportunities for gospel witness rather than deterrents. This vision-induced encouragement transitions seamlessly into further prophetic warnings at Tyre.

13.2 Agabus and Tyrian disciples predict imprisonment—Spirit both cautions and commissions

As Paul and his companions minister along the coast, they encounter disciples from Tyre who, through the Spirit, foretell that Paul will be bound in Jerusalem (Acts 21:4). The prophet Agabus later reenacts the binding, taking Paul's belt and tying his own hands and feet, declaring, "Thus says the Holy Spirit, 'This is how the Jews at Jerusalem will bind the man who owns this belt'" (Acts 21:11). These vivid enactments illustrate the Spirit's personal engagement in mission strategy—providing both clear warnings and implicit commissions. Despite repeated entreaties from the local church to avoid Jerusalem, Paul affirms, "I am ready not only to be bound but even to die in Jerusalem for the name of the Lord Jesus" (Acts 21:13).

His resolute response underscores that Spirit-led missions may embrace suffering rather than circumvent it. The personal nature of these warnings—involving physical dramatizations and prophetic proclamation—demonstrates the Spirit's willingness to reveal future trials intimately. The Spirit's caution does not deter Paul but clarifies the cost of obedience. Recognizing costs in advance prepares missionaries for endurance, a principle that leads into Paul's determined journey to Jerusalem.

13.3 Paul's Spirit-constrained determination to reach Jerusalem

Despite the Spirit's cautions, Paul insists that he must go to Jerusalem because "none of these things will move me" (Acts 21:14). His determination is itself a product of Spirit-constrained resolve, rooted in the knowledge that God's purposes will prevail. The Spirit's personal role here is paradoxical: He warns, yet allows Paul the freedom to prioritize divine summons over personal safety. As Paul moves forward, the group carries out the temple purification rites to allay Jewish suspicions (Acts 21:26), demonstrating Spirit-led sensitivity to cultural ministry contexts. Even as Paul enters the temple, the Spirit's prior warnings seem eclipsed by a higher call—bearing witness in Jerusalem, despite impending arrest. The Spirit's personal dynamic thus balances caution with higher commissioning. Paul's willingness to face imprisonment exemplifies how Spirit-directed missions integrate prophetic warning with obedient determination. This tension prepares us for Paul's courtroom defenses before governors and kings.

14 Witness before Governors and Kings (Acts 22–26)

14.1 Spirit-aided defense in Hebrew on temple steps

When Paul is seized in the temple by a hostile mob, he is about to be scourged until he reveals his Roman citizenship (Acts 22:25–29). Addressing the crowd in Hebrew, he recounts his Damascus encounter and gospel commission "not to all people but to the Gentiles" (Acts 22:21). Speaking in the Aramaic dialect of his hearers, Paul demonstrates Spirit-enabled linguistic discernment, ensuring his message pierces their hearts. This Spirit-aided defense defuses immediate threats and commands attention from the Sanhedrin. His invocation of shared heritage—citing the hope of Israel—displays personal sensitivity to his audience's convictions. The Spirit's personal empowerment in speech equips Paul to navigate volatile crowd dynamics and transition to formal legal proceedings. This

120

strategic proclamation prepares the groundwork for his subsequent defenses before Roman officials.

14.2 Felix, Festus, Agrippa—Spirit-guided reasoned persuasion

At Caesarea, Paul defends himself before Governor Felix, recounting his unimpeded service to his people and affirming his faith in the resurrection (Acts 24:10–21). The Spirit's presence shapes Paul's measured tone, balancing respect for authority with boldness in truth. Felix defers judgment, leaving Paul under custody but granting freedoms for continued dialogue. Under Governor Festus, Paul appeals to Caesar, a Spirit-inspired legal maneuver protecting Paul from Sanhedrin plots (Acts 25:11). Festus then arranges a hearing before King Agrippa II and Bernice, where Paul delivers a comprehensive gospel defense (Acts 25:23–26:32). The Spirit's infusion of wisdom, courage, and rhetorical skill guides Paul's reasoned persuasion, such that Agrippa concludes, "In a short time would you persuade me to be a Christian?" (Acts 26:28). The Spirit's personal presence both convicts and commends, generating reflective responses from his hearers. Through these legal defenses, the Spirit uses established power structures as platforms for gospel advance. The complexity of these trials transitions us to Paul's journey to Rome.

14.3 Vision in prison—Spirit reaffirms Rome as ultimate stage

While under house arrest in Caesarea, Paul receives the visit of Luke and possibly other companions, sharing in Gospel proclamation with witnesses to governors and kings. Later, as Paul sails for Rome, he survives a shipwreck on Malta, where he ministers under "no small encouragement" from the Lord in a night vision: "Do not be afraid… for God has granted you all those who sail with you" (Acts 27:23–24). Though not explicitly called the Holy Spirit here, this reassurance reflects Spirit-sanctioned encouragement, reminiscent of earlier visions. The Spirit's personal affirmation amid crisis assures Paul that Rome is the appointed arena for final proclamation. Paul's resolve to proceed despite peril demonstrates the Spirit's sustaining presence in perilous contexts. This vision prepares Paul for his mission in the heart of the empire, highlighting Rome as strategic culmination of his apostolic journey. The narrative's shift to Malta miracles preludes the Spirit's credentials for credible gospel proclamation.

15 Rome without Hindrance: Open-Ended Mission (Acts 27–28)

15.1 Storm at sea—Spirit-delivered oracle of survival

During the perilous voyage to Rome, the crew endures a violent storm, and after days without food and hope, Paul reassures them based on the Spirit-sanctioned vision: "God has granted safety to all who are sailing with you" (Acts 27:24). Paul, guided by the Spirit's promise, counsels the crew to eat and lose cargo to lighten the ship. The storm narrative demonstrates the Spirit's personal authority even over natural forces and human despair. The sailors' eventual survival, achieved by Paul's Spirit-enabled strategies, underscores that the Advocate's guidance spans seas and circumstances. This miraculous deliverance sets the stage for further Spirit-directed works on Malta and in Rome. The transition from peril to safety models Spirit-guided crisis navigation.

15.2 Malta miracles—healing as Spirit credential for gospel credibility

On the island of Malta, Paul is bitten by a viper but suffers no harm (Acts 28:3–5), a sign interpreted by islanders as divine protection. Subsequently, Paul heals the father of Publius, the local chief, and many others who are sick (Acts 28:8–9). These miracles, empowered by the Spirit, serve as credentials validating gospel credibility among Gentile audiences. The Spirit's personal involvement in healing builds relational bridges for Paul's continued ministry. Word spreads rapidly, and islanders show extraordinary hospitality, sharing their resources until Paul's departure. The sequence on Malta reflects the Spirit's integration of humane relief, miraculous signs, and evangelistic opportunity. As Paul embarks for Rome, he carries with him the momentum of Spirit-empowered witness, priming the final stage of his mission.

15.3 House arrest evangelism—Spirit-empowered proclamation "boldly and without hindrance"

In Rome, Paul is permitted to live by himself under guard but receives all who visit, proclaiming the kingdom of God openly and without hindrance (Acts 28:30–31). The Spirit's personal presence in Paul's guarded quarters transforms confinement into a vibrant mission center. Paul's letters—Ephesians, Philippians, Colossians, Philemon—are written during this period, reflecting Spirit-guided theological elaboration and pastoral concern. Visitors receive Spirit-inspired instruction, impacting both Jewish and Gentile audiences. The Spirit's empowerment transcends physical limitations, ensuring that the gospel reaches beyond prison walls. Paul's boldness in Rome fulfills Jesus' promise that His witnesses would reach the empire's heart by Spirit mandate (Luke 24:47; Acts 1:8). This open-ended proclamation under house arrest signals that the Spirit's personal mission continues unimpeded, even in captivity. Recognizing this final phase readies us to survey thematic patterns across Acts.

16 Thematic Synthesis: Personal Agency of the Spirit in Acts

16.1 Verbs of speech, selection, and restraint—lexical survey

A close reading of Acts reveals that key verbs—*lalein* (to speak), *eklegomai* (to select), *apokrinomai* (to refuse or restrain)—are frequently predicated of the Spirit. The Spirit *speaks* in visions (Acts 10:19; 13:2), *selects* individuals for mission (Acts 13:4; 16:6), and *restrains* the missionaries from Asia (Acts 16:6). This lexical pattern underscores the Spirit's personal agency in guiding words, decisions, and boundaries. The consistent use of these verbs attributes deliberate, conscious activity to the Advocate—deciding, directing, and declaring. Recognizing this verb-based evidence strengthens the argument against impersonal pneumatology. The Spirit's personal interventions in speech and strategic choices pervade the narrative, revealing a divine Subject at work. This synthesis of Spirit-verb patterns transitions into analysis of relational interactions.

16.2 Relational interaction with believers and unbelievers alike

Throughout Acts, the Spirit interacts with a diverse cast: disciples praying in the upper room, Philip led to the Ethiopian eunuch, Saul's conversion, Jerusalem council deliberations, even obstruction of mission plans. These interactions display relational nuance: encouragement, correction, commissioning, warning, rebuke, empowerment. The Spirit discerns hearts (Acts 8:23), knows intentions (Acts 5:3), and offers comfort amid suffering (Acts 27:23–25). This personal engagement transcends simple illumination—He enters human relationships, shapes communal decisions, and fosters apostolic resilience. The Spirit's relational ministry with unbelievers (Cornelius, Lydia, the Philippian jailer) and with believers (disciples, apostles, churches) illustrates an expansive network of divine-human encounters. This relational mosaic prepares us to compare Spirit's ministry in the church with Jesus' own ministry.

16.3 Continuity with Jesus' ministry yet expansion through the church

Acts demonstrates that the Spirit continues Jesus' works—healing, teaching, casting out demons, baptizing with power—while empowering the church to expand beyond Israel to the Gentile world. The Spirit's ministry in Acts mirrors Jesus' earthly ministry but amplifies it in scope, scale, and diversity of context. Jesus healed and taught in Palestine; the Spirit heals and teaches from Jerusalem to Rome. Jesus resisted Satan's temptations; the Spirit restrains missionaries from misguided paths and exposes falsehood. Jesus commissioned Twelve; the Spirit commissions multiplies of apostles, prophets, and lay leaders across continents. This continuity-expansion dynamic shows that the Spirit-person actualizes Christ's mission in ever-new ways. Recognizing this pattern readies us to transition from narrative to doctrinal reflections in the Pauline epistles.

17 Bridge to Pauline Letters: The Spirit Who Builds and Gifts Communities

17.1 Antioch to Corinth—Acts-Pauline intersections

The narrative in Acts connects directly with Paul's epistles to churches founded or visited during his journeys. At Antioch, Paul's commissioning by the Spirit precedes his letters to the Galatians, where he emphasizes Spirit-baptism (Gal 3:14). In Corinth, Spirit-empowered signs and teachings transition into First and Second Corinthians, addressing spiritual gifts and communal dynamics (1 Cor 12; 14). Romans resumes the Jerusalem collection theme from Acts 24:17, framing it as Spirit-led generosity (Rom 15:25–27). These intersections reveal how narrative experiences under Spirit guidance inform Pauline doctrinal and practical instructions. Recognizing these links underscores that Spirit-person ministry is both event-driven and doctrinally synthesized. This seamless transition from Acts to epistles highlights the Spirit's ongoing role in both narrative and theological dimensions.

17.2 From narrative demonstrations to doctrinal elaborations

While Acts emphasizes demonstration—visions, miracles, direct speech—Paul's letters elaborate on these experiences to develop systematic pneumatology. Paul reflects on Spirit baptism (Rom 6:3–4), Spirit-led adoption (Rom 8:15), Spirit-guided sanctification (Gal 5:16–25), and Spirit-empowered unity (1 Cor 12:13). He addresses abuses—misuse of gifts (1 Cor 12–14), quenching the Spirit (1 Th 5:19)—providing corrective frameworks born from narrative precedents. Paul's doctrinal elaborations build on the Spirit's personal ministries witnessed in Acts, offering theological depth to narrative insights. This development illustrates the Spirit's personal influence on both practice and doctrine, shaping the church's understanding of divine empowerment. Recognizing this progression prepares readers for the deeper analysis of the Spirit's intellect, emotion, and will in Pauline writings.

Conclusion Throughout these opening acts, the Spirit emerges as a personal Director, Teacher, Advocate, Judge, and Purifier—guiding the church from its inception through crises and expansions. The narrative shows that divine strategy transcends human planning: leadership choices, missionary routes, and communal structures all bear the Spirit's imprint. This chapter has revealed the Spirit's relational involvement at every turn, ensuring that the church's mission is not self-driven but Spirit-directed. As Acts progresses beyond these foundational episodes, we will see how the Spirit safeguards community purity, empowers cross-cultural evangelism, and orchestrates global mission strategy. In the next chapter, we will trace the Spirit's continuing ministry in Paul's letters, where the Advocate's intellect, emotion, and will are reflected in doctrinal elaboration and practical counsel.

Chapter 6. Pauline Witness: Intellect, Emotion, and Will of the Spirit

Paul's letters offer a profound pneumatological theology, revealing the Holy Spirit's personal engagement in believers' minds, hearts, and wills. Unlike narrative accounts that describe the Spirit's external acts, Paul delves into the Spirit's internal workings—illuminating divine mysteries, shaping emotions, and exercising sovereign choice. Throughout his epistles, the Spirit emerges as a teacher who unveils God's depths, a communicator who inspires speech, an enabler of emotional transformation, and a director of spiritual gifts and mission. This chapter traces Paul's multifaceted testimony to the Spirit, showing how His intellect, emotion, and volition underpin the life and unity of the church.

1 Mapping Paul's Pneumatological Landscape

1.1 Chronological sweep—Galatians to the Pastorals

Paul's pneumatological reflections span from his earliest letter to the Galatians, where he contrasts life "in the Spirit" with bondage under the law (Gal 5:16–18), to his pastoral epistles that address Spirit-related abuses and affirmations in local churches (1 Tim 4:1–2; Titus 3:5–6). In Galatians, he pioneers the concept of Spirit adoption (Gal 4:6), while in Romans he develops a comprehensive theology of the

Spirit's role in new creation (Rom 8:1–17). First Corinthians examines Spirit-gifted worship and communal order (1 Cor 12–14), whereas Second Corinthians emphasizes the Spirit's sealing (2 Cor 1:22) and ministry of the new covenant (2 Cor 3:6–18). Ephesians and Colossians situate the Spirit within the triune mystery, illustrating cosmic reconciliation (Eph 2:18; Col 1:19). The Pastorals then address threats of false teaching by warning against spirits of error (1 Tim 4:1) and affirm Spirit-baptism as central to regeneration (Titus 3:5). This chronological panorama shows Paul's evolving reflection on the Spirit-person, adapting to diverse ecclesial contexts and challenges. His letters trace thematic development: initial proclamation of Spirit freedom, deepening in theological exposition, and eventual pastoral safeguarding of Spirit truth. Recognizing this sweep prepares us to examine Paul's key vocabulary clusters.

1.2 Vocabulary clusters: *pneuma, charis, koinōnia, dynamis*

Paul's pneumatology is articulated through recurring terms that form interlocking semantic fields. *Pneuma* (Spirit) appears over 150 times, denoting not impersonal force but a personal agent active in revelation, empowerment, and fellowship. *Charis* (grace) frequently accompanies Spirit references, linking Spirit-baptism to unmerited favor (Rom 3:24; 6:14). *Koinōnia* (fellowship/participation) underscores communal sharing in Spirit life (2 Cor 13:14; Phil 2:1), reflecting relational depth. *Dynamis* (power) conveys the Spirit's energizing presence for mission, witness, and transformation (1 Cor 4:20; Titus 2:11–12). Together, these clusters reveal the Spirit as the wellspring of God's grace, the agent of fellowship, and the source of transformative power. Paul's consistent pairing—Spirit and grace, Spirit and fellowship, Spirit and power—reinforces a cohesive pneumatology. This technical vocabulary moves readers from narrative impressions to doctrinal clarity, enabling precise articulation of the Spirit's personal ministries. Having mapped these clusters, we turn to Paul's frequent triadic doxologies.

1.3 Triadic doxologies situating the Spirit with the Father and the Son

Paul anchors his pneumatology within Trinitarian praise, crafting benedictions that invoke Father, Son, and Spirit in mutual relation. Romans 1:7 greets believers "from God our Father and the Lord Jesus Christ," with implicit Spirit mediation. Romans 16:25–27 expands to "God...through Jesus Christ...according to the revelation of the mystery...by the command of the eternal God, to bring about the obedience of faith for the sake of his name, to the only wise God be glory forevermore through Jesus Christ! Amen." Here the Spirit is implicit in revelation and obedience. First Corinthians 12:4–6 delineates diversities of gifts, services, and workings "but the same Spirit...same Lord...same God who empowers." Second Corinthians 13:14 proclaims "The grace of the Lord Jesus Christ and the love of God and the fellowship of the Holy Spirit be with you all." Ephesians 4:4–6 similarly affirms "one Spirit, one Lord, one God and Father." These triadic formulas highlight the Spirit's equal standing, relational integration, and distinct personhood within the Godhead. They also establish the Spirit's central role in blessing, fellowship, and mission. By embedding the Spirit in liturgical practice, Paul ensures that congregations experience pneumatology as doxology. From these doxological peaks we move to Paul's hermeneutical method.

1.4 Hermeneutical method—story-shaped theology in epistolary form

Paul's approach to Scripture and life is narrative-shaped: he reads Israel's story as a framework for understanding Christ and the Spirit. In Romans 15:4, he asserts that "whatever was written in former days was written for our instruction, that through endurance and through the encouragement of the Scriptures we might have hope." The Spirit's role in illuminating the scriptural story is implicit here, guiding interpretation. Paul's letters themselves follow a narrative arc— gospel proclamation, conversion account, ethical exhortation, eschatological hope—mirroring the meta-narrative of redemption. He often weaves Old-Testament quotations (e.g., Hab 2:4 in Rom 1:17; Isa 28:16 in 1 Cor 3:11) into Christological and pneumatalogical reflections, demonstrating the Spirit's continuity in revelation. This story-shaped theology transforms ethical commands into participation in Christ's life by the Spirit. Paul's epistolary theology thus becomes a hermeneutical model: texts are signs of God's Spirit-led narrative, interpreted by the same Spirit who inspired them (2 Tim 3:16–17). Recognizing Paul's method sets the stage for examining the Spirit's intellectual work in knowing and teaching.

2 The Spirit's Intellect: Revelatory Knowing and Teaching

2.1 Searching the depths of God (1 Cor 2:10–11)

Paul declares that "the Spirit searches everything, even the depths of God," emphasizing the Spirit's personal intellect and omniscient capacity (1 Cor 2:10). The Greek *zētēsei* (searches) evokes a deliberate inquiry, not a blind force. Just as only a person can engage in complex exploration, the Spirit's role here discloses divine mysteries inaccessible to human wisdom. By contrast, worldly philosophers rely on natural reasoning; only the Spirit knows God's mind. Paul uses this motif to justify Spirit-revealed wisdom as superior to human rhetoric (1 Cor 2:4–5). The Spirit's search also undergirds spiritual discernment within the church, empowering believers to grasp deep truths. This function anticipates the Spirit's teaching ministry, moving congregations from elementary truths to profound insights. Recognizing the Spirit as investigator highlights His personal initiative in revelation. From searching to illuminating, we transition to the Spirit's role in apostolic proclamation.

2.2 Illuminating apostolic proclamation (1 Th 1:5; 2 Cor 4:13)

Paul characterizes his proclamation to the Thessalonians as "with power of the Spirit and full conviction" (1 Th 1:5), indicating that the Spirit's personal presence gives both content and force to the message. The Greek *kratos* (power) here links to the Spirit's dynamic movement, making divine truths compelling. Similarly, in 2 Corinthians 4:13, Paul cites Psalm 116:10—"I believed, and so I spoke"—asserting, "We also believe, and so we speak," with faith infused by the Spirit. The Spirit's illumination ensures that apostolic words carry divine authority, clarity, and conviction. This illumination is not mere emotional hype but cognitive clarity that persuades both mind and heart. The Spirit guides Paul in crafting arguments that resonate with human reason and spiritual sensitivity. This dynamic interplay of belief and proclamation underscores the Spirit's role as intellectual mentor. Having seen the Spirit illuminate the apostles, we turn to His revealing of the "mind of Christ."

2.3 Disclosing the "mind of Christ" to the mature (1 Cor 2:12–16)

Paul asserts that believers have "received the Spirit who is from God, that we might understand the things freely given us by God" (1 Cor 2:12). He contrasts natural persons, who receive not "the things of the Spirit of God, for they are folly to them," with spiritual persons who "judge all things" because they "have the mind of Christ" (1 Cor 2:14–16). The Spirit-person thus imparts Christ's own cognitive posture: humility, solidarity with God's will, and discernment of spiritual realities. This mental conformity involves personal teaching, enabling believers to navigate complex ethical, doctrinal, and communal issues. The mature Christian, guided by the Spirit's mind, avoids both arrogance and naiveté. The Spirit's revealing of Christ's mind fosters unity, since all Spirit-taught believers share the same perspective. This mystical cognition transitions to the Spirit's unveiling of Gentile inclusion in Ephesians.

2.4 Unveiling the mystery of Jew–Gentile unity (Eph 3:4–6)

Paul explains that by reading his letter, "you can perceive my understanding in the mystery of Christ, which was not made known to the sons of men in other generations as it has now been revealed to his holy apostles and prophets by the Spirit" (Eph 3:4–5). The Spirit-person here functions as divine communicator, disclosing the previously hidden truth that Gentiles are fellow heirs and members of one body (Eph 3:6). This revelation, termed a *mystērion*, underscores the Spirit's personal agency in revealing God's universal plan. The Spirit's unveiling bridges ethnic divides and establishes the church's identity. By situating Jewish–Gentile unity in the Spirit's wisdom, Paul affirms that only a personal divine agent can dissolve ancient hostilities. The Spirit's intellectual ministry thus has significant ecclesiological ramifications, forming a unified body. Having explored the Spirit's cognitive roles, we now turn to His communicative agency in speech and witness.

3 Communicative Agency: Speaking and Bearing Witness

3.1 Orchestrating prophetic speech in gathered worship (1 Cor 14:29–33)

Paul provides detailed instructions for prophecy in church gatherings: "Let two or three prophets speak, and let the others weigh what is said" (1 Cor 14:29). The Spirit-person empowers prophetic utterances by individuals, yet requires communal discernment, highlighting relational accountability in Spirit communication. Paul clarifies that "God is not a God of confusion but of peace" (1 Cor 14:33), indicating that Spirit-inspired speech maintains order and clarity. Prophetic speech under the Spirit's direction edifies the body, exhorts, and consoles (1 Cor 14:3), evidencing the Spirit's personal involvement in corporate worship. The guidelines ensure that Spirit-led prophecy serves the community's spiritual health rather than individual aggrandizement. Paul's detailed regulations reflect a high view of the

Spirit's communication, balancing spontaneity with structure. Recognizing the Spirit's orchestration in worship prepares us to see His role in Scripture's inspiration.

3.2 Providing verbal inspiration for Scripture (*2 Tim 3:16–17* cf. *2 Pet 1:21*)

Paul affirms that "all Scripture is inspired by God" (*theopneustos*) "and profitable for teaching, for reproof, for correction, and for training in righteousness" (2 Tim 3:16). The term *theopneustos* literally means "God-breathed," indicating that the Spirit—a divine Person—communicated through human authors. Peter corroborates this in 2 Peter 1:21: "prophecy never had its origin in the will of man, but men spoke from God as they were carried along by the Holy Spirit." These texts identify the Spirit as the divine communicator who moves authors to speak God's words, ensuring scriptural reliability. The Spirit's verbal inspiration secures the church's doctrinal foundation, guiding teaching and practice. By attributing Scripture's origin to the Spirit-person, Paul and Peter integrate pneumatology with bibliology. This divine authorship underscores the Spirit's personal intention in revealing God's truth across generations. Having established the Spirit's role in Scripture, we move to His direct speech in missionary contexts.

3.3 Direct speech in missionary settings ("the Spirit says…," 1 Tim 4:1)

Paul warns Timothy that "in later times some will depart from the faith by devoting themselves to deceitful spirits and teachings of demons" (1 Tim 4:1), attributing these departures to "the Spirit" speaking lies. Conversely, he also quotes Spirit-inspired commands, such as "Do not forbid to marry" (1 Tim 4:3). This usage indicates that the Spirit communicates specific guidance to the church's leaders, shaping ethical and doctrinal priorities. The Spirit's direct speech in pastoral contexts demonstrates His personal involvement in regulating communal life. Rather than leaving Timothy to infer principles, the Spirit-person authoritatively addresses controversies. This pattern echoes the prophetic "thus says the LORD," adapted for church governance. Recognizing the Spirit's direct communication equips leaders to discern true versus false directives. Having surveyed Spirit speech, we examine how the Spirit seals apostolic authority.

3.4 Sealing apostolic authority through Spirit-empowered signs (Rom 15:18–19)

Paul boasts that he "fully preached the gospel of Christ... by the power of signs and wonders, by the power of the Spirit of God" (Rom 15:19). His method involves not only persuasive speech but also verifiable supernatural signs—healings, exorcisms, miracles—that authenticate apostolic authority. The Spirit's personal empowerment ensures that the gospel proclamation is accompanied by divine approval, compelling belief. These Spirit-wrought signs build credibility among both Jews and Gentiles, substantiating the message's origin. Paul's emphasis on Spirit power contrasts with reliance on human eloquence, underscoring the Spirit-person's primacy in mission. By sealing apostolic words with signs, the Spirit-person fosters trust and paves the way for communal acceptance of foundational doctrines. This combination of word and power showcases the Spirit's communicative agency in both content and context. As we move from communication to emotion, we witness how the Spirit also shapes believers' affective life.

4 Affective Life: Joy, Love, Jealousy, and Grief

4.1 Pouring God's love into believers' hearts (Rom 5:5)

Paul declares that "God's love has been poured into our hearts through the Holy Spirit who has been given to us" (Rom 5:5). The metaphor of pouring indicates personal action: the Spirit, like an agent with intention, infuses believers with divine affection. This love is not an abstract cosmic force but relational warmth that bonds believers to the triune God. The Greek *ekcheo* (poured out) evokes divine hospitality, as if the Spirit opens the heart's capacity to receive love. This experiential love undergirds all aspects of Christian life—assurance (Rom 8:15), unity (Eph 4:2), and mission (2 Cor 5:14). By attributing love to the Spirit's personal activity, Paul affirms that believers' affection is both gift and indicator of Spirit presence. This transformation of the heart leads to joy and peace under Spirit influence.

4.2 Producing joy and peace as kingdom hallmarks (Rom 14:17; 15:13)

Paul writes that the kingdom of God is "righteousness and peace and joy in the Holy Spirit" (Rom 14:17), rooting kingdom experience in the Spirit-person's emotional ministry. Joy and peace here are not circumstantial but Spirit-derived dispositions sustained by divine presence. In his benediction, he prays that "the God of hope fill you with all joy and peace in believing, so that by the power of the Holy

Spirit you may abound in hope" (Rom 15:13). The Spirit's personal interventions foster steadfast joy amid trials and peace amid conflict. These emotions become hallmarks of kingdom ethics, signaling spiritual maturity. The Spirit-person thus functions as a counselor who nurtures believers' emotional well-being, enabling them to witness hope to the world. From joy and peace, we turn to the Spirit's jealous yearning for fidelity.

4.3 Yearning jealously for covenant fidelity (Jas 4:5 echoed in Pauline ethos)

Though primarily Pauline, the motif of the Spirit's jealousy finds resonances in Paul's warnings against idolatry. While James states, "Or do you suppose that it is to no purpose that the Scripture says, 'He yearns jealously over the spirit that he has made to dwell in us'?" (Jas 4:5), Paul echoes this zeal in his pastoral care. He rebukes the Galatians for turning to a different gospel (Gal 1:6–9), demonstrating a Spirit-impelled zeal for doctrinal purity. Paul's forceful language—"I am astonished that you are so quickly deserting him who called you in the grace of Christ" (Gal 1:6)—reflects the Spirit's personal jealousy for believers' devotion. The Spirit's jealous yearning protects the church from spiritual adultery, demanding exclusive loyalty to Christ. Paul's pastoral fervor thus mirrors the Spirit's protective passion. Understanding this jealousy prepares us to consider the Spirit's capacity for grief over communal sin.

4.4 Grieving over community-destroying sins (Eph 4:30)

Paul explicitly warns, "And do not grieve the Holy Spirit of God, by whom you were sealed for the day of redemption" (Eph 4:30). The verb *lupeō* (to grieve) attributes personal emotion to the Spirit—He experiences sorrow when believers exhibit bitterness, anger, and slander (Eph 4:31). This grief is relational, indicating that the Spirit-person is intimately connected to the church's emotional health. Grieving the Spirit jeopardizes the seal of redemption, emphasizing the seriousness of sin within the community. Paul's pastoral exhortation—put off old self and put on new self (Eph 4:22–24)—aims to prevent such grief. The Spirit's capacity for grief underscores His personal engagement and moral sensitivity. This somber emotion transitions to the Spirit's volitional sovereignty over gifts and mission, which we explore in the next chapter.

5 Volitional Sovereignty: Choosing, Distributing, Directing

5.1 Allocating charismata "as He wills" (1 Cor 12:4–11)

Paul emphasizes that though there are diversities of gifts, services, and workings, "it is the same one Spirit, distributing to each one individually as He wills" (1 Cor 12:4–11). This verb *thelō* ("as He wills") underscores the Spirit's personal volition in the allotment of spiritual gifts, distinguishing divine sovereignty from human choice. No believer can demand a particular gift; rather, the Spirit, in His personal freedom, bestows gifts according to divine purpose. The enumeration of nine gifts—from word of wisdom and knowledge to discernment and various tongues—reflects the Spirit's intentional provision of varied ministries for the common good. Paul's repeated "to each one" affirms that individuals receive unique callings, preventing uniformity that would stifle diversity. By attributing gift distribution to the Spirit's will, Paul guards against pride and resentment in the community. Each believer learns to receive with humility, acknowledging the Spirit's personal discernment of church needs. The theological implication is profound: the Spirit's sovereign will undergirds communal flourishing, ensuring that every gifting aligns with His overarching mission. This section transitions naturally to how the Spirit personally directs leadership appointments.

5.2 Setting leaders in place through congregational discernment (*Acts 20:28*; 1 Cor 12:28)

Paul instructs that God has appointed first apostles, second prophets, third teachers, then miracles, gifts of healings, helps, administrations, and various kinds of tongues (1 Cor 12:28), illustrating an ordered sequence grounded in the Spirit's personal design. In Acts 20:28, the Ephesian elders are told they were entrusted by the Holy Spirit to oversee the church of God, highlighting that pastoral leadership originates from Spirit bestowal. Leadership recognition thus rests on Spirit-informed criteria, not mere human selection. Congregational discernment—testing spirits and observing fruit—uncovers the Spirit's personal choice of leaders. The laying on of hands for ordination symbolizes Spirit-transmitted authority. Paul warns against quenching or despising the Spirit (1 Th 5:19–21), a caution that includes disregarding His chosen servants. By grounding leadership in the Spirit's personal entrustment, Paul affirms that ecclesial order flows from divine initiative. This section's emphasis on Spirit-originated authority transitions into His directional role in mission geography.

5.3 Regulating missionary geography (Acts 16:6–7, reflected in Paul's reports Rom 15:22–32)

Acts 16:6–7 reports that Paul and his companions were "forbidden by the Holy Spirit to speak the word in Asia" and "attempted…to enter Bithynia, but the Spirit of Jesus did not allow them." These prohibitions reveal the Spirit's personal agency in guiding apostolic routes, restraining efforts that could hamper mission effectiveness. Paul's subsequent decision to turn toward Europe aligns with Spirit-led adjustment rather than human ambition. In Romans 15:22–32, Paul explains that he was hindered from visiting many regions, indicating recurring experiences of Spirit-constrained plans. He frames his missionary travel as moves "in the will of God," connecting divine will with Spirit direction. This volitional regulation prevents fruitless labor and directs resources to receptive fields. The Spirit's personal guidance in strategic redirection demonstrates His intimate involvement in global mission planning. Believers learn to test directional impulses against Spirit confirmation through prayer and prophetic counsel. Having surveyed geographic regulation, we turn to corporate decisions shaped by Spirit consensus.

5.4 Orchestrating corporate decisions—"seemed good to the Holy Spirit and to us" ethos applied (*Acts 15:28*; 1 Cor 7:40; Phil 1:27)

The Jerusalem council declares that it "seemed good to the Holy Spirit and to us" to impose minimal requirements on Gentile believers (Acts 15:28), placing Spirit discernment on par with apostolic judgment. Paul echoes this ethos in recommending widows "remain as I am" if it "seems good to them…and to me" (1 Cor 7:40), implicitly grounded in Spirit-enabled insight. In Philippians 1:27, he exhorts believers to "conduct yourselves in a manner worthy of the gospel of Christ," implying Spirit-shaped communal comportment. The phrase "it seemed good" reflects the Spirit's personal imprimatur on collective decisions, signaling communal alignment with divine will. This principle extends beyond first-century councils into every congregational assembly facing doctrinal, ethical, or missional choices. By acknowledging the Spirit's personal agency in consensus-building, Paul models a decision-making process that honors divine sovereignty and human responsibility. This triadic harmonization—Spirit, apostles, community—ensures that corporate actions remain rooted in the Advocate's guidance. Concluding volitional sovereignty, we next explore the Spirit's intercessory intellect and empathy.

6 Intercessory Intellect and Empathy

6.1 Groanings too deep for words (Rom 8:26–27)

Paul teaches that "we do not know what to pray for as we ought, but the Spirit Himself intercedes for us with groanings too deep for words" (Rom 8:26). The Spirit's intercessory ministry combines intellectual sensitivity—knowing divine will—with empathetic emotional resonance—groaning in harmony with human weakness. The term *sugchōn* (groanings) conveys profound emotional involvement, highlighting the Spirit's personal solidarity with believers' struggles. The Spirit discerns the mind of the Father, shaping intercession according to perfect divine intellect. This synergy of cognitive insight and emotional empathy underscores the Spirit's personal nature: He feels with us and knows before us. The intercessory activity ensures that believers' inadequacies do not hinder communion with God. The Spirit's intercession also models Christian prayer, encouraging reliance on the Advocate rather than self-sufficiency. Recognizing this dual ministry prepares us to examine how divine will and human weakness are harmonized.

6.2 Harmonizing divine will and human weakness

Paul affirms that the Spirit "knows the mind of God, because the Spirit searches everything, even the depths of God" (1 Cor 2:10–11). When interceding, the Spirit aligns believers' prayers with divine will, compensating for human ignorance and emotional volatility. This harmonization involves the Spirit's personal agency in transforming prayer intentions, so that petitions ascend in accord with God's purposes. In contexts of suffering, the Spirit channels believers' laments into redemptive groans, weaving raw emotion into divine tapestry. The Spirit's empathy never overrides human responsibility; rather, He empowers believers to pray with authenticity and trust. This cooperative dynamic affirms both human participation and divine primacy. The Spirit's harmonization of wills reveals a deeply relational interplay that sustains believers through weakness. From empathic intercession, we turn to the Spirit's anticipatory pledge of redemption.

6.3 Anticipatory pledge of final redemption (Eph 1:13–14)

Paul calls the Spirit the "seal" and "guarantee" of our inheritance until we acquire possession of it, to the praise of His glory (Eph 1:13–14). The Spirit-person functions as a down payment (*arrhabōn*), personally securing believers' eschatological hope. This pledge involves cognitive certainty—assurance of future redemption—and affective security—peace that God will fulfill His promises. The Spirit's presence within believers serves as continuous reminder of their adoption and future transformation. He also intercedes in the "last days" (Acts 2:17) for ultimate fulfillment of God's redemptive plan. The Spirit's dual role as empathic intercessor and earnest pledge underscores His comprehensive relational ministry. Understanding this anticipatory function transitions us into the Spirit's work in adoption and assurance.

7 Adoption and Assurance: The Spirit Who Cries "Abba"

7.1 Spirit of sonship replacing fear (Rom 8:15)

Paul contrasts the spirit of slavery leading to fear with "the Spirit of adoption as sons, by whom we cry, 'Abba! Father!'" (Rom 8:15). This replacement underscores the Spirit-person's personal ministry in reorienting believers from anxious servitude to intimate filial confidence. The Aramaic *Abba* evokes childlike trust, reflecting a relational shift accomplished by the Spirit. This cry is not a ritual formula but a spontaneous expression of personal devotion. The Spirit's facilitation of this heartfelt address highlights His empathetic, emotionally nuanced engagement. By redefining believers' self-understanding, the Spirit fosters liberty and identity within the Father's household. This experience of adoption flows from the Spirit's intentional activity, anchoring assurance in personal relationship. Transitioning from sonship, we examine the Spirit's testimony within the believer.

7.2 Witnessing with our spirit that we are God's children (Rom 8:16)

Paul asserts, "The Spirit Himself bears witness with our spirit that we are children of God" (Rom 8:16). Here *bears witness* (*sumpnisthe*) implies a synergistic testimony: the Spirit affirms internally mediated conviction. This Spirit-person function involves cognitive confirmation—an inner knowing—and emotional assurance—peace of mind in belonging. Believers thus possess both objective status and subjective experience as God's children. The Spirit's personal witness serves as ongoing verification, safeguarding against doubt. This inner testimony unites intellect and emotion in the assurance of salvation. Recognizing the Spirit's dual testimony prepares us to explore His role as guarantee of inheritance.

7.3 Guaranteeing eschatological inheritance (2 Cor 1:22; 5:5)

Paul writes that God "has anointed us, set His seal of ownership on us, and put His Spirit in our hearts as a deposit guaranteeing what is to come" (2 Cor 1:21–22). Similarly, "He who prepared us for this very thing is God, who gave us the Spirit as a guarantee" (2 Cor 5:5). The Spirit's role as *arrhabōn* and seal conveys both protective ownership and forward-looking pledge, embodying personal assurance. Believers, under house arrest or on perilous journeys, could rely on the Spirit's personal guarantee of resurrection and new creation. This intimate function binds the present and future in a relational continuum. Understanding the Spirit as guarantee leads us to His liberating work from legal slavery.

7.4 Liberating from legal slavery (Gal 4:4–7)

Paul teaches that when the fullness of time came, God sent forth His Son "to redeem those who were under the law, so that we might receive adoption as sons" (Gal 4:4–5). He adds that "because you are sons, God has sent the Spirit of His Son into our hearts, crying, 'Abba! Father!'" (Gal 4:6). The Spirit's personal descent emancipates believers from legal bondage, establishing them as heirs rather than servants. This liberation combines legal emancipation—no longer under the law's sentence—and relational adoption, conveyed by the Spirit's emotional witness. Believers transition from fear-based obedience to freedom-driven devotion. The Spirit's liberating agency thus undergirds the entire trajectory from legal requirement to familial privilege. This segues into the Spirit's transformative work in character formation.

8 Transforming Character: Fruit and Freedom

8.1 Walking by the Spirit versus gratifying flesh (Gal 5:16–18)

Paul exhorts, "Walk by the Spirit, and you will not gratify the desires of the flesh" (Gal 5:16). Walking indicates ongoing personal cooperation with the Spirit's guidance. The Spirit alerts believers to fleshly inclinations and empowers them to resist. By cultivating a

Spirit-led lifestyle, believers experience freedom from sin's dominion. This dynamic involves daily relational engagement: discerning Spirit promptings and acting accordingly. The Spirit's personal presence shapes moral choices, disrupting habitual patterns of self-indulgence. He does not coerce but invites cooperation, highlighting personal agency within divine empowerment. This ethical formation prepares for the cultivation of Spirit fruit.

8.2 Cultivating the nine-fold fruit (Gal 5:22–23)

Paul lists the fruit of the Spirit—love, joy, peace, patience, kindness, goodness, faithfulness, gentleness, self-control (Gal 5:22–23)—as evidence of Spirit-indwelt transformation. Each attribute reflects a personal quality emanating from the Spirit's character. Believers cultivate these qualities through relational dependence: yielding to the Spirit's work within. The fruit contrasts with the works of the flesh (Gal 5:19–21), illustrating two distinct lifestyles. The Spirit's role is not just to empower behavior but to shape moral dispositions at the root. Over time, these traits coalesce into Christlike character. Recognizing the Spirit's formative ministry leads us to His renewing action on the inner person.

8.3 Renewing the inner person day by day (2 Cor 4:16 – 5:5)

Paul declares, "Though our outer self is wasting away, our inner self is being renewed day by day" (2 Cor 4:16). This ongoing renewal results from the Spirit's personal work, transforming the believer's inner nature even as physical limitations persist. The Greek *anakainōsis* (renewal) suggests fresh infusion of divine life, countering decay. Paul's future hope of a heavenly dwelling (2 Cor 5:1–5) is anchored in the Spirit as deposit guaranteeing bodily transformation. This inner renewal under Spirit agency sustains believers through suffering and mortality. The Spirit's personal ministry thus encompasses not only moral formation but existential renewal. From inner renewal, Paul moves to the Spirit's conforming of believers to Christ's image.

8.4 Forming Christ's image from glory to glory (2 Cor 3:17–18)

Paul asserts that "where the Spirit of the Lord is, there is freedom" (2 Cor 3:17), and that believers, beholding the Lord's glory with unveiled faces, "are being transformed into the same image from one degree of glory to another" by the Spirit (2 Cor 3:18). The Spirit-person facilitates progressive sanctification, enabling believers to reflect

Christ more fully. The transformation unfolds "from glory to glory," indicating incremental, sustained change rather than instantaneous perfection. This process involves personal relational engagement with the Spirit, who unveils Christ's presence through Scripture and community. The freedom provided by the Spirit liberates believers to pursue this ongoing metamorphosis without fear. Recognizing this transformative pattern concludes our exploration of the Spirit's personal intellect, emotion, and will in Paul's witness.

9 Building Unity: Fellowship (*Koinōnia*) of the Spirit

9.1 One body, one Spirit, one hope (Eph 4:1–6)

Paul prays that the Ephesians "lead a life worthy of the calling to which you have been called" by maintaining the unity of the Spirit in the bond of peace (Eph 4:1–3). He identifies seven markers of this unity: one body, one Spirit, one hope, one Lord, one faith, one baptism, one God and Father of all (Eph 4:4–6). These repeated "ones" underscore the Spirit-person's role in forging a singular, cohesive community from diverse members. The Spirit accomplishes this unity by baptizing individuals into one body (1 Cor 12:13), by distributing gifts for the building up of the body (Eph 4:12), and by producing mutually reinforcing virtues—humility, gentleness, patience, and love (Eph 4:2). The Spirit's personal agency in creating and sustaining fellowship transcends ethnic, social, and gender divides (Gal 3:28). Tensions and conflicts within the church are therefore violations of Spirit-unity, calling for repentance and reconciliation. The Spirit-person invites each believer to participate actively in this unity by bearing with one another, entrusting the community's health to His enabling presence. This corporate koinōnia flows naturally into Paul's immediate concern for baptismal unity.

9.2 Baptized by one Spirit into one body (1 Cor 12:13)

In Corinth, Paul emphasizes that "by one Spirit we were all baptized into one body—Jews or Greeks, slaves or free—and all were made to drink of one Spirit" (1 Cor 12:13). Here *baptized* (*baptizō*) refers not only to water baptism but to Spirit-baptism, an immediate divine act that incorporates believers into Christ's body. The Spirit's personal volition initiates this baptism, effecting a fundamental relational transformation. Each believer's identity shifts from atomic individuality to organic interdependence, grounded in Spirit communion. The imagery of drinking from one Spirit conveys both unity and shared sustenance—each member partakes equally in the Advocate's life-giving presence. This Spirit baptism creates a spiritual kinship that empowers mutual care, accountability, and mission. The Corinthians, prone to factionalism over gifts and personalities, are reminded that the Spirit's purpose is unity, not division. Recognizing Spirit baptism as the foundation of ecclesial unity sets the stage for maintaining the bond of peace.

9.3 Maintaining the bond of peace (Eph 4:3)

Paul urges believers to be "eager to maintain the unity of the Spirit in the bond of peace" (Eph 4:3). The term zēloō (be eager) suggests passionate personal commitment to nurture Spirit-wrought unity. The bond (*syndesmos*) conveys both relational connection and mutual restraint, tying members together in love. Peace (*eirēnē*) is not mere absence of conflict but the Spirit-generated harmony that arises from shared allegiance to Christ. The Spirit's personal ministry involves reconciling estranged parties (Eph 2:14–16) and cultivating dispositions—patience, kindness, forgiveness—that preserve community cohesion. When disagreements surface, the Spirit's continuing presence enables godly confrontation and restoration rather than fragmentation. Believers learn to appeal to the Spirit within one another to reconcile misunderstandings, reflecting corporate maturity. This maintenance of peace under Spirit guidance naturally leads to mutual edification.

9.4 Participating in mutual edification (*Phil 2:1; 1 Th 5:19–21*)

Paul exhorts the Philippians, "If in Christ there is any encouragement from his love, any participation in the Spirit, any affection and sympathy, complete my joy by being of the same mind" (Phil 2:1). The phrase "participation in the Spirit" (*koinōnia pneumatos*) highlights communal sharing in the Advocate's presence as the basis for mutual encouragement. In Thessalonica, he warns, "Do not quench the Spirit. Do not despise prophecies, but test everything; hold fast what is good" (1 Th 5:19–21). These instructions show the Spirit-person at work in congregational edification: encouraging, guiding, exposing, and validating gifts. The Spirit fosters a learning community where prophetic words and practical deeds coalesce into collective growth. Believers exercise discernment under the Spirit's guidance, ensuring that mutual edification reflects divine truth. This synergy of participation and discernment seals the Spirit's fellowship ministry and prefaces discussions of the Spirit's eschatological functions.

10 Eschatological Firstfruits and Resurrection Power

10.1 Spirit as down payment of the new creation (Rom 8:23)

Paul describes believers as "those who have the firstfruits of the Spirit" (Rom 8:23), employing the agricultural metaphor of first portion guaranteed before the full harvest. The Spirit-person here functions as the *arrhabōn*, an advance pledge of the future resurrection and renewal of creation. As firstfruits once consecrated Israel's harvest (Lev 23:10–14), the Spirit confirms the sanctity and destiny of redeemed humanity. This Spirit-down payment establishes identity and hope in the present, anchoring believers amid suffering. The personal guarantee ensures that the full redemption will be realized in bodily resurrection. The Spirit's eschatological pledge reinforces both communal perseverance and individual assurance. From firstfruits we move to the Spirit's role in raising life.

10.2 Life-giving power raising Jesus and believers (*Rom 8:11*; *1 Cor 15:45*)

Paul declares that "if the Spirit of Him who raised Jesus from the dead dwells in you, He who raised Christ Jesus will also give life to your mortal bodies through His Spirit who dwells in you" (Rom 8:11). The Spirit's personal power is thus the same that overcame death in Jesus, now active within believers' frail bodies. The designation "living Spirit" in 1 Corinthians 15:45 connects the Spirit's life-giving role to the "last Adam" who became a life-giving spirit. The Spirit-person animates natural life and resurrected life, bridging present mortality with future glorification. This personal power assures that death does not have the final word for those indwelt by the Spirit. Believers experience glimpses of resurrection power—physical healing, spiritual renewal—pointing to the consummation. Recognizing the Spirit's personal life-giving agency grounds current hope in future realities. From resurrection power we shift to how the Spirit energizes hope amid suffering.

10.3 Energizing hope amid present suffering (Rom 8:18–27)

Paul contrasts present afflictions with future glory, asserting that "the creation waits with eager longing for the revealing of the sons of God…we ourselves…groan inwardly as we wait eagerly for adoption" (Rom 8:19, 23). The Spirit intertwines with creation's longing and human groaning, directing hope toward redemption. The Spirit's intercession with groanings too deep for words (Rom 8:26) channels suffering into anticipatory prayer, fueling resilient hope. This dynamic underscores the Spirit-person's personal solidarity with both believers and all creation, promising that present hardships are part of the Spirit's redemptive narrative. The Spirit's engagement transforms suffering into a context for deeper communion and anticipation of future vindication. This eschatological hope transitions into the Spirit's cosmic liberation guarantee.

10.4 Guaranteeing cosmic liberation (*Eph 1:10, 22–23*; *Col 1:19–20*)

Paul proclaims that God's plan is "to unite all things in him, things in heaven and things on earth" under Christ, "in whom...God was pleased to have all his fullness dwell" (Col 1:19–20). Ephesians adds that the church is "the fullness of him who fills all in all" (Eph 1:23). The Spirit-person actualizes this cosmic reconciliation, working in believers and through the church to extend Christ's lordship. The Spirit empowers missional witness that anticipates creation's restoration and moral order. This cosmic dimension of the Spirit's personal agency elevates local churches' work to universal significance. Understanding the Spirit's role in cosmic liberation prepares us to examine His ethical empowerment and spiritual warfare.

11 Ethical Empowerment and Spiritual Warfare

11.1 Putting to death deeds of the body (Rom 8:13)

Paul exhorts, "If by the Spirit you put to death the deeds of the body, you will live" (Rom 8:13). The Spirit-person empowers believers to overcome fleshly impulses that lead to death, enabling ethical transformation. This putting to death (*anaptein*) is a deliberate act of cooperation with the Spirit, who convicts of sin and grants strength for victory. The Spirit's personal ministry integrates moral discipline with relational transformation, turning convictions into consistent behavior. The ethical empowerment extends to a vast array of sins—sexual immorality, envy, anger—showing the Spirit's concern for holistic holiness. By harnessing the Spirit's enabling presence, believers participate in the Spirit's personal work of sanctification. This empowerment leads into a new way of service.

11.2 Serving in the "new way of the Spirit" versus old letter (Rom 7:6)

Paul contrasts serving "in the new way of the Spirit" with "the old way of the written code" (Rom 7:6). The Spirit-person ushers believers into a dynamic relationship with Christ, where moral guidance comes from Spirit promptings rather than external compulsion. This new way fosters intrinsic motivation—love, joy, peace—rather than fear of legal penalty. The Spirit's personal presence writes God's law on hearts (2 Cor 3:3), enabling spontaneous obedience aligned with God's will. Believers thus serve not under threat but out of grateful devotion. The Spirit-person's relational guidance prevents legalism and cultivates genuine freedom. This new way equips believers for the spiritual armor that follows.

11.3 Spiritual armor and Spirit-directed prayer (Eph 6:10–18)

Paul instructs believers to "be strong in the Lord and in the strength of his might…having put on the whole armor of God" and to "pray at all times in the Spirit" (Eph 6:10–18). The Spirit-person supplies divine strength (*dunamis*) as believers equip themselves with truth, righteousness, readiness, faith, salvation, and the Word. Each piece of armor reflects the Spirit's enabling: truth illumines, righteousness empowers, faith fortifies, and the Spirit-sharpened Word deflects falsehood. Prayer "in the Spirit" (*en pneumati*) suggests Spirit-led intercession and warfare, aligning believers' petitions with divine strategy. The Spirit's personal presence thus transforms spiritual combat from human effort to cooperative encounter. This Spirit-directed warfare prepares the community for discernment of spirits and prophetic testing.

11.4 Discernment of spirits and prophetic testing (*1 Cor 12:10*; *1 Th 5:19–22*)

Paul ascribes to the Spirit the gift of *diakrisis pneumaton* (discernment of spirits) among the charismata (1 Cor 12:10), enabling identification of authentic versus counterfeit spiritual activity. He also commands the Thessalonians not to quench the Spirit or despise prophecies but to test everything and hold fast to what is good (1 Th 5:19–21). The Spirit-person here functions as both gift-giver and ethical standard, guiding believers to evaluate prophetic utterances and spiritual phenomena. Discernment involves intellectual acumen and moral sensitivity imparted by the Spirit. Believers learn to weigh messages, charisms, and experiences against apostolic witness and communal edification. This Spirit-enabled testing preserves doctrinal integrity and prevents exploitation. Having examined spiritual warfare, we now move to discipline and restoration under the Spirit's personal care.

12 Discipline, Judgment, and Restoration

12.1 Delivering to Satan for redemptive purposes (1 Cor 5:3–5)

Paul instructs the Corinthian church to expel the incestuous brother and "deliver such a one to Satan for the destruction of the flesh, so that his spirit may be saved in the day of the Lord" (1 Cor 5:5). This radical measure, under the Spirit's authority, aims at disciplinary restoration rather than mere punishment. The Spirit-person authorizes the church's judgment to sever communal fellowship temporarily, allowing the offending individual to experience conviction and repentance. The ultimate goal is spiritual salvation ("his spirit may be saved"), demonstrating that Spirit-driven discipline seeks redemption, not retribution. This corrective process highlights the Spirit's pastoral concern for individual and corporate purity. Having seen disciplinary action, we examine how the Spirit grants godly sorrow.

12.2 Spirit-granted godly sorrow leading to repentance (2 Cor 7:9–11)

Paul contrasts worldly sorrow, which leads to death, with godly sorrow, which leads to repentance and a desire to amend (2 Cor 7:10). He rejoices that the Corinthians exhibited such sorrow when he wrote his previous severe letter (2 Cor 7:8–9). This godly sorrow, prompted by the Spirit's conviction, produces earnestness, eagerness to clear themselves, indignation at sin, fear of God, longing, zeal, and vindication of righteousness (2 Cor 7:11). The Spirit-person thus orchestrates a complex emotional response that culminates in moral transformation. Godly sorrow attests to the Spirit's personal ministry of repentance, leading to renewed fellowship. This repentance process readies the community for comfort.

12.3 Warning against quenching or despising the Spirit (1 Th 5:19)

Paul commands, "Do not quench the Spirit" (1 Th 5:19), cautioning against stifling Spirit-led initiatives in worship, prophecy, and ministry. He immediately follows with "Do not despise prophecies, but test everything" (1 Th 5:20–21), linking quenching with disregard for Spirit communication. The Spirit-person's agency therefore demands attentive engagement rather than rejection. Quenching the Spirit occurs when believers resist His convictions, stifle spiritual gifts, or neglect corporate discernment. Such quenching undermines relational solidarity with the Spirit-person and hampers communal vitality. This warning prepares the ground for comforting the repentant.

12.4 Comforting the penitent and reaffirming love (2 Cor 2:5–11)

After a brother's transgression and discipline, Paul urges the Corinthians to forgive and comfort him, "lest such a one be overwhelmed by excessive sorrow" (2 Cor 2:7). He reminds them not to "grieve the Spirit of God" by withholding love, since forgiveness and reaffirmation prevent the adversary from gaining ground (2 Cor 2:10–11). The Spirit-person here works through communal empathy to restore the repentant brother's spirit. Paul's instruction merges divine and human agency: the Spirit prompts repentance and communal warmth secures restoration. This cycle of discipline, sorrow, and comfort exemplifies the Spirit's personal care for individuals and the community. Having traced discipline and restoration, we are ready to explore hermeneutical implications of Spirit versus letter.

13 Spirit versus Letter: Hermeneutical Implications

13.1 Covenant contrast—ministry of death versus ministry of life (2 Cor 3:6–9)

Paul contrasts the old covenant written on stone, which he calls "the ministry of death, carved in letters on stone" (2 Cor 3:7), with the new covenant "ministry of the Spirit" that brings life. The "letters" here signify the written code, external regulations that condemn transgression without providing inner transformation. By describing the old ministry as glorious yet fading, Paul acknowledges its historic significance while exposing its limitations: adherence to the law produces guilt, not genuine righteousness. In contrast, the Spirit's ministry is depicted as genuinely liberating, engraving God's will on human hearts (2 Cor 3:3). The Spirit's personal agency makes the believer a "letter" known and read by all, reflecting internalized divine character rather than external compliance. This shift from letter to Spirit reframes biblical interpretation: true understanding arises from the Spirit's illumination of Scripture, not merely intellectual assent to its words. The hermeneutical implication is that readers must seek the Spirit's guidance when engaging Old-Testament texts, allowing the Advocate to actualize life-giving power rather than legalistic judgment. Recognizing this covenantal contrast sets the stage for exploring how believers can read Scripture with unveiled faces.

13.2 Reading Scripture with unveiled face (2 Cor 3:14–17)

Paul observes that "when Moses is read, a veil lies over their hearts," a barrier removed only in Christ (2 Cor 3:14). The Spirit-person functions as the remover of this veil, granting the capacity to see and reflect God's glory. Believers who turn to the Lord "are being transformed into the same image from one degree of glory to another, which comes from the Lord who is the Spirit" (2 Cor 3:18). The process involves the Spirit-person empowering readers to move beyond literal interpretation into spiritual insight. This spiritual reading requires humility, openness, and dependence on the Advocate's illumination. Paul's metaphor suggests that each encounter with Scripture under Spirit guidance deepens understanding and fosters transformation, rather than mere accumulation of facts. The presence of the Spirit in the interpretive community ensures that Scripture's transformative intent is realized. As readers are no longer hindered by the veil, they participate in an interpretive act that is both cognitive and relational, reflecting the image of God. This Spirit-enabled reading lays the groundwork for using Spirit-taught words in communicating spiritual realities.

13.3 Spirit-taught words comparing spiritual realities (1 Cor 2:13)

Paul declares that "we impart this in words not taught by human wisdom but taught by the Spirit, interpreting spiritual truths to those who are spiritual" (1 Cor 2:13). The Greek *diēgoumenoi* ("interpreting" or "comparing") indicates the Spirit's role in using language to convey intangible realities. This interpretive process involves selecting analogies, metaphors, and arguments that resonate with listeners' hearts. The Spirit imparts vocabulary and structure, enabling speakers to articulate theological truths—such as justification, sanctification, and adoption—in ways that penetrate both mind and conscience. The Spirit's personal guidance prevents misrepresentation, ensuring that language remains anchored in Christ's redemptive work rather than human speculation. As a result, communities grasp not only propositional truths but experiential dimensions—joy, hope, love—that accompany those truths. This Spirit-taught communication transforms communal discourse into a participatory encounter with divine reality, fostering deeper fellowship. Having explored linguistic mediation, we now turn to contemporary implications for interpretation.

13.4 Implications for contemporary biblical interpretation

The contrast between letter and Spirit challenges modern interpreters to prioritize the Advocate's role in exegesis. Academic methodologies must be complemented by spiritual discernment, inviting the Spirit-person to illuminate texts' theological intent. Congregational Bible studies should incorporate prayerful dependence on the Spirit, rather than treating Scripture as a mere historical artifact. The Spirit's guidance calls for an interpretive posture marked by humility, listening, and communal engagement. Misuses of Scripture—proof-texting, ideological twisting—are forms of quenching the Spirit's transformative work. Conversely, Spirit-led interpretation yields ethical transformation, therapeutic restoration, and missional vision. Embracing the Spirit's hermeneutical primacy fosters reading practices that align with the kingdom's values, ensuring that the church's encounter with Scripture remains a living, dynamic fellowship with the Advocate. This sets the stage for celebrating triune patterns in Pauline benedictions.

14 Triune Relational Patterns in Pauline Benedictions

14.1 Grace, love, and fellowship formula (2 Cor 13:14)

Paul's closing blessing in Second Corinthians encapsulates triune relational dynamics: "The grace of the Lord Jesus Christ and the love of God and the fellowship of the Holy Spirit be with you all" (2 Cor 13:14). Each element corresponds to a person of the Trinity: grace flows from the Son's redemptive work, love from the Father's covenantal affection, and fellowship (*koinōnia*) from the Spirit's personal communion. The ordering highlights the Spirit's unique role in mediating relational intimacy, transforming believers into participators in divine life. This formula becomes a liturgical and theological pattern, embedding triune fellowship into the church's worship and identity. The Spirit's fellowship promise ensures that grace and love yield tangible communal experiences. Recognizing this triadic structure deepens appreciation for the Spirit-person's integrative role in the relational economy of God. Having seen the benediction's relational architecture, we explore the Spirit's role in Christ's ongoing faithfulness.

14.2 Spirit's role in Christ's faithfulness (*Gal 2:20*; *Phil 1:19*)

Paul declares, "I have been crucified with Christ… yet I live, no longer I, but Christ who lives in me" and adds, "The life I now live in the flesh I live by faith in the Son of God, who loved me and gave himself for me" (Gal 2:20). This indwelling of Christ is effected by the Spirit-person, whose presence enables Christ's life and faithfulness within believers. In Philippians, Paul expresses confidence that "this will turn out for my deliverance through your prayer and the supply of the Spirit of Jesus Christ" (Phil 1:19). Here the Spirit-person is explicitly named as the source of internal strength that sustains Paul amid trial. The Spirit's personal participation ensures that Christ's faithfulness is not a historical event alone but an ongoing reality within the church. Believers thus experience Christ's love and sacrifice internally, mediated by the Spirit. This experiential dynamic deepens the church's trust in the triune God's continual provision. Having seen the Spirit's participatory role, we turn to Spirit-energized Eucharistic thanksgiving.

14.3 Eucharistic thanksgivings energized by the Spirit (1 Th 1:2–5)

Paul thanks God "always for all of you, constantly mentioning you in my prayers, remembering before our God and Father your work of faith and labor of love and steadfastness of hope in our Lord Jesus Christ" (1 Th 1:2–3). He attributes the Thessalonians' reception of the gospel "in power and in the Holy Spirit and with full conviction" (1 Th 1:5). In the context of communal meals and remembrance, the Spirit-person energizes gratitude and mutual encouragement. The Spirit's personal presence transforms ordinary gatherings into eucharistic experiences, where shared thanksgiving becomes an act of koinōnia. This Spirit-energized thanksgiving fosters communal resilience and worshipful remembrance of Christ's sacrifice. The interplay of faith, love, hope, and Spirit power in thanksgiving meals anticipates the fully realized doxological praise we examine next.

14.4 Doxological ends—Spirit's glory with Father and Son (Eph 3:21)

Paul concludes his grand doxology by ascribing glory to the triune God: "to him be glory in the church and in Christ Jesus throughout all generations, forever and ever. Amen" (Eph 3:21). Though the Spirit is not explicitly named here, the surrounding context (Eph 3:14–19) describes the Spirit's role in empowering believers to grasp Christ's love and fullness. The Spirit-person thus undergirds the doxological focus on Father and Son by realizing their purposes in the church. This triune glory culminates the pneumatological journey: intellect, emotion, will, fellowship, eschatology, ethics, discipline, hermeneutics, and relational patterns all converge in Spirit-enabled worship. Recognizing the Spirit's contribution to doxological ends completes our exploration of Pauline pneumatology. We now synthesize and transition to the next thematic chapter.

Conclusion Paul's witness paints the Spirit as a fully personal divine Agent—illuminating minds, inspiring speech, shaping affections, and exercising sovereign will. From narrative integration across his letters to precise vocabulary clusters, Paul constructs a comprehensive pneumatology that grounds Christian identity and mission. The Spirit's intellect unveils mysteries, His communication secures revelation, His emotional ministries foster love and zeal, and His volitional choices direct gifts and gatherings. Recognizing the Spirit's multifaceted personhood equips the church to experience and honor the Advocate's ongoing presence. As we transition to Chapter 7, we will examine how relational attributes—love, fellowship, and jealous yearning—further reveal the Spirit's personal depth across the New Testament.

Chapter 7. Relational Attributes: Love, Fellowship, and Jealous Yearning

The Holy Spirit's relational attributes—love, fellowship, and jealous yearning—reveal His deeply personal engagement with God's people. Across the Old and New Testaments, the Spirit emerges not as an impersonal force but as the divine Lover, Companion, and Covenant-Keeper whose intimate affections drive redemption, community life, and passionate fidelity. In this chapter, we will trace how prophetic promises of covenant love find fulfillment in Pauline and Johannine writings, how the Spirit forges unity within the Trinity and the church, and how divine jealousy safeguards pure devotion. We will also explore the Spirit's hospitality—welcoming all into divine presence—and His peacemaking work in conflict and reconciliation. Through careful exegesis, we will see that relational dimensions of the Spirit form the beating heart of Christian experience, guiding believers toward perfected fellowship with God and one another.

1 Love Poured Out: The Spirit as Divine Affection

1.1 Covenant Love in Prophetic Promise (Isa 63:9–14; Hos 11:8–9)

Isaiah recalls that in Israel's distress, the "angel of his presence saved them; in his love and in his pity he redeemed them" and led them like a flock through the wilderness (Isa 63:9–14), depicting the Spirit's protective affection. The prophet Hosea wrestles with divine sorrow over unfaithfulness yet declares that God will not execute His fierce anger, for He is "God and not man, the Holy One in your midst, and I will not come in wrath" (Hos 11:8–9). Both passages personalize God's love with emotional nuance—tenderness, sorrow, protective zeal—attributes of the Spirit's covenant affection. The Spirit's love is neither aloof nor detached but enters Israel's anguish, shares its vulnerabilities, and steadfastly upholds covenant promises. These prophetic images anticipate the Spirit's New-Testament outpouring of love into believers' hearts (Rom 5:5). The Spirit's divine affection grounds Christian assurance: God's love pursues even wayward hearts. The prophetic promise also implies that this love enables repentance, inviting return through compassionate longing. Recognizing the Spirit's covenant affection prepares us for Paul's testimony to love "shed abroad" in the believer's heart.

1.2 Pauline Testimony: Love "shed abroad" in our hearts (Rom 5:5)

Paul boldly affirms that "God's love has been poured into our hearts through the Holy Spirit who has been given to us" (Rom 5:5), employing the same metaphor of pouring to describe covenant intimacy. This divine plumbing of the heart indicates the Spirit's personal involvement: He takes the initiative, not waiting for human affection to arise. The verb *ekcheo* ("poured out") connotes abundance, suggesting that God's love overwhelms self-centered tendencies. This love generates assurance, bonding believers to the Father's heart and sustaining them through trials. The Spirit's affection disrupts fear-based relationships, replacing anxiety with confidence in divine acceptance. This love is both objective—rooted in Christ's sacrificial work—and subjective—experienced as warmth and attraction to God. The Spirit's personal ministry thus creates a new locus of desire, orienting affections toward Christ. This poured-out love also fuels ethical imperatives: love of neighbor and enemy alike. It unifies the community, for all who share the Spirit share the same love. The Spirit's divine affection therefore becomes the engine of mission and moral life. As this love expels fear, it leads seamlessly into the next subsection.

1.3 Sanctifying Affection that Drives Out Fear (Rom 8:15; 2 Tim 1:7)

Paul contrasts the Spirit-given "spirit of adoption" with a "spirit of slavery to fear" (Rom 8:15), highlighting that divine affection liberates believers from bondage to guilt and anxiety. This adoption entails an inner confession—crying "Abba! Father!"—an unguarded address possible only through the Spirit's personal love. Timothy's pastoral charge reinforces this: "for God gave us a spirit not of fear but of power and love and self-control" (2 Tim 1:7). The triad—power, love, self-control—flows from Spirit indwelling and dismantles paralyzing fears. This sanctifying affection moves the believer from performance-driven religion to freedom-driven devotion. The Spirit's personal love becomes the motivating force behind courage in witness, perseverance in suffering, and bold ethical living. As fear recedes, the believer's affectionate trust deepens, enabling risk-taking for Christ's sake. The Spirit's affection also fosters compassion within the community, encouraging members to support one another courageously. This dynamic of love overcoming fear naturally gives rise to missionary impulse.

1.4 Missional Impulse: Spirit-compelled Love for the Nations (Acts 13:2–4; Rom 15:30)

In Antioch, the Spirit commands, "Set apart for me Barnabas and Saul for the work to which I have called them" (Acts 13:2), and the church, moved by divine affection for the lost, fasts, prays, and lays hands on them (Acts 13:3–4). The Spirit's personal command emerges from loving compassion for unreached peoples. Later Paul implores the Romans, "I appeal to you, brothers, by our Lord Jesus Christ and by the love of the Spirit, to strive together with me in your prayers to God on my behalf" (Rom 15:30). Here *love of the Spirit* is the motivating factor behind intercession for missions. The Spirit's affection not only warms the believer's heart but also compels outward action, turning internal devotion into global outreach. Love ignited by the Spirit shapes missionary strategies: going "to the Jew first" then to the Gentile (Rom 1:16), reflecting God's reconciling love for all. The Spirit's personal love thus becomes the engine of cross-cultural gospel advance, uniting prayer, commissioning, and perseverance. Mission arises not from human ambition but from the Spirit's unquenchable love. As this love propels evangelists, we transition to the Spirit's work in forging fellowship within the Trinity and the church.

2 Fellowship of the Spirit: Koinōnia Within the Trinity and the Church

2.1 Triadic Benedictions and Mutual Indwelling (2 Cor 13:14)

Paul's benediction—"The grace of the Lord Jesus Christ and the love of God and the fellowship of the Holy Spirit be with you all" (2 Cor 13:14)—offers a concise summary of triune fellowship. The triad unites grace, love, and koinōnia, attributing each to a distinct Person yet weaving them into a relational tapestry. Grace flows from Christ's redemptive work, love from the Father's heart, and fellowship from the Spirit's active presence. Mutual indwelling—Father in Son, Son in believers, Spirit in believers—reflects perichoretic life spilling over into the church. This triadic fellowship is not static but dynamically ongoing, sustaining believers in communal worship and mission. The Spirit's fellowship dimension invites participation in divine life, making the church a living extension of Trinitarian communion. Recognizing the Spirit's role here sets the stage for exploring unity across Jew–Gentile lines.

2.2 Spirit-Created Unity Across Jew–Gentile Lines (Eph 2:18–22; 4:3–6)

Ephesians underscores that through Christ and by one Spirit, both Jews and Gentiles have access to the Father (Eph 2:18). The Spirit creates a new humanity, abolishing enmity and forming a "holy temple" where diverse stones are joined together (Eph 2:19–22). Believers—once strangers—become fellow citizens and members of God's household by Spirit fellowship. Paul commands them to "make every effort to maintain the unity of the Spirit in the bond of peace" (Eph 4:3), relying on the Spirit-person's work to sustain this unity. The Spirit's personal agency melds distinct cultural streams into one river of life. This unity is more than administrative; it is organic, rooted in Spirit indwelling that transcends socio-ethnic barriers. The Spirit's fellowship thus becomes the locus of reconciliation, integrating varied gifts and backgrounds into a unified community. From unity we move to shared sufferings and consolation.

2.3 Shared Suffering and Consolation in the Spirit (Phil 2:1; 1 Pet 4:14)

Paul appeals to the Philippians, "If in Christ there is any encouragement from his love, any participation in the Spirit, any affection and sympathy, complete my joy by being of the same mind" (Phil 2:1). Shared suffering—"to be like-minded, having the same love, being one in spirit and of one mind"—stems from Spirit participation. The Spirit-person binds hearts in mutual empathy amid trials. Peter likewise exhorts believers, "if you are insulted for the name of Christ, you are blessed, because the Spirit of glory and of God rests upon you" (1 Pet 4:14), identifying the Spirit as companion in persecution. This Spirit-based consolation affirms that suffering is not endured alone but within Trinitarian fellowship. The Spirit's personal consolation fuels perseverance, creating a communal refuge in hardship. Shared suffering becomes a sacrament of unity, forging deeper fellowship under the Advocate's care. This intimate solidarity leads into sacramental communion shaped by the Spirit.

2.4 Sacramental Communion: Baptism and Eucharist as Spirit-Wrought Participation (1 Cor 12:13; 10:16)

Paul teaches that "we were all baptized by one Spirit into one body" (1 Cor 12:13), indicating that Spirit baptism is both a sacramental incorporation into Christ and koinōnia with all believers. Baptism marks the Spirit's handprint on one's identity, uniting diverse members in one living body. The Eucharistic "cup of blessing" is described as participation in the blood of Christ, and the bread as participation in the body of Christ, "because there is one bread, we who are many are one body, for we all partake of the one bread" (1 Cor 10:16–17). This sacramental participation depends on Spirit presence to make the elements effective signs of real fellowship. The Spirit-person transforms physical symbols into spiritual realities, uniting worshipers with Christ and one another. Together, Spirit baptism and Spirit-led Eucharist enact divine fellowship, forging communal identity through ritual participation. This sacramental dimension of koinōnia transitions us to the Spirit's jealous yearning for exclusive devotion.

3 Jealous Yearning: Covenant Zeal of the Spirit

3.1 Old-Testament Background: Divine Jealousy for Exclusive Worship (Ex 34:14; Zech 8:2)

Exodus warns, "For you shall worship no other god, for the LORD, whose name is Jealous, is a jealous God" (Ex 34:14), attributing divine jealousy to Yahweh's covenant love that demands exclusive affection. Zechariah echoes this zeal, calling God "Jealous for Zion with great jealousy" (Zech 8:2), a passion to preserve covenant purity and communal identity. This divine jealousy is not petty envy but protective zeal, safeguarding the covenant relationship against spiritual adultery. The Spirit of God embodies this jealous yearning, reacting against idolatry and half-hearted devotion. This Old-

Testament covenant context informs New-Testament portrayals of the Spirit's jealousy, highlighting that a fervent guarding of hearts is a sign of divine love. Recognizing this foundation prepares us to see James's articulation of the Spirit's desire for faithful hearts.

3.2 James 4:5 and the Spirit's Desire for Faithful Hearts

James declares, "Or do you suppose it is to no purpose that the Scripture says, 'He yearns jealously over the spirit that he has made to dwell in us'?" (Jas 4:5). Here the Spirit's personal yearning underscores His deep desire for believers' undivided hearts. James uses covenant jealousy to warn against friendship with the world— "You adulterous people!" (Jas 4:4)—and to call for repentance. The Spirit-person's jealous longing compels believers to examine loyalties and realign with God. This divine zeal is not vindictive but restorative, aimed at reclaiming wayward devotion. The Spirit's yearning thus becomes a catalyst for moral revival and communal purity. Recognizing this yearning leads naturally into how the Spirit confronts and judges sin within the community.

3.3 Guarding Holiness: Confronting Sin in the Community (Acts 5:1–11; Eph 4:30)

When Ananias and Sapphira lie "to the Holy Spirit" (Acts 5:3), Peter confronts them with prophetic precision, and the Spirit swiftly executes judgment (Acts 5:5, 10). The Spirit's personal jealousy for communal holiness refuses complicity with deceit. Similarly, Paul warns, "Do not grieve the Holy Spirit of God, in whom you were sealed" (Eph 4:30), equating sin with wounding the Advocate's affections. The Spirit-person thus functions as both loving guardian and judge—calling out hypocrisy and protecting fellowship. Confrontation of sin is not punitive vindictiveness but an expression of jealous covenant care, aimed at communal restoration. The Spirit's involvement in church discipline underscores that purity is non-negotiable in His relational economy. Understanding this protective jealousy transitions into how positive zeal provokes undivided devotion.

3.4 Positive Jealousy: Provoking Believers to Undivided Devotion (2 Cor 11:2–3)

Paul expresses apostolic zeal by saying, "I feel a divine jealousy for you, since I betrothed you to one husband, to present you as a pure virgin to Christ" (2 Cor 11:2). This positive jealousy models the Spirit's longing for believers' exclusive allegiance to Christ. The marriage metaphor underscores relational fidelity: just as a wife's undivided devotion honors her husband, so believers' loyalty pleases the Spirit. Paul fears that false teachings may corrupt this devotion—"I am afraid I may have labored over you in vain" (2 Cor 11:2)—indicating protective zeal. This proactive jealousy spurs vigilance in doctrine, worship, and ethical living. The Spirit's positive yearning thus motivates apostolic care and communal purity. From jealous yearning, the chapter moves to the Spirit's hospitality as divine host.

4 Hospitality of the Heart: The Spirit as Divine Host

4.1 Indwelling as Sacred Welcome (1 Cor 3:16; John 14:23)

Paul reminds the Corinthians, "Do you not know that you are God's temple and that God's Spirit dwells in you?" (1 Cor 3:16), portraying each believer as a sacred dwelling for the Spirit-person. This indwelling signifies a personal welcome, where the Spirit—like a divine guest—takes residence in human hearts. Jesus similarly promises, "If anyone loves me, he will keep my word, and my Father will love him, and we will come to him and make our home with him" (John 14:23). The triune God becomes a heavenly household within believers, initiated by the Spirit's entry. This divine hospitality transforms ordinary bodies into living tabernacles, sanctified spaces of relationship. The Spirit's personal indwelling thus creates perpetual fellowship, echoing the tabernacle's sacred welcome in Israel's wilderness. Recognizing this sacred hospitality naturally extends to human expressions of welcome.

4.2 Making Room for the Other: The Spirit and Christian Hospitality (Rom 12:13; Heb 13:2)

Paul exhorts Romans to "contribute to the needs of the saints and seek to show hospitality" (Rom 12:13), linking hospitality with Spirit-enabled love. The writer to the Hebrews commands, "Do not neglect to show hospitality to strangers, for thereby some have entertained angels unawares" (Heb 13:2), recalling divine visitations to Abraham and Lot. Christian hospitality thus becomes responding to the Spirit's welcoming presence by opening one's home and table. The Spirit-person inspires empathy for the outsider, reflecting divine impartial welcome. Such hospitality extends relational warmth initiated by the Spirit's divine welcome. By practicing generosity and kindness, believers mirror the Advocate's heart toward sinners and strangers. This hospitality fosters community bonds, demonstrating the Spirit's personal ministry in everyday life. From human hospitality we turn to how spiritual gifts serve as relational table-settings.

4.3 Spiritual Gifts as Relational Table-Settings (1 Pet 4:9–11)

Peter enjoins believers to "show hospitality to one another without grumbling" and to "use [gifts] to serve one another, as good stewards of God's varied grace" (1 Pet 4:9–10). Spiritual gifts function like place settings at a banquet, each uniquely arranged by the Spirit to serve others. Whether hospitality, teaching, encouragement, or generosity, each gift facilitates relational interaction—welcoming, instructing, comforting, and sharing. The Spirit-person distributes these gifts with personal knowledge of believers' capacities and communal needs. When exercised in love, gifts become expressions of divine hospitality around Christ's table. This relational dynamic models the Spirit's divine hospitality at work in the church. From table-settings we move to worship gatherings as encounters with the living Guest.

4.4 Worship Gatherings as Encounters with the Living Guest (1 Cor 14:24–25)

Paul notes that if all prophesy in a church gathering, unbelievers and inquirers are convicted, "and as many as have fallen asleep in the Lord are comforted," because God's secrets are disclosed by the Spirit (1 Cor 14:24–25). Worship thus becomes an occasion where the Spirit-person visits, convicts, reveals, and comforts—like a gracious host meeting guests. The presence of the Spirit transforms collective worship into a personal encounter with the divine Guest. Believers anticipate His coming in song, prayer, and proclamation, preparing hearts to receive His relational benefit. Such Spirit-wrought worship builds corporate identity as a fellowship of pilgrims in divine hospitality. Recognizing worship as an encounter with the living Guest completes our exploration of the Spirit's hospitality and paves the way to His peacemaking role.

5 Conflict and Reconciliation: The Spirit's Peacemaking Role

5.1 Quenching and Grieving the Spirit in Relational Breakdowns (1 Th 5:19–20; Eph 4:30–32)

Paul's stern admonitions—"Do not quench the Spirit" (1 Th 5:19) and "Do not grieve the Holy Spirit of God, by whom you were sealed" (Eph 4:30)—underscore that interpersonal strife can stifle or sadden the

Advocate. Quenching, literally "to extinguish," portrays the Spirit as a flame that believers can inadvertently snuff out by resisting His promptings or suppressing spiritual gifts. Grieving employs the metaphor of a personal entity experiencing sorrow over relational wounds caused by bitterness, wrath, anger, clamor, and slander (Eph 4:31). Such behaviors fracture trust, impede communal worship, and hinder the Spirit's encouragement. Paul's contrast between grieving and "putting away all bitterness" (Eph 4:31–32) reveals the Spirit's desire for restorative cultures marked by kindness and forgiveness. The Spirit-person is deeply affected by the church's emotional climate; unresolved conflict can choke His gentle voice, impede prophetic word, and damage unity. Believers are called to recognize relational breakdowns as offenses against the Spirit's personal presence, prompting both confession and active peacemaking. By honoring the Spirit's emotional sensitivity, communities maintain openness to His guidance, ensuring that conflict becomes a catalyst for reconciliation rather than division. This awareness of the Spirit's affective ministry lays the groundwork for restorative practices.

5.2 Restoring the Fallen in a Spirit of Gentleness (Gal 6:1–2)

In Galatians Paul instructs, "If anyone is caught in any transgression, you who are spiritual should restore him in a spirit of gentleness" (Gal 6:1). The qualifier "you who are spiritual" implies those led by the Spirit possess the discernment and humility necessary for restorative intervention. Gentleness (*prautēs*) reflects the Spirit's personal disposition—strength under control—ensuring that correction proceeds from love rather than condemnation. The imagery of "bearing one another's burdens" (Gal 6:2) parallels the Spirit's intercessory role, bridging individual weaknesses with communal support. Restoration involves empathic listening, prayerful counsel, and practical assistance, mirroring the Spirit's own ministry to convict and comfort. The Spirit's personal methodology preserves the dignity of the fallen, fostering repentance and reintegration. This process underscores that discipline, when guided by the Spirit's gentleness, does not alienate but heals. The restored individual then participates fully in community life, reflecting the Spirit's reconciliation. Such restoration practices prepare the congregation for deeper cycles of forgiveness and mutual care.

5.3 Mediating Forgiveness and Comfort (2 Cor 2:5–11)

After severe discipline for sin, Paul encourages the Corinthians to forgive and comfort the offender, "lest he be overwhelmed by excessive sorrow" (2 Cor 2:7). He instructs, "Confirm your love for him" (2 Cor 2:8), equating forgiveness with active reaffirmation. This pastoral approach mirrors the Spirit's own reconciling work—first convicting of sin (Rom 8:16), then assuring pardon (Ps 32:5), and finally comforting wounded spirits (Isa 61:1). The admonition "do not grieve the Spirit" (Eph 4:30) echoes here: withholding forgiveness wounds the Advocate's affections. By commanding forgiveness "in the presence of Christ" (2 Cor 2:10), Paul situates reconciliation within Spirit-enabled communion. Comfort (*paraklēsis*) literally means "coming alongside," a function the Spirit embodies as Advocate. This Spirit-mediated comfort restores trust, prevents lingering guilt, and wards off Satan's accusations ("lest Satan gain an advantage over us," 2 Cor 2:11). The process demonstrates the Spirit's personal role in orchestrating both judgment and mercy, ensuring communal resilience and spiritual health. Such Spirit-guided forgiveness cycles deepen relational bonds and prepare the community for non-violent witness.

5.4 Spirit-Empowered Non-Violent Witness (Acts 7:55–60)

Stephen's martyrdom exemplifies Spirit-empowered non-violent witness: "But he, full of the Holy Spirit, gazed into heaven...'Lord, do not hold this sin against them'" (Acts 7:55–60). Even under stoning, Stephen's Spirit-filled vision sustains his compassionate intercession for persecutors. His non-retaliatory love, modeled after Christ's own forgiveness, demonstrates that the Spirit empowers believers to stand firm in truth without resorting to violence. The Spirit's personal enablement grants courage and serenity, transforming Christian witness into a living sermon of grace. Stephen's example set the pattern for early martyrs and non-violent resistors, affirming baptism into the cost of discipleship (Matt 16:24–25). The Spirit's presence in suffering not only vindicates the righteous but also softens hearts of witnesses—some present at Stephen's death "were cut to the heart" (Acts 7:54). Non-violent witness thus becomes a strategic Spirit-guided tool for conviction and conversion. Recognizing this dimension readies communities to integrate Spirit-empowered peacemaking into public engagement, transitioning into festivals of celebration.

6 Joyful Participation: Festivals of the Spirit

6.1 Pentecost as the Eschatological Feast of Fellowship (Acts 2:1–13)

Pentecost, originally a harvest festival, becomes the inaugural feast of the new covenant when the Spirit descends on the gathered disciples with wind and tongues of fire (Acts 2:1–3). This event inaugurates eschatological fellowship—crowds from every nation hear the disciples proclaiming the mighty works of God in their native languages (Acts 2:4–11). The festival's agricultural roots—celebrating firstfruits—are recast as cosmic celebration, with the Spirit personally pouring out life and unity. The communal joy generated by this feast foreshadows the "banquet of the King" (Matt 22:1–14), where invitation extends to all. Believers' shared participation in this festival models Spirit-wrought community—diverse yet unified. As the harvest speaks of God's provision, Pentecost signals the Spirit's abundant outpouring upon all flesh (Joel 2:28). The feast thus becomes a recurring motif of joy and solidarity, leading into expressions of praise and prophetic celebration.

6.2 Song, Dance, and Prophetic Praise (Eph 5:18–20; Ps 150)

Paul exhorts, "Be filled with the Spirit, addressing one another in psalms and hymns and spiritual songs, singing and making melody to the Lord with your heart" (Eph 5:18–19). The Hebrew Psalter's climactic call—"Let everything that has breath praise the Lord!" (Ps 150)—echoes in Spirit-led worship that integrates song, instrumental praise, and prophetic utterance. Dance, implied in Lev 23:40's festival celebrations, likely accompanied early gatherings, expressing embodied joy. Prophetic praise (*paraklēsis*) flows from the Spirit's personal ministry, inspiring words that comfort, exhort, and declare God's deeds. Such vibrant worship spills beyond congregation to public streets, testifying to the Spirit's personal presence. The integration of arts and prophecy in Spirit-led praise builds communal identity and sustains joy amid trials. This celebratory ethos prepares the ground for corporately discerning and celebrating spiritual diversity.

6.3 Corporate Discernment and Celebration of Diversity (1 Cor 14:26–33)

Paul instructs Corinthians to let each one contribute, so that "all may learn and all be encouraged" (1 Cor 14:31). This corporate discernment in gatherings—whether through teaching, prophecy, or tongues—demonstrates the Spirit's personal facilitation of diverse expressions under ordered worship. Guidelines ensure that each gift builds up the body without chaos (1 Cor 14:26–33). Celebrating diversity reflects the Spirit's sovereign distribution of gifts (1 Cor 12:4–

11) and fosters mutual appreciation. The church learns to distinguish genuine Spirit-led contributions from mere emotionalism, exercising both freedom and order. This balanced celebration nurtures joy, unity, and spiritual growth. Collective discernment thus becomes a festival of the Spirit's manifold grace, leading worshipers forward in relational harmony. From festive discernment we anticipate ultimate celebration.

6.4 Anticipating the Marriage Supper — Spirit and Bride Say "Come" (Rev 22:17)

John records the Spirit and the Bride issuing a joint invitation: "The Spirit and the Bride say, 'Come'" (Rev 22:17). This eschatological feast of intimacy anticipates the marriage supper of the Lamb (Rev 19:9), where Spirit and church unite in calling the redeemed to final communion. The dual voice underscores relational synergy: the Spirit-person and the Bride—the church—together extend hospitality. The repeated "come" evokes festival language, summoning the thirsty to living water (John 7:37). This final festival affirms that the Spirit's personal ministry culminates in perfected fellowship, where desire, participation, and celebration converge. The eschatological festival thus frames all current Spirit-led gatherings as foretaste of the age to come, preparing believers for consummated joy. This prophetic invitation naturally leads into the Spirit's marking of the people of God.

7 Ecclesial Identity: The Spirit Marks the People of God

7.1 Sealing and Ownership (Eph 1:13–14; 4:30)

Believers are "sealed with the promised Holy Spirit" (Eph 1:13), a legal and relational mark of ownership indicating personal possession by God. The seal (*sphragis*) conveys authenticity and permanence, akin to a royal signet ring. This sealing ensures that believers belong to the triune God, protected from spiritual forgery. Conversely, grieving the Spirit (Eph 4:30) is tantamount to violating one's own seal, an offense against the divine Host. The Spirit's personal inscription on each heart establishes ecclesial identity beyond ethnicity or class. This seal also guarantees future redemption, linking present identity to eschatological consummation. Recognizing the Spirit's sealing ministry affirms the church's corporate unity under divine ownership.

7.2 Temple Imagery: Living Stones Built Together (1 Pet 2:4–5)

Peter addresses believers as "living stones...built up as a spiritual house" (1 Pet 2:4–5), drawing on Ezekiel's temple vision where Spirit-filled stones form God's dwelling. The Spirit-person functions as the master builder, shaping individual stones—believers—into a unified structure. Each stone's placement depends on Spirit-enabled growth in holiness and faith. The living temple thus becomes the locus of Spirit worship (1 Cor 3:16) and sacrificial spiritual offerings (1 Pet 2:5). This temple imagery situates ecclesial identity within Spirit-wrought architecture, where relational bonds are consecrated by divine presence. The Spirit's personal craftsmanship affirms both individual value and corporate purpose.

7.3 Holy Priesthood and the Aroma of Christ (2 Cor 2:14–16)

Paul describes believers as a "fragrance of Christ among those who are being saved and among those who are perishing" (2 Cor 2:15). As a holy priesthood (1 Pet 2:5), the church offers spiritual sacrifices pleasing to God (1 Pet 2:5), mediated by the Spirit's intercession. The aroma imagery suggests a palpable Spirit-presence that emanates from worship and witness. The Spirit-person transforms mundane lives into sacrificial offerings, broadcasting Christ's presence to the world. This priestly identity transcends Temple boundaries, embedding worship in everyday life. The Spirit's personal marking of the church as priesthood underscores both access to God and responsibility to mediate grace.

7.4 Global Family Beyond Ethnicity and Class (Col 3:11; Acts 2:39)

In Christ there is "neither Greek nor Jew...for you are all one in Christ Jesus" (Col 3:11). The Spirit-person dissolves social barriers, forging new familial bonds that transcend ethnicity, gender, and class. Peter's Pentecost sermon affirms that the Spirit's promise is "for you and your children and for all who are far off" (Acts 2:39), extending family lines to every generation and nation. The church becomes the global family under Spirit parentage, experiencing brotherly love across cultural divides. The Spirit's personal ministry knits together disparate members into one household, ensuring that ecclesial identity reflects divine inclusivity. This family identity under the Spirit leads seamlessly into pastoral practices for relational sensitivity.

8 Pastoral Implications: Cultivating Relational Sensitivity to the Spirit

8.1 Practicing Attentive Listening in Prayer and Community

Cultivating Spirit sensitivity begins with attentive listening, as exemplified by Elijah's encounter not in the wind or earthquake but in a "still small voice" (1 Kings 19:12). Prayer gatherings should incorporate spaces of silence, allowing the Advocate to speak personally. Small-group meetings benefit when leaders model listening to spontaneous promptings—prophetic words, convicting impressions, or pastoral insights. Training in spiritual listening equips believers to discern the Spirit's voice amid competing narratives. Attentive listening fosters mutual respect and honors the Spirit's presence in diverse contributions. This practice transitions to examining motives behind ministry.

8.2 Discernment of Motives — Love versus Self-Promotion in Ministry

Jesus warns against practicing righteousness "before others to be seen" (Matt 6:1). The Spirit-person helps believers examine whether gifts and service stem from genuine love or desire for recognition. Pastors and lay leaders must regularly test motives through communal accountability and Scriptural reflection under Spirit guidance. Encouraging mentorship and peer evaluation prevents self-promotion from quenching the Spirit. When motives align with divine love, ministries flourish; when they diverge, the Spirit's jealous longing convicts and redirects. Discernment of motives thus safeguards holistic relational sensitivity, preparing communities for rhythms of confession.

8.3 Rhythms of Confession and Reconciliation to Avoid Grieving the Spirit

Regular rhythms—corporate liturgies of confession, small-group accountability, and restorative conversations—prevent the build-up of bitterness that grieves the Spirit (Eph 4:30). Incorporating confession into worship services and small groups fosters transparency. Leaders should guide congregations through structured reconciliation processes (Matt 18:15–17; Gal 6:1–2) under the Spirit's gentleness. Rituals of forgiveness—laying on of hands, communal absolution— reflect the Advocate's reconciling ministry. These rhythms maintain the Spirit's unhindered presence, ensuring relational health and communal vitality. From confession we move to designing liturgical spaces.

8.4 Liturgical Spaces that Welcome the Spirit's Relational Presence

Physical and virtual worship spaces should facilitate personal encounter with the Advocate. Designs—open seating, interactive prayer stations, spaces for communal art or written petitions—invite believers to inhabit relational intimacy. Liturgies incorporating silence, prophetic pausing, and Spirit-led testimonies establish a hospitable environment. Multi-sensory elements—candles, incense, visual art— evoke the Spirit's presence beyond mere auditory stimuli. Technology can extend these spaces online, creating virtual rooms for communal listening. By intentionally crafting environments that signal divine welcome, leaders honor the Spirit's hospitality, enabling congregations to experience relational depths.

9 Eschatological Consummation: Perfected Fellowship in the Age to Come

9.1 Firstfruits Now, Full Harvest Later (Rom 8:23; 2 Cor 5:5)

Paul's metaphor of the Spirit as "firstfruits" conveys a present taste of the redeemed life to come, marking believers as heirs of God's future harvest (Rom 8:23). Firstfruits in Israelite worship signaled God's covenant faithfulness, and the Spirit's down-payment functions similarly—ensuring that what has begun in the believer will reach its full consummation. This partial experience of eschatological reality prompts both patient endurance in suffering and joyful anticipation of final redemption. The promise of full harvest later inspires present holiness, for believers know their final glorification is secured by the Advocate's pledge. In 2 Corinthians Paul again underscores the Spirit's guarantee: "He who has prepared us for this very thing is God, who has given us the Spirit as a guarantee" (2 Cor 5:5). This dual imagery of firstfruits and guarantee situates the Spirit as both the initial and continuing witness to God's completion of His redemptive plan. Believers thus live in a tension of "already" and "not yet," carefully stewarding present gifts while awaiting future glory. The Spirit's personal presence bridges this tension, transforming uncertainty into confident hope. This confidence shapes disciples' daily choices, aligning them with their destined inheritance. As firstfruits point toward fullness, the narrative of the Spirit's future work unfolds in the vision of a Spirit-saturated new creation.

9.2 Spirit-Saturated New Creation (Rev 21:3; Isa 32:15–18)

Revelation's climactic vision—"Behold, the dwelling place of God is with man...he will dwell with them" (Rev 21:3)—portrays the culmination of Spirit indwelling: no temple needed because the Spirit-filled bodies of saints become God's eternal abode. Isaiah similarly foretold that the Spirit poured out would transform desolate lands into flourishing oases, "justice will dwell in the desert, and righteousness remain in the fruitful field" (Isa 32:16–17). These Old-Testament and apocalyptic visions converge to depict a new creation wholly animated by the Spirit's sustaining presence. In this renewed cosmos, relationships are perfected: there is no mourning, crying, or pain, because the Spirit's personal ministry has eradicated the effects of sin. The rivers of living water, flowing from the throne of God and of the Lamb, symbolize continuous Spirit outpouring (Rev 22:1), ensuring that the new creation remains ever fresh and life-giving. This eschatological hope transforms present discipleship, as believers begin to live in ways that reflect coming realities—justice, peace, and abundance. The Spirit's future saturation of creation inspires present engagement in justice and environmental stewardship, anticipating the full reconciliation of all things. The promise of Spirit-saturated new creation seamlessly leads us into the belief that knowledge and love of God will deepen without end.

9.3 Ever-Deepening Knowledge and Love within the Triune Life

Eschatological consummation entails not merely restored relationships but an ever-deepening participation in the life of the Trinity. Paul speaks of knowing the love of Christ that surpasses knowledge (Eph 3:19), suggesting a trajectory of ever-expanding understanding and affection. In the age to come, the veil that now obscures divine mysteries will be fully removed (1 Cor 13:12), enabling unmediated communion with the triune God. The Spirit, as the Spirit of truth, will continually lead believers into deeper insights and love, reflecting the perpetual interchange among Father, Son, and Spirit. This dynamic fellowship—the divine perichoresis—will become the believer's constant experience, transcending spatial and temporal limitations. Worship will no longer be a finite act but an unending, participatory immersion in the triune dance of love. The progressive transformation "from glory to glory" (2 Cor 3:18) hints at this unending journey, where each new revelation fuels deeper relational intimacy. The Spirit's personal ministry thus extends beyond initial conversion into eternal maturing, guaranteeing that love's well never runs dry. Believers anticipate not static bliss but dynamic covenant life, reflecting the Spirit's ongoing activity with the Father and the Son. This vision of perpetual relational growth sets the stage for the transition to the Spirit's personal ministries as Teacher, Guide, Advocate, and Intercessor.

Conclusion In exploring the Spirit's relational attributes—divine affection, fellowship, jealous yearning, and hospitality—we have glimpsed the Advocate's deeply personal engagement in covenant love, communal unity, and passionate fidelity. These attributes shape every facet of Christian life: from the outpouring of love that drives mission to the sacred welcome that transforms bodies into divine tabernacles. The Spirit's covenant zeal guards purity, His hospitality fosters authentic community, and His fellowship embeds believers within the triune life. As we move into the next chapter, we will examine the Spirit's concrete personal ministries—Teacher, Guide, Advocate, and Intercessor—that operationalize these relational depths in the everyday life of the church.

Chapter 8. Personal Ministries: Teacher, Guide, Advocate, Intercessor

In this chapter, we move from the Spirit's relational attributes to His concrete personal ministries—how the Advocate functions as Teacher, Guide, Advocate, and Intercessor in the life of the church. These ministries are the operational dimensions of His personhood, shaping doctrine, discerning Scripture, directing disciples, defending the faithful, and praying on their behalf. By examining key biblical narratives and theological articulations, we will uncover how the Spirit continues Christ's pedagogical work, illuminates hearts, charts missionary strategy, and upholds believers in trial. This exploration demonstrates that the Spirit's involvement is not merely an abstract power but a deeply personal presence active in every facet of Christian formation, worship, and mission.

1 The Pedagogue of Truth: The Spirit as Teacher

1.1 Paraklētic Promise Fulfilled — John 14:26 and the Post-Easter Classroom

Jesus promises that the Spirit "will teach you all things and bring to your remembrance all that I have said to you" (John 14:26), inaugurating a new mode of instruction beyond physical presence.

After Easter, the disciples find themselves in a living classroom where Jesus' words are continually unpacked by the Spirit. The Greek term *paraklētos* here highlights the Spirit's role as both comforter and instructor, combining pastoral care with doctrinal clarity. In Acts 1–2, the same disciples who struggled to recall Jesus' predictions find themselves preaching with bold accuracy, indicating that the Spirit's teaching fulfills the Paraclete promise. This post-Easter pedagogy relies on personal indwelling: believers internalize Jesus' teachings through Spirit-wrought insight rather than second-hand notes. As the early church formed creeds and catechisms, they trusted the Spirit to safeguard orthodoxy, ensuring that the Gospel message remained true to the Master's intent. The Spirit's teaching ministry thus becomes foundational for church councils, councils' rulings, and subsequent doctrine. This continual instruction extends to every generation, as believers throughout history experience personal illumination of Christ's words. Understanding the Spirit as the living Teacher prepares us to explore His unveiling of Scripture's deepest truths.

1.2 Illumination of Scripture — Unveiling "the Deep Things of God" (1 Cor 2:10–13)

Paul explains that "the Spirit searches everything, even the depths of God...and we impart this in words taught by the Spirit" (1 Cor 2:10–13). This metaphor of searching suggests deliberate exploration by a Person who knows the divine counsels and shares them with human minds. Scripture, while written under divine inspiration, requires the Spirit's personal illumination to reveal its full meaning. The Spirit opens eyes to the Christ-centered narrative woven through Torah, Prophets, and Writings—showing how Old-Testament types and shadows find fulfillment in the Gospel. This revelatory teaching transforms dusty ink on pages into living encounters, enabling believers to apply ancient truths to contemporary challenges. Early church fathers credited the Spirit with guiding them through the difficult passages of Isaiah, Daniel, and Revelation, confirming that no text is immune to Spirit insight. In our own context, Spirit-led Bible study integrates prayer, historical awareness, and openness to surprise, ensuring that Scripture remains a dynamic Word. The Spirit's personal teaching prevents both fundamentalist rigidity and moralistic reading, balancing fidelity to text and freedom for application. Recognizing this ministry moves us to consider how the Spirit equips communities to discern and weigh prophetic words.

169

1.3 The Anointing that "Teaches All Things" (1 John 2:27) and Safeguards Orthodoxy

John assures his readers that "the anointing you received from him abides in you, and you have no need that anyone should teach you" (1 John 2:27). This *chrism*—the Spirit's anointing—guarantees ongoing guidance in truth, safeguarding the early church against false teachers who denied Christ's incarnation. The personal presence of the anointing enables disciples to discern true doctrine from heretical deception, relying on internal conviction rather than external authority alone. In contexts of Gnostic intrusion and emerging canonical debates, this Spirit-given teacher ensured continuity with apostolic teaching. The Spirit's anointing also preserved integrity in transmission of the Gospel, as teachers and scribes depended on Him to retain and relay authentic content. In contemporary theological education, this principle underwrites the necessity of cultivating spiritual awareness alongside academic rigor. Professors and pastors who honor the Spirit's anointing cultivate communities that receive teaching as a shared, Spirit-mediated event rather than top-down instruction. The abiding anointing thus becomes the church's ultimate orthodoxic guardrail, preparing believers for communal discernment of the Spirit's diverse charismata.

1.4 Didactic Charismata — Teaching and Prophecy as Spirit-Distributed Gifts (Rom 12:7; 1 Cor 12:28)

Paul enumerates teaching and prophecy among the Spirit's distributed gifts: "If it is teaching, let him teach; if it is prophecy, let him prophesy" (Rom 12:7); "And God has appointed in the church first apostles, second prophets, third teachers..." (1 Cor 12:28). These roles demonstrate that the Spirit not only acts through inspired Scripture but also through Spirit-gifted individuals who provide ongoing instruction and exhortation. Prophets, under Spirit influence, address both future revelations and immediate pastoral needs, while teachers systematically articulate doctrine and guide discipleship. The presence of both gifts ensures that proclamation and explanation work in tandem, reflecting the Spirit's comprehensive pedagogy. Communities flourish when these gifts are exercised in mutual submission, accountability, and love, preventing abuses of authority. In missionary contexts, teaching gifts equip new believers to understand Scripture, while prophetic gifts warn against syncretism. The interplay of teaching and prophecy models the Spirit's holistic educational strategy, blending orthodoxy and edification. This spectrum of didactic charismata prepares the church to navigate

170

changing cultural landscapes while remaining anchored in truth. Having seen the Spirit's teaching ministry, we now turn to how He shapes hermeneutics in the church.

2 Hermeneutics in the Spirit

2.1 Spiritual versus Merely Rational Reading — The Unveiled Heart (2 Cor 3:14–17)

Paul contrasts the veiled reading of Moses's law with Spirit-enabled interpretation: "But when one turns to the Lord, the veil is removed...for where the Spirit of the Lord is, there is freedom" (2 Cor 3:16–17). This removal of the veil signifies that the Spirit-person transforms biblical engagement from dry legalism into liberated insight. A merely rational approach treats Scripture as historical text; a spiritual reading, empowered by the Spirit, exposes living truths that shape heart and will. In practice, this means combining exegetical methods with prayerful dependence on the Advocate's inner witness. The Spirit unveils moral imperatives embedded in narrative, opening avenues for theological creativity without compromising core meaning. Pastors trained in both critical scholarship and spiritual discernment exemplify this balance, guiding congregations to read with both mind and heart. The Spirit's unveiling also fosters humility, acknowledging that human understanding remains partial without divine illumination. Recognizing this dynamic equips readers to approach challenging texts—law, poetry, prophecy—with openness to the Spirit's corrective and creative insights. This unveiled hermeneutic sets the stage for communal practices of weighing prophetic words.

2.2 Communal Discernment — Weighing Prophetic Words (1 Cor 14:29)

In Corinth, Paul mandates that "two or three prophets speak, and the others weigh what is said" (1 Cor 14:29), placing communal discernment at the heart of Spirit-led interpretation. Discernment (*diakrisis*) involves testing prophetic utterances against apostolic tradition, Scripture, and the fruit of the Spirit. The process prevents authoritarian claims to private revelation, ensuring that the Spirit's personal guidance remains accountable to the broader body. Communities practice discernment through structured dialogues— small groups, eldership boards, or prophetic councils—each member bringing Spirit-empowered wisdom. Historical precedents, such as the Bereans who "received the word with all eagerness, examining

171

the Scriptures daily" (Acts 17:11), demonstrate the early church's commitment to this balance of openness and testing. Modern congregations can emulate these patterns by providing frameworks for prophetic feedback, teaching critical thinking alongside spiritual receptivity. The Spirit's personal ministry in communal discernment thus protects the church from stray doctrines and cultivates collective spiritual maturity. This relational hermeneutic leads us to guardrails against private illuminationism.

2.3 Guardrails against Private Illuminationism and Authoritarian Claims

While affirming the Spirit's inner teaching, Paul warns against quenching and despising the Spirit (1 Th 5:19–20), indicating that communities must guard against suppressing genuine revelation or elevating private interpretations above communal discernment. Authoritarian claims to unique Spirit-given insight risk eclipsing the authority of Scripture and history, fracturing unity. Early councils— Jerusalem (Acts 15) and later ecumenical synods—modeled how Spirit guidance operates within accountable structures. The rule of faith—summaries of apostolic teaching—served as guardrails for first- and second-generation believers. Contemporary churches can adopt similar guardrails: doctrinal statements, accountability teams, and peer review for prophetic ministry. These measures do not deny the Spirit's personal activity but provide checks that honor communal wisdom. By preserving both freedom and order, the church remains open to the Spirit's fresh insights while upholding shared convictions. Such balance fosters healthy growth and prevents the abuses that can arise from unchecked private illumination. Having set these guardrails, we turn to contemporary models of Spirit-shaped study.

2.4 Contemporary Models of Spirit-Shaped Bible Study and Catechesis

Spirit-shaped hermeneutics has found expression in modern approaches like the *Bible in the Life* model, which integrates lectio divina with small-group discussion, and *Ignatian* spiritual exercises that meld Scripture reading with imaginative prayer. In catechetical programs, the *Catechism of the Catholic Church* emphasizes the Spirit's role in interpreting the faith (*Sacred Tradition and Sacred Scripture*) under the Magisterium. Protestant traditions have developed *Inductive Bible Study* methods that incorporate prayerful reflection at each stage: observation, interpretation, application. Charismatic communities utilize *Scripture prophecy* sessions, where participants first pray silently, then share impressions, and finally test them through communal discernment. Academic institutions increasingly offer courses in *Spiritual Hermeneutics*, training students to combine rigorous exegesis with sensitivity to the Spirit's lead. Digital platforms now include prayer-prompted reading plans, where daily passages are accompanied by reflective prayer guides. These models all underscore that true understanding comes not from technique alone but from reliance on the Advocate's teaching. As believers experience the Spirit's guidance in interpretation, they grow in both knowledge and intimacy with the Word-Person, setting the stage for daily Shepherding guidance.

3 The Shepherding Guide: Daily Direction and Moral Formation

3.1 "Led by the Spirit" — Filial Guidance in Rom 8:14 and Gal 5:18

Paul declares, "For all who are led by the Spirit of God are sons of God" (Rom 8:14), and urges, "But if you are led by the Spirit, you are not under the law" (Gal 5:18). The imagery of leading evokes a shepherd guiding sheep along green pastures and still waters, ensuring both nourishment and safety. Filial guidance implies that the Spirit cares for believers as a Father cares for children, directing their steps in moral and vocational decisions. This leadership is personal and relational, not impersonal direction; the Spirit engages with human wills, offering promptings, warnings, and confirmations. In practice, disciples cultivate sensitivity through prayer, journaling, and spiritual companionship, discerning daily decisions—career moves, relational choices, ethical dilemmas—through Spirit promptings. The Spirit's guidance safeguards freedom, for true guidance never overrides conscience but aligns it with divine intention. As believers grow in discernment, they learn to recognize the Advocate's voice amid competing influences. This filial guidance flows into broader decision-making processes involving Scripture and community counsel.

3.2 Inner Witness, Scriptural Norms, and Ecclesial Counsel in Decision-Making

Effective discernment integrates the Spirit's inner witness with objective norms and communal wisdom. Paul commends Timothy to "keep as the pattern of sound teaching" (2 Tim 1:13), indicating that

Scripture provides normative boundaries. Yet, Paul also testifies to Spirit-driven visions and impressions—heeding prophetic voices in Antioch (Acts 13:2). Decisions that harmonize personal promptings with biblical principles and counsel from mature believers reflect a balanced approach. Historical examples—such as the Council at Jerusalem (Acts 15) combining prophetic testimony and Scripture—model this tri-factor discernment. In local churches, elders and spiritual mentors guide less-experienced believers in interpreting inner promptings, ensuring that the Spirit's direction aligns with the Gospel. Training programs in spiritual direction and discernment groups teach participants to distinguish impressions originating from the Spirit versus self-will or external pressures. By valuing the Advocate's inner ministry alongside Scripture and ecclesial counsel, communities cultivate robust moral formation. This integrated discernment approach naturally flows into narrative case studies of Spirit guidance.

3.3 Narrative Case Studies: Philip (Acts 8:29) and Paul (Acts 16:6–10)

Philip's encounter with the Ethiopian eunuch illustrates Spirit guidance in micro-mission: "The Spirit said to Philip, 'Go over and join this chariot'" (Acts 8:29). Philip's immediate obedience leads to a life-changing baptism, demonstrating the Spirit's personal care in individual evangelism. Conversely, Paul's second journey experience—being forbidden by the Spirit to preach in Asia and redirected by a Macedonian vision (Acts 16:6–10)—shows macro-strategic guidance. The Spirit's leadership in Philip's case is quiet and immediate, prompting Philip's movement into an unplanned context. Paul's redirection involves both prohibition and invitation, indicating the Spirit's sovereignty over ministry geography. In both narratives, the Spirit's personal agency navigates between human intention and divine mission, ensuring that the gospel advances strategically and relationally. Modern disciples can learn from these stories: to expect personal promptings, to test them against Scripture and community prayer, and to embrace both micro and macro assignments with equal trust. These case studies illustrate that the Advocate guides holistically—across individual decisions and global strategies. From narrative examples, we transition to cultivating habitual responsiveness.

3.4 Walking in the Spirit — Cultivating Habitual Responsiveness and Virtue (Gal 5:25)

Paul exhorts believers to "keep in step with the Spirit" (Gal 5:25), depicting discipleship as an ongoing walk characterized by attentiveness and alignment. This idiom evokes rhythm and coordination—a dance between divine initiative and human response. Cultivating such habitual responsiveness involves spiritual disciplines: daily prayer, silence, Scripture meditation, and journaling to record promptings and follow-throughs. Spiritual formation communities practice *Listening Prayer*, offering structured times to listen for the Spirit's voice and commit to obedience. Over time, patterns of virtue emerge—compassion, honesty, generosity—as the Spirit integrates moral character within the believer. This process counters moralism by rooting virtue in relational communion rather than external rules. As disciples learn to recognize the Advocate's gentle nudges, they become more adept at discerning right paths quickly. This Spirit-guided virtue formation naturally extends into corporate life and into mission strategy under the Spirit's oversight.

4 Strategist of Mission and Church Planting

4.1 Antioch's Commissioning Moment (Acts 13:2–4) — Prayerful Listening that Launched a Movement

In Antioch, the church's leadership gathered for worship, fasting, and prayer, when the Holy Spirit spoke: "Set apart for me Barnabas and Saul for the work to which I have called them" (Acts 13:2). This commissioning emerged from communal spiritual disciplines rather than boardroom deliberations. The Spirit's voice was perceived collectively by prophets and teachers, leading to a liturgical act of laying on hands. This moment exemplifies how prayerful listening to the Advocate can birth global movements; Barnabas and Saul's mission would plant churches across the Mediterranean. The Spirit's strategic direction required patience—fasting and prayer preceded the call—and communal consent, reinforcing shared ownership of mission. This model of prayer-saturated commissioning contrasts with purely human-driven mobilization, ensuring that mission flows from divine initiative. Contemporary churches can replicate this pattern, creating rhythms of worship, intercession, and prophetic attentiveness that discern the Spirit's mission directives. By prioritizing the Advocate's call, ecclesial strategies remain adaptive and aligned with divine purposes. This commissioning scene sets the tone for navigating redirected roads.

4.2 Redirected Roads and Open Doors — From Asia to Macedonia (Acts 16:6–10)

Paul's second journey illustrates the Spirit's strategic flexibility: forbidden to preach in Asia, he and his team attempted Bithynia before Paul received a vision of the Macedonian man pleading for help (Acts 16:6–10). The Spirit orchestrated both prohibition and invitation, steering the mission toward Europe's unreached regions. This directional flexibility prevented wasted effort and positioned the gospel for maximum impact. The Spirit's strategy combines both negative guidance—restraining movement—and positive guidance—providing vision—demanding that missionaries remain vigilant to Divine leadings. Modern mission agencies learn from this pattern by balancing long-term plans with readiness to pivot when the Spirit opens new doors or closes others. This Spirit-led agility requires spiritual maturity and corporate discernment to avoid flippant shifts or rigid persistence. Understanding how the Advocate enables intelligent redirection empowers leaders to remain faithful stewards of mission opportunities. From geographic strategy we transition to how corporate vision casting under Oversight can sustain the church.

4.3 Corporate Vision Casting under the Spirit's Oversight Today

Vision casting in churches and mission organizations must be rooted in ongoing Spirit guidance rather than human aspiration alone. Regular *Spirit Summits*—gatherings for extended prayer, Scripture immersion, and prophetic input—provide spaces for discerning next steps. Vision teams include worship, teaching, and prayer streams that allow diverse voices to sense the Advocate's direction together. By periodically pausing strategic initiatives to seek fresh Spirit affirmation, communities avoid mission drift and maintain alignment with divine priorities. Case studies of congregations that recalibrated their focus—transitioning from local programs to global partnerships—demonstrate how Spirit oversight fosters missional adaptability. Leaders train members in *Spiritual SWOT* analyses, evaluating strengths, weaknesses, opportunities, and threats through prayerful filters. Incorporating Spirit feedback loops into strategic planning embeds personal ministry of the Advocate into every organizational layer. This Spirit-informed corporate casting flows naturally into the need for contextual flexibility without quenching the Guide.

4.4 Missiological Flexibility: Contextualizing the Gospel without Quenching the Guide

Contextual mission requires adapting methods and language to varied cultures while maintaining doctrinal fidelity under the Spirit's personal guidance. The apostolic pattern—Paul in Athens engaging Stoic and Epicurean audiences (Acts 17:22–34)—demonstrates how the Spirit leads workers to contextualize without compromising Christ's message. Modern practitioners employ *contextualization grids* tested through Spirit-led prayer, ensuring that translations, metaphors, and worship forms remain faithful. The Spirit guards against syncretism by convicting workers of deviations and affirming authenticity through fruit of repentance and unity. This ongoing dialogue between contextual innovation and Spirit oversight prevents both cultural irrelevance and doctrinal dilution. Training in cultural intelligence combined with spiritual discernment equips missionaries to read both people and Spirit promptings accurately. Embracing the Advocate's personal guidance ensures that dynamic missional flexibility remains a Spirit-empowered enterprise, preserving the integrity of the gospel in every context.

5 The Advocate (Paraklētos): Legal Defender and Consoler

5.1 "Another Advocate" beside the Father (John 14:16) — continuity with Jesus' own advocacy

Jesus promises, "I will ask the Father, and he will give you another Advocate to be with you forever" (John 14:16), presenting the Spirit as a distinct legal defender who continues Christ's own intercession. The term *another* (allos) indicates the Spirit is of the same kind as Jesus—another personal helper rather than a replacement force. This continuity means the Spirit embodies the same compassion, authority, and presence that defined Jesus' ministry on earth. Early Jewish courtroom imagery viewed an *advocate* as one who stands beside the accused, speaks on behalf of the innocent, and secures acquittal. The Spirit-paraklētē serves this role before the Father, ensuring that believers are never left to face divine judgment alone. Just as Jesus pleaded for Peter's faith after his denial (Luke 22:32), the Spirit pleads on behalf of every sinner who calls on Him. This advocacy is legal in that it petitions for mercy under the new covenant of grace, not under the condemnation of the law (Rom 8:1). Patristic writers like Athanasius interpreted the Spirit's role as securing divine pardon and ecclesial unity. In this way, the Spirit carries forward Christ's legal advocacy into every trial, both judicial and relational. Recognizing the Spirit as Advocate frames subsequent ministries of conviction and consolation as extensions of this courtroom function.

From legal defense, we move to the Spirit's worldwide convicting work.

5.2 Convicting the World of Sin, Righteousness, and Judgment (John 16:8–11)

Jesus describes the Advocate's public ministry: "He will convict the world concerning sin and righteousness and judgment" (John 16:8). The Greek *elenchein* (convict) implies forensic examination and moral exposure, revealing the world's unbelief as sin, Christ's righteousness as the only path to life, and upcoming judgment for rejecting Jesus. The Spirit thus serves as cosmic prosecutor, making God's standards clear and indicting all who refuse the gospel. This conviction is sovereign and personal: the Spirit selects the timing, method, and depth of exposure, whether through conscience, Scripture, or the witness of the church. In Acts, Spirit-driven conviction prompts thousands to ask "What shall we do?" (Acts 2:37), demonstrating the power of this ministry. Contemporary evangelists testify that the Spirit's conviction precedes true repentance, not mere guilt trips but life-changing awareness of truth. The Advocate's convicting role therefore serves both as judicial function and as catalyst for evangelistic breakthrough. This cosmic legal ministry transitions into assurance in hostile courts.

5.3 Assurance in Hostile Courts — Spirit-given words under persecution (Luke 12:11–12; Acts 4:8–13)

Jesus assures disciples, "When they bring you before synagogues … do not worry about how you should defend yourselves, or what you should say, for the Holy Spirit will teach you in that very hour what you ought to say" (Luke 12:11–12). This promise parallels Peter's Spirit-filling before the Sanhedrin, enabling fearless speech (Acts 4:8–13). The Advocate assures believers in hostile legal or social settings by providing both content and boldness. Historical accounts of martyrs note that Spirit-inspired defense often disarmed accusers and led to conversions. Today, Christians facing censorship or interrogation report experiencing sudden clarity and courage, attributing it to Spirit intervention. This ministry underscores that the Spirit is both lawyer and confidant, guiding Words under pressure. As the Spirit defends the gospel in courts and cultures, He also consoles those who suffer for justice.

5.4 Consolation for Suffering Saints — spreading hope and endurance (Rom 15:13; Phil 1:19)

Paul prays that "the God of hope fill you with all joy and peace in believing, so that by the power of the Holy Spirit you may abound in hope" (Rom 15:13), illustrating the Advocate's consoling role. In Philippians, he expresses confidence that his imprisonment will turn out for deliverance "through your prayer and the help of the Spirit of Jesus Christ" (Phil 1:19). This help (*boētheia*) underscores the Spirit's merciful support in affliction. The Spirit consoles by infusing hope, by orchestrating communal prayers, and by providing inner peace that transcends circumstances. Desert fathers and mothers recounted experiences of the Spirit's warmth in solitude, confirming divine companionship. In communal worship, Spirit-inspired hymns and testimonies offer solace to grieving hearts. This personal ministry of consolation flows directly from the Advocate's promise to never leave nor forsake (Heb 13:5), completing His role as both legal defender and compassionate comforter. From the Advocate's consoling work, we turn to the Spirit's intercessory prayers.

6 Intercessor of the Saints: Prayer Partner and High-Priestly Ally

6.1 Groanings Too Deep for Words — Spirit's empathetic prayer within us (Rom 8:26–27)

Paul acknowledges human weakness in prayer—"we do not know what to pray for as we ought"—but assures that "the Spirit Himself intercedes for us with groanings too deep for words" (Rom 8:26). This depiction portrays the Spirit as an empathetic intercessor who understands believers' deepest needs and translates them into divine petitions. The term *sugchōn* conveys shared sighs, signifying relational solidarity: the Spirit groans alongside our groans. Patristic commentators saw in this ministry the Spirit's participation in human vulnerability, bridging earthly frailty and heavenly strength. In corporate prayer contexts—such as prolonged vigils—believers detect Spirit-led shifts in tone and emphasis, resonating with communal burdens. In private devotion, individuals sensing unspoken longings often attribute clarity of heart to Spirit intercession. This empathetic intercession guarantees that no prayer is lost or misunderstood. From personal groanings, we move to corporate Spirit-led prayer practices.

6.2 "Praying in the Spirit" — corporate vigilance and perseverance (Eph 6:18; Jude 20)

Paul exhorts, "Praying at all times in the Spirit, with all prayer and supplication" (Eph 6:18), and Jude urges believers to "build yourselves up in your most holy faith…praying in the Holy Spirit" (Jude 20). Praying in the Spirit implies dependence on the Advocate's guidance in selecting topics, timing, and posture. Corporate *Spirit-led prayer* gatherings—such as all-night watches or prayer chains—combine fasting, Scripture reading, and dynamic prayer, trusting that the Spirit will prompt specific intercessions. Historical revivals often trace back to congregations committed to Spirit-led prayer before anything else. The Spirit's personal ministry in corporate prayer sustains perseverance when petitions seem unanswered, reminding participants of His ongoing advocacy. Discernment in prayer intentions—testing for self-will versus Spirit leadings—ensures that collective prayers align with divine purposes. This persistent, Spirit-empowered intercession readies the church for Spirit-given charisms of tongues and song.

6.3 Tongues and Prophetic Song as Modalities of Spirit-Empowered Intercession (1 Cor 14:14–15)

Paul explains, "For if I pray in a tongue, my spirit prays but my mind is unfruitful… I will pray with my spirit, but I will pray with my mind also" (1 Cor 14:14–15), indicating that Spirit-inspired utterances can serve as intercessory prayers beyond human language. This form of prayer offers direct communication between the Spirit and the Father on behalf of the community. Prophetic songs—melodic proclamations inspired by the Spirit—combine musical and prophetic ministries, creating an atmosphere where intercession transcends rational constraints. Early church testimonies record breakthroughs following extended periods of tongues and prophetic worship, attributing conversions and healing to this mode of prayer. Contemporary worship movements practice *praying in the Spirit* during conferences, enabling participants to intercede corporately for global issues. This modality underscores the Spirit's personal involvement in both form and content of prayer, weaving together heart and mind. From these Spirit-led intercessions, we anticipate the eschatological longing where Spirit and Bride unite.

6.4 Eschatological Longing — Spirit and Bride crying "Come" (Rev 22:17)

Revelation portrays the Spirit and the Bride in unison: "The Spirit and the Bride say, 'Come'" (Rev 22:17), expressing eschatological intercession that welcomes Christ's return. This dual voice symbolizes the Spirit's intercession joined with the church's yearning, creating a powerful petition for consummated fellowship. The Spirit's role here transcends individual or corporate prayer; it is the anticipatory cry of creation itself. Liturgically, churches mark seasons—Advent—by echoing this cry, combining prophetic expectation and worship. This eschatological intercession aligns present longing with future hope, reminding believers that the Spirit's advocacy extends beyond this age. The Spirit's personal ministry thus encompasses retrospective forgiveness, present sustenance, and forward-looking anticipation. Recognizing this final plea of the Advocate prepares us to explore the Spirit's role as worship leader.

7 Worship Leader and Liturgical Animator

7.1 Spirit-and-Truth Worship beyond Geographic Temples (John 4:23–24)

Jesus tells the Samaritan woman that true worshipers "will worship the Father in spirit and truth, for the Father is seeking such people to worship him" (John 4:23–24). The Spirit's role as worship leader liberates worship from physical temples, enabling genuine encounter anywhere the Spirit is welcomed. This Spirit-and-truth worship combines heartfelt devotion (*pneumati*) with doctrinal integrity (*alētheia*). In Acts, believers worship in homes, public squares, and prisons, guided by Spirit promptings rather than temple schedules. Contemporary worship services that emphasize open forums for spontaneous prayer, testimony, and prophetic song reflect this spiritual flexibility. The Advocate orchestrates liturgies that blend historical creeds with fresh expressions, ensuring that worship remains rooted in truth while sensitive to Spirit movement. This dynamic liturgical animation prepares the way for Spirit-sparked songs and psalms.

7.2 Psalms, Hymns, and Spiritual Songs — Melody Sparked by the Spirit (Eph 5:18–20)

Paul urges, "Be filled with the Spirit, addressing one another in psalms and hymns and spiritual songs, singing and making melody to the Lord with your heart" (Eph 5:18–20). The triad of song forms—psalms (Scriptural), hymns (theological compositions), spiritual songs (spontaneous utterances)—captures the Spirit's multifaceted direction in worship. The Spirit-person inspires choice of Scripture passages, theological themes, and impromptu lyrics that reflect current needs. In the early church, hymns like the Magnificat (Luke

1:46–55) and Christological canticles accompanied liturgy under Spirit guidance. Modern worship leaders practice *Spirit-led song writing* sessions where prayer and reflection yield new lyrics. This melodic ministry fosters corporate unity and provides theological depth. By shaping both content and emotion, the Advocate ensures worship remains doxological and transformative. This musical animation sets the stage for epiclesis in Eucharistic tradition.

7.3 Epiclesis in Eucharistic Tradition — Invoking the Spirit upon Bread, Cup, and Congregation

"Epiclesis" refers to the liturgical prayer that calls the Spirit to descend upon the Eucharistic elements and the assembly. Early liturgies—such as those of Hippolytus and in Byzantine rites—contain explicit epicleses asking the Spirit to transform bread and wine into Christ's body and blood. This calling recognizes the Spirit-person as the agent of real presence and communal participation. The epiclesis underscores that the sacraments are not mere symbols but Spirit-wrought means of grace. Contemporary liturgical scholars emphasize the necessity of epiclesis to maintain sacramental integrity, countering purely memorialist approaches. When congregations pray for the Spirit to "fill this table" and "unite us to Christ," they enact ancient patterns of Spirit invocation. The Advocate's personal ministry thus animates both elements and participants, ensuring that the Eucharist remains a living encounter. This sacramental animation leads naturally into discerning Spirit manifestations during praise.

7.4 Discernment of Spirit Manifestations during Gathered Praise (1 Cor 14:26–33)

Paul provides order for Spirit manifestations: "When you come together, each one has a hymn…let all things be done for building up" (1 Cor 14:26). Discernment involves distinguishing between genuine Spirit-led expressions—prophecies that edify, tongues that require interpretation, songs that exhort—and mere emotional excess or disorder. Church leaders develop *liturgical discernment teams* that observe, reflect, and provide feedback on corporate worship experiences, ensuring the Spirit's activity remains constructive. Historical councils addressed manifestations—such as Montanist prophecies—by evaluating consistency with apostolic Gospel. In modern contexts, worship teams balance openness to new songs and spontaneous prayers with adherence to doctrinal benchmarks. This practice prevents quenching or exploitation of Spirit gifts, fostering worship that truly builds up the body. Through careful discernment, the Advocate's presence animates gatherings without confusion, preparing communities for responsible testing of spirits in daily life.

8 Tester of Spirits: Discernment and Boundary-Setting

8.1 Christological Criterion — Confessing Jesus Come in the Flesh (1 John 4:1–3)

John warns, "Beloved, do not believe every spirit, but test the spirits to see whether they are from God…" and provides the Christological test: "every spirit that confesses that Jesus Christ has come in the flesh is from God" (1 John 4:1–3). The Advocate-person empowers this discernment by illuminating truth and exposing error. In the early church, heresies like Docetism were repelled by this Spirit-enabled test. Churches today apply the criterion by evaluating teachings on Jesus' humanity and atoning work. Training in *Spirit-led discernment* helps believers recognize deviations from orthodoxy, preventing spiritual abuse. This boundary-setting honors the Spirit's personal ministry in preserving the faith. Having established the Christological filter, we turn to affective fruit as authenticity markers.

8.2 Fruit versus Flash — Love, Joy, Peace as Authenticity Markers (Gal 5:22–23)

Paul contrasts Spirit manifestations governed by sound love, joy, and peace (Gal 5:22–23) with superficial displays of power or novelty. Genuine Spirit activity produces character transformation; flash without fruit signals deception or emotionalism. Leaders encourage post-worship reflection on whether gatherings left participants with increased love for one another and peace of conscience. Historical revivals accompanied societal reforms—abolition movements, social justice—evidence that true Spirit movement bears fruit beyond meetings. Contemporary contexts remind churches to measure manifestations against community well-being over time. The Advocate's personal ministry thus insists on sustainable growth rather than momentary spectacle. This fruit-based testing guides churches in responsible openness, bridging spiritual freedom and accountability.

8.3 Avoiding Both Quenching (1 Th 5:19–22) and Gullibility — Balanced Openness

Paul's warning—"Do not quench the Spirit. Test everything. Hold fast what is good. Abstain from every form of evil" (1 Th 5:19–22)—frames a middle path between suppressing Spirit gifts and gullibly embracing all phenomena. Balanced openness requires both enthusiastic reception of genuine promptings and critical evaluation of questionable experiences. Churches implement *prophetic covenant* agreements, defining mutual commitments to love, truth, and submission to Scripture. Leaders model humility by admitting limitations in discernment, seeking multiple confirmations. This approach honors the Advocate's personal ministry while protecting the flock from deception. Such balanced openness fosters an environment where innovation and tradition coalesce under Spirit guidance. The final subsection offers practical discernment frameworks.

8.4 Practical Discernment Frameworks for Leaders and Communities

Effective frameworks integrate biblical criteria, communal processes, and reflective spiritual practices. One model involves four steps: *Initial receptivity* (openly receiving promptings in prayer), *Scriptural alignment* (checking against clear biblical teaching), *Communal verification* (seeking counsel from mature leaders), and *Experiential validation* (observing fruit and life changes over time). Workshops and retreats train leaders in these steps, using case studies from Acts and Paul's epistles. Digital tools—online discernment forums—facilitate wider community input, ensuring diverse perspectives. Ongoing evaluation of prophetic words and worship innovations through periodic *Spirit reviews* helps communities adjust. This practical framework operationalizes the Advocate's personal ministry, equipping the church to navigate contemporary challenges.

Conclusion Chapter 8 has unveiled the Advocate's distinct personal ministries—teaching, guiding, advocating, and interceding—that operationalize His relational attributes within the church. We have seen how the Spirit completes Jesus' pedagogical work, illuminates Scripture, shepherds believers through life's decisions, strategizes global mission, defends the faithful, and prays on their behalf. By participating in these ministries, the church cooperates with the Advocate's ongoing presence, ensuring that doctrine, ethics, mission, and devotion remain anchored in divine initiative. In Chapter 9, we will trace how these personal ministries emerge from and underpin Trinitarian processions and missions, revealing why the Spirit carries out His work as Teacher, Guide, Advocate, and Intercessor in perfect unity with the Father and the Son.

Chapter 9. Trinitarian Dynamics: Processions and Missions

At the heart of Christian theology lies the dynamic interplay between God's eternal being and His redemptive actions. Nowhere is this interplay more profoundly expressed than in the relationship between the Spirit's eternal procession within the Trinity and His historical mission in salvation history. Chapter 9 will define key terms, trace biblical foundations, survey the patristic articulation, and examine the landmark Filioque debate. We will see that understanding how the Spirit proceeds from the Father (and, in Western theology, through the Son) illuminates why and how He is sent into the world to empower incarnation, baptism, resurrection, and the church's mission. By grounding mission in the Spirit's inner-Trinitarian life, we gain both doctrinal depth and practical vision for worship, witness, and unity.

1 Setting the Terms

1.1 Procession (ἐκπόρευσις / processio) versus Mission (missio / πέμψις)

In Trinitarian theology, *procession* (Greek *ekporeusis*) refers to the Spirit's eternal origin from the Father, a metaphysical relation within the Godhead that belongs to God's immanent life. By contrast,

186

mission (Latin *missio*; Greek *pempsis*) describes the Spirit's sending into the created order for the purposes of redemption and sanctification. The distinction safeguards the monarchy of the Father—only the Father is the source of the Son and Spirit in classical Eastern theology—while affirming that all three persons equally participate in the economic work of salvation. Procession speaks to "who" the Spirit is eternally; mission speaks to "where" and "why" the Spirit acts temporally. Without differentiating these, one risks confusing divine ontology with soteriological action, leading to modalism or subordinationism. Early theologians insisted that procession is unchanging and internal, whereas mission is contingent upon the Father's will to redeem humanity. Yet mission cannot be divorced from procession: only the Spirit who eternally proceeds can be sent to dwell in believers (John 15:26). Recognizing this duality provides clarity for subsequent creedal formulations and patristic debates, as we now explore the Creed's language.

1.2 Nicene–Constantinopolitan Creed and the Phrase "Who Proceeds from the Father"

The Nicene–Constantinopolitan Creed affirms that the Holy Spirit "proceeds from the Father" (ἐκ τοῦ Πατρὸς ἐκπορευόμενος), enshrining procession as a defining article of faith. This phrase sought to preserve the Father's monarchy against Arian claims and to articulate the Spirit's unique origin. The Creed's language emerged from controversies over the Son's divinity, extending Nicene boundaries to include the Spirit's co-equality. Eastern churches maintained that procession alone belonged to the inner life of the Trinity, cautioning against additions that might imply double sourcehood. The Creed's precise wording underscores the importance of theological vocabulary: *ekporeusis* (procession) differs from *pempsis* (sending). This distinction shaped Eastern liturgy, hymnography, and theology, highlighting that the Spirit's essence is from the Father, while His mission arises from both Father and Son. The Creed thus frames all subsequent Trinitarian reflection, setting the terms for Athanasian rule and the Cappadocian clarifications to follow.

1.3 Athanasius's Rule: The Economic Reveals—but Never Exhausts—the Immanent

Athanasius of Alexandria articulated the foundational principle that "the economic Trinity does not exhaust the immanent Trinity; it rather reveals it." By "economic Trinity," he meant the Father's work in creation and redemption; by "immanent Trinity," he referred to the Father–Son–Spirit's eternal relations. Athanasius insisted that while mission reflects eternal processions, it cannot define the Spirit's inner being. His rule protects against reducing God to His works—knowing what God does in history informs who God is, but never comprehensively defines His essence. Athanasius applied this rule in combating Arianism, arguing that the Son and Spirit, though sent, are truly God and consubstantial with the Father. This maxim underlies all orthodox Trinitarian theology, demanding humility and caution: our economic knowledge of God, mediated through Scripture and Spirit, is real yet analogous. Athanasius's insight bridges biblical revelation and creedal precision, preparing us to trace the biblical roots that inspired these theological constructs.

2 Biblical Roots of Procession

2.1 John 15:26 — "From the Father" and "From Alongside the Father"

In Jesus' Farewell Discourse, He promises, "When the Advocate comes, whom I will send to you from the Father, the Spirit of truth who proceeds from the Father, he will testify about me" (John 15:26). The double prepositional construction—*sent from the Father* (economic mission) and *proceeds from the Father* (eternal procession)—lays a nuanced foundation for later theology. The Greek *ek tou Patros* for procession denotes the Spirit's personal origin, while *ap' tou Patros* for sending indicates the Father's commissioning. Some manuscripts even reflect Johannine variants that stress the Spirit's joint procession from Father and Son, foreshadowing Western debates. This verse thus anchors Trinitarian vocabulary in the Gospel's own words, demonstrating that biblical testimony suffices to articulate the inner life of God. By distinguishing the Spirit's procession and mission, John ensures that readers recognize both who the Spirit is and what He does. The early church, meditating on this passage, discerned the need for precise language to express divine relations without dividing the Trinity's unity. From this Johannine basis, we turn to Pauline affirmations of Spirit-sending.

2.2 Galatians 4:6 — The Spirit "Sent into Our Hearts" Crying "Abba"

Paul writes, "Because you are sons, God has sent the Spirit of his Son into our hearts, crying, 'Abba! Father!'" (Gal 4:6). The verb *sent* (*apesteilen*) indicates the Spirit's economic mission, while His origin—*of his Son*—implies relational dynamics within the Trinity. Though Paul does not employ *procession* language, he presupposes that the Spirit's sending from the Son derives from shared divine life. The Spirit's arrival into believers' hearts fulfills His eschatological role, producing filial assurance. This verse strengthens Johannine testimony by showing that the Spirit's mission participates in Christ's sending. The Spirit's personal cry, "Abba," reveals both His role in adoption and His intimacy with believers. Early Christian exegetes used this text to nuance mission theology: the Spirit is sent in virtue of procession, linking immanent and economic aspects. This Pauline affirmation deepens our understanding of Trinitarian sending before we explore revelatory breath imagery.

2.3 Revelatory "Breathing" Imagery (Gen 2:7; John 20:22) and Its Limits

Genesis 2:7 depicts God forming Adam and "breathing into his nostrils the breath of life," while John 20:22 narrates Jesus "breathing on" the disciples, saying, "Receive the Holy Spirit." These *pneuma*-based images connect the Spirit's origin with life-giving action. The Hebrew *nishmat chayim* and the Greek *empsuchos* provide analogies for the Spirit's impartation of life, yet they do not articulate eternal procession. They emphasize mission—Spirit gives new creation in believers—rather than ontological origin. The breath metaphor underscores divine intimacy: as breath animates the body, the Spirit animates the new humanity in Christ. Patristic writers like Irenaeus and Gregory Nazianzen reflect on these texts as illustrations of mission but caution against equating breath with procession. Recognizing the power and limitations of this imagery prevents conflating metaphor with metaphysics. The life-giving breath prepares us for the Cappadocian clarity that follows.

3 Patristic Trajectories

3.1 Cappadocian Clarity: Basil, Gregory, and the ἐκ τοῦ Πατρός Formula

Basil the Great, Gregory of Nazianzus, and Gregory of Nyssa—the Cappadocians—provided decisive theological precision by insisting that the Spirit proceeds *ek tou Patros* (from the Father) alone. They argued that *ekporeusis* is unique to the Father's monarchy, distinguishing the Spirit's origin from the Son's generation. In Basil's

On the Holy Spirit, he writes that the Spirit's procession is "from the Father, not outside of the essence, but by which the essence remains whole." Gregory of Nazianzus, in his Fifth Theological Oration, emphasizes that procession is an eternal relation, inseparable from the Father's identity. Their consensus established orthodox language that the Eastern churches would enshrine in liturgy and theology. This formula resolved earlier conflations and laid groundwork for later ecumenical dialogues. Their work demonstrates the critical role of precise patristic definitions in safeguarding both the monarchy of the Father and the co-equality of the Spirit. From this Cappadocian ground, we turn to Augustine's relational taxis.

3.2 Augustine's Relational Taxis: Gift-Love Mutually Breathed

Augustine of Hippo, while affirming the Spirit's procession from the Father, introduced the concept of a *taxis*—an ordered communion of the Trinity—whereby the Spirit is the mutual love between Father and Son. In *De Trinitate*, Augustine describes the Spirit as the "bond of love" (*culos vinculum*) proceeding from both, without implying two sources. He uses psychological analogies—memory, understanding, and will—to illustrate the Trinity's internal relations. For Augustine, *procession* and *gift* (*donum*) coincide: the Spirit eternally proceeds as the gift of love and is missionally sent as the outpouring of grace. This relational taxis enriched Western reflection, providing analogies that connected procession to the mutual indwelling of the persons. Augustine's model influenced Latin theology's acceptance of the *filioque* clause—as an expression of the Spirit's procession *through* the Son—while preserving monarchical order. His insights into gift-love continue to inform contemporary Trinitarian models that emphasize relational perichoresis. Having surveyed Augustine, we turn to Syriac and Alexandrian emphases.

3.3 Syriac and Alexandrian Emphases on Father as Fountainhead (πηγή / pēgē)

Syriac theologians—such as Aphrahat and Ephrem the Syrian—and Alexandrian thinkers like Athanasius and Cyril of Alexandria emphasized the Father (*pēgē*, fountainhead) as the sole source within the Trinity. In Syriac liturgy, the Spirit is invoked as coming "from the Father who is the source of all." Ephrem's hymns poetically speak of the Spirit as the river flowing from the Father's bosom. Alexandrians, steeped in Platonic imagery, likened the Father to the primal source of unbegotten being, sending forth the Son and the Spirit in ordered mission. Their theological texts underscore that any language of Spirit origin *through* the Son must not compromise the Spirit's eternal origination from the Father alone. This emphasis provided a counterbalance to Western mutual procession models, reminding the church that even while celebrating shared operations, one must uphold the Father's monarchy. The Syriac and Alexandrian testimonies thus enrich the tapestry of early Trinitarian reflection, leading us into the historical Filioque controversy.

4 The Filioque Controversy

4.1 Historical Insertion in the Latin Creed (Toledo 589)

The addition of *filioque* ("and from the Son") to the Nicene Creed in the Third Council of Toledo (589) arose in defense of Christ's divinity and unity against Arianism in Spain. Latin churches began reciting that the Spirit "proceeds from the Father and the Son," reflecting Augustine's relational taxis and combating local theological errors. This insertion spread in the West, appearing in Charlemagne's reign to solidify ecclesial uniformity. However, it was never ratified by an ecumenical council, setting the stage for divisive tension with Eastern churches that held strictly to *ek tou Patros*. The political and pastoral motives intertwined with deep theological convictions, creating enduring ecclesial rifts. Understanding this historical context clarifies why *filioque* remains a key liturgical and doctrinal watershed. From its Latin origins, we examine Eastern objections.

4.2 Eastern Objections: Safeguarding the Monarchy of the Father

Eastern theologians objected to *filioque* on the grounds that it compromised the Father's unique role as the sole source of the Spirit's procession, thus undermining the monarchy and unity of the Trinity. Photios of Constantinople, in the 9th century, penned an extensive refutation, insisting that the Creed's language must remain unchanged. He argued that any notion of Spirit procession from the Son implied a dual fountainhead, threatening the immutable order of divine relations. Eastern liturgies and theological manuals continued to pray the original creed, emphasizing that mission from the Son does not entail eternal procession. These objections highlight the nuanced difference between economic mission and eternal relations, underscoring the precise language required in Trinitarian theology. The East's steadfast defense of the monarchy of the Father preserved vital Orthodox identities that still inform dialogues today. From Eastern critique, we survey modern rapprochements.

4.3 Modern Rapprochements: "Through the Son" as Mediating Language

Late 20th-century ecumenical dialogues—such as ARCIC II and the North American Orthodox–Roman Catholic consultations—proposed that "the Spirit proceeds from the Father through the Son," harmonizing Eastern emphasis on the Father's monarchy with Western affirmation of the Son's role. This mediating formula employs *dia tou Huiou* (through the Son) rather than *kai tou Huiou* (and the Son), preserving single sourcehood while acknowledging the Spirit's economic mission through the Son's redemptive work. Both communions recognized that this language accurately reflects patristic nuance and biblical patterns (e.g., John 15:26; Gal 4:6). Representing theological convergence, these proposals suggest that mutual breathing of love between Father and Son can be expressed as a single procession from the Father through the Son. While not universally adopted, these rapprochements demonstrate a shared desire to reconcile centuries-old disputes using precise, Christologically centered language. As these modern dialogues suggest, careful philological and theological work can build bridges without sacrificing doctrinal integrity.

4.4 Ecumenical Documents (e.g., Clarification on the Filioque, 1995)

In 1995, the North American Orthodox–Catholic Theological Consultation published "The Filioque: A Church-Dividing Issue?" and "Clarification on the Filioque," acknowledging both traditions' legitimate doctrinal concerns. These documents affirm the Father's monarchy and the Son's unique role in mission, proposing that the creed's original text be honored while recognizing Western theological expressions. They recommend that each communion respect the other's nomenclature and continue dialogue. The documents emphasize that the filioque controversy need not obstruct deeper unity, as both sides confess the same Trinity in substance. Such ecumenical statements model the Spirit's personal ministry of reconciliation, guiding the church toward unity in diversity. Emerging from these proposals is a shared commitment to integrate procession and mission in ways that reflect the Advocate's own perichoretic life. This ecumenical progress sets the stage for exploring the economic missions in redemptive history.

5 Economic Missions in Redemptive History

5.1 Incarnation: Spirit Overshadows Mary (Luke 1:35)

The angel's declaration that "the Holy Spirit will come upon you, and the power of the Most High will overshadow you" (Luke 1:35) portrays the Spirit's mission as the divine architect of the Incarnation. This military metaphor of *overshadowing* (Greek *episkiazei*) evokes God's protective and creative presence, recalling the cloud that sheltered Israel in the wilderness (Exod 13:21). Mary's *fiat*—her obedient consent—does not initiate the Spirit's work; rather, the Spirit's personal initiative precedes human assent, ensuring that the Son's conception is wholly divine. Early theologians saw in this event the first economic mission of the Spirit: to bring about the God–Man union without violating either divine or human natures. The Spirit's personal agency here underscores His integral involvement in the mystery of the Word become flesh. Patristic hymns extol this moment as the Spirit's greatest act of creation since Genesis 1. This economic mission inaugurates salvation history, setting a pattern for the Spirit's subsequent works at baptism, passion, and resurrection. Recognizing the Spirit's foundational role in the Incarnation transitions us into His visible descent at the Baptist's ministry.

5.2 Baptism: Spirit Descends, Father Speaks (Matt 3:16–17)

At Jesus' baptism, narrative symmetry unfolds: the heavens open, the Spirit descends "like a dove," and the Father's voice declares, "This is my beloved Son" (Matt 3:16–17). The Spirit's mission here confirms Jesus' identity and inaugurates His public ministry. The dove imagery echoes Noah's post-Flood peace and Israel's prophetic imagery of Spirit-restored land (Isa 44:3–4). The Spirit-person descends bodily, emphasizing personal presence rather than mere power. The Father's audible commendation vindicates this mission: the Spirit confirms the Son's messianic calling in real time. This triune epiphany demonstrates economic roles: the Son inaugurates ministry, the Spirit anoints, and the Father affirms. The baptismal event becomes paradigmatic for Christian initiation: believers are baptized into Christ's death and resurrection by the Spirit (Rom 6:3–4). The Spirit's personal descent at baptism foreshadows His mission to dwell in all believers, knitting them into Christ's body. This seamless connection between Incarnation and baptism leads us into the Spirit's mission at the cross.

5.3 Crucifixion: Christ Offers Himself "Through the Eternal Spirit" (Heb 9:14)

The author of Hebrews describes Christ's sacrificial offering "through the eternal Spirit" (Heb 9:14), highlighting that Jesus' atoning death was empowered and applied by the Spirit-person. The Spirit, sustaining Christ in obedience and purity amid suffering, ensures the efficacy of His blood for redemption. This economic mission reveals that the Spirit's presence was active even in the Passion, enabling Jesus to fulfill the righteous will of the Father (Matt 26:39). The term *eternal* signifies that the Spirit's operation in the crucifixion participates in God's timeless life. Early exegetes noted that the Spirit accompanied Jesus from conception through death, underscoring continuous divine involvement. The Spirit's mission at the cross also inaugurates the new covenant temple: Christ's body becomes the ultimate sanctuary, indwelt by the Spirit's presence. Believers partake in this offering through Spirit-united faith, sharing in Christ's death and life. Understanding the Spirit's role in the crucifixion prepares us for His mission in resurrection and exaltation.

5.4 Resurrection and Exaltation: Spirit Raises Jesus (Rom 8:11)

Paul asserts that "if the Spirit of him who raised Jesus from the dead dwells in you, he who raised Christ Jesus...will also give life to your mortal bodies through his Spirit" (Rom 8:11). The Spirit's resurrection work is personal and powerful: He is the agent who conquered death, affirming both Jesus' divine Sonship and the future hope of believers. Early creedal statements—"by the power of the Holy Spirit, he was raised from the dead"—root the Resurrection in the Spirit's personal action rather than impersonal cosmic forces. The Spirit's mission extends the Resurrection to all believers, guaranteeing participation in new creation. This Spirit-led exaltation completes the economic mission triad: overshadowing at conception, anointing at baptism, and vindication at resurrection. The risen Christ's Sonship and Lordship are confirmed by the Spirit's power, inaugurating the church's mission era. From resurrection we naturally flow into Pentecost as the great unveiling of the Spirit's processional mission to the world.

6 Pentecost: Manifest Mission of the Processional Spirit

6.1 "Poured Out" from the Exalted Son (Acts 2:33)

Luke connects the Spirit's mission at Pentecost to the exalted Son: "Being therefore exalted at the right hand of God, and having received from the Father the promise of the Holy Spirit, he has poured out this that you yourselves are seeing and hearing" (Acts 2:33). The *pouring out* language (Greek *ekcheō*) recalls eschatological prophecy (Joel 2:28) and firstfruits imagery, indicating an irreversible, abundant mission of the Spirit. The Spirit's sending is a direct consequence of Christ's ascension and reception of the promise—an economic extension of eternal processions. This moment publicly discloses the intimate link between immanent procession and mission: the same Spirit who eternally proceeds now empowers the church's birth. The Spirit's presence in wind and fire symbolizes both transcendent power and personal intimacy. Jewish pilgrims witnessing this event recognized divine judgment mitigated by mercy, prompting Peter's convicting sermon. From this universal outpouring we turn to the Spirit's bridge between Babel and Pentecost.

6.2 Spirit-Speech in Many Tongues — Reversing Babel, Fulfilling Joel

Pentecost's multilingual proclamation reverses Babel's linguistic dispersion (Gen 11:1–9) by enabling "each one to hear them speaking in his own language" (Acts 2:6). This Spirit-led reversal fulfills Joel's prophecy that sons and daughters would prophesy and foreigners receive visions (Joel 2:28–29). The Spirit's personal mission thus includes breaking down communication barriers, uniting diverse peoples in the gospel. The tongues phenomenon underlines that the Spirit's biased power is always reconciliation, never fragmentation. Early missiologists saw this as the paradigm for cross-cultural witness: spiritual gifts adapt to the hearer's context under Spirit control. Communities learning to test and interpret tongues practice balanced openness, ensuring that this gift builds up the body (1 Cor 14:26). From Babel's judgment to Pentecost's reversal, the Spirit shows Himself as the divine renegade of division, unifying creation. This unifying mission prepares us to consider the link between exaltation and effusion.

6.3 Link between Exaltation (Doxology) and Effusion (Gift)

Peter's sermon emphasizes that Jesus' exaltation—His enthronement at the Father's right hand—results in the Spirit's effusion: "God has made him both Lord and Christ... Therefore let all the house of Israel know for certain that God has made him both Lord and Christ... let the whole house of Israel therefore know that God has made him both Lord and Christ, this Jesus whom you crucified" (Acts 2:36). Thereafter, the believers receive the Spirit, demonstrating that doxological exaltation and ecstatic gift are inseparable. The doxology offered by the Father in raising and exalting the Son precipitates the effusion of the Spirit. Early liturgies reflect this dynamic in henotactic chants linking *Glory to the Father* with *Glory to the Son* and *Glory to the Holy Spirit*. Modern worship movements incorporate Spirit-empowered praise that emerges naturally from doxological reflection on Christ's lordship. Recognizing this link underscores that every outpouring of the Spirit flows from Trinitarian worship, shaping the church's continuous mission. This dynamic reveals how processions and missions interweave, leading us to mutual glorification without confusion.

7 Mutual Glorification without Confusion

7.1 Spirit Glorifies the Son (John 16:14)

Jesus affirms, "He will glorify me, for he will take what is mine and declare it to you" (John 16:14), indicating that the Spirit's missionally discloses the Son's character and work. The Spirit's personal ministry involves selective revelation—highlighting Christ's righteousness, obedience, and sacrificial love—ensuring that worship and doctrine remain Christocentric. This glorification does not diminish the Spirit's role but integrates it within the Trinity's cohesive purpose. Patristic commentators like Cyril of Alexandria emphasized that the Spirit's glorifying work validates Christ's nature against heretical misrepresentations. In liturgical contexts, Spirit-inspired preaching and songs focus on exalting Christ, illustrating that genuine Spirit presence never obscures the theological center. The Spirit's personal aim in mission is always to point away from Himself to the Son, underscoring the unity of purpose within the Trinity. From the Spirit's glorifying work we move to how the Son sends the Spirit for the Father's glory.

7.2 Son Sends the Spirit for the Father's Glory (John 17:1; 20:21–22)

In His high-priestly prayer, Jesus prays, "Father, the hour has come; glorify your Son that the Son may glorify you" (John 17:1), setting a reciprocal framework: the Son's glorification of the Father is enabled by Spirit mission. After resurrection, Jesus breathes on the disciples—"Receive the Holy Spirit" (John 20:21–22)—personally commissioning them under the Spirit's power for Father-glorifying witness. This breath motif recalls Creation and signifies new creation for Christ's community. The Spirit's mission from the Son testifies to the Father's name in the world (John 17:6,26), forging a liturgical and missional chain: Father sends Son, Son sends Spirit, Spirit enables church. Early eucharistic prayers evoke this flow, invoking the Spirit to make Christ present so that believers may glorify the Father. This mutual glorification functions without confusion of persons, displaying perfect perichoresis. Understanding this reciprocal mission prepares us to articulate the indivisible works of the Trinity.

8 Spirit as Mediator of Communion

8.1 "Through Him We Both Have Access … by One Spirit" (Eph 2:18)

Paul declares that "through him we both have access in one Spirit to the Father" (Eph 2:18), portraying the Spirit as the mediator of divine-human communion. The preposition *through* (*dia*) highlights that fellowship with the Father and Son is unobtainable apart from the Spirit's personal mission. This Spirit involvement overturns ethnic separations, granting both Jews and Gentiles equal access. Eastern liturgies often emphasize this verse in prayers of entrance, acknowledging the Spirit's role as gatekeeper and host. Paul's context—reconciliation of two peoples—illustrates that the Spirit-person actively removes barriers to communion. This mediative function echoes the High Priest's role in the temple, but surpasses it by entering the believer's heart. As the personal Spirit dwells in each, He ensures perpetual access to the Father, not limited to ritual precincts. Recognizing the Spirit as mediator of communion leads us naturally to His indwelling presence.

8.2 Indwelling that Makes Believers Temples (1 Cor 3:16; 6:19)

Paul proclaims, "Do you not know that you are God's temple and that God's Spirit dwells in you?" (1 Cor 3:16), reiterating that the Spirit's mission includes indwelling believers as sacred habitations. This indwelling parallels Old-Testament tabernacle theology but personalizes it: every believer becomes a living temple. The Spirit's personal presence sanctifies bodies and communities, making them loci of divine encounter. This mission underscores the Spirit's commitment to intimate relationship rather than distant oversight. Early monastic writings treat the heart as inner sanctuary, cultivated through prayer and ascetic disciplines to honor the Spirit's residence. Paul's further warning, "You are…not your own, for you were bought with a price. So glorify God in your body" (1 Cor 6:19–20), demonstrates that indwelling carries ethical responsibilities. The Spirit's indwelling thus merges soteriology with ethics, ensuring that

197

mission results in sanctified living. From individual temples we shift to the Spirit's role in communal fellowship.

8.3 Fellowship (Koinōnia) with Father and Son (2 Cor 13:14; 1 John 1:3)

Paul's benediction—"The fellowship of the Holy Spirit be with you all" (2 Cor 13:14)—and John's affirmation that "our fellowship is with the Father and with his Son Jesus Christ" (1 John 1:3) together indicate that the Spirit-person is the bond linking believers to the entire Trinity. This fellowship is not static membership but dynamic participation in divine life. The Spirit's personal presence creates communion patterns mirroring Trinitarian perichoresis: mutual indwelling, shared love, and unified purpose. Baptism initiates believers into this fellowship, while the Eucharist sustains it. The Spirit enables experiential knowledge of God—"we know that he abides in us" (1 John 3:24)—transforming doctrinal assent into relational intimacy. This fellowship confers identity and mission: as the church participates in Trinitarian life, it witnesses the invisible God to the world. Understanding the Spirit as mediator of communion paves the way for exploring the church's mission in the Spirit.

9 Mission of the Church in the Spirit

9.1 Father sends the Son; Father and Son send the Spirit; Spirit sends the Church

The Gospel opens with the Father's initiative in sending the Son into the world (John 3:16), establishing the first sending within the economic Trinity. At the conclusion of His earthly ministry, Jesus commissions His disciples, declaring that just as the Father sent Him, He in turn sends His followers (John 20:21). Simultaneously, the Father and the Son send the Spirit to empower this community for mission (John 15:26; 16:7). This Trinitarian relay highlights the personal agency of each divine Person: the Father as source, the Son as incarnational envoy, and the Spirit as missionary enabler. It is the Spirit-person who imparts the necessary gifts—boldness, wisdom, love, and power—for the church's witness (Acts 1:8; 4:31). By sending the church, the Spirit extends the Trinity's life into every context, creating a living network of divine presence. Theologically, this pattern reflects the perichoretic unity of the Godhead—each Person participates in the others' mission without confusion or division of wills. Missiological practice flows from this Trinitarian sending: missionary strategies must be rooted in prayerful attunement to the Spirit's personal directives, rather than purely human planning. Contemporary movements that emphasize *mission as divine sending* draw directly on this sequence, ensuring that every local outreach stands under the Spirit's commission. Understanding this relational sending informs our reflection on the Antioch blueprint for mission.

9.2 Antioch Blueprint — "Set Apart for Me" (Acts 13:2)

In the church at Antioch, leadership—prophets and teachers—gathered for worship, fasting, and prayer when the Holy Spirit said, "Set apart for me Barnabas and Saul for the work to which I have called them" (Acts 13:2). This phrase, *set apart* (*aphorizō*), indicates the Spirit's personal choice in commissioning missionaries, distinguishing them from the community for a specific purpose. The Antioch blueprint combines corporate spiritual disciplines—prayer, fasting, worship—with attentive listening, modeling how congregations discern Spirit-led mission. The community responds by laying hands on the chosen pair and sending them off in joyous release (Acts 13:3), demonstrating that mission requires both divine calling and communal consent. This pattern contrasts with top-down appointment; the Spirit's voice initiates, and the church affirms. Modern mission agencies replicate this blueprint by embedding discernment retreats and prayerful commissioning services into missionary pipelines. The Antioch event underscores that mission originates in Spirit-person directives, is ratified by the church, and is empowered by communal prayer. This narrative also highlights that the Spirit's sending extends to both Jew and Gentile contexts, foreshadowing global outreach. From Antioch's commissioning, we derive a hermeneutic that reads Scripture through the lens of divine sending.

9.3 Missional Hermeneutic: Scripture Read in Light of the Sending God

A missional hermeneutic interprets every biblical text as part of God's sending narrative. Genesis's promise that all nations will be blessed through Abraham (Gen 12:3) finds its fulfillment in the Spirit's empowering of believers for cross-cultural witness (Gal 3:14). The *Great Commission* (Matt 28:18–20) is not an isolated command but the culmination of redemptive sending: Father → Son → Spirit → Church → nations. Prophetic books like Isaiah and Joel, which envision Spirit outpouring and global worship (Isa 49:6; Joel 2:28–32), become missional manuals when read through the sending motif. Psalm 2's declaration that the Son's rule extends to the ends of the earth (Ps 2:8) anticipates the Spirit's mission in Acts. A missional hermeneutic empowers preachers and teachers to frame exegesis around divine commissioning, ensuring that local congregations see themselves as participants in an ongoing sentness. Bible study curricula built on this approach foster a sense of calling, connecting ancient texts with present-day mission. By reading Scripture through the sending God, the church aligns its identity and purpose with the Spirit's historic and eternal mission. This theological foundation leads into contemporary Trinitarian models that guide communal ethics.

10 Contemporary Trinitarian Models

10.1 Social Trinity and Its Promise for Communal Ethics

Modern theologians have revived the *Social Trinity* model, emphasizing the relational life between Father, Son, and Spirit as a paradigm for human community. Thinkers like Jürgen Moltmann and Stanley Grenz describe the Father–Son–Spirit communion as a dynamic fellowship characterized by mutual love, shared glory, and coequality. If the Trinity is a *divine society*, then human societies— churches, families, nations—can image this by embodying equality, mutual service, and shared purpose. The Spirit's procession and mission, rooted in perichoretic love, form the template for ethical community life: no hierarchy of persons, no domination, but mutual submission and hospitality. Ethicists draw on this model to address issues from racial reconciliation to economic justice, arguing that Spirit-led communities must reflect Trinitarian justice. Critiques of individualism and authoritarianism find a robust alternative in a social doctrine that grounds ethical norms in the Spirit's personal relationships within the Godhead. By seeing the Trinity's inner life as normative, the church gains both theological clarity and moral impetus for communal transformation. This social paradigm also invites scrutiny regarding functional subordination.

10.2 Objections to Functional Subordinationism

Some contemporary theologians caution against *functional subordinationism*, the idea that within the Trinity, the Spirit or Son might be eternally subordinate in will or authority to the Father. Critics argue this undermines coequality and risks sliding into subordinationism. They emphasize that economic roles—incarnation, mission, intercession—never imply ontological inferiority. The Cappadocians and Augustine both insisted on unity of essence despite functional distinctions. Modern analytic theologians reaffirm

200

that procession relations do not entail any hierarchy of being or value. They stress that terms like *through the Son* in the West denote order of mission rather than hierarchy of essence. Responses to subordinationist tendencies include robust affirmations of perichoresis, where each Person equally wields divine attributes even as they relate in ordered missions. This debate highlights the need for careful theology: honoring functional distinctions without compromising coequal deity. Recognizing these objections refines our understanding of analytic and Latin Trinitarian resurgences.

10.3 Analytic and Latin Trinitarian Resurgences — Prospects and Cautions

Late 20th-century *analytic theology* revitalized classical doctrine by applying precise philosophical tools to concepts like personhood, relation, and procession. Analytic theologians such as Alvin Plantinga and Kevin Timpe have clarified the difference between ontology and economy, affirming the Spirit's procession without conflating it with mission. Latin Catholic scholars continue to develop *relational models* that integrate Augustine's mutual love with Eastern monarchy, using *through the Son* language as a theologically balanced descriptor. These resurgences promise deeper dialogue, mutual enrichment, and robust defenses of orthodox teaching in secular academic contexts. Yet they also carry cautions: overemphasis on philosophical categories can abstract the Trinity from biblical narrative, and ecclesial identity may suffer if theology becomes overly technical. Churches engaging with these models must ensure that laypeople receive doctrine in accessible forms, preserving pastoral sensitivity. When analytic clarity and Latin nuance converge with patristic wisdom, the church gains a richer vocabulary for liturgy, education, and ecumenical engagement, poised to live out procession theology in contemporary contexts. Having surveyed these models, we now turn to worship and prayer implications.

11 Worship and Prayer Implications

11.1 Addressing the Father through the Son in the Spirit

Christian prayer tradition roots itself in Trinitarian structure: prayers are directed to the Father as *Father*, through the Son as *high Priest*, and in the Spirit as *intercessor*. Jesus models this pattern by praying "Father, glorify your Son" (John 17:1), and by instructing believers to pray "in my name" (John 14:13–14). The Spirit's personal ministry ensures that prayers ascend rightly—Spirit prays *through* Christ, guaranteeing access to the Father (Eph 2:18). Liturgical prayers often begin "Almighty God, Father of our Lord Jesus Christ…" and end with a Spirit invocation, reflecting this directionality. Pentecostal and charismatic services emphasize *spontaneous Spirit-led prayers*, while historic liturgies maintain *collects* that mirror Trinitarian sending. This prayer structure safeguards against arbitrary invocation and fosters reverence: God is Father, but only through the Son, and the Spirit enables communion. Recognizing this pattern deepens both corporate and private devotion, leading us to the epiclesis.

11.2 Epiclesis in Eucharistic Liturgy — Invoking the Processional Spirit

In historic Eucharistic liturgies—the Roman Canon, Eastern Anaphoras, Reformed liturgies—an *epiclesis* invokes the Spirit to transform bread and wine into Christ's body and blood and to sanctify the assembly. The epiclesis articulates the Spirit's mission as the Agent of presence: "Send down your Holy Spirit upon us and these gifts…" (Roman Canon). Eastern rites often place the epiclesis immediately before communion, emphasizing the Spirit's procession into the gifts and the people. This act re-enacts the ancient sending: Father → Son → Spirit → people. Theologically, the epiclesis connects procession with mission: the same Spirit who eternally proceeds is missionally sent to effect transubstantiation and communal participation. Pastors trained in liturgical studies teach that neglecting the epiclesis impoverishes sacramental theology by reducing the Eucharist to memorial. When congregations understand the epiclesis as Trinitarian participation, the liturgy becomes a foretaste of the heavenly banquet where Spirit-procession and mission converge. Having considered epiclesis, we examine doxological patterns.

11.3 Doxological Pattern: "Glory to the Father, through the Son, by the Holy Spirit"

Traditional doxologies follow the triadic pattern: *Glory to the Father, through the Son, in the Holy Spirit*. This formula, found in apostolic writings (Eph 3:21) and liturgies, encapsulates the sending order: the Father originates, the Son mediates, and the Spirit personalizes. Worshipers affirm divine agency in sequence: the Father's source, the Son's redeeming work, and the Spirit's empowering presence. Eastern Orthodox hymnody often expands this pattern with elaborate poetic stanzas, while Western canticles maintain brevity. These doxologies shape corporate identity, reminding the church that all glory flows inwardly and outwardly through the Trinity's mutual missions. Modern worship services include this pattern in benedictions and service conclusions, anchoring every act of praise in Trinitarian sending. Understanding the doxological pattern enables believers to worship with theological depth, bridging liturgy with mission praxis. From worship we now turn to the pastoral payoff of living in the flow of sending.

12 Pastoral Payoff: Living in the Flow of Sending

12.1 Embracing Adoptive Confidence — Crying "Abba" in Daily Prayer

Paul teaches that "you did not receive the spirit of slavery...but you have received the Spirit of adoption as sons, by whom we cry, 'Abba! Father!'" (Rom 8:15). This Spirit-given assurance shapes daily prayer: believers approach God with childlike confidence, knowing they are truly His. Pastoral ministries incorporate this by teaching congregants to begin each devotional with the intimate "Abba," fostering a relational posture rather than liturgical formulae alone. Small-group studies on Romans guide participants through exercises of prayer that internalize Spirit-birthed adoption. Counseling models emphasize the Advocate's personal witness to hearts struggling with guilt, restoring familial assurance. Embracing adoptive confidence under the Spirit's sending flow transforms spiritual formation, replacing legalism with filial freedom. This confidence fuels both personal piety and communal outreach, as children of God boldly share their Father's love. Recognizing this intimate adoption leads us to vocational discernment.

12.2 Vocational Discernment as Cooperative Listening to the Sending Spirit

Vocational guidance ministries now incorporate *Trinitarian discernment*: believers seek to hear how the Father, through the Son, and in the Spirit guides their life's calling. Spiritual directors facilitate conversations that map Scripture's sending narratives onto individual trajectories—calling parallels between Barnabas, Paul, and modern professionals. Workshops use *Ignatian exercises* to simulate the sending flow: imagining being sent by the Father, through Christ, and propelled by the Spirit into workplaces, families, and communities. Denominational bodies provide prayer retreats for pastoral candidate selection, ensuring that vocational norms align with Spirit's personal callings rather than institutional demands. This cooperative listening respects both corporate affirmation and individual conviction, reflecting the Antioch blueprint. As congregations practice such discernment, they embody the Spirit's sending flow in every aspect of life. From vocational listening we shift to unity-for-mission.

12.3 Unity-for-Mission: Procession Theology as Antidote to Ecclesial Tribalism

Procession theology emphasizes that the Spirit's origin in the Father and mission through the Son creates a model of unity that transcends denominational, ethnic, and ideological boundaries. When churches recognize that they are all sent by the same Spirit, their tribal loyalties give way to cooperative mission partnerships. Ecumenical initiatives grounded in procession theology—joint worship services, combined relief efforts, and shared church plants—demonstrate the Spirit's unifying power. Denominations that once competed now collaborate under the banner "one Spirit, one body" (Eph 4:4–6), reflecting the Father's singular source and the Son's singular mediation. Pastors report that joint mission trips or prayer networks under the Spirit's guidance break down historical prejudices. By framing unity as participation in Spirit-sending, procession theology serves as an effective antidote to ecclesial fragmentation. This unity-for-mission completes our pastoral payoff and prepares us for synthesis.

Conclusion Chapter 9 has traced the intimate connection between the Spirit's eternal procession within the Trinity and His historic mission in salvation, balancing precise theological vocabulary with biblical testimony and patristic insight. From defining procession and mission to examining the Creed's language, Athanasian rule, biblical roots, Cappadocian and Augustinian trajectories, and the enduring Filioque debate, we see that understanding the Advocate's origin enriches our grasp of His work in incarnation, baptism, Pentecost, and the church's sending. This Trinitarian clarity undergirds ecclesial worship, prayer, and unity, ensuring that the Spirit's personal ministries flow from His eternal relations. In Chapter 10, we will explore how the same Spirit who proceeds and is sent now transforms believers' hearts and communities through indwelling and sanctification.

Chapter 10. Indwelling and Sanctification: The Spirit's Interior Presence

The Spirit's indwelling presence marks the culmination of God's mission to draw near to His creation, transforming Eden's promise into a dynamic reality within every believer. Far from a distant power, the Advocate resides intimately in hearts and communities, making them living temples where divine and human life converge. This chapter explores how the Spirit fulfills the temple motif, writes God's law within, fashions Christlike character, and energizes ethical holiness. We will trace the contours of positional and progressive sanctification, examine the Spirit's sealing work of assurance, and consider the charisms and communal rhythms that foster growth. Throughout, the emphasis remains on the Advocate's personal engagement—His gracious residence, transformative touch, and careful cultivation of both individual and corporate holiness.

1 The Temple Motif Fulfilled

1.1 Eden, Tabernacle, and Solomon's Temple as Progressive Dwelling Paradigms

From the moment God breathes life into Adam in Eden (Gen 2:7), Scripture portrays humanity as God's intended dwelling place. Eden's garden functions as the first temple, where God walks "in the cool of the day" (Gen 3:8), establishing divine–human fellowship in a cultivated sanctuary. Israel's wilderness tabernacle then echoes Eden, a portable dwelling where God meets Moses, with the Spirit overshadowing the mercy seat (Exod 25:22). Its intricate design—courtyard, Holy Place, Holy of Holies—foreshadows deepening access, culminating in Solomon's temple, where cedar and gold manifested heavenly craftsmanship (1 Kings 6). Here the Spirit's presence descended upon the glory cloud (2 Chron 5:14), signifying full habitation. Yet even Solomon's temple, glorious though it was, could not contain God fully (1 Kings 8:27), pointing forward to a more intimate indwelling. Each stage reveals progressive residence: from Eden's openness to Israel's mediated approach and finally to the Spirit's unmediated entrance into human hearts. Recognizing these paradigms prepares us to see the gathered church as the new temple.

1.2 Corporate Sanctuary: The Gathered Church as God's Holy House (1 Cor 3:16–17; Eph 2:19–22)

Paul declares believers collectively to be "God's temple" (1 Cor 3:16), warning that destruction of this holy house grieves the Spirit who dwells within. The Corinthian congregation, prone to division, learns that corporate worship and unity are vital, for God resides among them when assembled. Ephesians paints the church as a "holy temple in the Lord," built on apostolic foundation, with Christ as cornerstone and believers as living stones (Eph 2:19–22). This imagery conveys that the Spirit's indwelling is neither generic nor solitary but communal: every gathering becomes a sanctuary where God's presence shapes prayers, preaching, and fellowship. Early Christian architecture—basilicas oriented east–west—echoed temple design, centering liturgy around the Spirit's presence in the altar and assembly. Contemporary congregations that emphasize Spirit-led corporate prayer and worship experience this corporate indwelling tangibly, reporting increased relational depth and supernatural unity. The Spirit's personal habitation in the church body demands that local assemblies cultivate holiness, reverence, and mutual care. From corporate sanctuary we turn to the individual's sacred space.

1.3 Individual Bodies as Spirit-Made "Holy of Holies" (1 Cor 6:19–20)

Paul's pointed question—"Do you not know that your body is a temple of the Holy Spirit within you?" (1 Cor 6:19)—transfers the temple motif from building to being. Each believer's body becomes the "holy of

206

holies," the innermost sanctuary where God dwells personally. This radical indwelling elevates bodily integrity: sexual immorality now defiles the temple (1 Cor 6:18), and self-care becomes sacred stewardship. Early ascetic writers like Clement of Alexandria interpreted this as a call to bodily discipline and chastity. Modern spiritual formation integrates yoga, breath prayer, and somatic awareness, acknowledging the Spirit's residency. Medical ethics rooted in this passage affirm the sanctity of life and the body's dignity. The Spirit's choice to make individual bodies His dwelling underscores the personal dimension of sanctification—every thought, word, and action matters. Recognizing our bodies as holy of holies sets the stage for the ultimate temple.

1.4 Eschatological Temple in the New Jerusalem where God Is All-in-All (Rev 21:22–23)

John's vision of the New Jerusalem offers the final temple motif: "I saw no temple in the city, for its temple is the Lord God the Almighty and the Lamb" (Rev 21:22). Here the Spirit's indwelling culminates in a fully transparent, all-pervasive sanctuary where God's presence lights the city. The river of life flows through its streets, and the tree of life heals the nations (Rev 22:1–2), symbolizing the Spirit's healing and unifying mission across the renewed cosmos. This eschatological temple abolishes any boundary between Creator and creature, individual and community—God becomes all in all (1 Cor 15:28). Liturgical practices that incorporate this vision—anticipatory hymns, immersive worship environments—invite believers to live in tension between "already" indwelling and "not-yet" consummation. The Spirit's personal presence in the New Jerusalem amplifies current indwelling, assuring believers that the temple journey will reach its perfect end. This eschatological hope transitions into the reality of new-heart transformation.

2 New-Heart Reality

2.1 Prophetic Promise of Internal Law-Writing (Jer 31:33; Ezek 36:26–27)

God's covenant with Israel envisages a future when He will "put my law within them, and I will write it on their hearts" (Jer 31:33). Ezekiel expands this promise: "I will give you a new heart, and a new spirit I will put within you; I will remove your heart of stone…and I will put my Spirit within you" (Ezek 36:26–27). These prophetic passages reveal that true holiness arises from internal transformation, not external compliance. By promising new hearts and Spirit-infused desires, God ensures that obedience flows from relationship rather than obligation. Jewish midrash interpreted these texts as visions of a Messianic age, fulfilled in Christ and the outpouring at Pentecost. Christian teaching links these promises to regeneration: at conversion, the Spirit renovates the believer's moral faculties—will, mind, emotions—making them receptive to divine love. Spirit-led therapies and inner healing ministries often draw on these prophecies to facilitate lasting change. The prophetic blueprint thus guides contemporary discipleship towards cultivating Christlike affections from within. From internal law-writing, we examine how heart circumcision relates.

2.2 Circumcision of Heart versus External Ritual (Rom 2:28–29)

Paul asserts that true Jews are those "who are one inwardly"—true circumcision is "of the heart, by the Spirit" (Rom 2:28–29). He contrasts external marks—foreshadowed by Abraham's physical circumcision—with the Spirit's inward work that marks believers as God's covenant people. This inward circumcision yields genuine devotion that supersedes ritual observance. Early Christian communities debated the role of Jewish law, concluding that Spirit-circumcision inaugurates the new covenant community (Col 2:11). Spiritual practices like fasting, confession, and accountability groups function as rites that foster inner transformation. The Spirit's personal surgery on the heart ensures that moral progress is not superficial but rooted in renewed motivations. Recognizing the superiority of heart circumcision leads disciples to value authenticity over ceremony. This inner transformation naturally produces liberated affections.

2.3 Liberated Affections that Delight in God's Will (Rom 7:22; Ps 40:8)

Paul laments his struggle with sin but declares, "For I delight in the law of God, in my inner being" (Rom 7:22), expressing that the Spirit's indwelling liberates affections to relish divine precepts. This delighted obedience mirrors the psalmist's commitment: "I delight to do your will, O my God; your law is within my heart" (Ps 40:8). The Spirit-person renews desires so that God's will becomes the believer's deepest pleasure, transforming duty into joy. Spiritual formation programs incorporate *delight practices*—reframing commands as invitations, memorizing Scripture to meditate on its beauty, and journaling instances of joy in obedience. This reframing counters legalism and fosters sustainable holiness. By internalizing the law, believers find rest for their souls and purpose-driven living.

Recognizing this shift from burden to delight sets the stage for ongoing inner renewal.

2.4 Ongoing Renewal of the Inner Person Day by Day (2 Cor 4:16)

Paul contrasts the decaying outer self with the inner person which "is being renewed day by day" (2 Cor 4:16), highlighting sanctification as a daily process. The Greek *anakainōsis* suggests continual revitalization, a natural byproduct of the Spirit's residence. Practices like daily examen, breath prayers, and Scripture meditation function as channels for this renewal. Early monastic traditions—lectio divina followed by contemplative silence—modeled rhythms of inner transformation. Contemporary retreats emphasize *interoception*, cultivating bodily awareness to sense the Spirit's renewing touch. Communities that integrate morning devotionals with evening reflections often report noticeable spiritual progress. The Advocate's personal ministry ensures that believers grow incrementally, reflecting the Trinity's patient shaping of human character. Understanding sanctification as ongoing renewal prepares us to consider the deeper transformation into Christ's image.

3 Transformation into Christ's Image

3.1 "From Glory to Glory" by the Lord-Spirit (2 Cor 3:17–18)

Paul exhorts that "as we behold the glory of the Lord, we are being transformed into the same image from one degree of glory to another, which comes from the Lord who is the Spirit" (2 Cor 3:17–18). The process is dynamic: each act of gazing upon Christ—through Word, sacrament, or prayer—initiates personal metamorphosis under the Spirit's hand. The Spirit-person functions as the divine sculptor, chiseling away sin and carving Christlike features. Spiritual disciplines serve as mirrors reflecting the Lord's glory, prompting the Spirit's catalytic work. Artistic expressions—icons, worship art—also aid this beholding, engaging the imagination in transformation. Believers become ever more conformed to Christ's character, moving beyond moral improvement to ontological participation in divine life. The incremental nature of this glory-to-glory process reminds us that sanctification is both gracious gift and cooperative endeavor. As believers participate in Christ's sufferings, they experience deeper conformity.

3.2 Conforming to the Son through Participatory Suffering (Rom 8:29; Phil 3:10)

Paul states that we are "predestined to be conformed to the image of his Son" (Rom 8:29), and in Philippians he yearns to "know Christ and the power of his resurrection...sharing in his sufferings" (Phil 3:10). The Spirit-person uses suffering as a sanctifying tool, forging perseverance, character, and deeper empathy. Redemptive suffering aligns believers with Christ's journey, producing holiness not through comfort but through perseverance. Historical examples—from early martyrs to modern persecuted churches—reveal how the Spirit sustains faith and fosters maturity amid hardship. Pastoral care now integrates *trauma-informed spirituality*, acknowledging the Spirit's comforting and transformative presence in pain. By participating in Christ's sufferings, believers enter a sanctification crucible where resilience and compassion are refined. This suffering-induced conformity naturally expresses itself as Spirit-produced fruit in relationships.

3.3 Fruit of the Spirit as Christ-likeness in Relationships (Gal 5:22–23)

The nine-fold fruit—love, joy, peace, patience, kindness, goodness, faithfulness, gentleness, self-control—embodies Christ's character in community (Gal 5:22–23). The Spirit-person plants and nourishes these attributes in relational soil, ensuring that personal holiness manifests in practical virtues. Small-group exercises—role plays, accountability partnerships, service projects—provide contexts for fruit maturation. Churches that prioritize relational health often see these virtues flourish, leading to robust community care ministries and effective conflict resolution. Movements emphasizing *community sanctification* teach conflict transformation and restorative justice as expressions of Spirit fruit. This relational holiness stands as visible evidence of Christ's image within believers. The growth of fruit naturally leads believers to practice mortification and vivification.

3.4 Mortification and Vivification—Putting Off and Putting On (Col 3:5–14)

Paul commands "put to death...immorality... but now you must put them all away: anger, malice, slander, and obscene talk" (Col 3:5,8) and then exhorts, "put on...compassion, kindness, humility, meekness, and patience" (Col 3:12). Mortification (putting off) and vivification (putting on) form twin strategies of sanctification under the Spirit's direction. Spiritual disciplines—fasting, confession, and accountability—assist in mortification, helping believers identify and renounce sins that grieve the Spirit. Simultaneously, vivification practices—daily gratitude lists, service in love, corporate worship—nurture new virtues. Monastic orders traditionally combined *night offices* of repentance with *daytime works* of compassion. Contemporary discipleship models integrate digital accountability apps and service-learning, enabling continuous cycles of mortification and vivification. The Spirit-person orchestrates these cycles, ensuring balanced growth. Transitioning from character transformation, we now examine the broader dynamics of sanctification.

4 Dynamics of Sanctification

4.1 Positional Holiness at Conversion and Progressive Growth Thereafter (1 Cor 1:2; 2 Cor 7:1)

Believers are declared holy the moment they are "called to be saints" (1 Cor 1:2), receiving a positional sanctification that separates them from the world. This definitive act is rooted in the Spirit's sealing, signifying corporate membership in God's holy people. Yet Paul immediately urges believers to pursue progressive holiness: "Since we have these promises, beloved, let us cleanse ourselves…from all defilement of body and spirit, perfecting holiness in the fear of God" (2 Cor 7:1). This dynamic establishes a two-tiered sanctification: one accomplished by Christ and the Spirit irrespective of human effort, and one requiring intentional cooperation. Spiritual formation curricula therefore begin with assurance of a new identity before introducing daily growth practices. This interplay of positional and progressive sanctification ensures that believers rest in grace while diligently pursuing transformation. From this dual reality we move to the Spirit's walking guidance.

4.2 Walking, Being Led, and Keeping in Step with the Spirit (Gal 5:16–25)

Paul's three metaphors—*walk by* the Spirit, *be led by* the Spirit, and *keep in step with* the Spirit (Gal 5:16,18,25)—depict sanctification as a journey of continuous responsiveness. To *walk by* signals habitual orientation; to *be led* emphasizes directional guidance; to *keep in step* suggests dynamic coordination. Spiritual disciplines—daily devotions, prayerful planning, and Spirit-directed decision-making—equip believers for this life in motion. Retreat participants practice silent walking meditations, learning to distinguish Spirit promptings as they move. Congregations that adopt *Spirit-formed rhythms*—regular fasting days, prayer watches, service projects—align corporate life with these scriptural commands. The Advocate's personal ministry thus encompasses both the individual's pace and the community's collective rhythm. As believers walk and keep step, they avoid grieving or quenching the Spirit in their midst.

4.3 Grieving, Resisting, and Quenching—The Dangers of Relational Neglect (Eph 4:30; Acts 7:51; 1 Th 5:19)

Paul's warnings—"Do not grieve the Holy Spirit" (Eph 4:30), Stephen's accusation—"You always resist the Holy Spirit" (Acts 7:51), and Paul's command—"Do not quench the Spirit" (1 Th 5:19)—highlight relational pitfalls that stunt sanctification. Grieving arises from sin that offends the Advocate's affections; resisting involves willful disobedience to Spirit promptings; quenching denotes suppressing Spirit gifts. These relational failures create spiritual blind spots, inhibiting both personal growth and corporate vitality. Pastoral care must address neglected relationships—bitterness, unrepented sins, silenced gifts—with restorative measures. Small-group exercises such as *grief confession circles* and *gift activation workshops* help communities identify and reverse these dangers. Spiritual mentors guide individuals through repentance and restoration processes, reinvigorating sanctification. Recognizing and remedying these relational breaches ensures the Spirit's continual flourishing presence. Having addressed relational neglect, we now explore divine discipline.

4.4 Divine Discipline as Filial Training in Holiness (Heb 12:5–11)

The author of Hebrews encourages believers to endure divine discipline: "My son, do not regard lightly the discipline of the Lord… for what son is there whom his father does not discipline?" (Heb 12:5–7). This discipline, though painful at first, "yields the peaceful fruit of righteousness" (Heb 12:11). The Spirit-person administers this training for the believer's good, reflecting Fatherly love. Spiritual directors interpret life's trials through this lens, helping disciples glean lessons and cultivate perseverance. Communities support one another through *life hardship support groups*, acknowledging God's refining hand rather than attributing suffering solely to misfortune. The Spirit's personal discipline shapes character, aligning affections and actions with divine standards. Embracing discipline as filial training secures lasting holiness and readies believers for the next stage of assurance and sealing.

5 Assurance and Sealing

5.1 Spirit as ἀρραβών—Down-Payment of the Inheritance (Eph 1:13–14; 2 Cor 5:5)

The Apostle Paul introduces the concept of the Spirit as *arrhabōn*, a down-payment guaranteeing the full inheritance yet to come (Eph 1:13–14). This metaphor echoes ancient Near Eastern practices, where a first installment assured the promise of greater wealth. In Pauline theology, the Spirit's indwelling presence is this first installment, assuring believers of their future resurrection and glorification. The Spirit's personal agency in sealing believers thus provides both present empowerment and future hope. Early church fathers—such as Augustine—explained that this heavenly pledge grants confidence amid trial, transforming fear into expectancy. The down-payment also secures community unity: all who share the Spirit share the inheritance, dissolving ethnic and social barriers (Gal 3:28; Col 3:11). Spirit-driven hope influences ethics: knowing that ultimate redemption is guaranteed inspires sacrificial generosity (2 Cor 8:14–15). The Spirit's seal marks believers as God's property, protecting them against spiritual theft by false gospels (2 Pet 2:1). Liturgically, confirmation rites in many traditions invoke the Spirit's sealing, uniting sacrament with Pauline promise. Pastors teach that this assurance is not a license for sin but a motivation for holiness, since believers belong irrevocably to Christ. Psychological ministries draw on the down-payment motif to foster spiritual resilience in suffering and loss. The *arrhabōn* thus anchors the Christian life in the Spirit's personal guarantee, sustaining faith through every season.

5.2 Witness with Our Spirit That We Are God's Children (Rom 8:16)

Paul writes that "the Spirit himself bears witness with our spirit that we are children of God" (Rom 8:16), depicting a synergistic testimony between the Advocate and our inner being. This internal witness is not merely emotional affirmation but cognitive-affective confirmation: the Spirit communicates divine identity to our deepest consciousness. Augustine interprets this as an inner echo of baptismal regeneration, where the Spirit's voice resonates in the soul. Spiritual formation practices—such as guided meditation on adoption texts—help believers tune their inner awareness to this witness. The *sumphōnia* (symphony) of Spirit and spirit silences doubt, offering immediate assurance beyond external proof. In pastoral counseling, this testimony is cited to counter impostor syndrome and spiritual anxiety. Communities cultivate this witness collectively through testimonies, where personal stories confirm the Spirit's work in diverse lives. The Spirit's personal bearing of witness also frames corporate liturgies: affirmations of faith and recitals of baptismal vows internalize this testimony. Psychological studies of religious experience acknowledge that inner conviction often correlates with long-term spiritual stability. The Spirit's witness precedes and sustains the believer's own confidence, enabling perseverance in uncertainty. By engaging both mind and heart, this ministry fosters holistic assurance.

5.3 Cry of "Abba, Father" Replacing Slavish Fear (Gal 4:6; Rom 8:15)

Paul contrasts a spirit of slavery with a spirit of adoption, enabling believers to cry *"Abba! Father!"* (Rom 8:15; Gal 4:6). The Aramaic *Abba* conveys intimate childlike address, signifying relational closeness rather than ritual formality. The Spirit's personal ministry transforms worshipers from timid servants into beloved children, uprooting fear-based obedience. Patristic commentators—Cyril of Jerusalem among them—note that this cry emerges spontaneously, evidencing genuine transformation rather than formulaic prayer. Contemporary spiritual disciplines encourage incorporating *Abba* into daily breath prayers, fostering immediate remembrance of the Spirit's adoption work. This cry shapes ethics: filial love motivates sacrificial service, contrasting with legalistic dread. In community settings, encouragement to share *Abba* prayers in small groups builds mutual vulnerability and trust. The Spirit's personal promptings to cry *Abba* interrupt anxious thought patterns, replacing them with relational confidence. This divine filial address also empowers believers to intercede boldly, knowing they stand before a loving Father. The transformation from slavish fear to filial boldness exemplifies the Spirit's sanctifying impact on identity.

5.4 Perseverance Empowered by Spirit-Borne Hope That Never Shames (Rom 5:5; 15:13)

Paul prays that "the God of hope fill you with all joy and peace in believing, so that by the power of the Holy Spirit you may abound in hope" (Rom 15:13). This triadic blessing connects the Spirit with enduring hope that "does not put us to shame" (Rom 5:5). The Advocate's personal indwelling sustains believers through trials, enabling joy and peace that defy circumstances. Early monastics spoke of the Spirit as the "comforter of sorrows," whose presence prevents shame in suffering. Spiritual direction draws on this promise to instill long-term endurance strategies—journaling answered prayers, communal lament, and renewal retreats. Psychological resilience frameworks parallel this: hope anchored in a reliable divine presence yields mental and spiritual well-being. In corporate worship, songs that proclaim Spirit-given hope foster communal courage, equipping congregations to navigate crises. The Spirit's sealing and witness converge here, as assurance fuels hope and hope reinforces assurance. This Spirit-borne hope thus functions as both anchor and sail, stabilizing belief and propelling mission.

6 Holiness Expressed Ethically

6.1 Sexual Integrity as Temple Stewardship (1 Th 4:3–8; 1 Cor 6:13–18)

Paul commands Thessalonians to abstain from sexual immorality, "for God has not called us for impurity but in holiness" (1 Th 4:3), and warns Corinthians that "your bodies are members of Christ…flee from sexual immorality" (1 Cor 6:15–18). Interpreting sexual integrity as stewardship of the Spirit-temple reframes chastity not as punitive prohibition but as protective care. The Advocate's personal indwelling makes self-control an act of love toward God and neighbor. Early church councils—e.g., Council of Elvira—issued strict canons against clergy immorality, reflecting Spirit-sanctified standards. Modern pastoral programs teach *smart chastity* and relational boundaries, integrating neurological research on habit formation with spiritual accountability. Retreats such as *Pure Desire* use Spirit-focused prayer to address deep-rooted affections, fostering renewal. Sexual ethics under Spirit-sanctification also impact congregational culture: open dialogue, recovery groups, and healing liturgies reunite broken individuals to community and Spirit. The Spirit's personal ministry thus transforms bodies from objects of desire into vessels of holiness. This sexual stewardship prepares believers for economic justice and generosity.

6.2 Economic Justice and Generosity Energized by the Spirit (Acts 4:31–35; 2 Cor 8:1–5)

After Peter's bold Spirit-filled speech, "they were all filled with the Holy Spirit and continued to speak the word of God" (Acts 4:31), and the early church "had all things in common" (Acts 4:32), selling possessions to meet one another's needs (Acts 4:34–35). Paul praises Macedonian churches for "overflowing joy and extreme poverty, wel did their abounding generosity abound in the riches of their liberality" (2 Cor 8:2–3). The Spirit's interior presence compels

215

ethical stewardship of resources, linking holiness with social justice. Historical monastic communities—like the Pachomians—practiced common purse, reflecting Spirit-driven generosity. Contemporary initiatives—community land trusts, microfinance in partnership with local churches—draw on Spirit-inspired communal models. Hospitality ministries and benevolence funds structure generosity as normative for Spirit-indwelt communities. Ethical frameworks taught in seminaries now incorporate Spirit empowerment as motive for economic justice. By interpreting wealth through Spirit sanctification, societies can address systemic poverty with compassionate participation. This Spirit-fueled generosity naturally extends into sanctified speech.

6.3 Speech Sanctified—Truth, Edification, and Gratitude (Eph 4:25–32; 5:18–20)

Paul exhorts believers to "put away falsehood…let each one speak the truth…be angry and do not sin…let no corrupting talk come out of your mouths, but only such as is good for edification" (Eph 4:25–29). He further commands to be "filled with the Spirit…addressing one another in psalms and hymns and spiritual songs" (Eph 5:18–19). The Advocate's interior presence governs both content and tone of speech. Spiritual formation workshops on *wholeness in speech* teach *breath praying* before speaking to ensure Spirit alignment. Restorative justice frameworks train congregations to use language that builds up rather than injures. Small-group norms—such as 'no gossip' covenants—create environments where Spirit's sanctification transforms conversation. Theological reflection on *the logos* as both Christ and Spirit-empowered word underscores speech's sacredness. Ethical diction in business and politics, under Spirit influence, fosters credibility and trust. The Spirit's personal ministry thus extends to every utterance, equipping believers to communicate with grace. This sanctified speech leads into the reconciling love embodied in community.

6.4 Reconciling Love that Embodies the Law of Christ (Gal 6:2; Col 3:12–15)

Paul commands, "Bear one another's burdens, and so fulfill the law of Christ" (Gal 6:2), and calls believers to put on "compassion, kindness, humility, meekness, and patience" and to let "the peace of Christ rule in your hearts" (Col 3:12–15). The Advocate's interior affections manifest ethically as reconciliation and forgiveness. Reconciliation ministries—such as *Peacemakers* training based on

Matt 18:15–17—equip participants to practice Spirit-led conflict resolution. Pastoral counseling integrates *Inner Healing* models to release resentment and foster empathy. Congregations implementing *restorative circles* experience the Spirit's transforming presence in real-time forgiveness. In marriage enrichment programs, Spirit-guided exercises on bearing burdens strengthen relational resilience. Community reconciliation initiatives partner churches across racial and socioeconomic lines, embodying Christ's reconciling love. The Spirit's personal indwelling thus turns doctrinal principles into living virtues that bind communities in holiness and justice, setting the stage for charisms that build up body.

7 Charisms for Edification and Growth

7.1 Gifts Distributed for the Common Good "as the Spirit Wills" (1 Cor 12:4–11)

Paul acknowledges one Spirit but "varieties of gifts...distributions of service...varieties of activities"—"all these are empowered by one and the same Spirit, who apportions to each one individually as he wills" (1 Cor 12:4–6,11). The Greek *as he wills* (*hos thelē*) affirms divine sovereignty and personal discernment in gift allocation. The Advocate's will governs the distribution of gifts—prophecy, healing, teaching, administration—for communal edification. Spiritual gift inventories in many churches begin with prayerful discernment, seeking confirmation rather than self-selection. Leaders train members to recognize gift promptings, ensuring that service aligns with Spirit's personal assignment. Historical mission orders—Franciscans, Jesuits—emphasized charism integration with communal needs. Communities that practice *gift circles*—regular meetings to share gift experiences—learn to harness the Spirit's will rather than institutional agendas. This Spirit-driven gifting fosters holistic maturity, leading into the mechanisms of mutual ministry.

7.2 Mutual Ministry Producing Maturity and Doctrinal Stability (Eph 4:11–16)

Paul describes gifts—apostles, prophets, evangelists, pastors, teachers—given "to equip the saints for the work of ministry, for building up the body of Christ, until we all attain...mature manhood" (Eph 4:11–13). The Advocate's personal allocation of these gifts ensures both doctrinal continuity and spiritual growth. Apostles establish foundations; prophets guard truth; evangelists expand outreach; pastors nurture; teachers clarify doctrine. This mutual ministry prevents both charismatic excess and doctrinal drift. Seminary programs now emphasize *team-based ministry models* combining these roles under Spirit supervision. Congregations implement *equipping schools* to involve laypeople in teaching and pastoral care. Regular doctrinal reviews by elders safeguard orthodoxy while leaving space for Spirit innovation. The synergistic interplay of diverse ministries under the Advocate's will produces stability and maturity. Understanding this pattern naturally leads to the ordering of gifts in gathered worship.

7.3 Discernment and Ordering of Gifts in Gathered Worship (1 Cor 14:26–33)

Paul instructs, "When you come together, each one has a hymn, a lesson, a revelation, a tongue, or an interpretation. Let all things be done for building up" (1 Cor 14:26). The Spirit-distributed gifts require communal discernment and ordering to prevent confusion. Modern worship teams use *service flow charts* that anticipate prophetic words, musical offerings, and teaching segments, allowing spontaneous input under pastoral oversight. Training in prophetic etiquette and interpretation guidelines ensures that Spirit gifts edify rather than disrupt. Role rotations and debrief sessions help communities reflect on how the Advocate's personal initiatives manifested in gatherings. Historical worship manuals—such as those of Hippolytus—provide templates for ordered charism use. This disciplined openness fosters environments where the Spirit can move freely yet constructively. Effective gift ordering thus strengthens corporate sanctification and transition to a balanced gift ecosystem.

7.4 Balance of Power-Gifts and Service-Gifts in Holistic Sanctification (Rom 12:6–8; 1 Pet 4:10–11)

Paul instructs, "Having gifts that differ according to the grace given to us, let us use them…he who prophecies, in proportion to his faith; he who serves, in his serving…" (Rom 12:6–7). Peter exhorts, "As each has received a gift, use it to serve one another…whoever speaks…as one who speaks the oracles of God; whoever serves…as one who serves by the strength that God supplies" (1 Pet 4:10–11). The Advocate ensures that power-gifts—miracles, healings, prophecy—are balanced by service-gifts—helps, administration, hospitality—avoiding charismatic imbalance. Churches that integrate *service gift tracks* alongside *power gift forums* cultivate both the spectacular and the mundane aspects of Spirit sanctification. Leadership pipelines encourage gift diversity, preventing gifted but untrained individuals from skewing community focus. Training programs combine theological instruction with practical apprenticeship, ensuring that power-gifts serve the body's needs rather than personal agendas. This balanced gift ecosystem epitomizes holistic sanctification, demonstrating the Spirit's comprehensive personal ministry.

8 Corporate Sanctification Practices

8.1 Baptism as Initiatory Participation in the Spirit's Body (1 Cor 12:13)

Paul affirms, "For in one Spirit we were all baptized into one body" (1 Cor 12:13), indicating that baptism not only initiates individual conversion but incorporates believers into the Spirit-wrought community of Christ. This sacramental participation is the foundational act of corporate sanctification, uniting diverse members under one Spirit. Historical baptismal liturgies—catechumenate processes of the early church—provided extended instruction and spiritual formation before immersion, ensuring that baptismal candidates understood the Spirit's communal implications. Contemporary baptism services often include corporate vows and baptismal sponsors, highlighting the collective responsibility for ongoing sanctification. The Spirit's personal involvement in baptism underscores both individual regeneration and communal identity, setting the tone for further practices such as the Eucharist.

8.2 Eucharistic Communion and the Spirit's Real Presence (1 Cor 10:16)

Paul describes the cup as "the participation in the blood of Christ," and the bread as "the participation in the body of Christ" (1 Cor 10:16), affirming that the Spirit-person actualizes Christ's presence in the elements. This sacramental real presence confirms that the church's holiness is grounded in Spirit-mediated communion. Early church fathers—Ignatius of Antioch, Justin Martyr—emphasize the Spirit's invocation (epiclesis) in transforming the gifts and uniting the congregation to Christ. Modern liturgical renewal movements integrate both the Word and Spirit in Eucharistic rites, ensuring that elements become conduits of sanctification. Trans-denominational dialogues on the Spirit's role in the Sacrament reinforce that the Eucharist remains a primary means of grace for corporate holiness. By regularly partaking, believers experience both forgiveness and empowerment for holy living. Recognizing the Spirit's personal presence in communion leads us to communal rhythms of confession and discipline.

8.3 Confession, Admonition, and Restorative Discipline (Jas 5:16; Matt 18:15–20)

James urges, "Confess your sins to one another and pray for one another…that you may be healed" (Jas 5:16), and Jesus outlines a process for church discipline leading to reconciliation (Matt 18:15–20). The Spirit's interior presence guides both personal confession and corporate admonition, ensuring that discipline is restorative rather than punitive. Churches that incorporate *penitential liturgies* provide space for communal accountability under Spirit-led grace. Training in *restorative justice circles* helps members practice confession and forgiveness in structured contexts. Admonition by peers, when guided by the Advocate's wisdom, heals divisions and cultivates mutual care. The Spirit's personal ministry thus orchestrates cycles of confession, discipline, and restoration, reinforcing corporate holiness.

8.4 Communal Rhythms of Scripture, Prayer, and Praise Fostering Shared Holiness (Col 3:16–17; Acts 2:42–47)

Paul urges, "Let the word of Christ dwell in you richly…singing psalms and hymns and spiritual songs, with thankfulness in your hearts to God" (Col 3:16), and Luke describes the early church devoted to teaching, fellowship, breaking of bread, and prayer (Acts 2:42). These rhythms—Scripture exposition, communal prayer, sacramental meals, and joyful praise—function as daily corporate sanctification practices under the Spirit's personal leadership. Historical monastic schedules—*horarium*—structured these activities at set hours, fostering disciplined community life. Contemporary congregations implement *church at home* rhythms—daily Bible readings via technology, midweek prayer gatherings, weekend worship services—to maintain shared holiness. Small groups that follow the *Acts 2 model* report stronger relational bonds and spiritual vitality. By aligning communal life with Spirit-led rhythms, the church experiences continuous formation in unity and love.

9 Eschatological Consummation

9.1 Firstfruits of Resurrection Life in Present Groaning (Rom 8:23)

Paul describes believers as "those who have the firstfruits of the Spirit" (Rom 8:23), invoking the Levitical festival of firstfruits (Lev 23:9–14) to illustrate present taste of future glory. The Spirit-person, as the down-payment, imbues Christians with resurrection life now, creating an anticipatory groaning that echoes creation's "eager longing" (Rom 8:19). This groan is not mere lament but Spirit-enabled hope that transforms suffering into expectant prayer. Early Christian writings—such as 1 Clement and the Didache—affirm the Spirit's firstfruits as the basis for holy living amid persecution. Liturgies on Easter vigil celebrate this firstfruits motif, emphasizing that the same Spirit who raised Christ dwells in believers already. Modern spiritual retreats incorporate *resurrection meditations*, inviting participants to sense firstfruits power. The Spirit's personal guarantee through firstfruits unites individual renewal with cosmic redemption. This dynamic hope propels ethical persistence, seamlessly leading into the reality of Spirit-raised bodies.

9.2 Spirit-Raised Bodies and Incorruptible Glory (Rom 8:11; 1 Cor 15:44–49)

Paul affirms, "If the Spirit of him who raised Jesus from the dead dwells in you, he who raised Christ...will also give life to your mortal bodies" (Rom 8:11). The Spirit's resurrection power extends to mortal flesh, promising incorruptible glory. In 1 Cor 15, Paul contrasts natural bodies with spiritual bodies, declaring that "flesh and blood cannot inherit the kingdom of God" but "we shall all be changed" (1 Cor 15:50,52). The Spirit-person thus transforms corporeality, preparing believers for eternal embodiment. Patristic homilies—especially by Gregory of Nyssa—meditate on the resurrection body's beauty wrought by the Advocate. Contemporary theology engages biotechnology ethics in light of Spirit-guaranteed resurrection, affirming dignity of bodies as future temples. Witnesses of near-death experiences often report luminous bodies, which theologians cautiously interpret as anticipatory glimpses of Spirit-formed glory. Liturgical art and iconography depict believers clothed in light, symbolizing the Spirit's work. This assurance of Spirit-raised bodies informs present stewardship of health and ethics regarding end-of-life care. From individual resurrection we turn to creation's liberation.

9.3 Creation's Liberation through Spirit-Filled Sons and Daughters (Rom 8:19–22)

Paul broadens the scope of redemption: "Creation waits with eager longing for the revealing of the sons of God...creature itself will be set free from its bondage to corruption" (Rom 8:19–21). The Spirit-person, poured out on believers, inaugurates cosmic liberation as "sons and daughters" manifest God's kingdom. Creation's groaning (Rom 8:22) joins human groaning (8:23), uniting all in the Spirit's redemptive work. Early Christian cosmology linked this to Genesis's curse (Gen 3:17–19) and envisioned Spirit-animated restoration of land, flora, and fauna. Modern ecological theology, inspired by this text, advocates for *creation care*, seeing environmental stewardship as Spirit-empowered mission. Worship services that include prayers for the earth reflect this cosmic consciousness. Scientific dialogues on climate justice sometimes integrate Spirit-based hope for creation's renewal. The Spirit's personal ministry thus extends beyond human hearts into the renewal of all creation, culminating in the New Jerusalem's vision. This cosmic hope prepares the church for unmediated communion with God.

9.4 Vision of God: Unmediated Fellowship in the Spirit's Light (Rev 22:1–5)

John's final vision portrays the river of life flowing from God's throne, with the "tree of life" yielding healing fruit, and "no night" because "the Lord God will be their light, and they will reign forever and ever" (Rev 22:1–5). The Spirit's personal presence transforms believers into living lamps reflecting God's glory directly, removing all mediation. This unmediated fellowship embodies the temple motif's consummation: God and the Lamb dwell with humanity (Rev 21:3), and the Spirit's light illuminates all. Patristic expositions by Augustine and Gregory the Theologian describe this vision as the apex of sanctification where the Advocate's indwelling reaches its fullest expression. Contemporary worship movements incorporate *candlelight vigils* and *immersive light installations* to symbolize the Spirit's illuminating presence. Theologically, this vision grounds eschatological preaching and shapes Christian ethos—living now as citizens of the city where darkness cannot fall. The unending reign in Spirit's light seamlessly transitions into practical pathways for sustaining such indwelling presence.

10 Pastoral Pathways for Hosting the Spirit

10.1 Practices of Vigilance: Examen, Breath Prayers, and Yielding Moments

Hosting the Spirit requires vigilant attention to His personal promptings. The *Examen*—a daily review of conscience originated by

Ignatius Loyola—guides believers to notice moments of consolation and desolation, attributing them to Spirit or self. Breath prayers—short invocations such as "Spirit, teach me"—integrate Spirit-awareness into everyday tasks. Christian mentors teach *yielding moments*—intentional pauses before decisions to invite the Advocate's guidance. Monastic vigils, held during the night office, historically trained monks to discern Spirit stirrings in quiet hours. Contemporary pastors adapt these practices in workplace chaplaincy, encouraging professionals to scan their commitments for Spirit-led adjustments. Counseling frameworks incorporate mindful spiritual attentiveness as tools for emotional resilience. By cultivating practices of vigilance, the church ensures the Spirit's continuous indwelling moves from passive possession to active partnership. These attentiveness practices naturally extend into hospitality for the Spirit in communal space.

10.2 Hospitality to the Spirit in Liturgical Space and Daily Routines

Creating hospitable environments for the Spirit involves both architectural design and liturgical intentionality. Worship spaces feature *breathing walls*, contemplative gardens, and interactive prayer stations that invite spontaneous engagement. Ancient basilicas oriented east–west signaled expectation of Christ's coming light; modern sanctuaries incorporate *light streams* and *soundscapes* fostering Spirit-attuned worship. Daily routines such as *morning blessings* over workstations and *table prayers* before meals acknowledge the Advocate's presence. Pastoral teams train congregants in *spiritual hospitality*—welcoming Spirit-driven visitors, discerning prophecies, and practicing nonjudgmental listening. Life rites—baptisms, weddings, funerals—are rituals of Spirit hospitality, marking thresholds with prayers invoking the Advocate's presence. By fostering these hospitable spaces—both sacred and secular—the church models indwelling as relational intimacy rather than transactional proximity. This hospitality paves the way for spiritual accompaniment and healing ministries.

10.3 Spiritual Accompaniment—Mentoring Believers in Spirit Awareness

Spiritual accompaniment—rooted in Ignatian *spiritual direction*—pairs experienced guides with seekers to track Spirit movements in life narratives. Directors listen for Spirit themes in scripture reflections, dreams, and daily experiences, guiding directees into deeper awareness. Training programs certify directors in *Spirit discernment* techniques, ensuring ethical and theologically sound accompaniment. Communities establish *direction circles* where multiple companions offer collective listening under Spirit guidance. Research in pastoral psychology correlates accompaniment with improved spiritual health and decreased anxiety. Seminary curricula now include supervised practicums in spiritual direction, integrating humanistic counseling with pneumatology. This mentoring fosters lifelong growth in Spirit awareness, bridging indwelling presence with personal transformation. From accompaniment we move to counseling and healing prayer.

10.4 Counseling and Healing Prayer that Cooperate with the Sanctifier

Pastoral counseling integrates *inner healing prayer* frameworks, inviting the Spirit to address deep wounds such as betrayal trauma, identity crises, and spiritual oppression. Trained prayer ministers lead individuals through guided dialogues, lifting burdens into the Advocate's compassionate presence. Ministries like *Healing Rooms* combine biblical anointing, confession, and Spirit-led proclamation of freedom. Clinical pastoral education programs incorporate Spirit-cooperative interventions alongside psychological models, ensuring holistic care. Biblical counselors instruct on the Spirit's role in renewing mindsets (Rom 12:2) and overcoming strongholds. Congregations host *prayer-walking* events, inviting the Spirit's healing over neighborhoods. By partnering with the Spirit in counseling and healing prayer, the church embodies sanctification's personal and communal dimensions.

Conclusion Chapter 10 has charted the Spirit's interior presence, revealing how indwelling fulfills temple patterns, writes God's law on hearts, and fashions Christlike character through ongoing renewal and trial. We have seen that positional sanctification and progressive growth intertwine, assured by the Spirit's sealing work, and realized through ethical expressions, charisms, and communal practices. By hosting the Advocate within bodies and assemblies, believers participate in God's own life, anticipating the fullness of new creation. As we move into Chapter 11, we will examine how the Spirit's gifting of believers for mission—the distribution of charisms—continues this sanctifying journey, empowering the church's growth and unity in the unfolding of redemptive history.

Chapter 11. Gifts, Callings, and Empowerment for Mission

The diverse gifts and callings bestowed by the Spirit constitute the engine of the church's mission, equipping every believer for participation in God's redemptive purposes. These charisms—ranging from teaching and mercy to healing and leadership—reflect the Trinity's generous nature, the Son's victorious purchase, and the Spirit's sovereign distribution. As we explore why gifts are given and how they are organized, we will see that they mirror the Body's unity-in-diversity, continue Christ's ministerial work, and foster mutual love and maturity. Grasping these principles provides a robust framework for discerning personal callings, deploying ministries wisely, and ensuring that the entire church advances the gospel effectively in every context.

1 Foundation: Why the Spirit Gives Gifts

1.1 Manifesting the Body's Unity-in-Diversity (1 Cor 12:4–7)

Paul emphasizes that though there are "diversities of gifts, the same Spirit," and "diversities of service, the same Lord," each believer is endowed with a gift "for the common good" (1 Cor 12:4–7). This divine arrangement manifests the body's structural unity: just as a human body comprises many parts with distinct functions, so the church flourishes when every member employs his or her unique gift. The Spirit distributes charismata not according to merit or preference but "as He wills," underscoring God's personal oversight. These gifts function in concert—no gift is self-sufficient, and no member is dispensable—so that the community testifies to Christ's incarnational solidarity. Early church councils drew on this analogy to structure episcopal, presbyterial, and diaconal ministries in proportion to needs. In contemporary congregations, gift inventories followed by communal affirmation ensure that members discern Spirit-led callings rather than pursue programmatic agendas. Ministries that neglect the Body metaphor risk elevating certain gifts at the expense of others, resulting in imbalance and disunity. When gifts operate in mutual support, the church embodies the relational perichoresis of the Trinity, demonstrating to the world the beauty of cooperative diversity under one Spirit. Recognizing this foundational purpose shapes our engagement with every subsequent gift category and call.

1.2 Continuing Jesus' Works through His Corporate Body (John 14:12; Acts 1:1–2)

Jesus promised, "Whoever believes in Me, the works that I do he will do also; and greater works than these he will do" (John 14:12). This assurance establishes a continuity: Christ's healing, teaching, and deliverance persist through His followers by the Spirit's empowering presence. In Acts 1:1–2, Luke recounts that the risen Jesus "presented Himself alive…by many infallible proofs, being seen by the apostles during forty days and speaking of the things pertaining to the kingdom of God." He then charged them not merely to remember His words but to share His Spirit-enabled ministry. This commission inaugurated the church's mission era, during which signs and wonders authenticated apostolic proclamation (Acts 4:30; 5:12). Christian communities, therefore, see their ministries—whether healing, exorcism, or teaching—as direct extensions of Jesus' own works, performed by His Body under Spirit guidance. Seminary curricula on spiritual gifts underscore the historical continuity of charismatic ministry from the first Christians to today. Ignoring this continuity relegates gifts to antiquarian fascination, rather than recognizing them as vital means for kingdom expansion. By embracing Spirit-empowered works, the church remains faithful to Christ's promise and practice, advancing His healing and justice into every sphere of society. This continuation naturally arises from the Trinity's generous outpouring.

1.3 Expressing Trinitarian Generosity—The Father's Promise, the Son's Purchase, the Spirit's Distribution

The Spirit's gifting flow traces back to the Father's promise and the Son's atoning purchase: the Father "will give you another Helper" (John 14:16), and Christ "gave Himself for us" so that "the promise of the Spirit...the gift of God" might be shared with all (Gal 3:14; Eph 4:7). In this economy, the Father initiates by promising, the Son secures by sacrifice, and the Spirit lavishly distributes charismata. This Trinitarian generosity underscores that gifts are not human achievements but divine endowments bestowed freely. Patristic writers likened the Spirit's distribution of gifts to the outpouring of streams from a fountain—ever abundant and life-giving. The Spirit's sovereignty in distribution prevents competition or hoarding; each gift emerges at God's appointed time and place. Liturgical prayers often echo this generosity, invoking the Spirit to grant "wisdom, understanding, counsel, fortitude, knowledge, piety, and fear of the Lord." Modern philanthropic expressions—church-based scholarship funds, community grant initiatives—reflect this divine pattern of giving, modeling the Spirit's abundance. By framing gift distribution as Trinitarian generosity, the church fosters gratitude and humility among recipients, encouraging stewardship rather than entitlement. This gracious economy grounds the gifts' purpose: cultivating love, maturity, and mission.

1.4 Cultivating Mutual Love, Maturity, and Mission (Eph 4:12–16)

Paul envisions that Christ gave "the apostles, the prophets, the evangelists, the shepherds and teachers, to equip the saints for the work of ministry, for building up the body of Christ" until all reach unity in faith and knowledge (Eph 4:11–13). This equipping produces mutual love, maturity, and effective mission: "We are no longer children...but speaking the truth in love, we are to grow up in every way into Him who is the head" (Eph 4:14–15). The Advocate's personal involvement ensures that gifted ministries do more than perform tasks; they shape character and unity. The synergy between diverse ministries fosters doctrinal stability—guards against false teaching—and communal flourishing—enhances relational depth. Mission arises naturally as mature believers, equipped in love, extend service beyond the church's walls. Contemporary training programs integrate theological education with community service, reflecting this Ephesian framework. Metrics for ministry effectiveness now include witness impact and relational health, not merely attendance or budget. By linking gifts to love, maturity, and mission, the Spirit's charismata become holistic catalysts for kingdom transformation. Understanding this multifaceted purpose leads us to map New-Testament gift lists in detail.

2 Mapping the New-Testament Gift Lists

2.1 Romans 12:6–8—Motivational Gifts and Everyday Service

In Romans 12 Paul introduces motivational gifts—*prophecy, service, teaching, exhortation, giving, leadership, mercy*—and urges, "Let him use it in proportion to his faith" (Rom 12:6–8). These gifts hinge on inner motivations: prophecy flows from faith, service from diligence, teaching from understanding, and mercy from cheerfulness. The Spirit's personal insight into each believer's temperament and capacity ensures that gifts align with natural inclinations and divine enabling. Unlike extraordinary manifestations, these motivational gifts undergird everyday service—small group leadership, hospitality, financial generosity, pastoral care—forming the backbone of congregational life. Early house churches depended heavily on these gifts to meet practical needs. Modern churches that emphasize service pathways—volunteer sign-ups matched with spiritual gifts assessments—see increased volunteer retention and satisfaction. Training sessions on *motivational gift activation* teach believers to identify and deploy their gift in daily contexts, such as workplace witness and neighborhood outreach. Integrating motivational gifts into daily routines fosters a culture where service becomes second nature, demonstrating the Spirit's personal empowerment for ordinary sanctification. This section frames our understanding of manifestation gifts that surface in gathered worship.

2.2 1 Corinthians 12:8–10—Manifestation Gifts for Gathered Worship

Paul lists manifestation gifts—*word of wisdom, word of knowledge, faith, gifts of healing, working of miracles, prophecy, discernment of spirits, tongues, interpretation of tongues*—and notes that all these are "worked by one and the same Spirit" (1 Cor 12:8–10). These extraordinary gifts are visible signs of the Spirit's direct intervention in communal gatherings, serving to authenticate the gospel and edify the church. The word of wisdom offers divinely inspired insight for complex situations; word of knowledge conveys supernatural awareness of hidden realities; faith ignites bold trust for extraordinary deeds; healing and miracles tangibly demonstrate God's reign. Prophecy and discernment maintain doctrinal purity, while tongues and their interpretation facilitate universal praise and personal edification. Early Corinthian abuses—unregulated tongues—prompted Paul's corrective teaching on order (1 Cor 14). Contemporary charismatic congregations implement *gift protocols*—volunteer chapels designated for prophecy, interpretation, and healing prayer—to harness these gifts responsibly. Training in *miracle guidelines* and *prophetic mentoring* helps ensure that manifestation gifts build up the community rather than provoke confusion. Understanding the Spirit's personal distribution of these gifts prepares us to survey ministry offices and functions.

2.3 1 Corinthians 12:28—Ministry Offices and Community Functions

In the same chapter, Paul outlines a hierarchy of roles: "God has appointed...first apostles, second prophets, third teachers, then miracles, then gifts of healings, helps, administrations, various kinds of tongues" (1 Cor 12:28). These offices—apostles, prophets, teachers—carry community functions beyond gifting: apostles pioneer and lay foundations; prophets guard covenantal direction; teachers cultivate deep theological understanding. The secondary list of miracles, healings, helps, administrations, tongues reflects both charismatic and service functions essential to church health. The Advocate's personal commissioning of these offices ensures that leaders possess both spiritual gifting and divine endorsement. Early church structures—the pentarchy model, monastic orders—drew on Paul's listing to organize missionary and pastoral networks. Modern denominations continue to wrestle with apostolic identity, prophetic authority, and administrative structures in light of this text. Leadership training programs now integrate *apostolic praxis*, *prophetic oversight*, and *administrative stewardship* under Spirit supervision. Recognizing the interplay of offices and gifts helps churches allocate resources and responsibilities effectively, setting the stage for the distinct equipping vocations of Ephesians 4.

2.4 Ephesians 4:11—"Five-Fold" Equipping Vocations

Paul identifies five equipping vocations—*apostles, prophets, evangelists, shepherds, and teachers*—given "to equip the saints for the work of ministry" (Eph 4:11–12). This five-fold model emphasizes that equipping vocations function within an interdependent economy: apostles ensure faithfulness to mission; prophets provide ongoing revelation and direction; evangelists catalyze new commitments; shepherds tend and protect congregations; teachers deepen understanding of Scripture. The Spirit's personal empowerment undergirds each vocation, granting both the necessary gifting and spiritual authority. Historical church movements—such as Wesleyan societies—employed itinerant evangelists alongside local pastors and teachers, reflecting this model. Contemporary church-planting coalitions apply the five-fold framework to develop leadership pipelines, ensuring that new congregations have apostolic vision, prophetic counsel, evangelistic zeal, pastoral care, and instructional clarity. Seminary curricula incorporate *five-fold ministry modules*, training students in each distinct vocation under Spirit mentorship. By mapping these gift lists, we appreciate the comprehensive equipping machinery the Spirit employs for bodybuilding and mission, leading us naturally into specific speaking gifts.

3 Speaking Gifts: Communicating God's Heart

3.1 Prophecy—Forthtelling, Not Fortune-Telling (1 Cor 14:1–5)

Paul exhorts, "Pursue love...and earnestly desire the spiritual gifts, especially that you may prophesy" (1 Cor 14:1), clarifying that biblical prophecy serves edification rather than predicting the lottery. Prophecy in the New Testament primarily means *forthtelling*—Spirit-inspired declaration of divine truth, exhortation, and consolation. The prophet stands alongside Scripture, articulating God's current word for a congregation's situation (Acts 11:28; 13:1). Early church orders required prophets to submit messages to apostolic oversight, safeguarding doctrinal consistency. Contemporary prophetic ministries distinguish *corporate prophecy*—words directed to the whole assembly—from *personal prophecy*—words addressed to individuals—both requiring interpretation by recognized elders. Training in *prophetic listening* teaches participants to discern tone, content, and timing under the Advocate's guidance. Prophecy's primary aim is building up the church (1 Cor 14:3), revealing God's heart in matters of justice, faith, and communal direction. Misuse—presuming to foretell private futures—undermines credibility and grieves the Spirit. Responsible prophetic practice thus remains a vital conduit for the Spirit's personal communication, transitioning us to tongues and interpretation.

3.2 Tongues and Interpretation—Sign and Edification (1 Cor 14:26–28)

Paul instructs that "if any speak in a tongue, let there be only two or at most three...and each in turn, and let someone interpret" (1 Cor

14:27). Tongues function as both personal prayer (1 Cor 14:14) and corporate sign, especially to unbelievers (1 Cor 14:22). The Advocate uses tongues to bypass linguistic barriers, conveying spirit-level intercession that builds up the speaker (1 Cor 14:14–17). Interpretation, when Spirit-enabled, renders the message intelligible to the assembly, aligning tongues with prophecy in service of edification (1 Cor 14:5,12). Early church liturgies often included periods of tongues followed by prophetic interpretation, ensuring orderly worship. Modern charismatic gatherings employ *interpretation teams*, rotating roles under pastoral oversight to maintain balance. Training sessions on *discerning interpretation* cover biblical criteria— accuracy to Scripture, consonance with previous revelation, pastoral benefit. Properly practiced, tongues and interpretation exemplify the Spirit's personal ministry in enabling both personal intimacy with God and mutual building up, preparing us to consider teaching and exhortation next.

3.3 Teaching and Exhortation—Spirit-Illuminated Scripture Delivery (Rom 12:7; Acts 11:23)

Teaching and exhortation serve as twin speaking gifts: teaching expounds doctrine, while exhortation applies truth to stir obedience and encouragement. Paul lists teaching among motivational gifts (Rom 12:7), and in Acts 11:23 the church in Antioch is commended for teaching with "all steadfastness, for the Lord was with them." The Advocate as Teacher illuminates Scripture's depth (1 Cor 2:10–13), equipping teachers to articulate theological insights and moral applications. Exhorters, often emerging from prophetic gifting, challenge the community toward repentance, faith, and love (Acts 14:22). Early catechetical schools—such as those in Alexandria— blended teaching and exhortation under Spirit guidance, training new converts. Contemporary seminaries emphasize *Spirit-empowered pedagogy*, encouraging professors to pray for illumination before lectures and to invite Spirit-led discussion in classrooms. Exhortation in pulpit and small groups prompts congregational action—service, evangelism, reconciliation—reflecting the Spirit's nudge. Together, teaching and exhortation communicate God's heart and guide the church toward obedience, leading naturally to evangelistic proclamation.

3.4 Evangelistic Proclamation in Cross-Cultural Contexts (Acts 8:35; Eph 4:11)

Philip's approach to the Ethiopian eunuch—"Philip...opened his mouth, and beginning with this Scripture he told him the good news about Jesus" (Acts 8:35)—exemplifies evangelistic proclamation tuned to cultural context. As a gift, evangelism involves both Spirit-driven boldness and strategic contextualization, bridging cultural gaps without theological compromise. Paul lists evangelists among equipping vocations (Eph 4:11), underscoring their role in initiating new faith communities. The Advocate's personal guidance directs evangelists to appropriate methods—public preaching, relational witness, media outreach—sensitive to audience languages and customs. Early Christian apologists—Justin Martyr, Gregory of Nyssa—demonstrated evangelism through dialogue with Greek philosophy, adapting the Gospel's message to local thought forms. Today, missionary training programs integrate *cross-cultural communication* with Spirit-led itinerancy, using interpreters and technology to span linguistic divides. Evangelistic campaigns under Spirit direction avoid coercive tactics, relying instead on genuine relationships and prayerful dependence. This Spirit-empowered proclamation ensures that mission reflects Christ's heart for all peoples, setting the stage for exploring service gifts.

4 Service Gifts: Embodying Compassion and Order

4.1 Mercy Ministries—Spirit-Empowered Empathy (Rom 12:8)

Paul exhorts those with the gift of mercy to "do it with cheerfulness" (Rom 12:8), highlighting that mercy ministries flow from Spirit-imbued empathy and compassion. Mercy gifts manifest in caring for the sick, comforting the bereaved, and advocating for the oppressed. The Advocate's personal empathy enables ministers to "weep with those who weep" (Rom 12:15) and to discern unspoken needs. Early deaconesses—Phoebe (Rom 16:1)—embodied mercy ministries, providing relief in homes and prisons. Modern mercy ministries include hospital chaplaincy, refugee resettlement, and trauma recovery groups, all calling upon Spirit-led discernment and endurance. Training in *compassion fatigue prevention* and *spiritual self-care* draws on Psalms as Spirit-inspired texts for consolation. Mercy ministries function best when integrated into congregational structures—care teams, prayer networks, support groups—ensuring systematic compassion. The Spirit's personal empowerment in mercy sets the stage for practical helps and hospitality.

4.2 Helps and Hospitality—Practical Love that Reveals God's Welcome (1 Pet 4:9–10)

Peter instructs, "Show hospitality to one another without grumbling...as each has received a gift, use it to serve one another" (1 Pet 4:9–10), linking helps and hospitality with stewardship of God's grace. The Spirit-person equips servers to anticipate needs—preparing meals, arranging transportation, organizing assistance—demonstrating God's welcome in tangible ways. The Greek *diakonia* (service) conveys deacon's ministry in both liturgical and social contexts. In monastic communities, hospitality to pilgrims and the poor modeled Gospel welcome. Contemporary church service ministries—home repair teams, community meals, newcomer hospitality—draw on Spirit guidance to adapt offerings to local cultures. Hospitality training includes cross-cultural sensitivity, dietary awareness, and trauma-informed care. The Acts 2 community's sharing of possessions (Acts 2:44–45) inspires modern food pantries and co-housing initiatives. The Spirit's personal anointing for practical love ensures that hospitality ministries mirror Christ's open table. From hospitality we turn to administration's strategic vision.

4.3 Administration (kubernēsis)—Spirit-Given Strategic Leadership (1 Cor 12:28)

Paul names *kubernēsis* (administration) among the gifts God appoints in the church (1 Cor 12:28), recognizing the need for strategic coordination of resources, programs, and people. The Spirit's personal insight equips administrators to cast vision, manage logistics, and allocate finances wisely. Early church councils—Council of Jerusalem (Acts 15)—demonstrated Spirit-guided decision-making in complex doctrinal and cultural matters. Modern church administrators use *mission alignment frameworks* and *prayer-based strategic planning* to ensure that programs reflect Spirit priorities. Training in nonprofit management, coupled with spiritual discernment practices, helps administrators balance efficiency with humility. Ethical governance models under Spirit direction guard against bureaucratic drift and mission creep. The Spirit's personal involvement in administration ensures that organizational structures serve the Body's flourishing rather than dominate it. This strategic leadership complements craftsmanship and creative arts in embodying gospel beauty.

4.4 Craftsmanship and Creative Arts—Echoes of Bezalel's Anointing (Ex 31:1–5)

In Exodus 31 God fills Bezalel "with the Spirit of God, with skill, ability, and knowledge in all kinds of crafts" (Ex 31:1–5), commissioning him to construct the tabernacle's sacred furnishings. The Spirit's anointing for craftsmanship extends to music, visual arts, architecture, and digital media—creative gifts that shape worship and cultural engagement. Early Christian art—catacomb frescoes, iconography—expressed Spirit-inspired theology for illiterate communities. Contemporary artists sense Spirit promptings in composition of songs, design of sacred spaces, and production of film and literature. Training in *spiritual aesthetics* encourages artists to cultivate contemplative practices that invite the Advocate's inspiration. Arts ministries within churches commission Spirit-led projects, from stage plays to murals honoring community history. By embodying theological truths in tangible forms, craftsmanship and creative arts serve as powerful witnesses, reflecting the Spirit's personal creativity. This concludes our detailed exploration of section four, setting the stage for power gifts.

5 Power Gifts: Demonstrating the Kingdom's Reality

5.1 Gifts of Healings—Wholeness as Sign and Mercy (1 Cor 12:9, 28)

The Spirit empowers believers to minister healing in physical, emotional, and spiritual realms, demonstrating that the gospel brings wholeness. Paul lists "gifts of healings" among manifestation gifts, highlighting the Advocate's compassion for human suffering. These healings serve as signposts of the coming kingdom, pointing beyond mere medicine to divine restoration. In Mark's Gospel, Jesus commissions the Twelve to heal the sick as part of their mission (Mark 6:13), and Acts records similar practices by apostles—Peter healing the lame man (Acts 3:1–10) and Paul restoring Eutychus (Acts 20:9–12). The continuity between Christ's miracles and Spirit-enabled healings underscores that the Advocate's power continues Christ's ministry. Theological reflection understands these gifts as both mercy ministries and apologetic demonstrations, authenticating the gospel message. Training in healing prayer often includes biblical study of Elijah's and Elisha's ministries (1 Kings 17; 2 Kings 5) and practical guidance on laying on of hands (James 5:14). Churches that incorporate healing services create space for testimonies of deliverance, encouraging faith in divine possibility. Pastoral counseling integrates healing prayer with psychological care, acknowledging that the Spirit works holistically. Ethical guidelines warn against manipulation or false promises, affirming that genuine healings rely on Spirit sovereignty, not human formulae. The unpredictability of outcomes reminds ministers to depend on the Advocate's timing and will. Recognizing the relational dynamics—listening deeply to the sufferer, praying empathy-laden petitions—reflects the Spirit's personal care. Embodying healing gifts thus becomes a powerful catalyst for evangelism, leading communities to trust in God's active presence and preparing the ground for miracles and special faith.

5.2 Workings of Miracles—Including Exorcism and Nature Interventions (Acts 19:11–12)

Beyond healings, the Spirit distributes "workings of miracles" that transcend natural laws, ranging from exorcisms to nature interventions. Acts 19:11–12 recounts extraordinary deeds through Paul's handkerchiefs, illustrating that objects touched by the apostolic instrumentality of the Spirit can convey power. Exorcisms, such as Jesus' liberation of demoniacs (Mark 1:23–28) and Paul's expulsion of the spirit from a girl in Philippi (Acts 16:16–18), signify spiritual warfare—overcoming the cosmic powers that enslave humanity. Nature miracles—multiplying loaves (John 6:1–13), commanding storms (Mark 4:35–41)—reveal the Advocate's authority over creation, proclaiming the owner's sovereignty. These gifts invite deep theological engagement: they expose spiritual realities behind physical phenomena and confirm the Creator's supremacy. Training in deliverance ministries emphasizes biblical literacy, pastoral sensitivity, and communal discernment to prevent sensationalism. Church practices often include *prayer labyrinths* or *outdoor retreats* to witness nature interventions, blending creation care with charismatic expectation. Missionaries report that miracles in cross-cultural contexts open hearts resistant to mere words, demonstrating the gospel's power to transform both spirits and circumstances. Ethical reflection cautions against exploiting these gifts for personal gain or platform-building. Ultimately, the Spirit's personal orchestration of miracles points back to Christ's victory over sin and death, bridging the gap between earthly suffering and eschatological hope. From cosmic interventions we move to the special faith that undergirds extraordinary acts.

5.3 Special Faith—Spirit-Ignited Confidence for Extraordinary Tasks (1 Cor 12:9)

Among charismata, Paul includes a "special faith" distinct from general faith that saves; this gift endows individuals with extraordinary confidence to undertake tasks beyond natural ability. Examples include Peter stepping out of the boat to walk on water (Matt 14:28–31) and Stephen standing firm under lethal opposition (Acts 7:55–60). Special faith often accompanies healings and miracles, providing the bold trust necessary for impossible endeavors. Spiritual mentors identify this gift by observing individuals who exhibit marked expectation of direct divine action. Training in *faith development* includes studying Abraham's call and Isaac's birth (Rom 4), cultivating trust in God's promise even when circumstances contradict. Communities that foster *faith-labs*—structured opportunities to pray for bold interventions—encourage this gift's discernment. The Spirit's personal igniting of faith testifies that God equips certain servants for front-line breakthroughs. Yet such faith must remain submission to divine will, lest confidence devolve into presumption. Discernment frameworks evaluate outcomes and alignment with Scripture to ensure authenticity. Recognizing special faith's role in divine strategy naturally prepares us to harness prophetic insight in critical moments.

5.4 Word of Knowledge and Word of Wisdom—Prophetic Insight for Critical Moments (1 Cor 12:8)

The Spirit imparts "word of knowledge" and "word of wisdom," complementary gifts that provide supernatural insight into hidden facts or timely guidance. The word of knowledge reveals specific information unknown to the speaker—Peter's awareness of Ananias' deceit (Acts 5:3)—while the word of wisdom applies truth to solve complex dilemmas—Jesus advising the lawyers on paying taxes to Caesar (Mark 12:13–17). These gifts function in both evangelistic and pastoral contexts, enabling precise interventions when human reasoning falters. Churches train *prophetic councils* to steward these insights, ensuring they align with Scripture and benefit the community. In crisis prayer gatherings, words of wisdom guide strategic decisions—from planting new congregations to navigating social justice initiatives. Modern psychospiritual research correlates intuitive insights with Spirit promptings, encouraging balanced integration of heart and mind. Ethical teaching warns against using these gifts for manipulation, advocating transparency and accountability. Recognizing the Spirit's personal impartation of insight highlights the Advocate's role as divine counselor, equipping believers for critical mission junctures.

6 Vocational Callings and Five-Fold Equippers

6.1 Apostles Today—Pioneering, Foundation-Laying Servants (Eph 2:20; 4:11)

Ephesians describes the church as "built on the foundation of the apostles and prophets, Christ Jesus Himself being the cornerstone" (Eph 2:20) and names apostles among the equipping gifts (Eph 4:11). Contemporary understanding of apostolic ministry encompasses pioneering church planters, network catalysts, and theological innovators who establish foundational structures for gospel advance. The Spirit commissions modern apostles to discern unreached frontiers—geographical, cultural, or digital—and to plant new communities. Historic examples include Augustine's mission to England and William Carey's to India, both Spirit-led initiatives that reshaped mission history. Training for apostolic ministry integrates missiological strategy, leadership development, and spiritual formation, ensuring that architects of new works remain rooted in prayer and Scripture. Apostolic teams provide oversight for emerging congregations, offering doctrinal guidance, resource allocation, and conflict resolution. Discernment for apostolic calling involves communal affirmation, spiritual fruit examination, and often visionary confirmation, modeled on Barnabas' encouragement of Paul (Acts 13:1–3). Contemporary apostolic networks foster collaborative rather than competitive models, reflecting the Advocate's relational nature. Apostolic ministry thus ensures the church's adaptive expansion, setting up successive ministries of prophets and evangelists.

6.2 Prophets—Guardians of Covenant Faithfulness and Direction (Acts 11:28; 13:1)

The five-fold model includes prophets as essential equippers, providing corporate direction and covenant vigilance. In Antioch, prophets like Agabus warned of famine (Acts 11:28) and the Spirit directed Paul and Barnabas (Acts 13:1), demonstrating prophecy's strategic role. Modern prophetic ministries encompass both corporate word (guidance for the church at large) and personal word (counsel for individuals), always subject to communal testing (1 Cor 14:29). Training programs in prophetic ministry stress biblical grounding in Old and New Testament prophets, emphasizing forthtelling over fortune-telling. Schools of prophetic ministry often include field mentoring, prophetic etiquette, and integration with pastoral oversight. Prophets safeguard doctrinal purity by confronting deviations from apostolic faith, mirroring Nathan's confrontation of David (2 Sam 12). They also provide fresh vision for mission, calling communities to new initiatives aligned with the Advocate's leading. Prophetic intercessions prepare congregations for forthcoming challenges, serving as spiritual radar. Properly balanced, prophetic ministries deepen the Body's sensitivity to the Spirit and shape a culture of open yet accountable expectation. Prophetic equipping leads naturally to understanding evangelistic callings.

6.3 Evangelists—Bridge-Builders to the Unreached (Acts 21:8)

Philip is called "the evangelist" in Acts 21:8, illustrating the distinctive gifting of those who "stir up waters" to cross cultural and religious boundaries. Evangelists possess both Spirit-induced boldness and contextual wisdom, bridging the gospel to those outside the faith community. They often pioneer local outreach strategies—street evangelism, digital campaigns, relational networks—tailored to specific cultures. Training in cross-cultural communication equips evangelists to navigate language barriers and worldview differences, reflecting the Spirit's personal adaptation of methods. Partnerships between evangelists and local congregations ensure that new believers are quickly integrated into Body life. Mentoring relationships help evangelists maintain spiritual health amid high-pressure contexts. In Acts, evangelistic breakthroughs—Samaritan revival (Acts 8:5–8) and Ethiopian conversion (Acts 8:26–39)—demonstrate the Spirit's orchestrated approach: combining public proclamation, supernatural signs, and personal connection. Contemporary movements like digital missions harness technology under Spirit guidance to reach global audiences, while preserving relational depth. The Spirit's personal empowerment of evangelists thus accelerates kingdom expansion in both geographic and demographic frontiers, preparing the church for sustained pastoral care.

6.4 Pastors-Teachers—Shepherding, Feeding, and Protecting the Flock (Eph 4:11; 1 Pet 5:1–4)

Pastors-teachers combine two vocations: the shepherd's relational care and the teacher's doctrinal instruction. Paul assigns pastors-teachers "to equip the saints for the work of ministry" (Eph 4:11), and Peter exhorts elders to "shepherd the flock...serving as overseers, not by constraint, but willingly" (1 Pet 5:1–2). The Advocate calls these leaders to cultivate both spiritual maturity and community cohesion. Training programs in pastoral theology emphasize theological depth, counseling skills, and leadership competencies, always undergirded by Spirit-dependence. Pastors-teachers conduct hospital visits, funeral services, small-group oversight, and preaching—all expressions of Spirit-enabled care. Courses in *shepherding hearts* teach active listening and spiritual discernment to address congregants' struggles. Pastors-teachers also model holiness through personal disciplines, reflecting the Spirit's sanctification.

Administrative support structures—deacon boards, pastoral assistants, care teams—allow pastors-teachers to focus on relational and teaching priorities. The Spirit's personal equipping of pastors-teachers ensures that congregations receive both sound doctrine and heartfelt care, sustaining the entire Body's health and mission efforts.

7 Discerning, Confirming, and Deploying Gifts

7.1 Personal Desire, Communal Affirmation, and Providential Fruit

Discerning a gift begins with personal desire—the Spirit often stirs within an individual to serve in a particular area, as Paul's longing to proclaim Christ illustrates (Phil 1:20). Yet desire alone is insufficient; communal affirmation—elders, peers, and existing ministry leaders affirming the gift—is essential (1 Tim 4:14). Observing providential fruit—lasting positive impact, spiritual growth in beneficiaries, and inner joy—confirms authenticity. The Spirit's personal involvement ensures that gifts bear eternal fruit rather than mere organizational success. Discernment retreats often include spiritual gifts assessments, prayer walks, and supervised ministry experiences to test callings. Historical practices—such as Benedictine postulancy and novitiate periods—modeled extended discernment before vows. Contemporary programs adopt *triangulation*: subjective experience, objective affirmation, and external outcomes converge to validate gifts. This process builds confidence and accountability, preventing premature deployment and burnout. Confirmed gifts then transition to commissioning rites involving laying on of hands.

7.2 Laying on of Hands and Prophetic Commissioning (1 Tim 4:14; Acts 13:2–3)

Scripture portrays laying on of hands as the primary means for commissioning gifts—Paul received Timothy's gift through elders' hands (1 Tim 4:14), and Barnabas and Saul were set apart by Spirit-timed laying on of hands at Antioch (Acts 13:2–3). This physical act symbolizes spiritual transfer and communal blessing. Commissioning services include prayer, prophetic words, and symbolic gestures, formally authorizing individuals for ministry. Training in commissioning liturgies emphasizes theological coherence and cultural sensitivity. Some traditions incorporate *anointing oil* to signify Spirit presence sustained over anointing (James 5:14). Commissioning also involves accountability covenants: clear expectations, mentoring relationships, and periodic review. The

Spirit's personal seal in commissioning reinforces the communal nature of gift deployment, ensuring that no minister operates in isolation. From commissioning, ministries proceed into ongoing testing and review.

7.3 Testing Spirits and Motives (1 John 4:1; 1 Cor 13:1–3)

John cautions, "Beloved, do not believe every spirit, but test the spirits" (1 John 4:1), while Paul warns that gifts without love are empty (1 Cor 13:1–3). Testing involves examining whether gift expressions align with Scripture, bear fruit of love, and uplift Christ's reputation. Discernment teams—composed of mature leaders and prophets—evaluate prophetic words, miracles, and teaching segments for doctrinal accuracy and pastoral benefit. Criteria include consistency with previous revelation, transparency of process, and evidence of humility. Practices such as *prophetic debriefs*, *gift feedback sessions*, and *shadow supervision* help monitor gift use. The Spirit's role in testing is personal, imparting conviction to both gift-givers and recipients. Proper testing prevents spiritual abuse, cultic drifts, and gift-driven divisions. With tested authenticity, ministries move into long-term deployment under periodic review.

7.4 Periodic Review—Guarding against Gift-Drift and Burnout

Long-term gift deployment requires regular reflection and recalibration. *Periodic reviews*—annual evaluations by mentoring teams—assess alignment with initial calling, spiritual health, and ministry fruit. Burnout prevention strategies include sabbaticals, peer support groups, and continuing education to rekindle vision and rest the Spirit's anointing. Historical monastic *chapter meetings* functioned as periodic audits of vows and conduct; modern equivalents include pastoral retreats and leadership conferences. Metrics for review encompass spiritual vitality, community impact, and personal well-being. When gifts drift—when vision narrows or pride surfaces—reviews enable timely realignment or rest. The Spirit's personal care in oversight ensures that ministers remain faithful stewards, sustaining empowerment for mission. This thorough deployment cycle leads into practical empowerment for evangelism and church planting.

8 Empowerment for Evangelism and Church Planting

8.1 Spirit-Boldness in Witness (Acts 4:31)

Following Peter and John's release, the believers "were all filled with the Holy Spirit and continued to speak the word of God with boldness" (Acts 4:31). This empowerment supplies courage to confront skepticism, prejudice, and persecution. The Spirit-person equips evangelists and church-planters to overcome fear, articulate faith clearly, and persevere amid opposition. Training for missionary candidates includes *boldness workshops*—role plays simulating hostile contexts—and *prayer mobilization* to request Spirit intervention. Modern testimonies of legal counsel under trial, marketplace testimony in secular industries, and online apologetics attest to the Spirit's boldness gift. By depending on the Advocate, witnesses transcend introversion, cultural barriers, and institutional resistance, laying foundations for new faith communities. Spirit-uplifted boldness thus sparks the initial entry point for church planting.

8.2 Signs Confirming the Gospel among Unreached Peoples (Rom 15:18–19)

Paul prides that among the Gentiles he "fully preached the gospel of Christ, and [have] made it evident by the signs and wonders that God did through me" (Rom 15:18–19). The Spirit empowers church planters to confirm truth with tangible miracles, bridging gaps of doubt in unreached contexts. The synergy of message and sign parallels Israel's wilderness signs, testifying to divine authority. Missionaries report that Spirit-enabled healings and exorcisms frequently open closed communities to the Gospel. Training in *contextualized miracle ministry* equips planters to minister sensitively, ensuring cultural respect and biblical fidelity. Partnership with local leaders fosters sustainable follow-up after signs. Ethical guidelines prohibit manipulation, affirming that signs serve genuine invitation rather than spectacle. The Advocate's personal endorsement through signs accelerates the parable of the kingdom—seed falling on receptive soil emerging rapidly (Mark 4:26–29).

8.3 Contextualizing Gifts across Cultures without Syncretism

Effective church planting requires adapting gifting expressions— worship styles, teaching idioms, healing approaches—to local cultures. The Spirit guides planters in winning strategies: using indigenous music, storytelling formats, and symbolic practices that resonate with local worldviews. Yet contextualization must avoid syncretism; the Advocate's convicting ministry exposes false blends and protects core gospel truths. Historical missionaries—such as Matteo Ricci in China and Hudson Taylor in China inland—modeled deep cultural engagement under Spirit supervision. Cross-cultural training includes *inculturation seminars* and *ethnographic immersion*, complemented by Spirit-led prayer for discernment. Churches adopting contextual practices conduct *cultural feedback loops*, consulting local believers to refine methods. The Spirit's personal direction in contextualization ensures that the church remains authentically Christian while genuinely indigenous, leading into a case study of Antioch.

8.4 Case Study: Antioch to Asia Minor—Dynamic Deployment of Diverse Charisms

Antioch's church, propelled by Spirit leadership, sent out Paul and Barnabas (Acts 13), who evangelized Cyprus, Pisidian Antioch, Iconium, Lystra, and Derbe, employing diverse charisms— evangelistic preaching, prophetic guidance, signs, and service ministries. Prophets in Antioch provided initial direction; evangelists proclaimed in synagogues and marketplaces; healers confirmed messages; teachers established elders in new congregations (Acts 14:21–23). The Spirit's personal distribution of gifts enabled flexible strategies: Philip in Samaria (Acts 8), Peter among Cornelius' household (Acts 10), and Paul's Macedonian call (Acts 16). This case demonstrates how multiple gifts interweave—prophecy leads, evangelism initiates, service undergirds, and administration sustains. Analyses of Antiochite patterns inform modern church-planting networks, which replicate layered charism deployment: initial evangelists, follow-up pastors, care teams, and visionary apostles. The Advocate's personal orchestration of gifts ensures dynamic adaptability, contextual sensitivity, and sustainable growth. Learning from Antioch equips contemporary mission movements to synergize charismata for maximum gospel fertility.

9 Marketplace and Public-Square Charisms

9.1 Entrepreneurial Wisdom for Societal Blessing (Prov 8:12–21; Acts 16:14–15)

The Spirit-person bestows wisdom upon entrepreneurs who, under His guidance, create businesses that serve communities and reflect kingdom values. Proverbs portrays Wisdom as calling, "I, wisdom, dwell with prudence, and I find knowledge and discretion" (Prov 8:12). In Acts, Lydia's merchant trade facilitated the Philippian church's establishment (Acts 16:14–15). Under Spirit-inspired discernment, entrepreneurs identify societal needs—affordable housing, ethical technology—and develop sustainable solutions. Business incubators within the church provide mentoring, prayer support, and accountability, ensuring ventures align with gospel purposes. Training programs integrate spiritual disciplines—prayerful business planning, Sabbath rest practices—with market analysis. Marketplace charisms also include risk-taking faith, where Spirit-imbued confidence prompts investments in underserved areas despite uncertainty. Theological reflection on stewardship reframes profit as resource for generosity rather than personal gain. Case studies of mission-driven startups—microfinance co-ops, fair-trade cooperatives—illustrate how Spirit-led entrepreneurship fosters community uplift. Ethical frameworks challenge leaders to avoid exploitation, ensuring labor dignity and environmental care. Corporate prayer breakfasts and marketplace prayer networks become venues for mutual encouragement and intercession. The Spirit's personal engagement in market activities demonstrates that vocation and mission converge in public life, bridging to governmental and societal service.

9.2 Governmental Service and the Spirit of Counsel (Isa 11:2; Dan 6:3)

Isaiah foretells that the Messiah will be endowed with "the Spirit of counsel and might" (Isa 11:2), empowering wise governance. Daniel's exemplary service under multiple rulers (Dan 6:3) shows Spirit-enabled integrity and strategic insight in public office. Believers in governmental roles can receive Spirit-led counsel to craft just policies, defend the vulnerable, and oppose corruption. Spirit-counselled legislators draw on prayerful deliberation, citizen consultation, and moral conviction. Training for Christian public servants includes scriptural study on justice (Micah 6:8), conflict resolution, and policy analysis fused with Spirit sensitivity. Ethics committees in parliaments or city councils incorporate devotional elements—litanies, brief Scripture readings—before decision-making. Mentorship by seasoned Christian statespersons cultivates humility and discernment, ensuring that political power remains a means of service. The Spirit's personal guidance in governance transcends partisan divides, uniting leaders around common goods: human dignity, peace, and flourishing. Such Spirit-empowered statesmanship models the Advocate's reconciling work, setting the stage for academic and technological innovation.

9.3 Academic and Technological Innovation as Spirit Creativity (Ex 31:3; James 3:17)

Scripture describes Bezalel as "filled with the Spirit of God...in all manner of workmanship" (Ex 31:3), establishing craftsmanship as Spirit-inspired art and science. In modern contexts, academic researchers and technologists equipped by the Advocate pioneer breakthroughs—medical therapies, information systems, renewable energy—that serve human needs. Spirit-led scholarship pursues truth with humility, recognizing that "the wisdom from above is first pure, then peaceable..." (James 3:17). Universities and research centers can institutionalize *Spirit centering* through chapel services, prayer breakfasts, and interdisciplinary dialogues on faith and science. Academic conferences incorporate worship segments and prayer rooms, inviting the Spirit's creativity. Tech incubators hosted by churches provide seed funding and spiritual mentorship for socially responsible innovations. Ethical oversight committees, guided by Spirit principles, evaluate emerging technologies—AI, biotechnology—for human impact and moral alignment. Spirit-animated scholarship resists the temptations of elitism and reductionism, seeking holistic understanding of creation. Recognizing technological innovation as Spirit creativity prepares us to explore ethical witness in commerce and law.

9.4 Ethical Witness—Spirit-Formed Integrity in Commerce and Law (Mic 6:8; Acts 24:16)

The prophet declares, "He has told you, O man, what is good; and what does the Lord require of you but to do justice, love kindness, and walk humbly" (Mic 6:8). Paul, when defending himself before Felix, asserts, "I strive always to keep my conscience clear before God and man" (Acts 24:16), reflecting Spirit-formed integrity. Believers in commerce and law serve as ethical witnesses, upholding transparency, fairness, and compassion. Spirit-counselled lawyers advocate for the marginalized, reform unjust statutes, and promote restorative justice models. Business leaders implement fair wage policies, responsible sourcing, and environmental stewardship, avoiding practices that exploit people or the planet. Corporate governance under Spirit guidance features anti-corruption measures and whistleblower protections. Training in *biblical justice frameworks* equips professionals to navigate dilemmas—labor disputes, environmental regulation, consumer rights—with moral clarity. Accountability networks, such as Christian legal associations and business roundtables, offer peer review and prayer support. The Spirit's personal indwelling shapes character for integrity, ensuring that public square charisms testify to the kingdom's righteousness and mercy. These marketplace and public vocations naturally lead into inclusivity in gift distribution.

10 Inclusivity: Gender, Generation, and Culture in Gift Distribution

10.1 "Your Sons and Daughters Shall Prophesy" (Joel 2:28; Acts 2:17)

Joel's prophecy—that God will pour out His Spirit so that "your sons and daughters shall prophesy" (Joel 2:28)—and Peter's citation in Acts (2:17) affirm that Spirit-gifting transcends gender barriers. The early church witnessed female prophets—Philip's daughters (Acts 21:9) and the prophetess Anna (Luke 2:36)—exercising authority. Modern churches reclaim this biblical precedent by affirming women's gifting in teaching, prophecy, and leadership, guided by contextual exegesis and Spirit discernment. Training programs ensure that women receive equitable opportunities for theological education and charism deployment. Mentorship networks connect seasoned female leaders with younger sisters in the faith, fostering confidence and skill development. Inclusive policies in ordination and lay ministry reflect the Advocate's impartial distribution of gifts. The Spirit's personal endowment on both sons and daughters enriches the Body's resource pool and testifies to the kingdom's reversal of societal prejudices, leading to honoring elders and empowering youth.

10.2 Honoring Elders' Wisdom, Empowering Youth's Vision (Acts 21:9; 1 Tim 4:12)

While Philip's four daughters prophesied, Paul urges Timothy—not to let anyone despise his youth but to set the believers an example in speech, conduct, love, faith, and purity (1 Tim 4:12). The Spirit distributes wisdom and vision across generations: elders receive the gift of sagacity born of experience, while youth bring fresh zeal and innovative approaches. Healthy communities create structures for mutual mentoring: sabbath dialogues where elders share stories and youth present new ideas under prayerful discernment. Intergenerational retreats foster cooperative planning, ensuring that church initiatives benefit from both seasoned insight and generational relevance. Recognition of Spirit-given gifts in all ages prevents ageism and empowers every generation to contribute fully. Pastoral training includes modules on cross-generational communication and conflict resolution. The Spirit's personal agency ensures that the Body remains dynamic—rooted in tradition yet open to renewal—transitioning into global cultural synergy.

10.3 Cross-Cultural Synergy—Gifts Flourishing in Global Diversity (1 Cor 12:13; Rev 7:9)

Paul asserts that "by one Spirit we were all baptized into one body…whether Jew or Greek" (1 Cor 12:13), and Revelation envisions "a great multitude from every nation, tribe, people, and language" (Rev 7:9). The Advocate empowers gifts to take on culturally appropriate forms: songs sung in local idioms, sermons illustrated with indigenous stories, healing ministries attuned to vernacular traditions. International leadership exchanges—missionary residencies, theological partnerships—cultivate sensitivity to global charism expressions. Training in *cultural hermeneutics* helps gift bearers discern how to adapt without diluting biblical substance. Ethnographic studies of Spirit gifts in diverse settings—Africa, Asia, Latin America—reveal patterns of relational prophecy, communal tongues, and group healing rituals. Celebrating this cross-cultural synergy affirms that the Advocate's personal presence transcends ethnolinguistic boundaries, knitting a tapestry of global holiness. Shared festivals—World Day of Prayer, international worship nights—offer glimpses of the Body's multifaceted unity. This inclusive vision ensures accessibility and full participation of all believers in gift distribution.

10.4 Accessibility for Believers with Disabilities—Spirit Strength Perfected in Weakness (2 Cor 12:9)

Paul's summary of his thorn—"My grace is sufficient for you, for My power is made perfect in weakness" (2 Cor 12:9)—provides theological foundation for gifting among those with disabilities. The Spirit distributes gifts without regard to physical or cognitive limitations, often manifesting power gifts through those whom society deems weak. Churches that prioritize *accessible ministry* install ramps, offer sign-language interpretation, and adapt worship elements for neurodiverse participants. Training in *disability theology* engages pastors and gift mentors in understanding how the Spirit enables prophetic, teaching, or healing ministries within adaptive contexts. Stories abound of individuals with Down syndrome whose simple songs carry heavy Spirit anointing in worship. Support groups for disabled believers provide community and affirmation of gifts, countering marginalization. The Spirit's personal empowerment ensures that every member's contribution shines in communal life, showcasing that divine strength transcends human weakness and transitioning us into stewardship and accountability.

11 Stewardship, Accountability, and Common Pitfalls

11.1 Servant-Minded Use versus Platform-Building Pride

The Advocate distributes gifts to cultivate servant-hearted ministry, yet misuse can shift focus from God's glory to personal prominence. Peter warns against "lording it over those in your charge," emphasizing humble service (1 Pet 5:3). Gift stewards practice periodic self-examination—Are my motivations God-honoring or self-exalting? Churches implement *peer accountability groups* where leaders share challenges and receive corrective feedback. Pastoral supervisors observe public ministry for signs of pride: emphasis on personal brand over gospel message. Spiritual disciplines—lectio divina on Philippians 2:1–11—remind gift bearers of Christ's humility. When pride emerges, prophetic friends expose the root and pray for confession, preventing gift-driven cults of personality. Cultivating servant-minded use sustains faithful witness.

11.2 Guarding against Consumerism and "Charismatic Celebrity" Culture

In consumer societies, believers accustomed to passive reception risk treating gifts as commodities—seeking sensational experiences rather than genuine encounter with God. The Spirit's personal ministry counters this by calling communities to responsible participation, not mere spectatorship. Churches that track attendance versus engagement metrics—testimony sharing, ministry involvement—can identify consumerist patterns. Teaching on Romans 12:3 challenges "thinking more highly of himself than he ought," urging realistic gift assessment. Gift-focused events include participatory stations—prayer booths, prophetic dialogue tables—rather than spectator performances. Prophetic councils and elder teams monitor for "celebrity ministry" tendencies, ensuring that gifts serve rather than entertain. Emphasizing cost of discipleship (Luke 14:27) realigns gift expectations toward sacrificial service. This vigilance prepares congregations for financial integrity in power-gift ministries.

11.3 Financial Integrity in Power-Gift Ministries (Acts 8:18–23; 2 Cor 8:20–21)

Simon's attempt to buy the Holy Spirit's gift elicited Peter's rebuke, "May your silver perish with you" (Acts 8:18–23), highlighting the perils of corrupting gift stewardship. Paul commends the Macedonians for entrusting their offering to "honorable people" (2 Cor 8:20–21). Gift-driven ministries—healing crusades, prophetic conferences—often attract financial temptation: paid appointments, merchandise sales, promise of prosperity. The Spirit-person calls ministers to transparent budgeting, third-party audits, and clear giving policies. Training includes *financial ethics* courses, examining biblical models of temple finance, firstfruits (Prov 3:9), and widow's mite (Mark 12:41–44). Congregations adopt *giving covenants* ensuring offerings support ministry impact rather than personal enrichment. Financial accountability teams oversee event revenues, travel stipends, and honoraria. Embracing fiscal integrity preserves trust and reflects the Advocate's holiness.

11.4 Restorative Processes for Gift Misuse and Moral Failure (Gal 6:1–2)

When gift misuse or moral failure occurs, the Spirit-person calls for restorative correction, not mere punitive action. Paul instructs, "If someone is caught in any transgression, you who are spiritual should restore him in a spirit of gentleness" (Gal 6:1). Church policies for handling misconduct—abuse, financial malfeasance—combine even-handed investigation, protective measures for victims, and compassionate restoration for offenders. Restorative justice circles, biblical counseling, and supervised reinstatement programs model Spirit-led repair. Denominational protocols ensure that gift bearers undergo rehabilitation training, accountability partnerships, and ongoing evaluation. Public confession and communal forgiveness ceremonies can reflect the Advocate's reconciling ministry, healing congregational wounds. By integrating justice and mercy, churches embody the Spirit's personal approach to transformation.

12 Eschatological Horizon and Forward Look

12.1 Gifts as Interim Foretastes until "the Perfect Comes" (1 Cor 13:8–12)

Paul acknowledges that charisms are provisional: "When the perfect comes, the partial will pass away" (1 Cor 13:10–11). The Spirit's personal gifting offers glimpses of the fullness of redemption—a foretaste of direct divine encounter. These gifts, however, remain provisional, pointing toward the final consummation when believers see "face to face" (1 Cor 13:12). Understanding this horizon tempers both overreliance on gifts and neglect of their present value. Liturgies incorporate *capstone prophecies* on consummation, maintaining eschatological expectancy. Theological education balances charism engagement with hope in Christ's return, ensuring that gifts serve their intended transitional purpose. This horizon prepares the church for end-time revival imagery.

12.2 End-Time Revival Imagery—Spirit Poured Out on "All Flesh" in Fullness (Acts 2:17–21)

Peter's citation of Joel—"I will pour out my Spirit on all flesh" (Acts 2:17)—foreshadows a universal revival preceding the day of the Lord. This eschatological promise envisions an unprecedented outpouring across generations and cultures. Missions movements pray for global waves of the Spirit, employing 24/7 prayer towers, strategic city mapping, and intercession for unreached people groups. Revival training includes teaching on revival's marks—mass conversions, social renewal, renewed worship expressions—grounded in both Scripture and historical precedents. The Spirit's personal mission in end-time revival catalyzes communal transformation, preparing hearts for Christ's return. Recognition of this promise fuels perseverance amid setbacks.

12.3 New-Creation Vocation—Serving God with Undimmed Capacities (Rev 22:3–5)

Revelation assures that in the New Creation, God's servants will "see his face, and his name will be on their foreheads. Night will be no more...and they will reign forever" (Rev 22:4–5). The Advocate's personal equipping in this era includes unimpeded gifts—miracles, prophecy, worship—no longer provisional but perfected. Ministries that now labor under limitations will operate unhindered, serving God with full capacities. This vision shapes present vocational motivation: believers invest charisms in anticipation of perfect service, knowing that temporal sacrifices yield eternal fruit. Worship gatherings include eschatological songs envisioning this reign. Understanding our gifts as precursors to perfected service aligns present ministries with eternal calling, concluding our survey and transitioning into Chapter 12 on prayer in the Spirit.

Conclusion

In reviewing the Spirit's personal gifting—from the marketplace to the pulpit, from prophetic insight to pastoral care—we have seen that charisms are not optional adornments but essential instruments for mission and sanctification. Proper stewardship requires discernment, accountability, and a posture of humility, guarding against pride, consumerism, and misuse. Yet, even as gifts serve present needs, they point forward to the consummation when the perfect shall arrive and every capacity will be unhindered in God's presence (1 Cor 13:9–12; Rev 22:3–5). With this foundation in place, the church is poised to enter deeper into the Advocate's work through prayer in the Spirit—a practice that will sustain and amplify every calling and gift in the life of the Body.

Chapter 12. Prayer in the Spirit: Access and Advocacy

Prayer in the Spirit transforms our approach to God from duty to dialogue, inviting believers into a living relationship where access is granted, advocacy assured, and communion deepened. This chapter unfolds how the Advocate opens the way into the Father's presence, repositions us as beloved children crying "Abba," and intercedes with groans beyond words when our hearts falter. It explores the nature of Spirit-led petition—bold yet humble, structured yet spontaneous—and the ethical imperatives that shape our desires to match divine priorities. By learning to pray with the Spirit rather than merely to Him, we discover a rhythm of intimacy and intercession that fuels personal growth, corporate unity, and advancing mission.

1 Triune Pathway of Access

1.1 "Through Christ, in One Spirit, to the Father" (Eph 2:18)

The New Testament consistently portrays prayer as a threefold journey: we approach the Father through the Son, empowered by the Spirit. This formula emphasizes Christ's mediatorial role—His atoning work opens the way—while the Spirit's personal presence sustains our access. Believers draw near not by their righteousness but by Christ's perfect righteousness imputed to us (Rom 3:22). The Spirit

251

actively applies that righteousness in our hearts, enabling us to stand confidently before God (Rom 5:2). Early church liturgies reflected this pathway in their prayers, invoking the Trinity by name and sequence. In private devotion, Christians who pray "Father, in Jesus' name, empowered by Your Spirit" participate in the same pattern. This approach distinguishes Christian prayer from mere good wishes or pagan incantations, rooting it in covenant relationship. Pastors instruct new converts in this triune formula, modeling prayers that explicitly acknowledge each Person's role. Theologians note that this structure preserves both the unity of God and the distinct persons of the Trinity, preventing modalistic flattening. In communities where the formula is neglected, prayer may become flabby or self-centered; whereas, when embraced, it fosters reverence, intimacy, and doctrinal depth. Understanding this triune access sets the stage for exploring how the veil is removed and the throne is approached.

1.2 From Temple Veil to Throne of Grace (Heb 10:19–22)

The writer to the Hebrews draws a stark contrast: under the old covenant, only the high priest could enter the Holy of Holies, but Christ's sacrifice "opened a new and living way…through the curtain, that is, through His flesh" (Heb 10:20). This imagery transfers the temple veil into the believer's experience: Christ's body becomes both mediator and entrance. The Spirit then draws us into the presence of God, replacing fear with boldness "to enter the holy place" (Heb 10:19). Early Jewish Christians understood this as an eschatological shift from spatial limitations to perpetual heavenly access. In practice, Christians pray knowing they stand in the heavenly sanctuary, not a distant earthly temple. Liturgical prayers in Eastern traditions still refer to crossing the veil, while Western traditions emphasize "throne of grace" (Heb 4:16) as the locus of prayer. Spiritual formation programs encourage contemplatives to visualize approaching God's throne, fostering awareness of the Spirit's guiding hand. This transition from veil to throne underscores the Advocate's role in escorting believers into divine intimacy. It also roots prayer in Christ's finished work and the Spirit's ongoing ministry. Having removed the barrier, the Spirit now testifies to the new Exodus from bondage to approach the divine presence.

1.3 Spirit as Covenant Witness Sealing the New Exodus (Rom 8:2; 2 Cor 3:6)

Paul explains that "the law of the Spirit of life has set you free in Christ Jesus from the law of sin and death" (Rom 8:2), echoing the Exodus liberation motif. Here the Spirit-person acts as covenant witness, testifying internally to our status as freed people. In 2 Corinthians, Paul contrasts the old covenant's ministry of death with the new covenant's Spirit-enabled ministry of righteousness (2 Cor 3:6). The Spirit writes God's law on hearts, marking believers as citizens of the promised land of divine life. This sealing function assures us that prayer is not a renegotiation of terms but an expression of covenant fellowship. The Spirit's witness provides immediate confirmation of our freedom, silencing condemning thoughts and instigating gratitude. Early bishops taught catechumens that baptism represented crossing the Red Sea into Spirit-led freedom. In modern baptisteries, churches often incorporate testimonies of deliverance to illustrate the Spirit's liberating work. Pastors encourage congregations to recall personal memories of spiritual liberation when they pray, reinforcing the Spirit's testimony. This covenant witness transforms prayer from mere requests into relational dialogue. With barriers removed and freedom secured, believers now learn to pray with God rather than only to God.

1.4 Practical Implication: Praying With Rather Than Merely To God

Recognizing the Spirit's personal presence shifts prayer dynamics from a monologue of petition to a dialogue of mutual engagement. Praying "with" God means listening as well as speaking, expecting the Spirit to prompt, guide, and correct. Journaling spiritual impressions alongside petition entries fosters this conversational pattern. Early monastic rules—cell 'hours' of prayer—incorporated times of silence to hear the Advocate's voice. In corporate worship, interactive prayer forums allow Spirit-led interjections, transforming passive listening into active co-prayer. Spiritual directors teach directees to distinguish their thoughts from Spirit promptings by testing them against Scripture and community affirmation. This approach cultivates expectancy: believers anticipate God's responses, rather than merely citing a wish list. Ignoring the Spirit's role can reduce prayer to rote recitations; embracing it transforms prayer into dynamic fellowship. Transitioning from access to family intimacy, we now turn to the distinctive cry of adoption in prayer.

2 The Cry of Adoption: "Abba, Father"

2.1 Spirit of Sonship Replacing the Orphan Spirit (Rom 8:15–16; Gal 4:6)

Paul declares that "you did not receive a spirit of slavery leading to fear again, but you received a spirit of adoption as sons by which we cry, 'Abba! Father!'" (Rom 8:15–16). This spirit of adoption contrasts with the orphan's insecurity, signaling a fundamental identity shift. In Galatians he reiterates, "God has sent forth the Spirit of His Son into your hearts, crying, 'Abba! Father!'" (Gal 4:6), indicating that the Spirit himself initiates this familial relationship. Orphan mentality—feelings of abandonment, unworthiness, and alienation—gives way to the dignity and assurance of children in God's household. Early catechesis used the *Abba* cry as a baptismal confession, embedding familial language in liturgy. Contemporary prayer workshops invite participants to pray "Abba" slowly, allowing the Advocate to rewrite deep-seated narratives of insecurity. Pastoral care emphasizes that this cry arises spontaneously from the Spirit's own affirmation, not from emotional manipulation. Neuroscience of attachment theory confirms that spiritual adoption parallels healthy relational bonding, with the Spirit acting as the divine attachment figure. This new-heart reality grounds bold petitioning and intimate fellowship, preparing us to examine experiential assurance versus mere psychological projection.

2.2 Experiential Assurance versus Psychological Projection

While some psychological frameworks identify *parental-imago* projections in spiritual language, the New-Testament teaches that the Spirit alone provides genuine experiential assurance of adoption. Unlike mere wishful imagining, the Spirit's witness is objective—a divine testimony—to our sonship (Rom 8:16). Experiential assurance emerges as inner peace, unwavering hope, and consistent fruit of love, rather than fleeting positive feelings. Pastors caution against equating emotional highs with adoption evidence, instead pointing believers to the Advocate's steady unfolding work. Worship testimonies that recount Spirit-confirmed moments of calling or peace serve as communal affirmations of experiential adoption. Spiritual formation groups practice *assurance journaling*, tracking consistent patterns of the Spirit's witness over time. Discernment teams help distinguish between transient euphoria and substantive assurance rooted in the Spirit's presence. This clarity safeguards communities from psychological distortions and edge-of-the-seat emotionalism, leading naturally to the boldness that flows from filial address.

2.3 Filial Boldness in Petition (Matt 7:7–11; Heb 4:16)

Jesus encourages His followers to "ask, and it will be given to you" (Matt 7:7), framing God as a generous Father who delights in giving good gifts. The Spirit's sonship cry empowers believers to approach God with the confidence of children requesting needs from a loving parent. Hebrews echoes this, urging us to "draw near...with confidence" to the throne of grace (Heb 4:16), since our High Priest is both Son and Advocate. Filial boldness does not demand arrogance but presumes God's benevolence, asking unashamedly for healing, provision, and guidance. Historical prayer manuals—Augustine's *Confessions*—model this frank dialogue, recounting how he pleaded with God for mercy and understanding. Contemporary prayer ministries encourage *bold intercession workshops*, teaching believers to seize promised petitions. Training in spiritual warfare emphasizes that bold requests challenge demonic hindrances, as the Spirit amplifies our cries to heaven. Yet pastors guard against presumption, reminding congregations that true filial boldness submits to the Spirit's filtering of desires according to God's will (1 John 5:14). This dynamic boldness arises directly from the Spirit's personal adoption ministry and shapes pastoral rhythms that nurture family identity in daily prayer.

2.4 Pastoral Rhythms That Nurture Family Identity in Prayer

Churches cultivate family identity by embedding adoption language into communal practices—corporate prayers that begin with "Our Father," baptismal liturgies emphasizing spiritual parenthood, and mealtime blessings invoking *Abba*. Small groups often open sessions with personal prayers beginning "Father," reinforcing relational intimacy. Seasonal rhythms—Advent meditations on divine provision, Lent reflections on sonship through suffering—align personal adoption with the yearly church calendar. Mentorship programs pair older and younger believers, modeling filial dynamics in both prayer and life application. Pastoral letters and devotional guides provide weekly prompts to cry *Abba*, anchoring congregants in familial identity. Retreat centers offer *family-of-God* workshops, incorporating art, music, and silence to deepen sensory experience of adoption. Through these rhythms, the Spirit's personal work in adoption becomes woven into the fabric of corporate and private devotion, readying souls for intercession that transcends words. Having established our family access, we now turn to intercession with inarticulate groans.

3 Intercession with Inarticulate Groans

3.1 Romans 8:26–27 — Divine Empathy for Creaturely Weakness

Paul acknowledges human limitations in prayer—"we do not know what we should pray for as we ought"—but assures that "the Spirit Himself intercedes for us with groanings too deep for words" (Rom 8:26–27). This inarticulate intercession reveals the Spirit's divine empathy: He perfectly understands our needs when we cannot articulate them. Groans may arise from overwhelming grief, unspoken burdens, or complex dilemmas beyond vocabulary. The Spirit-person transforms our sighs and sobs into petitions aligned with the Father's will. Early church fathers taught that these groanings signify an intimacy so profound that language fails. In pastoral care, leaders encourage expressions of lament—tears, silent retreats, contemplative sighs—recognizing them as Spirit-led prayers. Liturgies sometimes incorporate communal laments, giving collective voice to groaning that resonates with Spirit intercession. Training in *lament theology* underscores that groanings are biblical prayers, validated by the Spirit's participation. This intercession bridges human frailty and divine omniscience, preparing us to explore the Trinity's searching of hearts.

3.2 Trinitarian "Searching of Hearts" and Alignment with God's Will

Alongside groanings, Paul notes that the Spirit "searches the hearts" (Rom 8:27), aligning our inner affections with God's intentions. This searching is an active divine examination, revealing motives and desires to ensure our prayers echo God's redemptive plan. The Trinity collaboratively scrutinizes and affirms: the Son's intercession, the Spirit's searching, and the Father's responsive listening (Rom 8:34). Pastoral ministries integrate *heart-assessment exercises*—journaling prompts that surface hidden motives and desires. Spiritual directors utilize guided questions, inviting the Spirit to illuminate underlying hopes or fears shaping prayer. Ancient monastic traditions practiced *examination of consciousness*, reflecting on thoughts and emotions under Spirit inspection. Contemporary cognitive-behavioral frameworks resonate with this searching process, encouraging recognition of thought patterns that hinder alignment with God's will. This divine heart-searching leads directly into Spirit-borne lament models in the Psalms.

3.3 Models of Spirit-Borne Lament in Psalms and Prophetic Prayers

The Psalms provide archetypal models for Spirit-borne lament—David's anguished cries in Psalms 13 and 22, the corporate laments of Asaph in Psalm 73, and prophetic intercessions like Jeremiah's confessions in Lamentations. These texts seamlessly blend complaint, pleading, and trust, revealing raw honesty under divine observation. The Spirit ensures that our laments maintain theological integrity—honesty without cynicism, grievance without despair. Early church liturgies included *Psalmody* of laments during Holy Week, aligning communal sorrow with Christ's suffering. Contemporary worship incorporates *lament services* where songs, readings, and silence facilitate Spirit-led emotional release. Pastors teach lament grammar—acknowledging injustice, naming pain, recalling divine acts—enabling congregations to pray fully. Mental health professionals recognize lament as spiritually therapeutic, reducing toxic shame. Through these models, the Advocate guides the church into lament that is both authentic and transformative, equipping communities to accompany sufferers when words fail.

3.4 Guidelines for Accompanying Sufferers When Words Fail

When individuals face trauma or grief, the Spirit's intercession via groans calls for compassionate accompaniment. Pastoral guidelines recommend silence, presence, and attuned listening rather than immediate problem-solving. Prayer partners practice *Holy Listening*, inviting the Spirit to intercede through their presence and touch rather than through words. Trauma-informed care protocols integrate spiritual lament with professional counseling, ensuring holistic support. Structured practices—like *breath prayer circles* and *laments in community*—provide frameworks for shared groaning. Ministers are trained to recognize when to hold space, when to pray for the Spirit's groanings, and when to offer scripture promises such as Psalm 34:18. Confidentiality covenants protect privacy, fostering trust that enables deeper Spirit-led intercession. By accompanying sufferers through Spirit-borne lament, the church embodies the Advocate's empathy, preparing hearts for the disciplined vigilance of Spirit-led warfare prayer.

4 "Praying in the Spirit" (Eph 6:18; Jude 20)

4.1 Exegetical Overview of the Phrase in Its Two Contexts

"Praying at all times in the Spirit" appears both in Ephesians 6:18—amid the call to put on the whole armor—and in Jude 20—exhorting believers to "build yourselves up in your most holy faith, praying in the

Holy Spirit." The phrase underscores Spirit-empowered prayer as essential to spiritual warfare and communal edification. In Ephesians, prayer serves as a weapon against demonic forces, requiring Spirit vigilance. In Jude, it builds faith, preserving doctrinal purity and mutual encouragement. Exegetes note that *pneumatō* functions adverbially—prayer characterized by Spirit involvement—rather than specifying a language like tongues. Historical commentators, such as Chrysostom, urged believers to integrate Spirit-led prayer into every life moment. Modern Greek lexicons confirm the phrase's consistency with Spirit-led orientation and dependence. Pastoral guides explain that praying *in* the Spirit encompasses adopting His perspective, sensitivity to His promptings, and reliance on His intercession. Teaching this exegetical nuance prevents conflating "praying in the Spirit" with any single spiritual practice, setting the stage for watchful perseverance.

4.2 Watchfulness, Perseverance, and Alert Spiritual Warfare

In the context of putting on the full armor of God, Paul admonishes, "Praying at all times in the Spirit, with all prayer and supplication. To that end keep alert with all perseverance" (Eph 6:18–19). Prayer thus becomes a sustained alertness to spiritual realities and demonic opposition. The Spirit equips believers to discern spiritual attacks— temptation, division, deception—and to respond with targeted petitions. Historical church fathers practiced *vigil prayers* at midnight, anticipating demonic activity in the watch hours. Contemporary prayer movements organize *24/7 prayer rooms* to maintain uninterrupted intercession, guided by the Spirit's leading. Training in *spiritual warfare* includes sensitivity exercises—recognizing oppressive atmospheres, interpreting dreams, sensing spiritual heaviness. Small-group watch ministries rotate teams to sustain prolonged intercession for communities, nations, and the church. Perseverance under pressure cultivates resilience, as believers experience Spirit-sustained hope and courage. Emphasizing watchfulness prevents prayer from becoming mechanical and readies the church for effective mission. From spiritual warfare we contrast Spirit-led prayer with rote recitation.

4.3 Contrast with Mechanical Recitation or Mindless Mantras

"Praying in the Spirit" stands in stark opposition to reciting words by rote or repeating mindless mantras devoid of consciousness. Mechanical prayer can become spiritual noise, desensitizing believers to the Advocate's voice. Jesus warned against empty phrases in Matthew 6:7, indicating that prayer must engage the heart and mind. The Spirit's personal involvement requires attentiveness, sincerity, and expectant listening. Liturgical traditions address this by alternating scripted prayers with spontaneous communal prayers, ensuring renewal. Prayer workshops teach *intercessory silence*— pausing after each sentence to invite the Spirit's response— transforming prayer from monologue into dialogue. Cognitive studies reveal that mindfulness in prayer enhances emotional regulation and spiritual awareness. Churches discourage "prayer chains" of unreflective shouting, replacing them with guided intercessions. This contrast establishes the necessity of integrating Scripture, silence, and spontaneity.

4.4 Integrating Scripture, Silence, and Spontaneity

A balanced practice of Spirit-led prayer weaves together biblical meditation, contemplative silence, and spontaneous utterance. Lectio divina invites slow, prayerful reading of Scripture, allowing the Spirit to illuminate verses for personal application. Silence creates space for the Advocate's promptings, fostering expectancy and receptivity. Spontaneity—heart-felt prayers rising in response to Scripture or communal need—reflects the Spirit's immediacy. Early monastics structured day and night into canonical hours combining these elements, recognizing the Spirit's work in each. Contemporary prayer gatherings use guided Scripture prompts followed by extended silent listening periods and open sharing. Digital prayer apps now intersperse Scripture notifications with silence timers, assisting individual integration. Training in *Spirit-aligned spontaneity* teaches believers to distinguish heart-led prayers from impulsive emotions, testing through community and Scripture. This integrative model ensures that prayer remains rooted in God's Word, sensitively attuned to divine presence, and flexibly responsive to unanticipated needs. Transitioning from personal prayer into communal practice, Chapter 12's remaining sections will explore tongues, corporate intercession, spiritual warfare, and missional momentum—all under the Advocate's personal advocacy.

5 Tongues and Prophetic Song as Private Devotion

5.1 Purpose of Glossolalia in Personal Edification (1 Cor 14:2, 4, 18)

The Apostle describes glossolalia as "speaking mysteries to God" (1 Cor 14:2), indicating a deeply personal prayer language unmediated by human understanding. This private devotions function primarily to build up the speaker's inner man, aligning the heart with the Spirit's intercession beyond the limitations of the mind. Paul affirms, "The one who speaks in a tongue edifies himself" (1 Cor 14:4), suggesting that tongues enable profound communion, strengthening faith, hope, and love from within. Early church fathers—such as Tertullian—testified that glossolalia accompanied times of intense spiritual refreshing and clarity. Contemporary charismatic movements echo this practice in personal altar times, where individuals yield to spontaneous prayer utterances inspired by the Advocate. Neurological research finds that repetitive, non-lexical vocalizations can induce meditative brain states, paralleling the Spirit's work in calming anxiety and fostering spiritual focus. Pastoral guidance emphasizes that personal tongues should be grounded in Scripture and Christ-honoring content, even when unintelligible to the mind. Believers often report that subsequent reflection on their glossolalic sessions reveals insights or resolutions to pressing issues, underscoring the Spirit's personal ministry. Private tongues thus serve as a condensate of intercession, worship, and sanctification, preparing the soul for communal expression. This inward edification naturally leads to consideration of interpretation for broader benefit.

5.2 Interpretation as Gateway to Communal Benefit (1 Cor 14:13–28)

Paul instructs those who speak in tongues to "pray that [they] may interpret" (1 Cor 14:13), underscoring interpretation's essential role in extending personal edification into communal building. Interpretation transforms individual utterances into intelligible messages, making the tongue-language a prophetic word for the entire assembly. The early church practiced this under apostolic oversight, ensuring that no message contradicted Scripture or sowed confusion. Modern practice often employs dedicated interpreters who, under pastoral and prophetic affirmation, relay the substance of tongues prayers in the gathered body. Training in interpretive gifting includes practicing mental quietude immediately after tongues, noting impressions or images that correspond to utterances. Accountability structures— prophetic councils—verify interpretations against biblical patterns, preventing speculative or spurious declarations. When interpreted tongues occur in worship services, congregants experience a corporate uplift, sensing the Spirit's unity and direction. Interpretation thus completes the private-to-public prayer cycle, linking personal devotion with communal edification and steering the Body toward corporate intercession.

5.3 Singing in the Spirit — Early Church and Contemporary Practice

The New Testament depicts corporate singing inspired by the Spirit: "Addressing one another in psalms and hymns and spiritual songs, singing and making melody in your heart to the Lord" (Eph 5:19). Early Christian assemblies recorded spontaneous chants and repetitive refrains that arose from the Spirit's prompting, blending scriptural psalms with new doctrinal lyrics. This "singing in the Spirit" functioned as both worship and intercession, carrying petitions and praises beyond human eloquence. Contemporary practices range from private devotional singing in tongues to corporate worship services allowing Spirit-driven songs without prewritten lyrics. Worship leaders equip congregations by modeling thematic spontaneity—introducing a scriptural motif and inviting fresh melody. Audio recordings of Spirit-led song sessions provide training examples, showing how melodic lines emerge organically from prayerful focus. Pastoral teams emphasize humility in Spirit-led singing, reminding worshipers to stay Christ-centered rather than performance-driven. The communal impact is significant: participants often testify to breakthroughs in personal struggle as Spirit-led melodies evoke deep emotional and spiritual responses. This blend of ancient pattern and modern application underscores tongues and prophetic song's vitality in private devotion, leading the way toward structured corporate intercession.

5.4 Pastoral Boundaries: Maturity, Humility, and Order

While private tongues and prophetic song offer rich spiritual resources, pastoral oversight establishes boundaries to prevent misuse. Maturity in gift use involves emotional stability, doctrinal grounding, and Christlike character—qualities pastors assess through mentorship and observation. Humility guards against self-aggrandizement; leaders encourage singers and speakers to redirect attention to Christ, not to personal abilities. Order requires that private devotions remain just that—private—unless interpreted or authorized for public worship. Churches implement guidelines: private practice in designated prayer rooms, scheduled times for shared spiritual song, and mentorship prerequisites before public participation. Accountability partners provide feedback on content and posture, ensuring that prophetic melodies and tongues align with the Spirit's character. When boundaries are honored, private tongues and song flourish as safe spaces for Spirit-led intimacy, enriching both personal devotion and corporate prayer life.

6 Corporate Prayer: Symphony of the Spirit

6.1 Pentecost Prayer Meeting Template (Acts 1:14; 2:42)

The Jerusalem believers "all joined together constantly in prayer" (Acts 1:14), devoting themselves to "the apostles' teaching and the fellowship...to the breaking of bread and prayers" (Acts 2:42). This template—intense, communal, Spirit-led intercession—ignited the Pentecostal outpouring. Early church gatherings combined Scripture reading, apostolic exhortation, confession, thanksgiving, and spontaneous Spirit-led petitions. Contemporary prayer movements replicate this template through *extended prayer convocations*—multi-hour vigils blending teaching, worship, and intercession. Prayer coordinators map out sessions: initial teaching on prayer principles, guided confession, focused petition for local and global needs, and open intercessory segments. Technology enables *24/7 virtual prayer chains*, maintaining perpetual petition around the clock. Such gatherings foster deep unity, as participants sense the Spirit moving across cultural and generational divides. Pastoral teams debrief after intense sessions, recording testimonies of breakthrough and direction. This Pentecost model grounds corporate prayer in historical precedent and Spirit expectation.

6.2 Discerning Consensus: "It Seemed Good to the Holy Spirit and to Us" (Acts 15:28)

During the Jerusalem Council, the church "decided by the Holy Spirit and to us" (Acts 15:28), illustrating Spirit-guided corporate decision-making. Discernment involves prayerful listening, open discussion, and sensitivity to prophetic confirmations. Modern church councils adopt similar processes: extended prayer before agenda items, periodic silence for Spirit promptings, and seeking unanimous affirmation before implementation. Facilitation methods—such as *Ignatian consensus*—allow space for minority voices and require communal testing of proposals against Scripture. Prophetic voices may surface in prayer times, offering insight that aligns with group discernment. Pastoral leadership then documents consensus decisions as Spirit-validated directions, reinforcing trust. This model prevents top-down decision-making and empowers the Body's collective wisdom. From consensus discernment, churches proceed to invoke the Spirit in worship through epiclesis.

6.3 Liturgical Epiclesis — Invoking the Spirit on Gathered Worship

Epiclesis—the formal invocation of the Spirit to consecrate the elements and the assembly—serves as a corporate petition for the Advocate's presence. Historic liturgies from the East and West include explicit epicleses: "Come, Holy Spirit, and sanctify these gifts…" and "Bestow upon us Your Spirit." This prayer recognizes that true worship and sacramental efficacy require the Spirit's descent. Contemporary liturgical renewal movements reclaim epiclesis in Eucharistic prayers, ensuring that congregations consciously invite the Advocate's transforming work. Worship leaders teach on the theological significance of epiclesis, linking it to Pentecost's power and Christ's promise of the Spirit (John 14–16). Music selections during epiclesis often shift to spontaneous songs, reflecting openness to the Spirit's movement. Small-group contexts incorporate mini-epicleses before prayer segments, normalizing Spirit invocation in every gathering. By prioritizing epiclesis, churches acknowledge that human planning and performance cannot replace the Spirit's personal anointing. This liturgical heartbeat leads naturally into small-group intercession circles.

6.4 Small-Group Intercession Circles and Prayer Rooms

Small-group intercession circles—gatherings of 6–12 believers committed to mutual prayer support—offer intimate venues for Spirit-led petition. Groups often follow structured rhythms: opening Scripture, personal sharing, communal intercession, prophetic insights, and closing thanksgiving. Prayer rooms—dedicated spaces within church buildings—operate as 24/7 houses of prayer, staffed by rotating teams who sense the Spirit's urgings for specific petitions. Technology-enhanced prayer walls allow participants to post requests and updates in real time, fostering connectedness. Facilitators train new intercessors in listening prayer, spiritual mapping of neighborhoods, and targeted prayer strategies for local issues such as homelessness or policing. Retreat centers adjacent to urban hubs host *silent prayer marathons*, enabling intercessors to sustain corporate petitions over days. Pastors integrate these small-group models into discipleship pathways, ensuring that every believer participates in corporate intercession. The Spirit's symphonic weaving of diverse voices in these venues mirrors heavenly worship, preparing the church for spiritual warfare responsibilities.

7 Spiritual Warfare and Watchful Intercession

7.1 Whole Armor Climax: "Praying … in the Spirit" (Eph 6:10–20)

Paul's armor metaphor culminates in the band of prayer: "Praying at all times in the Spirit, with all prayer and supplication" (Eph 6:18). The Spirit's personal involvement transforms prayer into an active defense and offense in spiritual warfare. Intercessors don the gospel belt of truth, the breastplate of righteousness, feet shod with readiness to share the gospel, shield of faith, helmet of salvation, and sword of Spirit-word (Eph 6:14–17), then wield prayer as the Spirit-energized approach to combat. Training in *armor application* includes mapping personal weaknesses, corporate needs, and adversarial strategies. Prayer gatherings incorporate strategic prayer points aligned with each armor piece—truth against deceit, righteousness against condemnation, etc. Spiritual warfare curricula emphasize dependence on the Advocate's power, not human force. Pastoral care teams support intercessors in ongoing battles, providing rest, debrief, and encouragement. The Spirit's personal empowerment in this context readies believers to stand firm in turbulent times, opening the way to discerning demonic resistance.

7.2 Discerning Demonic Resistance and Territorial Strongholds (Acts 16:16–18)

In Philippi, Paul and Silas confronted a spirit-possessed slave girl whose divinatory powers profited her owners (Acts 16:16–18). This incident illustrates the Spirit's role in exposing and overcoming demonic forces. Intercessors learn to pray for discernment of spiritual atmospheres—identifying oppression, legal claims, and territorial strongholds—through both biblical signs and Spirit promptings. Prayer mapping exercises chart geographic areas, community structures, and institutional influences to target intercession effectively. Training in *deliverance theology* equips teams to discern between mental illness and demonic influence, ensuring appropriate referral to healthcare. Police chaplaincies sometimes join these prayers, combining spiritual discernment with civic advocacy for justice. The Spirit's personal guidance protects intercessors from arrogance, ensuring that freedom ministry remains Christ-centered. Awareness of occult practices and cultural spiritualities informs contextual strategies. Discerning resistance guides the church into fasting and sustained vigilance.

7.3 Fasting, Night-Watches, and Sustained Vigilance

Jesus taught that some demons are driven out only by prayer and fasting (Mark 9:29). Fasting intensifies prayer by subduing the flesh, heightening spiritual sensitivity to the Spirit's leadings. Early church vigil practices—praying through the night—unguarded hours associated with demonic activity—exemplify sustained watchfulness. Modern prayer watches adopt lunar calendars for strategic timing, while congregations schedule community fasts preceding major decisions or evangelistic campaigns. Retreat centers host "40-hour fasts" combining continuous worship, prayer, and fasting in the Spirit's guidance. Training in fasting includes health considerations, spiritual disciplines to withstand temptation, and systems of accountability. Pastors advise gradual fasting progression—partial, absolute, Daniel-style—to suit individual capacity. Intercessors report breakthrough guidance and mountain-moving prayers during these intensified seasons, testifying to the Spirit's personal empowerment. Fasting and night-watches flow naturally into balanced vigilance that avoids triumphalism.

7.4 Avoiding Triumphalism: Weakness as Strategic Posture

While spiritual victory is assured, Paul cautions believers not to become "puffed up" but to remember the thorn in the flesh and the grace that sustains (2 Cor 12:7–10). True spiritual warfare maintains humility, acknowledging that victory depends on the Spirit's power, not human effort. Triumphalism—boasting of spiritual exploits—provokes the adversary and distorts gospel witness. Pastoral teaching emphasizes "weakness" as strategic posture, where believers boast in infirmities so that Christ's power may rest upon them. Prayer teams incorporate moments of confession and corporate lament to counter triumphalist tendencies. Spiritual directors monitor for signs of arrogance in intercessors—overconfidence, exclusivism, or lack of empathy. The Spirit's personal advocacy thrives in humility, ensuring that victories serve God's glory and the church's edification. From watchful intercession we transition seamlessly into missional momentum born in prayer.

8 Missional Momentum Born in Prayer

8.1 Antioch's Worship-and-Fasting Launchpad (Acts 13:1–4)

The Antioch church's prophets and teachers "fasted and prayed" before the Spirit directed, "Set apart for Me Barnabas and Saul" (Acts 13:2). This combination of worship, fasting, and prayer created a spiritual crucible for mission. The community's unified devotion sharpened collective sensitivity to the Advocate's voice, yielding clarity in commissioning. Contemporary mission agencies emulate this pattern through *prayer retreats* where potential church planters undergo periods of fasting, worship, and silence before formal appointment. Sponsoring churches hold commissioning services that involve corporate vows, prophetic prayers, and symbolic hand-laying. Mission sending teams conduct home assignments—mobilization phases integrating personal devotion with cross-cultural training. As in Antioch, Spirit-born mission momentum arises not from strategy alone but from Spirit-centered worship and fasting. This foundation leads to prayerful sensitivity in the face of open doors and closed roads.

8.2 Open Doors, Closed Roads — Prayerful Sensitivity on the Field (Acts 16:6–10)

Paul's missionary journey illustrates prayerful discernment of Spirit-open and Spirit-closed pathways: prohibited in Asia, turned back in Bithynia, and guided by a Macedonian vision (Acts 16:6–10). This pattern underscores that leaders must actively seek the Spirit's direction rather than impose predefined plans. On the field, prayer teams maintain *journey prayers* for travel routes, cultural entry points, and ministry partnerships, adapting to Spirit's redirects. Training includes *contextual prayer mapping*, assessing political climates, religious landscapes, and social networks. When doors close—visa denials, cultural barriers—missionaries pivot in prayer, seeking alternative strategies. Churches support through *redirect prayer updates*, keeping congregations informed and engaged in intercession. This dynamic responsiveness ensures that mission advances under the Advocate's personal orchestration rather than human ambition. From discerning pathways we explore prayer-care-share cycles.

8.3 Prayer-Care-Share Cycles in Contemporary Evangelism

Effective evangelism integrates cycles of prayer, care, and sharing: prayer opens the heart and environment, care builds authentic relationships, and sharing delivers the gospel message under Spirit guidance. Models such as *Evangelism Explosion* incorporate prayer as the foundational step, followed by service initiatives and relational invitations. Teams undergo training in *holistic evangelism*, combining medical camps, counseling services, and discipleship conversations. The Advocate's personal insight informs where to focus prayer and what care gestures to offer—meals for hungry families, tutoring for children, legal aid for immigrants. Shared testimonies from these cycles fuel further evangelistic vision, creating sustainable outreach rhythms. This integrated approach mirrors Jesus' ministry pattern of preaching, healing, and feeding, demonstrating Spirit-led mission vitality. Stories of revival ignited by concerted intercession set the stage for deepening chapters on ethics and eschatological horizon.

9 Ethics of Petition: Aligning Desires

9.1 "According to His Will" and the Spirit's Filtering Process (1 John 5:14)

Scripture assures that if we ask anything *according to His will*, God hears us (1 John 5:14). The Spirit-person plays a crucial role in aligning our petitions with the Father's intentions, filtering out selfish or shortsighted requests. Intercessors cultivate sensitivity to the Advocate's shaping of desires by testing their prayers against God's revealed purposes in Scripture—seeking justice, mercy, holiness, and the advance of the gospel. Early church theologians emphasized that God's will encompasses both His sovereign decree (His *decretive will*) and His ethical commands (His *preceptive will*). In practice, intercessors frame requests in phrases such as "Lord, if it aligns with Your will…," inviting the Spirit to adjust their heart's posture. Pastoral workshops teach *will alignment exercises* where prayer groups identify community needs and scripturally evaluate corresponding requests. Retreats incorporate *Scripture immersion*—extended reading of God's promises—before petitioning, ensuring that prayers spring from biblical convictions. The Spirit's personal advocacy also surfaces through inner impressions or prophetic words when petitions misalign, prompting repentance or revision. Over time, believers internalize God's values, resulting in prayers that reflect kingdom priorities rather than fleeting impulses. This maturation in petition leads naturally into recognizing and uprooting prayers born of lust or pride.

9.2 Lust, Pride, and the Quenching of Prayer (James 4:3–5)

James diagnoses misguided prayer: "You ask and do not receive, because you ask wrongly, to spend it on your passions" (Jas 4:3). Prayers motivated by lust—seeking selfish gratification—or pride—seeking status or control—quench the Spirit's fire and stall communion with God. Lust can masquerade as legitimate need, requiring intercessors to examine underlying motives: Is the petition driven by love of comfort or by compassion for others? Pride may cloak itself in piety: desiring answers to prove spiritual prowess. Pastors train congregations in *motives examen*—daily reflection on why they prayed certain requests, discerning entitlement from genuine dependence. Corporate confession times allow transparency, as believers confess pride-induced prayers and seek the Advocate's cleansing. Spiritual directors coach directees to cultivate humility through service-oriented prayers, redirecting focus from self to neighbor. The Spirit's personal discipline through conviction corrects unholy motives, safeguarding the integrity of petitions. This purification of prayer life paves the way for cultivating contentment and generosity in supplication.

9.3 Contentment and Generosity Shaped in Supplication (Phil 4:6–7; 1 Tim 6:17–19)

Paul urges, "Do not be anxious about anything, but in everything by prayer and supplication with thanksgiving let your requests be made known... and the peace of God will guard your hearts" (Phil 4:6–7). When prayer is infused with gratitude, it cultivates contentment, releasing anxiety's grip. The Spirit-person orchestrates this transformation, overlaying worries with remembrance of past mercies. Conversely, Timothy is instructed to command the wealthy "not to be haughty... but to do good, be rich in good works, generous and ready to share" (1 Tim 6:17–19). Generosity and prayer intertwine: as believers pray, the Spirit births compassion that prompts sacrificial giving. Churches implement *thanksgiving prayers* before petitions, embedding gratitude as a guardrail against entitlement. Community giving initiatives follow prayer services, allowing immediate outworking of generous impulses. Pastoral counseling on financial stewardship aligns budgets with Spirit-inspired convictions highlighted in prayer. Over time, believers report that prayerful gratitude lessens cravings, while Spirit-led generosity transforms their relationships with material resources. This ethical transformation in petitioning underlines the necessity of ongoing practices that examine motives and maintain communal accountability.

9.4 Practices: Examen of Motives, Communal Accountability

To sustain ethical petition, communities establish rhythms of *prayer motives examen*, modeled on the Ignatian Examen but focused on prayer life. Participants review their petitions over the week, noting shifts from self-centered requests to kingdom-oriented intercessions. Small groups incorporate *motive checks* in prayer time: before praying, each member briefly articulates why they are asking, inviting group feedback and Spirit-led discernment. Leadership teams hold periodic *prayer audits*, reviewing ministry prayer requests for alignment with mission values and Scriptural priorities. Mentors meet regularly with protégés to evaluate prayer journals, guiding them toward humility and generosity. Digital platforms can facilitate anonymous motive reflection, with Spirit-led prompts requesting reframe when self-serving patterns emerge. This blend of personal and communal practices ensures that prayer remains ethically sound, Spirit-empowered, and mission-focused, preparing the way for a sustained life of Spirit-guided prayer.

10 Cultivating a Life of Spirit-Guided Prayer

10.1 Breath Prayers, Jesus Prayer, and Lectio Divina in Spirit Key

Breath prayers—short, repeated phrases such as "Abba, Spirit, guide"—tower in their simplicity, syncing prayer with the body's rhythm and inviting continual Spirit presence. The ancient Jesus Prayer ("Lord Jesus Christ, Son of God, have mercy on me, a sinner") engages both mind and heart, fostering deep humility and ceaseless invocation. Lectio divina, with its fourfold rhythm of reading, meditation, prayer, and contemplation, provides structured space for the Advocate to illuminate Scripture. When practiced in Spirit key, these methods become more than exercises; they morph into Spirit-led dialogues, with practitioners pausing at each stage to sense the Spirit's promptings. Monastic communities have preserved these disciplines, combining them with communal chanting and silence. Contemporary retreats offer *guided breath prayer labs* where participants experiment with timing, posture, and short phrases under prayerful supervision. Spiritual directors teach *Scripture listening*— waiting in silence after reading to capture Spirit-inspired words or images. Integrating these methods into daily life grounds the believer in constant awareness of the Advocate's companionship, enabling prayer that flows spontaneously from Spirit attunement.

10.2 Daily Offices and Spontaneous Bursts — Balancing Structure with Flow

The daily offices—morning, midday, evening, and compline—provide a rhythmic scaffold for communal and individual prayer, historically anchoring believers in Psalmody and Scripture petitions. Yet the Spirit's personal advocacy also invites spontaneous bursts of prayer outside these appointed times—responses to sudden needs, urgent insights, or profound worship moments. Churches that maintain *prayer rhythms* encourage members to pray at set hours while leaving room for Spirit-led spontaneity. Smartphone apps now send *prayer hour alerts* paired with space for free-form journaling. Training in *rhythmic flexibility* helps believers avoid legalism or lethargy: structure ensures accountability, while openness to the Spirit's timing preserves vitality. Pastoral letters and small-group reminders reinforce the value of both disciplines, celebrating stories of midweek spontaneous breakthroughs as well as the steadiness of daily offices. This balanced approach fosters a robust prayer life, seamlessly transitioning into a listening posture that undergirds all Spirit-led prayer.

10.3 Listening Posture: Silence, Impressions, and Prophetic Journaling

Cultivating a listening posture involves intentional silence—pauses between prayers, days of silence, or extended retreats where words give way to expectancy. In these moments, practitioners note *inner impressions*: phrases, scriptures, visions, or feelings that arise under the Advocate's guidance. Prophetic journaling captures these impressions in real time, creating a record for later testing and community sharing. Early desert fathers called this *hesychasm*, the practice of stillness to hear God's whispers. Modern spiritual directors encourage *dream journaling* and *meditation logs*, helping directees discern between personal thoughts and Spirit prompts. Periodic reviews of prophetic journals aid in pattern recognition—identifying recurring themes or validations through scripture or community confirmation. This listening posture deepens intimacy with the Spirit, ensuring that prayers remain two-way conversations rather than monologues. Armed with these skills, believers are ready for mentoring relationships that sustain long-term growth.

10.4 Mentoring and Spiritual Direction for Sustained Growth

No one develops a mature prayer life in isolation; the Advocate often uses seasoned mentors and trained spiritual directors to refine His work in us. Mentors model Spirit-led prayer in daily life, offering guidance, accountability, and encouragement. Spiritual directors, trained in Scripture, theology, and pastoral care, provide confidential spaces for directees to explore prayer struggles, interpret inner promptings, and navigate spiritual transitions. Seminary and clinic programs now include supervised practicums in spiritual direction, ensuring that directors possess both theological acumen and pastoral sensitivity. Peer mentoring circles—triads or quads—enable reciprocal encouragement and prayer for discernment. Annual *prayer retreats with direction* offer extended immersion and reflection, reenergizing personal devotion. Evaluations of spiritual growth include self-assessments and mentor feedback, emphasizing progress over performance. The Spirit's personal mentorship through these relationships solidifies habits of listening, bold petitioning, and intimate fellowship, equipping believers to persevere in Spirit-guided prayer life.

11 Obstacles, Missteps, and Safeguards

11.1 Mysticism without Scripture — Danger of Subjective Drift

When prayer focuses solely on inner experience without tethering to Scripture, believers risk drifting into self-deception or fabricated spirituality. The Advocate forbids divorcing Scripture from Spirit-led prayer, as He never contradicts His written Word (2 Tim 3:16–17). Historical mystics like Madame Guyon suffered directionless exaltation when unguided by biblical anchors. Pastoral safeguards include requiring that prophetic words and impressions align with Scripture, using regular *Word checks* in prayer groups. Spiritual directors enforce *Scriptural accountability*, asking directees to cite relevant verses supporting their impressions. Congregational teaching emphasizes that the Spirit "will glorify me, for he will take what is mine and declare it to you" (John 16:14), underscoring that all authentic spiritual insight magnifies Christ's Word.

11.2 Hyperintellectualism — Quenching Affective Dependence

Conversely, an overemphasis on cognitive analysis and theology without heart engagement can quench the Spirit's warm intercession. Prayer becomes a lecture rather than a duet. Augustine warned against "heartless sermons" that neglect the affections. To safeguard against hyperintellectualism, communities incorporate *affective practices*—guided journaling of emotional responses to Scripture, communal lament sessions, and worship times focused on experiential trust. Lay retreats include *sensory prayer*—using art, movement, and music—to reawaken emotional receptivity. Leaders model vulnerability by sharing personal testimonies of Spirit-led emotional breakthroughs, demonstrating the balance between mind and heart.

11.3 Performance Anxiety in Public Prayer

Public prayer can trigger performance anxiety, causing speakers to focus on applause or self-consciousness rather than Spirit-led sincerity. The Advocate counsels against seeking human approval (Gal 1:10), instead fostering prayers that emerge from genuine dependence. Pastors address this by rotating prayer roles among small groups, providing low-stakes environments for practice. Workshops on *prayer posture* and *voice coaching* help pray-ers gain confidence. Mentors provide constructive feedback focused on authenticity and Spirit sensitivity, not eloquence. Churches also offer *anonymous prayer booths* for those reluctant to pray aloud, encouraging participation without exposure. Over time, consistent practice under Spirit guidance reduces fear and nurtures heartfelt public intercession.

11.4 Accountability, Discernment Teams, and Theological Anchors

To maintain healthy prayer ministries, churches establish *discernment teams*—groups of spiritually mature leaders who vet prophetic words, oversee fasting initiatives, and counsel on prayer direction. Accountability structures include *counseling covenants* requiring prayer ministers to meet regularly with mentors for review of personal devotion and public ministry. Theological anchors—confessions of faith, creeds, and agreed doctrinal statements—provide frameworks for evaluating all prayer initiatives. Rituals of *covenant renewal*—occasional recommitment ceremonies—reinforce communal accountability and reaffirm devotion to Spirit-led prayer under Scripture's lordship. These safeguards ensure that prayer in the Spirit remains both vibrant and faithful.

12 Eschatological Horizon: "The Spirit and the Bride Say, 'Come'" (Rev 22:17)

12.1 Marana tha Spirituality — Groaning for Consummation

John's closing invitation, "The Spirit and the Bride say, 'Come!'" (Rev 22:17), unites the Advocate with the church in eschatological longing. *Marana tha* ("Our Lord, come!") prayer recurs in early Christian liturgies as a succinct cry for consummation. This spirituality transforms present prayer into anticipatory longing, fueling hope amid suffering. Worship services conclude with *Revelation chants*, embedding this cry in congregational memory. Spiritual formation programs teach *eschatological groaning practice*, where participants articulate both grief and expectation for Christ's return. This forward-looking posture shapes all other forms of prayer, anchoring them in the promise of redeemed creation.

12.2 Firstfruits of Communion Anticipating Face-to-Face Glory

While we await the fullness, the Spirit and the Bride experience firstfruits of communion—moments of revelatory intimacy in prayer, worship, and sacraments (Rom 8:23). These foretaste experiences foster deep longing for unmediated fellowship "face to face" (1 Cor 13:12). Retreats themed on *heaven's vision*—using art, silence, and Scripture—prepare believers for ultimate communion. Pastors integrate *anticipatory liturgies*, where prayers for the kingdom's arrival blend thanksgiving for present grace. This dual consciousness—present experience and future hope—imbues all Spirit-led prayer with both joy and yearning.

12.3 Intercession for Creation's Liberation (Rom 8:19–23)

Paul's depiction of creation groaning in anticipation of liberation (Rom 8:19–23) expands Spirit-led prayer beyond human concerns to cosmic restoration. Intercessors pray for environmental healing, species preservation, and ecological justice, aligning petitions with God's redemptive plan for the earth. Churches partner with conservation initiatives, organizing *creation care prayer walks* and *eco-fast days*. Climate justice forums include *liturgical prayers* invoking Spirit renewal over land and sea. This broadened intercession recognizes the Advocate's mission to reconcile all things, embedding creation care within the church's prayer identity.

Conclusion

As we have seen, the Spirit's personal ministry undergirds every dimension of prayer—opening the veil, securing adoption, translating our deepest longings, and sustaining vigilant intercession. This dynamic access builds a foundation not only for private devotions but also for unified corporate advocacy, vibrant worship, and strategic mission. With hearts attuned to the Advocate's guidance, our prayers become both foretaste and foretaste of the day when Spirit, Bride, and all creation will cry, "Come, Lord Jesus." In the next chapter, we will turn this intercessory momentum into expressions of worship and adoration, discovering how the Spirit's presence shapes every song, sacrament, and liturgical gesture toward eternal praise.

Chapter 13. Worship, Adoration, and the Spirit's Presence

Worship is more than ritual—it is the dynamic encounter between a Spirit-led people and their triune God, transforming spaces, hearts, and everyday rhythms into sacred acts of adoration. From the earliest tabernacle cloud to Pentecost's portable sanctuary, the Advocate has guided the church into new expressions of praise that transcend boundaries of place, culture, and tradition. Whether through ancient psalms or contemporary hymns, prophetic oracles or silent contemplation, artful architecture or digital innovation, genuine worship arises when every element submits to the Spirit's personal presence. This chapter explores how the Spirit animates every dimension of worship—liturgical structure, musical creativity, sacramental encounter, and communal diversity—drawing the faithful into deeper intimacy with the Father through the Son.

1 Foundations: Worship "in Spirit and Truth"

1.1 Johannine Mandate—Relocating Worship from Place to Presence (John 4:23–24)

Jesus' conversation with the Samaritan woman reorients worship from a physical locale to the reality of divine presence, declaring that true worshipers will worship "in Spirit and Truth." This shift underscores that external ritual, whether on Gerizim or in Jerusalem, becomes inadequate when the Spirit is poured out on all believers (Joel 2:28–29). Johannine theology thus grounds worship in personal encounter: the Spirit, as the breath of God, animates hearts to perceive God's realities beyond sensory space. Early Christian communities applied this by meeting in homes, caves, and gathered courts, trusting that the Advocate would make their midst holy. The church father Origen taught that "place" in John 4 symbolizes the human heart as the new temple. Contemporary worship leaders emphasize Spirit-led atmospheres rather than building-dependent experiences, reminding congregations that corporate gatherings simply provide occasions for divine visitation. Training in contextual worship includes exercises in sensing God's presence in outdoor or nontraditional venues. The Johannine mandate demands that all planning and structure must be subservient to the Spirit's dynamic movement, ensuring that worship remains authentic rather than programmatic. This foundational understanding of presence leads directly to recognizing the Trinitarian logic of worship.

1.2 Trinitarian Logic—Father Seeks, Son Mediates, Spirit Energizes (Eph 2:18)

The pathway of worship reflects the Trinity's relational dance: the Father initiates by seeking worshipers (John 4:23), the Son opens the way through atonement (Heb 10:19–20), and the Spirit empowers and energizes worship (Eph 2:18). Paul writes that "through Him we both have access in one Spirit to the Father," encapsulating the triune choreography. Liturgically, prayers often begin "Almighty Father," pass through "in the name of Jesus," and close "by the power of the Holy Spirit," modeling this theological sequence. The church's doxologies mirror this: "Glory to the Father, through the Son, in the Holy Spirit." Early doxographers expanded on this pattern, crafting hymns that trace the sending order of the Godhead. Worship planners integrate Trinitarian petitions, ensuring that songs, prayers, and sacraments acknowledge each Person's role. Seminars on worship theology teach how neglecting any Person distorts the experience— Father-focused devotions can become moralistic, Son-centered services risk Christological reductionism, and Spirit-exclusive emphases verge on emotionalism. Embracing the full Trinitarian logic produces balanced worship that both humbles and elevates. Having established this, we turn to the dual posture of holiness and filial confidence.

1.3 Holiness and Awe—Approaching the Consuming Fire with Filial Confidence (Heb 12:28–29)

The writer to the Hebrews exhorts believers to "draw near with a true heart in full assurance of faith" (Heb 10:22) because we serve "a consuming fire" (Heb 12:29). True worship thus balances reverence for God's holiness with the confidence granted by adoption (Rom 8:15). The Spirit's role is to calibrate this tension: He convicts us of sin, fostering awe, yet consoles us as our Advocate, nurturing bold approach. Early Jewish Christians likened this to the temple's holy fire: unpredictable and purifying. Worship environments reflect this dual posture through moments of silent awe—candles, veiled crosses—followed by exuberant praise. Training in corporate liturgy includes modules on reverent silence and Spirit-driven exuberance, preventing either irreverence or paralysis. Small-group practices incorporate *holy pause* exercises before communal prayer. The Spirit's personal ministry ensures that worshipers neither take familiarity for granted nor shrink from intimacy. This balanced awe naturally unfolds into living sacrifice.

1.4 Living Sacrifice—Daily Obedience as Doxological Lifestyle (Rom 12:1–2)

Paul's call to present our bodies as a living sacrifice—holy and acceptable—frames worship not as weekly performance but as continuous obedience. The Spirit energizes this consecration, empowering believers to offer every thought, word, and action as an act of praise. Daily routines—work, rest, relationships—become doxological opportunities, turning the ordinary into worship under Spirit guidance. Early monastic rules emphasized sanctifying mundane tasks—cooking, farming, copying manuscripts—as spiritual sacrifices. Contemporary spiritual formation programs integrate *sacrificial service* into vocational calling, encouraging professionals to view ethical choices as worship. Worship planners remind congregations that Sunday liturgy equips Monday obedience. The Advocate's sustaining power prevents sacrificial fatigue, transforming obedience into joy. This living sacrifice ethos transitions worship from personal devotion into the unfolding narrative of God's presence, setting the stage for the canonical trajectory of worship.

2 Canonical Trajectory: Tabernacle, Temple, Upper Room

2.1 Glory Cloud Filling Tent and Temple (Ex 40:34–38; 1 Kings 8:10–11)

God's presence descending as a cloud in the wilderness tabernacle (Ex 40:34–38) and later filling Solomon's temple (1 Kings 8:10–11) set the pattern for worship as a site of encounter. The *shekhinah* cloud signified divine immanence, guiding Israel on journey and anchoring worship in visible glory. This tangible presence taught that worship spaces shape and reflect holiness. Ancient architects oriented worship structures eastward toward dawn, symbolizing the morning advent of God's presence. Liturgical rituals—incense, veils, chanted Psalms—echoed the wilderness sensory experience. The Spirit's personal role emerges when the physical cloud gives way to the Indwelling—Pentecost's cloud-like wind and fire (Acts 2:2–4). Worship planners weave historical motifs into modern spaces—smoke machines, colored lights, processional pathways—reminding congregations of glory descending. Yet the Spirit's invisible work transcends spectacle, inviting hearts to perceive presence beyond sensory stimuli. This progression flows into the Exilic purification of worship motives.

2.2 Exilic Purification of Worship Motives (Ps 137; Ezek 11:16–20)

During exile, Israel's worship became dysfunctional—chants in foreign lands rang hollow, as Psalm 137 laments—"How shall we sing the Lord's song in a foreign land?" The prophets, especially Ezekiel, foresaw a purified worship community whose hearts would be circumcised (Ezek 11:16–20). The Spirit's future indwelling promised true worshipers whose motives aligned with God's heart rather than nationalistic ritual. This purification process illustrates that mere form without Spirit-led fervor breeds emptiness. Exilic reflections led Second Temple reforms under Ezra and Nehemiah, emphasizing Torah teaching and communal confession over elaborate offerings. Contemporary worship emphasizes authenticity over style, encouraging congregations to examine their motives—seeking God's glory rather than cultural trendiness. Worship leaders facilitate *corporate lament* services to process communal guilt and renew wholehearted devotion. The Spirit's personal cleansing paves the way for the portable sanctuary inaugurated at Pentecost.

2.3 Pentecost as Portable Sanctuary—Spirit Inhabits Believers (Acts 2:1–4)

Pentecost fulfills the prophetic promise: the Holy Spirit descends like a violent wind and tongues of fire upon each believer, creating a portable sanctuary within their hearts (Acts 2:1–4). No longer confined to a building, God's presence now fills the gathered community wherever they assembled. The early church experienced worship that overflowed from the upper room into streets and homes, demonstrating that the Spirit's habitation freed worship from temple walls. Worship planners today adopt *guerilla worship* approaches—flash mobs, street praise—embodying this portable sanctuary ethos. Training in *Spirit mobility* encourages intercession in various contexts—urban, rural, online—trusting that the Advocate energizes worship beyond brick and mortar. The portable sanctuary model underscores that every believer, as a living stone, carries the presence into daily life. This expansion into homes and courts marks the final stage in the canonical trajectory.

2.4 Early Church Gatherings in Homes and Courts (Acts 2:46; Rom 16:5)

Luke notes that the first Christians "broke bread in their homes and ate their food with glad and generous hearts" (Acts 2:46), while Paul greets Prisca and Aquila's house church (Rom 16:5), illustrating that early worship thrived in domestic settings. These gatherings blended table fellowship, singing of Psalms, teaching, and prayer, reflecting a holistic approach to adoration. Domestic architecture influenced worship patterns—circles of chairs around a meal table, acoustic niches for intimate singing, and shared meals fostering unity. Early charges to "not neglect meeting together" (Heb 10:25) included but were not limited to formal edifices. Contemporary house church movements reclaim this pattern, using living rooms, courtyards, and even cafes as worship venues. Leaders train hosts in setting worshipful atmospheres—lighting, Scripture displays, accessible instruments—while acknowledging the Spirit's role in filling any space. Understanding these home-based gatherings completes our canonical survey and informs Spirit-guided liturgical design.

3 Spirit-Guided Liturgy: Structure and Spontaneity

3.1 Fourfold Apostolic Pattern—Word, Table, Prayer, Fellowship (Acts 2:42)

The earliest Christian liturgy followed a fourfold rhythm: devotion to apostolic teaching (Word), fellowship around meals (Table), prayer, and communal life (Fellowship). This pattern honored both

278

structure—the teaching and table elements—and relational spontaneity—prayer and koinōnia. The Spirit oversaw this balance, ensuring that doctrinal clarity coexisted with relational warmth. Early worship manuals, such as the Didache, provided outlines for these elements without prescribing rigid sequences, allowing the Spirit to animate assemblies. Modern liturgical planners incorporate reading of apostolic texts, celebration of the Lord's Supper, corporate intercession, and small-group sharing within a single service. Training in *fourfold facilitation* equips leaders to recognize when to shift from planned readings to Spirit-led prophecy or testimony. This dynamic recipe fosters holistic worship that engages head, heart, and hands. It also sets the foundation for combining fixed and charismatic elements.

3.2 Fixed Elements: Creeds, Psalms, Readings, Blessings (Col 3:16; 2 Tim 4:13)

Fixed liturgical elements create continuity and doctrinal stability across generations. Recitation of creeds affirms shared beliefs; singing Psalms connects the church to the Spirit-inspired songbook; Scripture readings ensure the Word remains central; blessings impart divine favor. Paul instructs believers to let the word of Christ dwell richly, teaching and admonishing one another in all wisdom (Col 3:16), underscoring the place of fixed forms. Early church practice included the Rule of Faith—a proto-creed—and a lectionary for OT and apostolic writings. Contemporary worship services maintain these through printed bulletins, projection screens, and responsive readings. Liturgists teach that fixed elements provide theological guardrails, shaping expectations and guarding against drift. Music directors curate Psalm settings that span genres, and clergy craft blessings that resonate cross-culturally. This structural reliability frees the Spirit to move spontaneously within safe boundaries. From fixed forms we move to charismatic elements that enliven worship.

3.3 Charismatic Elements: Prophecy, Testimonies, Tongues (1 Cor 14:26–33)

Even within structured services, the Spirit impels unexpected expressions: prophecy that addresses present needs, testimonies that witness past mercies, tongues that express unspeakable yearnings. Paul regulates these gifts in 1 Corinthians 14 to ensure they edify without causing confusion. Early assemblies practiced *orderly openness*, appointing moderators to recognize and integrate Spirit-inspired contributions. Modern worship services allocate *spontaneity slots*—portions of the service where attendees may share a word, a story, or a prayer in tongues, moderated by team leaders. Training in *charismatic stewardship* equips teams to discern authenticity, timing, and theological alignment of these elements. By embracing charismatic expressions within the liturgical flow, congregations experience both structural solidity and Spirit-driven freshness. This synergy prepares hearts for the broader rhythm of worship preparation and sending.

3.4 Rhythm of Preparation, Encounter, and Sending (Isa 6:1–8; Luke 24:30–35)

Worship follows a triptych rhythm: preparation (penitence, Scripture meditation), encounter (Word proclaimed, Spirit's visitation), and sending (commissioning into mission). Isaiah's vision—his garments cleansed before divine commissioning—models the necessary preparation. The Emmaus travelers' hearts burned as the disciples broke bread, illustrating the encounter. Luke's account of Jesus' ascension and subsequent Spirit-sent mission underscores the sending dimension. Church services often mimic this: *confession* and *silence* open the service, followed by *preaching* and *worship*, and conclude with a *benediction* commissioning believers. Retreats extend this rhythm over days, deepening each movement. Worship design teams craft transition cues—lighting, music, liturgical posture changes—to move congregants through these phases under the Spirit's guidance. This tripartite rhythm fosters transformative worship that empowers daily mission, leading naturally into the musical expressions that give voice to adoration.

4 Musical Expressions: Psalms, Hymns, Spiritual Songs

4.1 Psalter as Spirit-Inspired Songbook (Eph 5:18–20)

Paul exhorts believers to be "filled with the Spirit, addressing one another in Psalms and hymns and spiritual songs," affirming the Psalter's primary role in worship. The 150 Psalms, composed under various Spirit-inspired authors, cover the full spectrum of human experience—lament, petition, praise, thanksgiving. Early Christian worship preserved psalmody in multiple languages—Hebrew, Greek, Syriac—ensuring that the Spirit's original inspiration transcended cultural boundaries. Modern worship leaders curate psalm-singing sets, alternating ancient translations with contemporary paraphrases, preserving theological depth while engaging current idioms. Breath prayer and chanting techniques help congregations internalize psalms for personal devotion and corporate worship. Seminars on *psalm mapping* teach how psalm themes correspond to liturgical seasons—Advent, Lent, Easter—ensuring that the Spirit's ancient words resonate with present contexts. This rich psalter foundation broadens into new-creation hymns.

4.2 New-Creation Hymns in the Apocalypse (Rev 5:9–14; 15:3–4)

Revelation offers visions of heavenly worship, with chapters 5 and 15 presenting new hymns of the Lamb—songs not recorded in the Old Testament but spontaneously arisen in the Spirit's presence. These new-creation hymns celebrate redemptive history's climax, combining biblical motifs—creation's song, covenant fulfillment, cosmic victory. Early worship traditions incorporated *apocalyptic canticles* into liturgies for Easter and Pentecost. Modern hymnwriters draw on Revelation's imagery—multitude from every tribe, the song of Moses, harps and bowls of incense—to craft fresh lyrics and melodies. Worship workshops help congregations compose their own new-creation songs, providing templates for scriptural poetic structures. Integrating these hymns into Sunday services inspires participants to glimpse the eschatological reality for which they long. The Spirit's personal inspiration thus births new doxologies, bridging canonical text and contemporary expression. This creativity extends to instrumentation.

4.3 Cultural Instrumentation—Harps to Electric Guitars under Spirit Discernment (Ps 150; 1 Cor 9:22–23)

Psalm 150 exhorts praise with ten categories of instruments—trumpet, harp, lyre, tambourine, dance, strings, pipe, cymbals—affirming the value of diverse musical textures. Paul's contextual approach—becoming "all things to all people" (1 Cor 9:22)—encourages worshipers to adopt culturally appropriate instruments, from medieval organ to African drums, from Irish flute to electric guitar. The Spirit's discernment guides communities in selecting instrumentation that glorifies God without introducing distractions or cultural syncretism. Worship teams conduct *instrument audit sessions* to evaluate how new instruments impact corporate focus and theological coherence. Ethnomusicologists sometimes consult with congregations to adapt indigenous rhythms and scales. Technology, including loop stations and digital mixing boards, expands possibilities, but requires Spirit-led restraint to prevent mere concert atmosphere. The goal remains unity of voice and Spirit. This musical diversity arrives at congregational participation.

4.4 Congregational Participation versus Spectator Performance (1 Cor 14:15–17)

Paul insists that when believers pray or sing, they should do so intelligibly, ensuring that the congregation "may be built up" rather than left bewildered (1 Cor 14:15–17). True worship invites all to participate—hymn verses, responsive readings, communal chants—rather than relegating the congregation to passive spectators. Early Christian assemblies practiced *antiphonal singing*, alternating groups and encouraging communal voice. Contemporary worship services include projected lyrics, printed song sheets, and assisted-learning for new songs. Leaders model participation, inviting less confident members to join in simple refrains. Small-group music workshops teach basic vocal and instrumental skills to expand participation. The Spirit's personal prompting often leads timid believers to venture a line or two, gradually integrating them into the full chorus. This participatory ethos ensures that worship remains the Body's collective expression rather than a stage performance, completing our exploration of the foundational, structural, and musical dimensions of Spirit-led worship.

5 Prophetic and Charismatic Dimensions of Worship

5.1 Spontaneous Oracles That Edify, Exhort, and Console (1 Cor 14:3)

Spiritual oracles within worship gatherings function as direct communications from the Advocate to the Body, addressing current needs with timely encouragement. The apostle Paul emphasizes that prophecy "speaks to people for their upbuilding and encouragement and consolation," framing spontaneous oracles as gifts of pastoral care rather than theatrical spectacle. In practice, worship services allocate specific moments for individuals sensitive to the Spirit to share brief prophetic words, always subject to communal testing under Scripture (1 Cor 14:29). Historical patristic accounts describe prophets in the Didache-era church delivering exhortations that corrected moral lapses or inspired generosity. Contemporary worship leaders train prophecy teams in discernment protocols: praying for clarity, jotting impressions in notebooks, and sharing only when confirmed by other mature believers. Oracles may call a congregation to repentance, warn of upcoming trials, or highlight unseen ministry opportunities. Each word must align with the gospel's tenor—never contradicting Scripture or sowing fear. As participants receive prophetic insights, they often respond with corporate prayers or practical follow-up, integrating the oracle into ongoing ministry. Pastoral debriefs after services help confirm or refine prophetic words, ensuring they serve the Body's welfare. The Spirit's personal ministry thus shapes the worship experience, linking divine voice with human hearts. This spontaneous dimension coexists with lament and warfare songs, which channel prophetic intensity into communal expression.

5.2 Spirit-Stirred Lament and Warfare Songs (2 Chr 20:21–22; Acts 16:25–26)

Corporate worship sometimes erupts into lament or spiritual battle hymns when the Advocate moves hearts to engage suffering or oppose evil. In 2 Chronicles 20, King Jehoshaphat appoints singers to praise God before military engagement, resulting in divine victory (2 Chr 20:21–22). Similarly, Paul and Silas prayed and sang hymns in Philippian prison at midnight, prompting an earthquake that opened the jail (Acts 16:25–26). These biblical precedents illustrate that lament can express deep sorrow while warfare songs declare trust in divine deliverance. Worship gatherings that include lament offer space for communal grief—over injustice, loss, national crises— inviting the Spirit to transform sorrow into hope. Worship leaders introduce structured lament liturgies: shared readings of Psalms like Psalm 13, periods of silence, and responsive singing guided by prophetic musicians. Warfare songs—rhythmic anthems invoking God's strength—often arise spontaneously as participants sense spiritual opposition. Training in spiritual warfare worship emphasizes refraining from melodramatic aggression; rather, songs focus on God's sovereignty, justice, and compassion. Technical teams adjust lighting and sound to support the atmosphere without overshadowing the worshipers' engagement. Pastoral teams remain vigilant for emotional safety, offering follow-up care for those processing deep trauma. The Spirit's personal prompting ensures that lament and warfare songs serve both emotional release and prophetic declaration, paving the way for embodied praise through dance and banners.

5.3 Dance, Banners, and Bodily Response—Embodied Praise (2 Sam 6:14; Ps 149:3)

Worship in Spirit and truth embraces the whole person—body included—as a vehicle for adoration. David's leaping before the Ark (2 Sam 6:14) and the psalmist's exhortation to "praise his name with dancing" (Ps 149:3) establish dance as an ancient and biblical form of bodily praise. Similarly, the use of banners or flags—biblical in its symbolism of victory and celebration—adds a visual dimension to worship. Churches today integrate choreographed and spontaneous dance teams, as well as flag ministries, to translate worshipers' inner joy into physical motion. Leaders provide training in safe movement, cultural sensitivity (avoiding non-Christian religious symbols), and theological grounding so that embodied praise remains Christ-centered. Worship spaces are configured to allow freedom of movement—sturdy floors, clear aisles, and padded walls where needed. Embodied praise practices often emerge organically during Spirit-led moments—worshipers sense warmth or exhilaration and respond with lifted arms, shouts, or dance. Pastoral oversight ensures that these expressions do not become performance or distraction: leaders remind participants that the focus remains on God rather than individual skill. In small-group worship settings, embodied praise fosters intimacy and mutual encouragement. The Spirit's personal presence transforms bodies into living instruments of worship, naturally flowing into the safeguarding of theology and order when prophetic expressions arise.

5.4 Safeguarding Theology and Order amid Prophetic Flow (1 Th 5:19–22)

While charismatic expressions enliven worship, they require theological and procedural safeguards to maintain coherence and guard against deception. Paul warns, "Do not quench the Spirit. Do not despise prophecies, but test everything; hold fast what is good" (1 Th 5:19–22). Churches implement multi-layered oversight: trained moderators discern the theological content of oracles, elders review shared revelations for biblical consistency, and small-group councils provide relational accountability. Prophetic words are weighed against core doctrines—Christ's lordship, the gospel's sufficiency, Scripture's authority—ensuring no departure into aberrant teachings. Periodic theological refresher courses equip worship teams, intercessors, and prophetic ministries to recognize error. Written guidelines outline acceptable forms of expression, clarifying when to pause and confer rather than immediately share a word. Discipleship pathways include modules on prophetic etiquette: listening prayer, respectful speech, and deference to pastoral leadership. Immediate misuse—sensationalism, prideful declarations, unscriptural prophecies—triggers remedial mentoring and potential temporary removal from ministry roles. By balancing openness with discernment, congregations create safe environments where the Spirit's personal gifts can flow without destabilizing the Body. These order-maintaining practices form a bridge to sacramental participation and epiclesis, where the Spirit's presence is invoked over tangible rites.

6 Sacramental Participation and Epiclesis

6.1 Baptism into One Body by the Spirit (1 Cor 12:13; Acts 10:44–48)

Baptism inaugurates believers into the Body of Christ through the Spirit's direct agency—Paul writes, "For in one Spirit we were all baptized into one body" (1 Cor 12:13), and Peter witnesses the Spirit falling on Gentile converts, prompting immediate baptism (Acts 10:44–48). This sacramental moment blends divine action with human response, as water and Spirit unite to mark new identity. Early church liturgies featured baptistery ceremonies replete with exorcism prayers, renunciations, and the laying on of hands to signify Spirit reception. Catechumens prepared through extended instruction on creeds and moral teaching, ensuring informed faith. Contemporary baptism services often include testimonies of Spirit-led callings, anointing with oil, and communal laying on of hands post-immersion to emphasize epiclesis—the Spirit's descent. Pastors and deacons pray over each candidate, asking the Advocate to seal them with the Spirit's gift. Churches offer follow-up baptismal classes to nurture foundational spiritual disciplines. Baptism's sacramental reality anchors the believer's lifelong participation in worship and community, leading into the epiclesis of the Eucharist.

6.2 Eucharistic Epiclesis—Invoking the Spirit over Bread, Cup, and People (1 Cor 10:16)

The New Testament portrays the cup as "participation in the blood of Christ" and the bread as "participation in the body of Christ" (1 Cor 10:16), highlighting the Spirit's role in actualizing Christ's presence. Epiclesis—the formal invocation of the Holy Spirit—transforms the elements into vehicles of grace and consecrates the assembled community. Early liturgies in both East and West featured explicit epicleses: "Come, Holy Spirit, and sanctify these gifts" and "Send Your Spirit upon us and these gifts." Contemporary Eucharistic prayers incorporate varied epiclesis formulas, ensuring that leaders explicitly call upon the Advocate's personal ministry. Training for celebrants includes theological reflection on the Spirit's role in making sacraments efficacious, as well as practical guidance on pacing, gestures, and congregation engagement. Lay eucharistic ministers also learn to invite Spirit presence in assistance to the presider. Worship planners position the epiclesis just before or after the words of institution, depending on tradition, to maintain theological coherence. The Spirit's descent in epiclesis unites the invisible and visible, consecrating both gifts and people for ongoing worship and mission, guiding us into other Spirit-charged rites.

6.3 Foot-Washing, Anointing with Oil, and Other Spirit-Charged Rites (John 13:14–15; Jas 5:14–15)

Jesus' mandate to wash one another's feet (John 13:14–15) and James' instruction to anoint the sick with oil in the Lord's name (Jas 5:14–15) exemplify how physical rites become Spirit-charged encounters. Foot-washing services, practiced in many traditions on Maundy Thursday, symbolize humility, forgiveness, and mutual care under Spirit influence. Anointing with oil—whether for healing, commissioning, or blessing—invites the Advocate's personal touch, as ministers pray for specific needs and sense Spirit empowerment. Worship communities train designated ministers in hygiene, pastoral sensitivity, and prophetic listening to accompany these rites responsibly. Cultural adaptations—using local oils, water, or symbolic gestures—reflect the Spirit's contextual flexibility. Rites are introduced with Scripture readings explaining their biblical roots, followed by prayers inviting the Spirit's presence. Pastoral care teams coordinate follow-up for those who receive anointing, ensuring that spiritual encounter leads to holistic support. These Spirit-charged rites reinforce the sacrament's nature as encounter, not mere symbol, leading us into the transformative power of sacramental communion.

6.4 Sacrament as Encounter, Not Mere Symbol—Spirit Turns Sign into Communion (Luke 24:30–31)

The Emmaus road narrative shows that Christ is made known in the breaking of bread (Luke 24:30–31), illustrating that sacraments transcend symbolic representation when the Spirit illumines hearts. In Eucharistic gatherings, the Advocate transforms the sign (bread and cup) into a real means of communion, effecting spiritual union with Christ and the church. Early theologians like Augustine emphasized *fective*—making effective—dimension of sacraments by the Spirit's power. Contemporary worship includes moments of contemplative silence after communion, inviting worshipers to sense Christ's presence. Small-group discussions on sacramental experience help participants articulate Spirit-led encounters beyond intellectual assent. Churches incorporate *communion meditation guides*—Scripture and artwork—focusing minds and hearts on the mystery at hand. Training for ministers stresses that sacraments require both correct form and Spirit agency to function as encounters with Christ. This sacramental encounter seamlessly transitions into the aesthetic expressions that shape worship atmosphere.

7 Aesthetic Inspiration: Art, Architecture, and Atmosphere

7.1 Bezalel's Spirit-Gifted Craftsmanship as Paradigm (Ex 31:1–5)

God fills Bezalel "with the Spirit of God…the ability to engage in all kinds of crafts" (Ex 31:1–5), establishing aesthetic beauty as integral to worship. His anointing manifested in intricate designs for the tabernacle's curtains, furniture, and sacred objects, demonstrating that artistry itself is a Spirit-originated gift. Worship spaces throughout history—Byzantine mosaics, Gothic cathedrals, Renaissance frescoes—embody Bezalel's paradigm, inviting worshipers into transcendent beauty. Contemporary church architects and artists view their work as ministry, seeking Spirit inspiration through prayer, scriptural reflection, and collaborative visioning sessions. Materials—from local stone to recycled metal—are chosen for both symbolic resonance and ecological stewardship, reflecting the Advocate's holistic creative care. Workshops on *sacred art theology* teach that aesthetic elements shape theology in worshipers' hearts, pointing to divine glory. Each brushstroke, carving, or installation becomes an offering of spiritual craft, leading communities to sensory encounters with the Spirit. This Spirit-inspired artistry finds expression in light, color, and space.

7.2 Light, Color, and Space Shaping Attentiveness to Glory (Rev 4:3–6)

John's vision of the throne room—jasper, carnelian, rainbow-like light, and sea of glass—provides a blueprint for using light and color to evoke awe (Rev 4:3–6). Worship architects harness natural light through windows, skylights, and reflective surfaces, symbolizing the light of Christ piercing human darkness. Colored glass and LED systems create dynamic atmospheres aligned with liturgical seasons—deep blues for Advent, radiant golds for Easter. Spatial design—high ceilings, thoughtfully placed seating, and clear sightlines—encourages upward gazing and communal cohesion. Many modern worship centers incorporate *immersive projection* of nebulae, stained-glass patterns, or biblical scenes, engaging multiple senses. Technical teams coordinate light cues with musical and spoken elements, ensuring that sensory stimuli enhance rather than distract from worship. Training in *environmental theology* helps planners understand how physical space communicates spiritual truths. These aesthetic choices, under Spirit discernment, prime worshipers for deeper engagement, preparing them for iconographic resonance.

7.3 Iconography and Visual Scripture in Historic Traditions (Ex 25:18–22; Col 1:15)

God commands cherubim imagery on the Ark's mercy seat (Ex 25:18–22), and Paul calls Christ "the image of the invisible God" (Col 1:15), sanctioning the use of visual representation in worship. Iconography in Eastern Orthodoxy employs canonical styles to convey theological truths—Christ Pantocrator, Theotokos, and saints—serving as "windows to heaven" under the Spirit's anointing. Western cathedrals feature stained-glass cycles depicting biblical narratives, teaching the faithful through light and color. Contemporary visual Scripture initiatives include large-scale murals, digital signage devices showing animated Bible stories, and projection art in worship spaces. Artists and theological advisors collaborate to ensure accuracy and doctrinal integrity. Icon-painting workshops incorporate prayerful preparation, fasting, and adherence to early church canons. Worshipers engage icons through veneration—standing, bowing, and lighting candles—practices facilitated by pastoral instruction. This visual theology invites contemplation of spiritual realities, bridging to digital and multimedia creativity.

7.4 Digital and Multimedia Creativity—Spirit Innovation for Modern Worship (Ps 96:1–3)

Psalm 96 urges "sing to the Lord, all the earth; declare his glory among the nations," a call that modern worship answers through digital platforms—live streaming, projection mapping, and interactive apps. Multimedia worship teams integrate video testimonies, lyric overlays, and ambient soundscapes to craft immersive experiences. Graphic designers produce thematic visuals aligned with sermon series, while animators create motion graphics that illustrate biblical concepts. Social media platforms host virtual prayer walls and worship playlists, extending communal praise beyond physical buildings. Training in *digital discipleship* teaches technical skills alongside spiritual discernment, ensuring content honors the Spirit's presence and avoids sensory overload. Technical rehearsals include prayerful testing phases, where teams discern which multimedia elements invite genuine engagement. This innovative use of technology under Spirit guidance expands the canvas of worship, setting the stage for unity and diversity at the table of praise.

8 Unity and Diversity at the Table of Praise

8.1 One Spirit, Many Members—Intercultural Harmonies (1 Cor 12:12–13; Rev 7:9)

The Body of Christ comprises many members, each with distinct cultural song-lines, yet unified by the one Spirit. Paul writes that "by one Spirit we were all baptized into one body" (1 Cor 12:13), and Revelation portrays a great multitude from every nation worshiping together (Rev 7:9). Intercultural harmonies emerge when congregations incorporate global songs—African choruses, Latin American boleros, Asian chants—into worship sets, inviting diverse voices to lead. Worship teams host *global music nights*, teaching congregants the languages, histories, and spiritual contexts of each tradition. Cross-cultural partnerships with overseas churches yield worship exchanges and joint recordings, fostering mutual enrichment. Pastors emphasize the theological basis for diversity: every culture bears Imago Dei creativity. Technical teams adjust sound mixes to blend instruments and voices authentically. Such harmonies testify to the Advocate's unifying work, paving the way for generational dialogue.

8.2 Generational Dialogue—Elders' Wisdom, Children's Wonder (Joel 2:28–29; Ps 8:2)

Joel's promise that "your old men shall dream dreams, and your young men shall see visions" (Joel 2:28) and David's praise that God uses "little children" to declare His praise (Ps 8:2) affirm generational contributions to worship. Elders bring depth—centuries of spiritual insight, theological reflection, and hymnody—while children infuse wonder—spontaneous shouts, simple refrains, and unselfconscious joy. Intergenerational worship services intentionally incorporate children's choirs, youth bands, and elders' choirs, alternating leadership roles. Family-friendly liturgies include storytelling segments where grandparents recall Spirit-led adventures and children respond with creative expressions—drawings, poems, dances. Training programs equip multi-generational teams in intergenerational facilitation—managing transitions and honoring each age's gifts. The Spirit's personal enlivening across ages nurtures mutual respect and shared discovery. This generational synergy prepares congregations for partnerships in prophecy and prayer across gender lines.

8.3 Gender Partnership in Prayer and Prophecy (Acts 21:9; 1 Cor 11:5)

Philip's four daughters prophesying (Acts 21:9) and Paul's acknowledgment that women may pray and prophesy with their heads covered (1 Cor 11:5) establish biblical grounds for gender partnership in worship. Women and men share equally in leading prayers, prophetic declarations, and intercession. Congregations draft inclusive liturgical roles—rotating male and female presiders, prayer leaders, and testimony sharers—to reflect the Spirit's impartial gifting. Training in gender-sensitive ministry addresses cultural barriers that inhibit women's full participation, offering theological clarity on complementarity rather than hierarchy. Worship education classes emphasize the prophetic role of women in church history—Miriam, Deborah, Anna—and contemporary examples. Pastoral guidelines ensure that all prayers and prophecies, regardless of gender, are tested for sound doctrine and fruitfulness. By honoring gender partnership, churches mirror the Advocate's universal outpouring of gifts, opening pathways for believers with disabilities to contribute fully.

8.4 Accessibility and Inclusion of Believers with Disabilities (Luke 14:21; 2 Cor 12:9)

Jesus' parable of the great banquet (Luke 14:21) instructs the church to invite the marginalized—those with disabilities—into the feast of worship. Paul's affirmation that God's power is perfected in weakness (2 Cor 12:9) underscores that Spirit presence shines through disabled bodies and minds. Worship spaces include ramps, hearing loops, large-print and braille song sheets, sign-language interpreters, and quiet rooms for neurodiverse participants. Worship planners engage disability advocates in design and programming, ensuring full participation in singing, prayer, prophecy, and sacraments. Assistive technology—captioned live streams, tactile worship aids, and accessible smartphone apps—extends inclusion. Training for worship teams emphasizes sensitivity to varied expressions of participation— from nonverbal worship to sculptural art responses. Congregations celebrate testimonies of disabled believers whose Spirit-led gifts— artistic, prophetic, intercessory—have deepened communal worship. By integrating accessibility and honoring weakness as a conduit for divine strength, the church embodies the Advocate's inclusive love, completing our exploration of worship's unity and diversity under the Spirit's vibrant presence.

9 Personal Devotion Overflowing into Corporate Praise

9.1 Daily Offices and Secret Prayer Fueling Sunday Worship (Dan 6:10; Matt 6:6)

Daily offices—morning, midday, evening—root believers in habitual communion, reminding them that each hour belongs to God. Drawing on Daniel's disciplined habit of praying three times daily (Dan 6:10), these prayer rhythms train the heart to turn toward the Father even amid work and routine. Secret prayer, as Jesus teaches, occurs in private closets where the Father, unseen, rewards openly (Matt 6:6). Over time, the personal intimacy developed in private devotion becomes the wellspring for Sunday's corporate adoration. Individuals who have tasted early-morning hymnody and midday breath prayers arrive at the assembly with hearts already saturated in Spirit-presence. Pre-service prayer teams often begin worship spacing with a mini-office, setting a tone of expectancy. Musicians who pray the daily office find their playing infused with reflective depth, resonating beyond technical skill. Pastors who model secret prayer encourage congregations to value solitude as a prelude to communal celebration. Devotional journals kept during secret prayers frequently yield spontaneous songs or prophetic words shared later on Sundays. The Advocate's personal ministry in private devotion thus becomes a catalyst for richer corporate expressions. As personal intimacy deepens, individuals discover that their hidden prayers find corporate echoes in the gathered Body's united voice. This overflow bridges naturally into the sung Scripture of lectio divina.

9.2 Lectio Divina and Sung Scripture (Col 3:16)

Lectio divina invites worshipers to read Scripture slowly—pondering, meditating, praying, and resting—allowing the text to speak by the

Spirit. Paul's exhortation to let "the word of Christ dwell in you richly…singing psalms and hymns and spiritual songs" (Col 3:16) links contemplative reading with vocal response. In practice, small groups meditate on a brief passage, then craft short refrains that capture its essence, transforming text into sung poetry. Worship leaders integrate these congregational refrains into services, sustaining personal insights within corporate gatherings. For example, meditating on John 15:5–6 yields a simple song: "Abide in Me, and I in you," sung between readings and exhortations. Retreat centers schedule lectio-divina-and-song workshops, guiding participants to discern how the Spirit melds word and melody. Seminary courses on liturgical arts include lectio-based hymn composition exercises. The result is worship anchored both in biblical depth and emotive expression. Pastors note that congregations formed through lectio-sung Scripture display heightened scriptural literacy and emotional engagement. These hybrid practices exemplify how private devotion shapes public praise, setting the stage for creative journaling and poetic responses.

9.3 Journaling, Art, and Poetic Response to the Spirit's Whispers (Ps 45:1)

The psalmist confesses, "My heart overflows with a good theme; I address my verses to the king" (Ps 45:1), modeling poetic response to divine inspiration. Journaling under the Spirit's prompting captures metaphors, prayers, and visions that arise during devotion. Many believers record fragments of spontaneous songs, prayers, or images—later refined into art or poetry for corporate sharing. Worship arts ministries host *spirit whisper* journaling sessions, supplying sketchbooks, oil pastels, and handbound journals in prayer rooms. Spiritual formation retreats allocate dedicated time for creative response: participants reflect on a Scripture passage and then produce a drawing, poem, or short piece of music. Periodic *artistic testimonies* in worship services allow individuals to present these works as offerings. Digital galleries on church websites showcase congregants' Spirit-inspired creations, encouraging others to adopt creative journaling. The Advocate's personal stirring of hearts thus results in diverse artistic expressions that enrich communal worship. Creativity coaching classes in churches teach theological grounding for art, ensuring that all works remain Christ-centered. This cultivation of creative response transitions smoothly into testimony times that build corporate encouragement.

9.4 Testimony Time—Private Encounter Becomes Corporate Encouragement (Mal 3:16; Rev 12:11)

Malachi notes "a book of remembrance…for those who fear the Lord and meditate on His name" (Mal 3:16), linking private devotion with collective memory. Revelation affirms that believers overcome by "the blood of the Lamb and by the word of their testimony" (Rev 12:11), highlighting testimony as spiritual weaponry and communal uplift. Testimony time in worship services offers a structured space where individuals share how private encounters with the Spirit have shaped their faith. Leaders guide testimonies to focus on God's action rather than personal drama, ensuring edification. Testimonies may include answered prayers, prophetic confirmations, or artistic offerings developed in devotion. The microphone is passed in small-group or large-gathering settings, moderated to maintain order and thematic focus. Training sessions teach how to craft concise, impactful testimonies tied to scriptural promises, preventing undue attention on self. Testimonies foster vulnerability, build trust, and inspire others to expect the Advocate's movement. After each testimony, the congregation often responds with prayer or a sung refrain that encapsulates the shared experience. Over time, testimony time becomes a corporate chronicle of the Spirit's personal work, deepening unity and anticipation for future encounters. This public sharing of private devotion leads seamlessly into discerning the Spirit's authority through order and oversight.

10 Discernment, Order, and Spiritual Authority

10.1 Elders and Worship Leaders as Spirit-Appointed Stewards (Acts 20:28)

The apostle Paul exhorts elders to "pay careful attention to yourselves and to all the flock, in which the Holy Spirit has made you overseers" (Acts 20:28), establishing pastoral leadership as a Spirit appointment. Elders and worship leaders share responsibility for safeguarding worship integrity, theological soundness, and communal care. The commissioning of elders involves prayer, laying on of hands, and prophetic affirmation, symbolizing Spirit empowerment for oversight. Worship committees operate under elder guidance, vetting liturgical elements—music selections, artistic expressions, service flows—to ensure alignment with biblical priorities and congregational health. Regular leadership retreats include spiritual direction for elders, focusing on personal prayer life, pastoral character, and visionary discernment. Training for emerging worship leaders covers both technical skills and theological foundations, preventing proficiency from overshadowing Spirit dependence. Elder councils review prophetic words, testimonies, and creative works, offering constructive feedback and safeguarding against error. This Spirit-appointed stewardship sets the framework for evaluating prophecies and manifestations.

10.2 Evaluating Prophecies and Manifestations (1 Cor 14:29; 1 John 4:1)

Paul mandates that "two or three prophets should speak, and the others should weigh what is said" (1 Cor 14:29), emphasizing communal testing of prophetic words. John warns believers to "test the spirits…to see whether they are from God" (1 John 4:1). Worship governance includes *prophetic advisory teams* comprising elders, theologians, and seasoned prophets who listen to public and private prophetic utterances, comparing them with Scripture and doctrinal standards. Written guidelines specify criteria: consistency with the gospel, confirmation by multiple witnesses, absence of self-exalting content, and beneficial impact on the Body. Whistleblower channels allow discreet reporting of suspected errors, triggering review processes. Training workshops equip participants to recognize hallmark features of authentic prophecy—clarity, relevance, and evidence of love—versus manipulative or sensational claims. Periodic *prophecy calibration sessions* rehearse case studies from church history and contemporary contexts, refining discernment skills. This culture of testing ensures that charismatic flow enhances rather than undermines corporate order, informing our approach to avoiding manipulative atmospherics.

10.3 Avoiding Manipulative Atmospherics and Emotionalism (Jer 23:16–22)

God indicts false prophets whose words lead people astray (Jer 23:16–22), warning against emotional manipulation under the guise of spiritual ecstasy. Worship planners and leaders guard against creating contrived atmospheres—overamplified sound, strobe lights, or suggestive staging—designed to elicit manufactured responses rather than genuine Spirit-led engagement. Technical teams undergo *ethics of environment* training, focusing on transparency of intent, sensitivity to diverse emotional states, and avoidance of sensory overload. Pastors monitor worship for emotional dependency, ensuring that experiences connect back to Christ and Scripture rather than brief highs. Congregations practice *post-worship debriefs* to process experiences, distinguishing authentic encounters from mere emotional contagion. Spiritual directors incorporate emotional health assessments, offering counseling for those who find emotional extremes disorienting. This disciplined approach prevents the quenching or grieving of the Spirit by maintaining theological anchors and liturgical sobriety.

10.4 Liturgical Repentance for Quenching or Grieving the Spirit (Eph 4:30; Rev 2–3)

Paul warns believers not to "grieve the Holy Spirit" (Eph 4:30), while Revelation's letters call churches to repent of worship deficiencies (Rev 2–3). Worship communities hold periodic *liturgical repentance services*, confessing corporate failures—ritualism, entertainment-driven gatherings, neglect of the suffering—and seeking the Spirit's forgiveness and renewal. These services include readings from Ephesian and Laodicean letters, communal confession prayers, and symbolic acts—foot washing, silence, or renewed vow of devotion. Worship leaders issue *pastoral letters* afterward, outlining action steps to restore vibrant, Spirit-honoring worship. Spiritual refreshers—retreats or day-long prayer intensives—often follow repentance liturgies, inviting the Advocate to reignite passion for true adoration. By integrating repentance into liturgical life, churches demonstrate humility and openness to the Spirit's corrective ministry, completing our exploration of ordered worship under spiritual authority.

11 Global Worship Movements and Missional Song

11.1 Songs of the Diaspora—Gospel Hymnody Crossing Frontiers (Acts 16:13–15)

Lydia's heart "opened by the Lord" in Philippi became a gateway for gospel song to permeate European soil (Acts 16:14–15). As believers migrated, they carried cherished hymns—African spirituals, Celtic chants, Latin American corridos—integrating them into new cultural contexts. These diaspora songs often blend indigenous musical idioms with biblical texts, creating hybrid forms that resonate powerfully across linguistic barriers. Modern global worship movements curate *Hymns of Migration* events, inviting expatriate communities to share their heritage songs. Record labels and online platforms distribute these recordings worldwide, fueling reciprocal adoption—African Yoruba hymns echoing in American churches, and vice versa. Mission agencies incorporate local hymn translations into discipleship materials, ensuring that new converts learn to worship in their mother tongues. The Spirit's personal guidance in diaspora hymnody testifies to gospel universality and prepares the church for contextualized rhythms in indigenous instruments.

11.2 Contextualized Rhythms and Indigenous Instruments (Ps 47:1; Isa 60:1–7)

Psalm 47 exhorts all peoples to "clap your hands" in praise, while Isaiah's prophecy envisions nations bringing gifts and praise to Zion (Isa 60:1–7), implying diverse offerings in worship. Contemporary worship embraces contextually appropriate rhythms—djembe drums in West Africa, tabla rhythms in South Asia, steel pans in the Caribbean—each under Spirit discernment to avoid syncretism. Music workshops equip local worship leaders to adapt global songs into indigenous meters and scales. Ethnomusicologists collaborate with churches to document traditional musical forms and craft spiritual lyrics, preserving cultural heritage while honoring biblical content. Mission teams resist one-size-fits-all worship models, instead encouraging local creativity under the Advocate's personal direction. Governments sometimes partner with churches to host *cultural worship festivals*, showcasing the Spirit's work through arts and music. These contextualized practices affirm the gospel's relevance to every culture and segue into justice-oriented worship fueling social transformation.

11.3 Justice-Oriented Worship Fueling Social Transformation (Amos 5:23–24; Luke 4:18–19)

Amos declares that God despises empty worship without justice—"let justice roll down like waters" (Amos 5:24)—and Jesus proclaims good news to the poor and freedom for captives (Luke 4:18–19). Worship that integrates prophetic calls for justice aligns song lyrics, liturgical prayers, and testimonies with social action. Churches compose *justice anthems* highlighting human trafficking, racial reconciliation, and environmental stewardship. Corporate worship services allocate segments for *prophetic sermons* on current injustices, paired with communal prayer and offering for relevant NGOs. Worship arts teams produce multimedia presentations—videos, art installations—that depict social issues, prompting Spirit-led compassion. Worshipers then respond in practical ways: letter-writing campaigns, community cleanups, volunteer drives. The Spirit's personal prompting in worship spurs the Body from contemplation to concrete advocacy, preparing hearts to embrace digital connectivity in prayer watches.

11.4 Digital Livestreams and Global Prayer Watches—Spirit Connective Tissue (Ps 19:4; Rom 15:6)

Psalm 19 attests that "their voice goes out through all the earth," and Paul prays that believers "with one mind and one voice may glorify the God and Father of our Lord Jesus Christ" (Rom 15:6). Digital livestreams enable churches to broadcast worship globally, creating *24/7 prayer watches* that span time zones. Platforms integrate real-time chat, prayer request boards, and interactive song requests, fostering immediate Spirit-led responses. Teams schedule *prayer shifts* staffed by intercessors from diverse cultures, ensuring continual coverage. Online worship nights feature international guest musicians and speakers, embodying the Advocate's connective role across boundaries. Training in *digital hospitality* prepares hosts to moderate diverse participants and to facilitate Spirit-led interactions. Security protocols protect vulnerable participants while maintaining an open invitation. These digital expressions become Spirit's digital connective tissue, knitting churches worldwide into a single chorus of praise, naturally leading into Sabbath rest as spiritual formation.

12 Sabbath, Rest, and Spiritual Formation

12.1 Spirit-Led Cease-Striving—Worship as Resistance to Busyness (Heb 4:9–11)

Hebrews affirms a perpetual Sabbath rest for God's people (Heb 4:9–11), countercultural in eras of relentless productivity. Sabbath worship under the Spirit's guidance interrupts the tyranny of tasks, inviting believers to cease striving and behold God's creative work. Families observe Sabbath by attending worship, sharing meals, and engaging in communal scripture reading rather than domestic chores. Worship spaces open as *rest retreats*, offering quiet corners for reflection, guided meditation, and whispered prayer—modeling how the Advocate invites repose. Workplaces adopt *corporate Sabbath afternoons*, pausing operations for communal worship gatherings and mental health practices. Spiritual formation curricula in seminaries include *Sabbath theology* modules, instructing future leaders on integrating rest into discipleship. Testimonials from burnout survivors highlight Sabbath as key to spiritual renewal. This restful worship ethos merges into silence and contemplative adoration.

12.2 Silence and Contemplative Adoration (Hab 2:20; Ps 62:1)

Scripture calls for "the Lord in His holy temple; let all the earth keep silence before Him" (Hab 2:20) and David declares, "Truly my soul finds rest in God; my salvation comes from him" (Ps 62:1). Silence prepares hearts for contemplative adoration, where God's presence speaks without words. Monastic traditions preserved *hesychia*—stillness practices involving repetitive prayer and extended quiet—to cultivate inner receptivity. Modern churches designate *silence zones* within sanctuaries and prayer gardens for personal adoration. Worship services may pause after prayers or hymns for several minutes of communal silence, allowing the Spirit's personal voice to resonate. Retreat centers offer *silence retreats* ranging from 24 hours to weeks, balancing instruction with free-form contemplative time. Spiritual directors guide novices in recognizing thoughts as potential Spirit promptings, teaching discernment in the silence. These practices underscore that worship includes both sound and stillness, transitioning into rhythms of feasting and fasting.

12.3 Rhythms of Feasting and Fasting (Joel 2:15–27; Matt 9:14–17)

Biblical feasts—Passover, Pentecost, Tabernacles—celebrate redemption events, communal joy, and divine provision (Joel 2:15–27), while Jesus notes that fasting remains appropriate amid somber seasons (Matt 9:14–17). Worship integrates these rhythms: joyous celebration services with shared meals and symbolic foods, and solemn fast days emphasizing prayer, confession, and almsgiving. Congregations observe *Feast of Tables* events that include Eucharistic feasts extended into fellowship meals, highlighting unity. Fasting congregations often combine abstention with intensified prayer and study, anticipating fresh Spirit anointing. Pastors schedule *fast-and-feast seasons* tied to liturgical calendars or mission initiatives. Spiritual formation courses teach theological foundations for fasting, including scriptural examples and health considerations. By alternating feasting and fasting, the church mirrors Israel's rhythms and Jesus' model, deepening Spirit-guided worship life. These embodied practices set the stage for retreats and pilgrimages that renew awe.

12.4 Retreats and Pilgrimages Renewing Awe (Luke 5:16; Ps 84:5–7)

Jesus often withdrew to solitary places to pray (Luke 5:16), modeling retreat for spiritual renewal. Pilgrims journeyed to Zion, praying "blessed are those whose strength is in you" (Ps 84:5–7), encountering God's presence in sacred geography. Modern worship incorporates *guided retreats*—weekend or week-long experiences—at monasteries, wilderness centers, or urban retreat houses. Pilgrimages to biblical holy sites facilitate embodied worship, as participants walk ancient paths and engage in site-specific liturgies. Preparation sessions include teaching on pilgrimage as metaphor for spiritual journey, fostering reflective diaries and group sharing. Upon return, corporate worship services feature *pilgrim testimonies* and symbolic processions that integrate the retreat's fruit into communal life. These intentional pauses in ordinary routines enable awe to be renewed and the Spirit's presence to be re-encountered, completing our exploration of Sabbath, silence, and spiritual formation in worship life.

13 Eschatological Horizon: Worship in the New Creation

13.1 Spirit-Inspired Chorus of Every Tribe and Tongue (Rev 7:9–12)

John's vision of a vast multitude "from every nation, tribe, people, and language" standing before the throne (Rev 7:9–12) shapes eschatological worship expectations. The Advocate orchestrates a global symphony, weaving diverse cultural expressions into a unified chorus. Worship leaders prepare congregations by exposing them to multicultural songbooks and inviting international worship teams. Translation teams work to provide multilingual projections, enabling hearing and seeing the praise in multiple languages. Virtual choirs compile video recordings from across the globe, layering voices into a single anthemic piece. Multicultural worship festivals model this future chorus, offering participants a foretaste of the New Creation's kaleidoscopic praise. Funding missions to under-resourced places includes training local worship teams, ensuring that all nations have stake in the global chorus. The Spirit's personal work across cultural boundaries anticipates the consummation where unity transcends diversity, segueing into Lamb-centered liturgy.

13.2 Lamb-Centered Liturgy and Unceasing Spirit Illumination (Rev 21:22–23)

Revelation describes the New Jerusalem where the Lamb's presence provides light, and the nations "will walk by its light" (Rev 21:22–23). Worship in that age will revolve entirely around Christ the Lamb, with no need for temple structures or sun. The Advocate continually illuminates hearts with unmediated revelation. Liturgical forecasts in current practice include repeated refrains—"Worthy is the Lamb"— and periods of radiant white light worship environments symbolizing the Bride's union with the Lamb. Artists create immersive installations depicting the city of light, inviting worshipers to sense the eschatological atmosphere now. Homiletics on Revelation focus on the Lamb's centrality, shaping all worship elements—song selection, prayers, sacraments—toward Christocentric focus. By foregrounding the Lamb, worship becomes an ongoing testimony of redemption's culmination, leading into creation's liberated symphony.

13.3 Creation's Liberated Symphony—Trees Clapping, Seas Roaring (Isa 55:12; Ps 98:7–9)

Isaiah prophesies that creation will "break forth into singing" (Isa 55:12), and the psalmist calls for the trees and seas to praise God (Ps 98:7–9). This vision of cosmic worship suggests that the New Creation itself will join the Lamb-centered liturgy in ecstatic chorus. Worshipers today incorporate *creation-based liturgies*—services in forests, by rivers, and on mountaintops—anticipating this liberated symphony. Liturgical calendars include *creation care Sundays*, combining environmental action with thematic worship. Artistic collectives compose *eco-psalms* and mount compositions for outdoor performance, blending natural acoustics with human voices. Retreat centers practice *forest church* gatherings, where the wind through branches becomes part of the worship soundtrack. Scientists and theologians collaborate on *bio-worship labs*, exploring how nature's rhythms mirror liturgical patterns. These experiential worship forms prepare hearts for the day when all creation will undimmedly declare the Creator's glory, transitioning us to the contemporary challenges of pneumatological renewal.

Conclusion

As we have seen, authentic worship in Spirit and truth weaves together biblical foundations, historical patterns, charismatic spontaneity, aesthetic beauty, and inclusive unity, all orchestrated by the Advocate's personal ministry. When believers learn to balance reverent awe with filial confidence, structured liturgy with Spirit-led innovation, and private devotion with corporate celebration, they participate in a living symphony that points toward the New Creation's unending praise. In the face of cultural shifts and secular pressures, this robust vision of worship equips the church to steward its heritage while remaining open to the Spirit's fresh wind. Chapter 14 will turn to the contemporary challenges confronting worship today and chart pathways for renewed pneumatological vitality so that the Spirit's presence continues to ignite genuine adoration across generations and nations.

Chapter 14. Contemporary Challenges and Pneumatological Renewal

In an era marked by rapid change and deep uncertainty, the church encounters unprecedented challenges to its understanding and experience of the Spirit's work. Technological revolutions, ideological shifts, and spiritual syncretism press the boundaries of traditional pneumatology, calling believers to reconsider how the Spirit is active in worship, witness, and community life. Yet alongside these challenges arise fresh stirrings of renewal—movements that transcend cultural divides and recapture the dynamic power of Pentecost. This chapter surveys the contemporary landscape, diagnosing obstacles to vibrant Spirit-led faith and pointing to emerging signs of pneumatological resurgence. By engaging with both threats and hopes, we prepare to chart courses for renewal that honor biblical precedent while innovating for today's context.

1 The Pneumatological Landscape Today

1.1 A Global "Charismatic Century": Growth Statistics and Shifting Centers of Gravity

Over the past century, Pentecostal and charismatic expressions have surged from a handful of Western enclaves to more than 600 million adherents worldwide, now constituting the fastest-growing segment of global Christianity. Surveys by the World Christian Database and Pew Research show that sub-Saharan Africa, Latin America, and Southeast Asia lead in Spirit-empowered movements, outpacing European and North American centers. This demographic shift reshapes theological conversation: voices from Nairobi, Manila, and São Paulo bring fresh emphases on deliverance, healing, and Spirit-filled worship. Seminary enrollments in Nigeria's Redeemer's University and Brazil's Faculdade Teológica Sul Americana underscore a new academic axis where pneumatology is studied in dialogue with local cultures. Mission strategies pivot accordingly: Western churches send fewer long-term missionaries and instead partner with vibrant majority-world sending movements. The Spirit's global vibrancy challenges Western paradigms that assumed cultural hegemony, prompting humility and reciprocal learning. These demographic realities invite deeper reflection on how the Spirit transcends ethnic and socioeconomic boundaries, leading us to consider barriers that still hamper credibility.

1.2 Lingering Questions of Credibility: Scandals, Fragmentation, Anti-intellectualism

Despite explosive growth, charismatic movements have sometimes been marred by high-profile financial and moral scandals. Televised "miracle crusades" that later exposed fundraising abuses have eroded public trust. In-charismatic circles, rival groups compete for followers, leading to fragmentation rather than unity—an irony given the Spirit's unifying mission (Eph 4:3). Academic critiques decry anti-intellectualism: some pastors dismiss theological education, equating experiential authenticity with rejection of rigorous doctrine. This creates a dichotomy where scholarly pneumatology and grassroots enthusiasm seem at odds. The result is a circus-style spirituality that fetishizes signs while neglecting discipleship, and academic pneumatology that can become sterile and detached. Restoring credibility requires transparent accountability structures, ethical guidelines for gift use, and partnerships between scholars and practitioners. Models like South Korea's Council for Charismatic Churches show that mutual accountability and shared doctrinal statements can heal fragmentation. Encouraging academic–church networks—seminaries that host "Spirit Practicum" labs—fosters both intellectual depth and experiential integrity. Addressing credibility crises sets the stage for engaging Western spiritual disaffection.

1.3 The Rise of the "Nones" and Functional Deism in the West

In Europe and North America, the category of religious "nones"—those claiming no religious affiliation—has risen above 25 percent in many surveys, reflecting a drift toward functional deism or secular humanism. These individuals may believe in a benign Creator or "force," but reject institutional religion and any notion of a personal Spirit actively intervening in history. This spiritual vacuum fosters skepticism toward supernatural claims, viewing charismatic practices as outdated or manipulative. Church attendance declines even among self-identified Christians, as worship services are perceived as irrelevant to daily life. Yet many "nones" gravitate toward mindfulness, yoga, and New Age modalities in a quest for transcendence, indicating a latent spiritual hunger. Evangelistic approaches that merely defend dogma fail to engage this demographic; instead, incarnational presence—hospitality, justice work, environmental stewardship—often moves their hearts. Spirit-empowered testimonies of transformation that resist sensationalism can cut through postmodern cynicism. Bridging the gap between deistic assumptions and Spirit-filled witness requires demonstrating the Spirit's personal care in tangible acts of compassion (James 2:17). This contextual challenge highlights the necessity of ecumenical convergence.

1.4 Hopeful Signs: Ecumenical Convergence around the Spirit's Gifts and Mission

Amid diversity, there is growing momentum for ecumenical agreement on core pneumatological convictions. The World Council of Churches' "Pentecostal-Charismatic Dialogue" and bilateral agreements between Pentecostal and mainstream Protestant bodies have produced consensus statements affirming Spirit gifts while respecting theological distinctives. Joint mission initiatives—such as global prayer networks for persecuted Christians—exemplify unity in intercession. Shared conferences on spiritual gifts, featuring Catholic, Orthodox, and Protestant scholars, showcase mutual respect and combined ministry strategies. Denominations once divided over charismatic renewal now collaborate on compassion projects, honoring one another's Spirit-wrought charisms. Emerging global communions, like the Renewalist branch of the Anglican Communion, integrate charismatic worship with historic liturgy, demonstrating creative convergence. These hopeful developments illustrate that the Spirit can overcome institutional barriers, forging unity that reflects the prayer of Jesus "that they may all be one" (John 17:21). Recognizing this convergence encourages us as we turn to the secular forces challenging transcendence.

2 Secularization and the Eclipse of Transcendence

2.1 Charles Taylor's "Immanent Frame" and the Closed Plausibility Structure

Philosopher Charles Taylor describes modernity's "immanent frame" as a cultural milieu that confines thought to naturalistic explanations, rendering transcendence "unlikely" within the closed plausibility structures of Western societies. Within this frame, spiritual experiences are easily dismissed as psychological phenomena. The church must learn to disrupt this frame, inviting people to consider realms beyond the empirical. The Spirit challenges immanence by surreptitiously collapsing scientific-religious divides; for instance, quantum physicists intrigued by consciousness studies cautiously note "non-material" dimensions, echoing biblical affirmations of a Spirit-wrought cosmos (Gen 1:2). Cultural artifacts—art installations, film narratives—sometimes regain transcendence by embedding symbols that evoke longings for the numinous. Spirit-led worship arts that surprise routine expectations can rupture immanent assumptions: a sudden Gospel proclamation in a secular festival can make audiences palpably aware of otherworldly presence. Recognizing the immanent frame compels us to cultivate "hidden transcripts" of transcendence—moments of awe that subtly reconfigure worldviews—setting the stage for deeper spiritual longing.

2.2 Therapeutic Spirituality Replacing Covenant Encounter

Modern culture often substitutes therapeutic spirituality—focused on self-esteem, personal fulfilment, and emotional well-being—for covenantal encounter with a holy God. While the Spirit indeed comforts and heals, reducing pneumatology to a feel-good therapy undermines doctrines of sin, repentance, and divine holiness. Therapeutic religion shifts power from the sovereign Spirit to consumer choice, where individuals "shop" for spiritual experiences. The result is shallow faith, easily bored or disillusioned when inner feeling wanes. The church must reclaim covenantal motifs— baptismal vows, Eucharistic covenant, solemn assemblies—that shape worship around divine promises and human commitments. Spirit-driven liturgies of confession and renewal nurture depth beyond self-help models. Retreats emphasizing covenant renewal, such as shared vows of discipleship, can reorient hearts from therapeutic self-centeredness to covenantal allegiance. Pastors who preach on Wesley's concept of "outward and inward holiness" invite congregations to embrace both Spirit-given transformation and disciplined obedience. Recognizing the drift toward therapeutic spirituality invites reclamation of a balanced pneumatology rooted in covenant relationship.

2.3 The Spirit as Re-enchanter of Ordinary Life and Vocation

In response to disenchantment, the Spirit re-enchanters the mundane, infusing daily vocations with divine meaning. Whereas secularization exalts the distinction between sacred and profane, the biblical vision (Col 3:23–24) sees every task—farming, teaching, parenting—as an arena for Spirit-led worship. Testimonies from Spirit-empowered believers in the marketplace recount sudden insights—combining prayer and project planning—that accelerate innovation and reflect the Spirit's creative agency. Movements like the "Theology of Work" advocate Spirit-restored vocational witness, emphasizing that God's call extends into offices and workshops. Practices such as midday prayer pauses, described in Psalm 119:164 and Acts 3:1, interrupt secular rhythms, inviting the Spirit to reclaim time for divine soundings. Artists discover fresh inspiration for creative work when they yield projects to Spirit promptings, finding their craft becoming ministry. Recognizing the Spirit as re-enchanter combats the spirituality-work divide and opens the door to practices of wonder.

2.4 Practices of Wonder that Pierce Disenchantment (Art, Silence, Creation Walks)

To dismantle the closed plausibility frame, the church cultivates practices that reawaken organic wonder in God's world. Art installations within worship spaces—kinetic sculptures that respond to breath or movement—invite participants to marvel at the Spirit's artistic touch. Communal times of meditative silence, rooted in monastic *hesychia*, create sacred intervals for the Spirit to speak (Psalm 46:10). Organized "creation walks" combine stewardship with sensory attunement, teaching participants to discern God's fingerprints in wind-whispered branches (Job 12:7–10). Seasonal sites—riverbanks for baptism renewals, mountain overlooks for sunrise prayer—leverage grandeur to evoke Spirit-ignited awe. Poetry slams that end with spontaneous Spirit-led testimonies blend creativity with adoration. Such wonder practices reposition believers as pilgrims in a Spirit-animated world, ready for deeper engagement with charismatic renewal. As these practices break through disenchantment, they prepare ground for addressing charismatic excess and cessationist neglect.

3 Charismatic Excess versus Cessationist Neglect

3.1 Spectacle Culture: Hype, Hype Fatigue, and Miracle Marketing

In some charismatic circles, ministry events become branded spectacles—mega-conferences with celebrity speakers, elaborate stage productions, and high-cost ticketing that commodify spiritual experiences. Promotional campaigns promising guaranteed miracles or emotional highs often lead to "hype fatigue," where participants grow cynical when expected outcomes fail to materialize. Social media amplifies this dynamic, with sensational clips circulating but deeper transformation neglected. This commercialization echoes Jesus's critique of the temple marketplace (John 2:14–16), warning against reducing sacred encounters to transactions. The church must rebuke spectacle-driven ministry by refocusing on patient disciple-making and sustained community care. Revival history teaches that genuine movements arise from grassroots prayer and simple obedience, not elaborate productions. Ministries like the Brownsville Revival eventually collapsed under a culture of sensationalism, prompting renewed calls for humility. Recognizing the pitfalls of spectacle culture prepares us to examine the opposite error: over-rationalized cessationist neglect.

3.2 Functional Cessationism: Doctrinal Assent without Experiential Reality

At the opposite extreme, some theologians affirm spiritual gifts in doctrine but deny their present-day operation, resulting in "functional cessationism." Churches may retain creedal statements about the Spirit's gifts yet cultivate environments where only scripted ministry is allowed. This produces congregations proficient in theological assent but bereft of experiential faith, where prayer meetings become routine rather than expectant. Ministers trained in seminary may feel ill-equipped to recognize or facilitate genuine Spirit activity, fearing doctrinal error. Consequently, believers hungry for encounter drift toward Pentecostal services or alternative spiritualities. Rebalancing requires fostering "ordered openness"—structured environments that honor biblical boundaries (1 Corinthians 14:40) while welcoming unpredictable Spirit manifestations. Voices like Sam Storms and D.A. Carson call for robust theological frameworks that underpin experiential pneumatology. Congregations practicing simple gift-sharing rituals—testimonies, prophetic words, healing prayer—build confidence in the Spirit's active presence. Recognizing functional cessationism as a barrier prompts exploration of a mediating way.

3.3 A Mediating Way: Ordered Openness Rooted in Scripture and Discernment

Scripture calls the church to "test everything; hold fast what is good" (1 Th 5:21), modeling a balance between openness to the Spirit and critical discernment. Ordered openness involves establishing guidelines—scripture conformity, communal testing (1 Cor 14:29), pastoral oversight—for integrating charismatic expressions. Churches can form Spirit-gift councils that pray, discern, and provide feedback on ministry proposals, ensuring prophetic words align with doctrine and character. Training programs on spiritual gift ethics and deliverance ministries help avoid abuses and superficiality. Regular rhythms of spontaneous prayer within set liturgies—such as allowing one or two prophetic prayers after a sermon—invite unpredictability without chaos. Incorporating debriefing sessions after Spirit-led events allows collective reflection on fruit and alignment with mission. Networks like the Global Awakening Commission exemplify how global practitioners share best practices under shared theological frameworks. Recognizing ordered openness affirms that the Spirit is both free and faithful, guiding us beyond extremes into healthy renewal. This balanced approach paves the way for historic churches to integrate contemporary renewal.

3.4 Case Studies of Balanced Charismatic Renewal in Historic Churches

Several historic denominations have successfully integrated charismatic renewal without abandoning their liturgical or theological heritage. The Church of England's Charismatic Renewal movement, beginning in the 1960s, combined ancient liturgies with Spirit-empowered prayer groups, yielding parish revitalization while maintaining sacramental integrity. In the Roman Catholic charismatic renewal, communities like the Focolare and Communion and Liberation emphasize adoration, healing services, and lay ministries under episcopal oversight, demonstrating unity of authority and charism. The Moravian Church's Lovefeast tradition, enriched by Spirit revival in the 18th century, pairs communal meals with hymn singing and testimonies—an early example of ordered openness. Lutheran renewal movements in Scandinavia balance Pietist spirituality with confessional theology, producing robust catechesis alongside vibrant prayer meetings. Detailed evaluations show these models share common features: rigorous theological grounding, transparent leadership, structured freedom, and communal accountability. Recognizing these case studies equips other historic bodies to embark on pneumatological renewal without losing their unique identities. As we celebrate examples of balanced renewal, we turn next to examine consumerism and prosperity distortions.

4 Consumerism, Prosperity Theology, and the Spirit of the Cross

4.1 Commodifying the Anointing: Conferences, Merch, and Paywalls

In a consumer-driven culture, spiritual experiences risk becoming packaged commodities: ticketed conferences promising guaranteed impartation, websites selling "anointed" music downloads, paywalled sermon archives. This economic model mirrors market logic rather than kingdom generosity, implying that Spirit gifts can be purchased rather than freely given (Luke 24:49). Ticket prices rising into the hundreds of dollars exclude lower-income believers, contravening the Spirit's democratizing work at Pentecost. Merchandising—anointing oils, T-shirts with prophetic slogans—can trivialize sacred realities and foster transactional mindsets. Digital platforms placing Spirit-filled teaching behind paywalls perpetuate information inequity, contradicting Paul's instruction to offer "gifts free of charge" (Matt 10:8). Churches must resist consumer models by foregrounding free resources, sliding-scale offerings, and open-access digital libraries. Spirit-led initiatives like "Open Worship Project" provide licensed worship tracks free for congregational use, embodying Spirit generosity. Recognizing commodification pitfalls helps the church re-center on sacrificial cross-shaped giving rather than profit-driven events, prompting reflection on authentic kenosis.

4.2 "Name-It-Claim-It" Distortions of Blessing and Suffering

Prosperity theology's "name-it-claim-it" rhetoric reduces the Spirit's work to a formulaic promise of health, wealth, and success, often leaving afflicted believers feeling spiritually defective when suffering persists. This distortion conflates covenantal blessing with material prosperity, neglecting biblical themes of cross-bearing (Matt 16:24), fellowship in suffering (Phil 3:10), and redemptive sorrow. New Testament examples—Paul's "thorn in the flesh" (2 Cor 12:7–10) and Jesus's own path of suffering (Isa 53)—underscore that Spirit-filled life includes endurance of hardship. Churches must teach a balanced theology of blessing that encompasses both deliverance and cruciform discipleship. Seminars on "Prosperity Myths" can unpack the Spirit's role in sustaining faith amid poverty, illness, and persecution, highlighting James's call to "count it all joy" when trials come (James 1:2). Recovery ministries for those disillusioned by prosperity promises witness to the Spirit's healing of spiritual disillusionment. Recognizing "name-it-claim-it" errors paves the way for embracing Pauline kenosis and cruciform power.

4.3 Pauline Kenosis and Cruciform Power (2 Corinthians 12:9)

Paul's experience of divine sufficiency—"my grace is sufficient for you, for my power is made perfect in weakness"—reveals a Spirit-shaped dynamic of strength through humility (2 Cor 12:9). The Spirit equips believers to embrace weakness, knowing that reliance on Christ's power transcends human capability. In practical ministry, leaders who share personal struggles of fatigue or doubt often find that the Spirit's empowerment deepens communal empathy and authenticity. Seminars on "Spirit and Suffering" incorporate silence and lament into worship, inviting the Spirit to sanctify affliction rather than bypass it. Projects like "Adaptive Church" study how small congregations flourish by leveraging Spirit-given resources rather than expanding to match consumer-driven ambition. Recognizing kenotic theology as Spirit-imparted counters triumphalism and cultivates cruciform witness, a posture that naturally critiques prosperity distortions and readies communities for economic justice engagement.

4.4 Economic Justice and Simplicity as Spirit-Formed Resistance (James 2:15–16; Luke 16:10–13)

The Spirit who empowers witness undergirds ethical mandates for economic justice. James warns that faith without care for the poor is dead, signaling the Spirit's concern for social equity (James 2:15–16). Jesus's parables—such as the unjust steward commended for prudence (Luke 16:8)—invite Spirit-led creativity in resource stewardship, prompting microfinance, fair-trade initiatives, and cooperative business models. Movements like "Simple Way" in Philadelphia practice Spirit-formed simplicity: shared housing, communal meals, and local commerce that challenges consumer culture. Advocacy organizations rooted in Spirit conviction—Micah 6:8 coalitions—lobby for living wages and ethical supply chains, viewing justice as integral to the gospel. Churches adopting alternative giving structures—resource pools, mutual aid networks—demonstrate Spirit-enabled generosity without market mindsets. Recognizing economic justice and simplicity as Spirit-shaped resistance enacts a gospel that embraces both cross-shaped humility and social transformation. Transitioning from critique to practice, these Spirit-formed efforts model tangible expressions of the Spirit of the cross in a consumerist age.

5 Syncretism and New-Age "Energy" Spiritualities

5.1 Reiki, Crystals, and the Language of Vibration in Popular Culture

Practices such as Reiki healing and crystal therapy employ terminology like "energy," "vibration," and "aura," borrowing Biblical language of spirit (*ruach*) but divorcing it from personal, biblical agency. Practitioners claim to channel universal life force through hand movements or gemstone placements, yet the Spirit of God is revealed as distinct Person in Scripture (John 14:16–17) rather than an impersonal energy field. The popularity of these modalities in wellness culture reflects deep human longing for tangible spiritual encounter, a gap sometimes unmet by church ministries. Social media influencers demonstrate crystal grids and chakra alignments, presenting these as paths to emotional balance and spiritual growth, often without any theistic framework. Churches that neglect engaging this vogue risk losing seekers to alternative spiritualities that promise immediate self-healing. Educators must equip believers to discern charismatic parallels—both speak of energy flows—but clarify that only the Spirit reveals Christ (John 16:13). Small-group discussions analyzing popular wellness trends can expose underlying presuppositions, helping participants articulate why personal communion with the Triune God surpasses impersonal mysticism. Testimonies of individuals transitioning from crystal therapy to Spirit-led healing ministries illustrate the Spirit's superior power to renew both mind and body. Recognizing cultural fascinations with "vibration" invites the church to offer deeper encounters through Spirit-empowered worship and prayer. As awareness grows of impersonal forces' limitations, we turn to respectful dialogue with indigenous practices.

5.2 Indigenous and Ancestral Spirit Practices—Respectful Dialogue, Clear Boundaries

Global Christianity often encounters indigenous rituals—ancestor veneration, spirit-medium ceremonies, ritual dances—that honor local worldviews of spiritual realms. In many contexts, these rites are conduits for community identity and perceived protection from malevolent forces. Mission theologians stress the importance of respectful dialogue, affirming the image of God in every culture (Gen 1:27) while discerning which practices conflict with biblical monotheism and the Spirit's unique lordship. Anthropologists partnering with missionaries note that indigenous leaders respond positively when invited to share cultural stories, provided the church does not immediately condemn every custom. Boundary clarity is essential: worship of ancestors as mediators infringes on Christ's sole mediatorial role (1 Tim 2:5). Churches that train cross-cultural workers in contextualization skills learn to translate the biblical narrative into local idioms without syncretistic compromise. Case studies in Melanesia demonstrate successful integration of indigenous music and symbolism in liturgy, after thorough Spirit-led evaluation of potential theological risks. Recognizing the Spirit's respect for cultural diversity within Christ's lordship readies mission teams to navigate ancestral rites with wisdom and compassion. As we honor local spiritual sensibilities, we maintain fidelity to the Personhood of the Spirit rather than impersonal forces.

5.3 Biblical Criteria for Distinguishing Person from Impersonal Force

Scripture provides clear markers to discern a personal Spirit from impersonal "energy." Persons act with volition—they speak, guide, comfort, convict—whereas impersonal forces lack mind and will (Rom 8:16; John 14:26). The Holy Spirit teaches truth (John 14:17), prays intercedes (Rom 8:26), and convicts of sin (John 16:8), all actions that presuppose personhood. Impersonal modalities offer no moral direction or relational comfort, often leaving participants without hope when practices fail. Biblical narratives—Elijah's encounter on Mount Horeb (1 Kings 19)—contrast God's "gentle whisper" with impersonal elements like wind and earthquake, asserting that Spirit is not nature but personal revelation. Churches should teach these distinctions through expository sermons and workshops, analyzing every claimed spiritual phenomenon against biblical categories of personhood. Deliverance ministries confirm that when demons are cast out, a personal spiritual adversary departs, distinct from inert energies. Recognizing these biblical criteria holds potential for apologetics: engaging skeptics who experience "energy" but remain open to a personal Spirit who offers relational transformation. This clear theological framework builds confidence for prophetic engagement with New-Age trends, leading to constructive evangelism rather than polemic.

5.4 Apologetic Approaches that Honor Common Longing yet Point to the Triune God

Effective apologetics begins by affirming the genuine longings behind New-Age practices—peace, healing, connection—then showing that the Triune God meets these deeper than any technique can. Paul's Athens sermon (Acts 17) commended idol searchers for their spiritual quest before introducing the living God; similarly, churches can acknowledge seekers' searches for "energy" before unveiling the Holy Spirit's personal love and authority. Storytelling that parallels biblical accounts of Spirit-outpouring with modern testimonies builds bridges of empathy. Equipping evangelists with both biblical clarity on personhood and compassion for seekers fosters trust, preventing immediate rejection of New-Age practitioners. Interfaith dialogues can include testimonies from former Reiki practitioners now healed and empowered by the Spirit. Worship services themed around "Encountering the Living Spirit" contrast stoic meditation practices with vibrant Spirit-led prayer. Recognizing New-Age longings as pointers to the Creator rather than dismissing them paves the way for relational proclamation of Christ who baptizes in the Holy Spirit (Matt 3:11). As this section concludes, we transition to the digital frontiers where these dynamics replicate in virtual spaces.

6 Digital Mediation and the Disembodied Gathering

6.1 Livestream Liturgies, Virtual Reality Prayer Rooms, AI Sermons

As churches expand online, they experiment with livestreamed liturgies, virtual reality prayer rooms, and even AI-generated sermon outlines. Livestream platforms allow worshipers confined by illness or geography to participate in real time, yet the Spirit's presence cannot be guaranteed by pixels alone. VR prayer rooms, where avatars kneel before a digital altar, create immersive settings, but the risk arises that participants equate high-fidelity graphics with genuine divine encounter. AI sermons, crafted by algorithms trained on vast theological corpora, can produce doctrinally consistent messages, though lacking the Spirit's personal unction. Tech-savvy ministries hire Spirit-led "digital chaplains" to monitor chat intercessions, pray for spontaneous requests, and pastor virtual participants in the margins of the platform. Observers note that Spirit's creative work sometimes subverts digital rigidity: unexpected healing testimonies posted in chat flood participants with consolation. Recognizing these emerging media's potentials and limits compels the church to develop digital pneumatology: theology of Spirit's presence that transcends screen technology and remains anchored in relational encounter. From these high-tech frontiers, we turn to opportunities they present.

6.2 Opportunities: Accessibility, Global Intercession Networks

Digital tools democratize access: remote communities can join global prayer networks, receiving Spirit-led insights from continents away. Platforms like online prayer walls and live-translated captions include non-native speakers, reflecting Acts 2's multilingual proclamation (Acts 2:6–8). Disability-accessible worship—captioned videos, screen-reader–friendly liturgies—enables Spirit-filled participation for all, fulfilling James's vision of "pure and undefiled religion" that cares for the vulnerable (James 1:27). Digital mission hubs connect frontline workers with prayer partners worldwide, coordinating 24/7 intercession that unleashes Spirit freighted breakthroughs. Tech-supported Bible apps, annotated by Spirit-led devotions, help believers engage Scripture on demand, fostering regular Spirit-led study. Recognizing digital accessibility as Spirit-facilitated inclusion drives investment in user-friendly platforms and global partnerships. As inclusion expands, we must remain vigilant against the risks inherent in disembodied gathering.

6.3 Risks: Screen Fatigue, Algorithmic Echo-Chambers, Sacramental Displacement

Excessive screen-based worship can lead to fatigue—diminished attention spans, online distractions, emotional detachment—hindering deep Spirit engagement (Heb 10:24–25). Algorithms that tailor content based on viewing history create echo chambers, reinforcing pre-existing beliefs and inhibiting the Spirit's correction (John 16:8) through diverse voices. Some participants substitute digital participation for embodied gathering, neglecting sacraments that require physical presence—baptism, Eucharist—and the Spirit-led mutual encouragement found in face-to-face fellowship. Cybersecurity breaches risk exposing personal prayer requests, undermining trust in digital confidentiality. Churches respond by setting healthy online-offline rhythms—limiting screen time, encouraging in-person small groups, safeguarding digital privacy.

Recognizing these risks underscores the need for a balanced digital pneumatology.

6.4 Toward a "Digital Pneumatology" of Presence, Participation, and Discernment

A robust digital pneumatology affirms that the Holy Spirit transcends technology to attend to hearts, guide collective worship, and intercede through online networks. Principles include intentional invitation—prayer begins with asking the Spirit to fill both physical and virtual rooms—and sacramental integrity—ensuring that baptisms and communions remain embodied even when live-streamed. Discernment practices teach participants to test digital promptings against Scripture, distinguishing genuine Spirit nudges from algorithmic manipulation. Hybrid liturgies integrate spontaneous digital prayer breaks where online chat prompts are read aloud and prayed over by in-person leaders. Ongoing training in digital literacy and spiritual discernment equips pastors to shepherd both analog and digital flocks. Recognizing digital pneumatology as distinct yet integrated prepares the church to leverage technology without compromising Spirit-led authenticity. As digital and in-person praxis unify under Spirit guidance, we turn to the toll of trauma and the Spirit's comfort.

7 Trauma, Mental-Health Crises, and the Comforter

7.1 Pandemic Aftershocks and Collective Grief

The COVID-19 pandemic unleashed waves of collective grief—lost loved ones, social isolation, economic hardship—that overwhelming traditional pastoral structures. The Spirit's role as Comforter (Paraklētos) became especially vital, interceding for hearts unable to articulate sorrow (John 14:16; Rom 8:26). Online grief support groups facilitated by trained prayer ministers saw participants report spontaneous peace mid-session, attributing it to the Spirit's presence. Prayer walls filled with anonymous laments, leading worship communities to host dedicated lament services where Spirit-led songs and readings validated communal pain. Research indicates that spiritual comfort reduces cortisol levels, aligning with biblical promises that God "binds up the brokenhearted" (Ps 147:3). Recognizing pandemic aftershocks as an arena for Spirit consolation highlights the need for integrated mental-health and spiritual care.

7.2 Spirit-Enabled Lament and the Language of the Groan (Romans 8:26–27)

Lament—honest expressions of sorrow and protest—is a Spirit-led gift often neglected in triumphalist settings. The Spirit's groan intercession (Rom 8:26–27) models wordless lament that Scripture invites communities to emulate (Lam 5). Lament services incorporate unstructured time for tears, silence, and spoken cries, with worship leaders occasionally offering Spirit-spoken phrases or scriptural echoes. Liturgies may include collective reading of Psalms of lament (Ps 13, 22, 88) followed by open mic prayers, allowing individuals to voice personal burdens. Mental-health integration encourages participants to journal emergent emotions and share them in confessional small groups, fostering mutual support and reducing shame. In contexts of racial trauma or political violence, public lament vigils become Spirit-mediated protest, blending justice and worship. Recognizing lament as Spirit-enabled advocacy prevents superficial positivity and invites genuine healing.

7.3 Integrating Psychology and Spiritual Direction: Safeguards and Synergy

Effective care for trauma requires collaboration between licensed counselors and Spirit-led spiritual directors. Professional psychologists provide diagnostic tools—PTSD screening, trauma-informed therapy—while spiritual directors listen for Spirit's guidance in matters of soul care. Confidential referral networks ensure that individuals with complex mental-health needs receive clinical care, with the Spirit guiding referrals and therapeutic prayer. Training programs for pastors increasingly include modules on trauma theology and psychological first aid, equipping leaders to discern when clinical intervention is needed. Spirit-led discernment flags red-flag symptoms—self-harm ideation, dissociative episodes—triggering immediate care. As clinical and spiritual approaches align under Spirit wisdom, churches develop holistic healing ministries.

7.4 Healing Communities that Embody Gentleness, Hospitality, and Hope

Communities shaped by the Spirit's comfort become sanctuaries for the wounded. Small groups prioritize safety through clear confidentiality covenants, Spirit-inspired compassionate listening, and soul care liturgies. Hospitality—shared meals, open homes, crisis housing—embodies the Spirit's gentleness. Hope-focused ministries train volunteers to speak life-giving truths under Spirit prompting, echoing Paul's encouragement to "encourage one another and build one another up" (1 Th 5:11). Narratives of post-traumatic growth—where suffering yields deeper faith—circulate as Spirit-called testimonies, reinforcing resilience. Recognizing such communities as Spirit-formed healing spaces underscores the Spirit's role in renewing hearts for mission, and prepares us to celebrate the global South's dynamism next.

8 Global South Dynamism and Western Malaise

8.1 Pentecostal Explosion in Africa, Asia, and Latin America

In the Global South, Pentecostalism's rapid spread—often outpacing population growth—reflects the Spirit's vibrancy in contexts of poverty, instability, and religious plurality. Churches plant wildly in informal settlements, with Spirit-led house fellowships multiplying spontaneously. Mass healing services attract thousands, demonstrating the Spirit's authoritative power amidst limited medical infrastructure. Indigenous leaders contextualize preaching using local symbols—drum rhythms in West Africa, street-theater in Latin America—invited by Spirit promptings. Mobilization of Spirit-empowered laity into entrepreneurial and social initiatives reveals how renewal extends beyond worship into holistic transformation. Recognizing this explosion highlights a contrast with Western youth exodus and aging congregations, urging cross-pollination of styles and convictions.

8.2 Contextual Theologies of Struggle, Joy, and Communal Deliverance

The Global South's lived realities—economic hardship, political oppression, spiritual warfare—shape pneumatologies that emphasize immediate Spirit intervention. Theologians develop contextual doctrines: in Brazil, "God in the Favela" movements affirm Spirit's presence among the oppressed; in the Philippines, deliverance prayer networks confront animist inheritance with apostolic boldness. Liturgies integrate Socratic lament, Spirit-empowered testimonies, and communal deliverance rites, resonating with Acts' multi-ethnic worship (Acts 10). Communal deliverance centers emerge, offering Spirit-led freedom rituals that engage collective curses and liberate entire villages. Recognizing these contextual theologies invites Western churches to adopt robust emphases on social liberation alongside doctrinal orthodoxy.

317

8.3 Mutual Gifts: Doctrinal Depth from North; Experiential Vitality from South

True ecumenism involves North–South partnership: Western scholarship offers centuries of doctrinal reflection—creeds, councils, systematic theology—while the Global South provides experiential vitality in Spirit-led worship, healing, and mission. Joint conferences like Lausanne III demonstrate synergy when Northern theologians and Southern pastors collaborate on mission strategies. Seminaries in the North invite Global South faculty for residencies focused on pneumatology, while Southern churches request Western lecturers on ecclesiology and ethics. Online platforms share courses on Spirit ministry recorded in Asia and translated for African contexts. Recognizing mutual gifts prevents paternalism and fosters reciprocal enrichment—a reflection of the Spirit's unifying purpose (Eph 4:3).

8.4 Polycentric Mission Led by Spirit-Filled Majority-World Voices

The future of global mission is polycentric: sending centers arise in Nairobi, Seoul, and São Paulo, coordinating teams that cross continents. These movements no longer depend solely on Western funding; Spirit-led bi-vocational workers support themselves while pioneering churches in Europe and North America. Networks like the Movement for Global Mission, convened by majority-world leaders, set strategic priorities under Spirit prayer gatherings. Shared training hubs emphasize quadrilateral partnerships—Global North, South, East, West—ensuring mission strategies reflect diverse contexts. Recognizing polycentric, Spirit-led mission movements embeds humility in Western churches and amplifies the Spirit's global mandate to renew all nations under Christ's lordship.

9 Ecological Crisis and the Spirit of New Creation

9.1 Groaning Creation Awaiting Spirit-Wrought Liberation (Romans 8:19–22)

Creation itself waits with eager longing for the revealing of the children of God, as Paul teaches, because it too is subject to futility and bondage to decay. The Spirit's role here is dual: first, to groan within creation, as He groans within believers, calling for liberation; second, to empower believers to join in creation's travail. Environmental degradation—deforestation, pollution, biodiversity loss—is experienced as creation's groans, resonating with the Spirit's deep intercession (Rom 8:26). Theologians have begun to speak of the Spirit as the "Cosmic Groaner," whose empathy for a wounded earth is as personal as His comfort of the afflicted. In practice, churches host "creation lament services," where readings from Isaiah 24 and laments from the Psalms are combined with silent meditation on endangered species. Practical ministries like river cleanups and reforestation efforts become acts of Spirit-drawn solidarity with creation's groaning. Pastors preach sermons that weave ecological statistics—species extinction rates, carbon emission figures—with the promise of Spirit-energized renewal. Children's Sunday-school curricula now include stewardship projects that invite the Spirit to awaken wonder and responsibility. Scientific conferences on climate change increasingly open with prayers led by interfaith groups invoking the Spirit for insight and courage. Recognizing the Spirit's cosmic groaning reframes ecological activism from political agenda to sacred calling, preparing communities for eco-theological reflection.

9.2 Eco-theology: Breath (Ruach) as Life-Network and Stewardship Mandate

The Hebrew word **ruach**—breath, wind, Spirit—images the interconnectedness of all life. Eco-theology draws on Genesis 2:7, where God breathes into dust to create life, and Ezekiel 37, where breath enters dry bones. The Spirit's breath permeates soil, water, and air, knitting ecological networks into a unified body of life. Theologians propose that stewardship is not only a moral duty but a sacramental response to the Spirit's indwelling of creation. Carbon footprints are now taught as spiritual footprints; each emission becomes a tangible sign of spiritual disconnection. Churches adopt "carbon fasts" during Lent, mirroring spiritual fasting with reduced fuel use, inviting the Spirit to deepen both environmental and spiritual discipline. Seminary courses on eco-theology include guided forest retreats where students pray with trees, listening for the Spirit's whisper in rustling leaves. Eco-justice advocates cite Colossians 1:16–17 to show that the Spirit upholds all things in Christ, empowering faithful care for creation as divine co-labor. Recognizing **ruach** as life-network extends the Spirit's fellowship beyond human community, framing environmental activism as neighbor love on a planetary scale. This conception transitions naturally into liturgies of repentance.

9.3 Liturgies of Repentance for Environmental Sin

Just as communal confession addresses social and personal sins, environmental liturgies repent on behalf of ecological harm—overfishing, deforestation, oil spills. Worship planners craft services that integrate readings from Amos 5 and Micah 6, condemning selfish exploitation, followed by prayers confessing corporate complicity. Symbolic acts—casting biodegradable seeds into a central bowl to represent new creation—invite congregations to witness the Spirit's power to transform wastelands into green sanctuaries. Music selections can include "For the Beauty of the Earth," reinterpreted in Spirit-saturated arrangements. After such services, many churches organize community greening days, linking liturgical repentance to practical action. The Spirit is invoked in the epiclesis: "Come, Holy Spirit, renew the face of the earth," echoing Psalm 104's creation praise. Liturgical seasons like Rogation Days, historically tied to agricultural blessing, are revived under Spirit guidance to pray for rains and soil fertility. Recognizing liturgical repentance as Spirit-led fosters continuity between worship and ecological advocacy, leading into grassroots initiatives.

9.4 Grass-roots Initiatives—Renewable Energy, Tree Planting, Environmental Advocacy

Inspired by Spirit-shaped repentance, churches launch renewable-energy co-ops that install solar panels on underused buildings, testifying to Odyssey's vision "You shall be as a garden, as a spring of water" (Isa 58:11). Tree-planting campaigns partner with local municipalities, engaging youth groups in restoring urban green spaces. Advocacy networks like "Creation Justice Ministries" mobilize congregants for legislative action on clean air and water, guided by Spirit-inspired petitions. Faith-based investment funds divest from fossil fuels, investing in community-owned wind farms as an act of prophetic witness. Intergenerational teams build community gardens in food deserts, combining ecological stewardship with food justice. Universities host conferences on "Faith and Sustainability," featuring Spirit-led keynote addresses that bridge scientific and theological wisdom. Recognizing these initiatives as Spirit-empowered praxis integrates theology with activism, setting the stage for addressing gender and power dynamics next.

10 Gender, Power, and the Spirit of Equality

10.1 Daughters Prophesy: Spirit-Empowered Women in Scripture and History

Scripture affirms that the Spirit falls on both sons and daughters: "Your sons and your daughters shall prophesy" (Joel 2:28; Acts 2:17). Women like Deborah (Judges 4–5), Miriam (Exod 15:20), Anna (Luke 2:36–38), and the Samaritan woman (John 4) illustrate Spirit-empowered leadership across roles. Church history records figures such as Teresa of Ávila and Katharina von Bora whose Spirit-driven reforms reshaped monastic and Protestant movements. Yet patriarchal structures have often suppressed women's gifts. Renewed pneumatology insists on scriptural equality: Galatians 3:28's "neither male nor female" marks the baptized community. Contemporary movements like "Restoring Women's Ministry" train congregations to re-embrace Spirit-given female vocations. Panels at seminary conferences feature female theologians articulating distinctive Spirit insights. Convenings like the Lausanne Women's Coalition highlight women missionaries forging new centers of gravity in the Global South. Recognizing daughters' prophetic place liberates gendered power structures, facilitating mutual submission under the Spirit's koinōnia. This balanced insight prepares churches to confront abuse scandals.

10.2 Confronting Patriarchal Systems and Abuse Scandals

The Spirit's personal advocacy extends to victims of abuse, calling the church to repentance for patriarchal distortions that have harmed women and children. Testimonies of survivors finding healing under Spirit-led counseling ministries underscore His comfort (2 Cor 1:4). Denominational commissions, guided by Spirit-sensed urgency, implement safeguarding protocols, mandatory reporting, and restorative justice processes. Liturgies of lament and renewal, featuring survivor-led readings, invite the Spirit's conviction upon leadership cultures steeped in silence. Workshops for pastors integrate Spirit-empowered empathy training, emphasizing listening for Spirit-given courage to address systemic abuses. Faith-based therapy programs combine trauma-informed care with Spirit-guided prayer, demonstrating synergy between clinical and spiritual renewal. Recognizing the Spirit's call to justice catalyzes structural changes—diaconal councils with parity in gender representation—that embody divine equality. Transitioning from confession of sin against the vulnerable to proactive empowerment readies the church for mutual koinōnia in the Spirit's next dimension.

10.3 Mutual Submission and Spirit-Generated Koinōnia (Ephesians 5:18–21)

Paul's command to "be filled with the Spirit...submitting to one another out of reverence for Christ" (Eph 5:18–21) frames church life as Spirit-enabled mutuality rather than top-down patriarchy. In Spirit-empowered communities, leadership teams practice shared authority models—elders and deacons of both genders co-lead—reflecting perichoretic fellowship. Decision-making processes employ Spirit-guided consensus, with extended prayer, listening, and prophetic testing protecting against power grabs. Norms like the "circle model," where each voice is heard in Spirit-led rounds, democratize governance. Pilot projects in urban churches replace male-only boards with equal-gender committees, citing Acts 6's inclusion principle. Retreats on "Servant Leadership in the Spirit" teach humility and mutual submission as pathways to healthy authority. Recognizing Spirit-generated koinōnia uproots hierarchical sin patterns, cultivating relational equality that mirrors divine communion. This Spirit-patterned fellowship transitions into mentoring frameworks.

10.4 Mentoring Frameworks that Release Gifts across Gender and Generation

The Spirit shapes mentoring relationships that transcend gender stereotypes and generational gaps. Older women and men, under Spirit direction, mentor younger believers, passing on charisms and vocation insights. Programs like "Women in Leadership" pair emerging female pastors with seasoned mentors, under Spirit-led covenant agreements. Multi-generational cohorts—combining teens, parents, grandparents—meet monthly for Spirit-guided skill-sharing: worship technology, discipleship methods, inner-healing practices. Safe-space protocols ensure that voice and initiative come first from the Spirit, not from cultural norms. Continuing education units for clergy include Spirit-directed modules on gender inclusivity and intercultural competency. Recognizing these mentoring frameworks as Spirit-wrought communities of practice ensures that every believer, regardless of gender or age, receives confirmatory gifts. This prepares the way for exploring pathways of renewal.

11 Pathways of Renewal: Scripture, Liturgy, and Contemplation

11.1 Slow, Spirit-Led Lectio Divina Countering Distraction Culture

In a world of constant stimuli, the ancient discipline of lectio divina offers Spirit-paced immersion in Scripture. Practitioners read a short biblical passage slowly—Psalm 1 or Mark 4—pausing between words to ask the Spirit, "What are You saying?" Small groups practicing Spirit-led lectio report that a single phrase like "Be still and know" (Ps 46:10) can become a dwell-spot for the Spirit throughout the week. Retreat centers host "Lectio Marathons," where participants linger over a single verse for hours, allowing Spirit insight to ripple through mind and body. Smartphone app reminders for lectio encourage brief pauses in hectic schedules, reminding users that the Spirit speaks in silence. Academic studies link slow reading with improved focus and emotional regulation, paralleling Spirit-enabled renewal of the mind (Rom 12:2). Recognizing lectio as a Spirit-directed pause counters the tyranny of the quick and readies hearts for sacramental imagination.

11.2 Sacramental Imagination Rekindled by the Spirit's Epiclesis

Renewing the imagination requires recovering the Spirit-invocative moment in every sacrament. Western rites often abbreviate or omit the epiclesis—the Spirit-calling prayer over bread and wine—yet ancient liturgies made this central. Recovering robust epicleses in Eucharistic prayers reconnects congregations to the Spirit's action in transforming elements into Christ's body. At baptism, explicit Spirit-calling prayers ask for anointing, sending, and empowerment. Retreat liturgies include Spirit-breathed blessings over meal times, reflecting Eucharist as anticipation of feast in the Spirit. Workshops on "Imagining Sacraments" explore how sensory details—water temperature, oil fragrance, chalice weight—become Spirit-eyed symbols. Recognizing epiclesis as Spirit's summons preserves mystery and invites congregants into living encounter rather than empty ritual. This sacramental rekindling leads into communal experiments in presence.

11.3 Monastic and Neo-Monastic Communities as Laboratories of Presence

Monastic orders have long exemplified Spirit-formed rhythms of prayer, work, and study. Neo-monastic communities transpose these rhythms into urban contexts: shared houses following Benedictine hours, weaving Spirit-led offices into daily life. These communities become "laboratories of presence," where the Spirit's work can be observed across seasons of stability and transition. Participants engage in shared meals, eucharistic hospitality, and community discernment circles guided by Spirit promptings. Urban monastic cells partner with local ministries—soup kitchens, youth mentoring—testing how Spirit formation in prayer flows into practical service. Academic studies of neo-monastic impact show increased spiritual depth, leadership sustainability, and missional creativity among residents. Recognizing these communities as Spirit laboratories confirms their role in testing and refining pathways of renewal for the wider church. Their lived experiments prepare us for convergence worship blended with ancient rhythms.

11.4 Convergence Worship Blending Charismatic Freedom with Ancient Rhythms

Convergence worship represents a synthesis of charismatic spontaneity and liturgical structure. Services begin with fixed-hour prayer elements—call to worship, confession, Scripture readings—then open to Spirit-driven moments of prophecy, free prayer, and spontaneous song. Music sets shift seamlessly from ancient chants to contemporary choruses, guided by Spirit-prompted transitions rather than rigid playlists. Communion is offered at multiple stations, inviting pilgrims to partake in small groups under Spirit guidance instead of a single procession. Testimonies and prophetic words are interwoven with corporate prayer, creating a tapestry of planned and unexpected encounters. Retreat weekends on convergence worship train teams to read congregational "atmosphere" under Spirit discernment, ensuring unity amid diversity. Recognizing convergence worship as Spirit-shaped fusion prevents either liturgical formalism or charismatic anarchy, offering a balanced pathway of renewal that draws on Scripture, liturgy, and contemplation as we close this chapter and prepare for daily discipleship in Chapter 15.

12 Justice, Reconciliation, and Prophetic Activism

12.1 The Spirit and Isaiah 61: Good News for the Poor, Liberty for Captives

In Luke 4, Jesus reads Isaiah 61, announcing the Spirit's mission: good news for the poor, liberty for prisoners, sight for the blind, and release for the oppressed. Contemporary justice ministries invoke this text as a pneumatological mandate. Spirit-led teams partner with anti-poverty organizations to address systemic injustice, combining evangelistic preaching with micro-enterprise development. In urban neighborhoods, churches offer legal aid clinics under Spirit prompting, aligning real-world advocacy with the biblical prophecy. Art installations in downtown spaces—interactive murals depicting Isaiah 61—invite passersby to pray for renewal. The Spirit's empowerment enables practitioners to speak truth to power, testifying that social transformation is integral to kingdom advance. Recognizing Isaiah 61 as Spirit-shaped activism prevents charity from stagnating into patronage and anchors justice in heralding the Spirit's arrival among the marginalized.

12.2 Race, Class, and the Ministry of Tearing Down Dividing Walls (Ephesians 2:14–18)

Paul proclaims that Christ "has broken down the dividing wall of hostility," creating one new humanity through the cross. The Spirit empowers reconciliation across race and class: worship services that integrate diverse ethnic musical traditions, leadership teams reflecting socio-economic variety, and shared table fellowships where stories of racial pain are heard and healed. Pilgrimages to historic sites of segregation—e.g., the U.S. civil-rights landmarks—become Spirit-guided pilgrimages of repentance and solidarity. Churches partner with local civic groups to advocate for criminal-justice reform, housing equity, and school desegregation, embodying Spirit-driven unity. Reconciliation seminars use experiential exercises—cross-cultural story circles, bias-awareness workshops—invoked by Spirit promptings for honest dialogue. Recognizing the Spirit's role in dismantling dividing walls situates reconciliation as central to the gospel rather than optional social outreach.

12.3 Non-violent Prophetic Protest Modeled on Acts 4 Prayer

After Peter and John's arrest, the early church prayed for boldness, not revenge, resulting in fresh Spirit empowerment (Acts 4:23–31). Similarly, modern prophetic activism incorporates non-violent protest with Spirit-guided prayer. Intercessors lead peaceful marches to capital steps, pausing for Scriptural declarations—"Righteousness exalts a nation" (Prov 14:34)—then praying for policymakers. Sit-ins at environmental orphans' conferences ask the Spirit to convict hearts rather than intimidate authorities. Campaigns for refugee rights include Spirit-led dialogues with community leaders, combining prophetic critique with hospitality invitations. Such activism avoids coercive tactics, embodying Jesus's methods of healing hearts before healing laws. Recognizing Spirit-empowered prayer as the catalyst for societal change reframes activism as worshipful obedience rather than secular protest.

12.4 Measuring Revival by Ethical Fruit, Not Only Ecstatic Experience

True pneumatological renewal bears fruit in justice, compassion, humility, and integrity—what Jesus called "good fruit" (Matt 7:16). Churches track metrics like poverty alleviation impact, racial reconciliation progress, and environmental improvements alongside baptism and attendance numbers. Testimonies of transformed lives are gathered not only in healing stories but in long-term rehabilitation of ex-offenders, reduction in local crime rates, and improved community health. Denominational renewal reports include case studies of businesses adopting living wages under Spirit conviction. Recognizing ethical fruit as the scoreboard of revival prevents an overemphasis on emotional highs and ensures that Spirit-driven renewal reshapes both heart and society.

13 Missional Imagination for a Spirit-Shaped Future

13.1 Fresh Expressions: Café Churches, Workplace Chaplaincy, Micro-Communities

The Spirit inspires innovative models—café churches where hosts brew coffee and biblical discussion flows organically; workplace chaplaincy that integrates prayer into corporate environments; micro-communities of 8–12 believers meeting in homes, parks, or co-working spaces. These fresh expressions reflect the Spirit's adaptability, meeting people where they are rather than expecting them to enter sanctuaries. Start-up teams spend time in local cafes, libraries, or markets seeking Spirit indicators—opened doors for gospel conversations or communities longing for sacred encounter. Successful café churches report that the aroma of fresh brew often becomes the Spirit's invitation to share living water (John 4:10). Workplace chaplains guided by the Spirit testify that impromptu prayer huddles before meetings transform organizational cultures. Recognizing these fresh expressions as Spirit-born innovations prevents rigid ecclesial forms from stifling the Spirit's creativity, paving the way for bivocational apostles and Spirit-driven entrepreneurship.

13.2 Bivocational Apostles and Spirit-Driven Entrepreneurship

Economic realities and Spirit promptings converge in bivocational apostles—individuals who maintain secular employment while pioneering new faith communities. This model reflects Paul's tentmaking (Acts 18:3) and the Spirit's equipping for mission without overbearing dependency on institutional salaries. Bivocational leaders report that daily workplace interactions become mission contexts, with Spirit-inspired prayers for colleagues yielding tangible opportunities for gospel witness. Spirit-driven entrepreneurs integrate kingdom values—justice, stewardship, community—into business ventures like social enterprises and ethical consulting, embodying the gospel in marketplace practices (Matt 5:16). Training networks for marketplace ministry offer Spirit-guided incubators where participants pray over business plans and test market viability under Spirit discernment. Recognizing bivocational and entrepreneurial models as Spirit-empowered pathways expands conceptions of discipleship beyond church walls into every sphere of life.

13.3 Signs and Wonders as Contextual Apologetics in Post-Christian Cities

In cities where secular narratives dominate, signs and wonders—healings, prophetic insights, marketplace miracles—function as contextual apologetics, authenticating the gospel's power. Mission teams prayer-walk urban districts, asking the Spirit to highlight open doors—perhaps a roadside healing or uncanny provision—that capture attention. A single documented miracle can open multiple neighborhoods to listening groups, as happened in Edinburgh's Holyrood Park revival. Evangelistic events in London's Greenwich Village featured free health clinics and deliverance prayer booths, yielding testimony media coverage that sparked curiosity. Recognizing signs and wonders as Spirit-led apologetics requires careful biblical discernment to avoid sensationalism, ensuring that miracles point to Christ's lordship (John 20:31). As contextual apologetics readies cities for gospel hearing, communities prepare for concluding synthesis toward daily discipleship.

Conclusion As we navigate the complex currents of contemporary culture—marked by demographic shifts, secularization, consumerism, and theological tensions—the Holy Spirit remains the divine Author of renewal. By diagnosing present challenges and highlighting vibrant signs of global, cross-cultural renewal, we see that the Spirit's work transcends human systems, inviting us into deeper reliance, balanced openness, and sacrificial witness. Whether confronting the immanent frame, resisting spiritual commodification, or embodying cruciform economic practices, the church is called to forge Spirit-led paths that honor biblical fidelity and contextual creativity. Moving forward, these reflections equip us to live "in step with the Spirit," translating pneumatological renewal into daily discipleship and missional imagination.

Chapter 15. Living in Step with the Spirit: Practical Implications

Living in step with the Spirit is not a lofty ideal reserved for spiritual elites but a daily invitation extended to every believer. As we move from theory to practice, this final chapter offers concrete habits, decision-making frameworks, communal rhythms, and personal disciplines that orient our entire lives around the Spirit's guidance. Rather than sporadic "spiritual experiences," we pursue an integrated discipleship in which prayer, work, rest, and relationships all become arenas of Spirit-led growth. By cultivating awareness, discerning rightly, forming Christlike virtues, and establishing sustainable daily patterns, we learn to navigate life's complexities with supernatural wisdom and power. These practical implications equip us to embody everything we have explored in previous chapters—ensuring that renewal is not merely an event but a lifelong journey of walking in the Spirit's footsteps.

1 Cultivating Spirit-Awareness

1.1 Slow Seeing: "Practicing the Presence" in Ordinary Tasks

Recognizing the Spirit in the mundane begins with intentional slowness: pausing at the sink to feel water's weight, breathing deeply before answering an email, or noticing the interplay of light and shadow on a walking path. Brother Lawrence's *Practice of the Presence* exemplifies how lifting every action into silent prayer turns dishwashing into altar ministry. Rather than rushing from task to task, believers learn to ask, "Where is the Spirit inviting my attention now?" during routine chores. In corporate meetings, one might begin by silently inviting the Spirit to illuminate each slide or spreadsheet, opening space for unexpected insight. Parents caring for small children can transform diaper changes into whispered prayers, sensing the Spirit's empowerment for patience and love. Students studying for exams may punctuate reading sessions with two or three Spirit-focused breaths, re-centering mind and heart. Slow seeing also applies to nature: a five-minute pause in the park can awaken awareness of the Spirit's creative artistry—Psalm 19's "heavens declare" come alive in every cloud formation. Over time, this cultivated slowness rewires neural pathways to expect divine invitation, creating a spontaneous readiness to respond. Communities practicing slow seeing report increased unity: shared awareness of Spirit promptings during common tasks deepens mutual attunement. Recognizing slow seeing as foundational awareness sets the stage for embodied prayer rhythms.

1.2 Breath Prayers as Embodied Reminders of Ruach Life

Short, two-phrase prayers—such as "Spirit, breathe" on the inhale and "renew me" on the exhale—anchor bodies and souls in the rhythmic flow of God's life-giving Spirit. These breath prayers harness the physiology of breathing to reinforce theological truth: God's **ruach** became our breath at creation (Gen 2:7), and the Spirit continues to animate our every moment. Professionals in high-stress environments find that embedding breath prayers in their workflow—reciting them while switching apps or before answering a phone—disrupts anxiety cycles and reasserts dependence on divine presence. Artists sketching or musicians tuning their instruments can sync creative impulses to Spirit-breathed petitions like "Teach me truth," inviting illumination mid-process. Breath prayers also serve families: setting a kitchen timer for 30-second prayer breaks throughout the day trains children to recognize divine comfort in fleeting pauses. Retreat leaders incorporate guided breath-prayer practices into silent sessions, noting that participants often report fresh clarity on persistent decisions. Over time, breath prayers transform into background music of the soul, reminding believers that every heartbeat is underwritten by the Spirit's sustaining power (Heb 12:1). Recognizing these simple prayers as embodied awareness

330

bridges ordinary tasks with deep communion, preparing hearts for reflective examen practices.

1.3 Noticing Consolations and Desolations—The Examen in Spirit Key

St. Ignatius's spiritual *examen* invites believers to review each day in the Spirit's presence, noting movements of consolation (joy, peace, love) and desolation (anxiety, agitation, disconnection). Conducted in four steps—gratitude, review, sorrow, and renewal—this practice becomes Spirit-attuned self-observation. In the evening, one might journal moments when a sudden delight in a friend's kindness signaled Spirit consolation, or when an uncharacteristic impatience with a coworker reflected desolation. Community groups developing *Ignatian circles* share consolidated examen insights, offering mutual discernment of recurring patterns. Therapists integrating spiritual direction report that clients gain emotional regulation by distinguishing feelings that arise from the Spirit's promptings versus base fears of the flesh. Over weeks, patterns emerge: consistent Spirit-led encouragement before major decisions or recurring desolation around specific relationships. Recognizing these patterns under Spirit guidance leads to targeted repentance and renewed trust, grounded in 1 John 4:1's call to test spirits. Examen thus becomes a continuous calibration tool, ensuring that subsequent prayers and actions align with the Spirit's movement. As discernment deepens, believers grow more confident in distinguishing God's voice amid life's noise.

1.4 Journaling Prompt: "Where Did I Sense the Spirit's Nudge Today?"

Simple journaling prompts focus awareness on daily Spirit interactions. At day's end, believers record instances of unexpected compassion, insight, or peace—moments when the Spirit "nudged" toward a kind word or a courageous step. Over time, these journals become crystallized evidence of the Spirit's faithfulness, fostering hope when seasons of apparent silence arrive. Leaders in small-group settings encourage cross-sharing of journal highlights, creating mutual affirmation and collective discernment of communal Spirit callings. Writers find that reviewing week-long entries sometimes reveals Spirit-led themes—perhaps a call to justice or a ministry opportunity—that guide future prayers and projects. Digital journaling apps with timestamp features allow patterns to surface via data analytics, though users must guard against over-reliance on metrics. Couples practicing joint Spirit-nudge journaling discover convergences that shape shared ministry visions. Recognizing journaling as a disciplined testament of Spirit presence grounds daily life in documented testimonies, segueing into frameworks for Spirit-anchored decision-making.

2 Discernment and Decision-Making

2.1 Three-Stranded Cord—Scripture, Community, Inner Witness

Effective decisions flow from intertwining three strands: the Word of God, communal wisdom, and the Spirit's inner witness. Scripture offers objective metrics—principles from Proverbs, commands from the Sermon on the Mount—that never contradict the Spirit. Community provides collective discernment: trusted mentors, prayer partners, and church leaders who listen for and test Spirit promptings together (Acts 13:2–3). Internally, the Spirit bears witness in the heart, often through a sense of peace or disquiet that arises when considering options (Col 3:15). A business owner facing expansion might first seek scriptural guidance on integrity, then consult a board of Spirit-led advisers, and finally weigh inner confirmations or reservations stirred by prayer. When all three strands converge, confidence is high; divergence prompts further reflection. Seminaries teach students to develop this tri-fold discernment, practicing case studies where one strand may momentarily dominate—say, a clear biblical injunction—yet the Spirit uses community to illuminate nuance. Recognizing the three-stranded cord as a resilient framework prevents lone-wolf decision-making and readies leaders for convergence and constraint considerations.

2.2 Convergence and Constraint: Closed Doors, Inner Peace, External Counsel

Discernment involves both affirmations and negations: the Spirit sometimes says "no" through closed doors—financial obstacles, relational blocks, unforeseen delays—that redirect plans. Inner peace functions as a green light, but its absence warrants caution. External counsel—wise advisors praying alongside—serves as a third check, guarding against self-deception or impulsive risk-taking. In Acts 16, Paul's team experiences a convergence of constraint: forbidden by the Holy Spirit to enter Asia, troubled by opposition in Bithynia, and finally led by a Macedonia vision (Acts 16:6–10). Churches today emulate this pattern by maintaining both open application processes and Spirit-listening retreats before new initiatives. Leaders track patterns of "no" by documenting obstacles and evaluating whether consistent barriers signal Spirit direction. Likewise, inner peace is assessed by noting bodily and emotional responses—rested optimism versus growing anxiety—after prayer. Recognizing that sometimes "no" is as Spirit-led as "go" prevents forced progress and cultivates healthy patience. Over time, adherence to convergence and constraint fosters mature obedience and reduces ministry burnout.

2.3 Discerning Timing as Well as Direction (Acts 16:6–10)

Timing is critical: the Spirit may direct a mission but withhold the season until hearts or contexts are ripe. Paul's delayed journey into Asia, followed by redirection to Macedonia, demonstrates discerning both where and when (Acts 16:6–10). Practically, believers test timing through "wait lists"—explicit periods of prayer during which no final decisions are made—and by watching for synchronized confirmations, such as repeated Scripture verses or unanimous community agreement. A church contemplating a new ministry might launch a small pilot program rather than a full-scale rollout, giving the Spirit room to confirm or modify timing. Seasonal calendars—harvest cycles, school years, fiscal quarters—are overlaid with prayer rhythms, ensuring that new initiatives coincide with community capacities. Recognizing misaligned timing often prevents wasted resources and spiritual discouragement. As timing and direction coalesce, decision-making moves from wishful thinking to Spirit-calibrated strategy.

2.4 Red-Flag Checklist to Detect Self-Deception or Spiritual Manipulation

To guard against false promptings—whether from personal ambition or demonic influence—believers use a red-flag checklist. Items include: "Does this contradict clear biblical teaching?"; "Is there a spirit of fear or compulsion rather than peace?"; "Are motives self-glorifying rather than God-exalting?"; "Does community feedback confirm or question this leading?"; "Is there pressure to move quickly without adequate counsel?" By routinely evaluating decisions against these flags, leaders avoid manipulation tactics—miracle marketing, guilt inducement, or pseudo-Spirit voices promising guaranteed success. Workshops train intercessors to pray through each red-flag category, inviting the Spirit to reveal hidden motivations or external deceptions. Recognizing and removing red flags upholds integrity and ensures that Spirit-led decisions remain gospel-centered, free, and wise. This vigilance prepares the way for forming virtues that reflect Spirit fruit.

3 Forming Virtues and the Fruit of the Spirit

3.1 Nine-Fold Fruit as Relational Litmus, Not Moral Scoreboard

Paul's list of the Spirit's fruit—love, joy, peace, patience, kindness, goodness, faithfulness, gentleness, self-control—serves as relational indicators, not legal checkboxes (Gal 5:22–23). Each quality functions as a litmus test in interactions: does this response flow from love or from contractual obligation? Is the peace I feel consistent with justice for the oppressed? When joy falters, is it due to external circumstances or a deeper lack of trust in God's promises? Communities can deploy peer feedback exercises, where partners share observations of fruit versus mere performance. Clarifying that fruit emerges organically from Spirit-infused life—not from rigid moralism—encourages grace in seasons of struggle. Recognizing fruit as relational litmus highlights the Spirit's priority: healthy connections over flawless conduct, preparing hearts for habit-formation strategies.

3.2 Habit Loops: Micro-Choices that Nurture Patience and Self-Control

Habits form through simple loops: cue, routine, reward. To cultivate patience, one might identify emotional triggers (cue), pause to breathe and pray (routine), then note relief or clarity (reward). For self-control, the cue might be temptation to overindulge; the routine is naming a breath prayer or texting an accountability friend; the reward is the Spirit's whispered affirmation of strength. Over weeks, these micro-choices rewire neural pathways, making Spirit-enabled responses more automatic. Apps can track habit completion and send congratulatory messages, but the ultimate reward is internalized Spirit confidence (Phil 4:13). Small-group "habit labs" provide mutual support: partners share daily wins and setbacks, pray over red-flag moments, and celebrate incremental progress. Recognizing habit loops as Spirit-assisted practices bridges virtue aspiration with concrete action patterns.

3.3 Replacing Vice with Spirit-Opposite (e.g., Greed → Generosity)

Rather than simply suppressing vice, believers replace it with the corresponding fruit. When greed surfaces, one responds with spontaneous acts of generosity—giving food to neighbors, donating a portion of income, or mentoring a needy friend. This replacement strategy aligns with Paul's command to "put on the new self" (Eph 4:24) by inwardly inviting the Spirit's countervailing power. Counseling ministries coach clients to identify triggers for vice—stress, envy, fear—and script immediate Spirit-opposite responses, such as reciting promises about God's provision (Phil 4:19). Over time, generosity replaces greed's drought with a cascade of blessing as resources flow outward. Recognizing vice-replacement as Spirit-driven transformation shifts focus from prohibition to positive growth, priming believers for tracking progress.

3.4 Tracking Progress: Testimonies, Accountability Partners, Celebration

Spirit-formed growth is celebrated communally through testimonies—regular "fruit-share" segments in small groups or services where individuals recount specific ways they have embodied the Spirit's fruit. Accountability partners maintain confidential logs of vice-replacement experiments, offering prayer and feedback. Quarterly "celebration liturgies" mark milestones: anniversaries of first breath prayers, days without reactive anger, or completed habit loops. Churches create digital "fruit walls" where members post short reflections or images illustrating their growth, fostering encouragement. Recognition events—potlucks, award ceremonies in the Spirit's name—underscore that virtue formation is both gift and joy. Recognizing spiritual progress through shared celebration cements communal bonds and models gospel hope for those still struggling. These communal disciplines transition naturally into daily rhythms and spiritual practices.

4 Daily Rhythms and Spiritual Disciplines

4.1 Rule of Life—Anchoring Prayer, Study, Rest, and Work

A *rule of life* is a personalized covenant outlining daily and weekly practices that balance prayer, Scripture study, physical rest, work responsibilities, and recreation. Inspired by monastic examples—Benedict's *ora et labora*—modern Christians craft rhythms that appoint fixed times for morning devotion, midday examen, evening communion, and Sabbath rest. Digital calendars can automate reminders, but participants are taught to pause the alerts in Spirit-led silence rather than reflexively dismiss them. Workdays begin with a two-minute breath prayer session, followed by Scripture velocity—reading a short passage with Spirit-attuned focus. Study periods integrate note-taking with Spirit-led journaling, asking, "Where is the

335

Spirit speaking?" Breaks involve brief creation walks or gratitude pauses. Sabbath delight is strictly observed: no work emails, family meals prioritized, beauty encountered in art or nature. Over months, the rule of life transforms chaotic schedules into sustainable patterns, enabling Spirit-led flourishing across all domains. Recognizing a rule of life as a covenantal framework ensures disciplines arise from devotion rather than duty.

4.2 Fasting as Amplifier of Dependence and Intercession

Fasting—voluntary abstinence from food, media, or other comforts—heightens spiritual appetite and intercessory focus. The Spirit's role is to bring awareness to areas of dependency that must be surrendered, revealing hidden idols of convenience or distraction. A corporate 24-hour fast preceding major decisions can sharpen communal reliance on Spirit guidance, as hunger pangs refocus prayers on divine provision (Matt 4:4). Individual fasting routines—once weekly partial fasts or seasonal fasts—heighten sensitivity to Spirit promptings in daily life. Journal prompts during fasts probe for inner cravings beyond physical hunger, unveiling deep-seated anxieties or unmet longings that only the Spirit can satisfy. Community fasts conclude with shared meals framed as vow renewals, celebrating Spirit-sustained dependence. Recognizing fasting as Spirit-invited practice deepens intercession and humility, setting the stage for Sabbath celebration.

4.3 Sabbath Delight: Play, Beauty, and Holy Uselessness

Sabbath is not merely rest from labor but delight in God's presence expressed through play, beauty, and "holy uselessness." Under the Spirit's lead, communities designate one day each week—or a quarterly "Sabbath week"—for activities that renew creativity and relational joy: art workshops, nature excursions, board-game festivals, or music jams. Churches partner with local artists to host gallery exhibits or open-mic evenings, celebrating beauty as a divine gift (Exod 31:3). Families dedicate Sunday afternoons to co-creating poetry, cooking new recipes, or simply lounging in hammocks, resisting productivity pressures. Spiritual directors emphasize that spiritual transformation often emerges in unhurried laughter rather than earnest devotion alone. Recognizing Sabbath delight as Spirit-empowered resistance to workaholism fosters holistic rest and anticipates the eternal Sabbath to come (Heb 4:9–10).

4.4 Digital Silence Blocks for Undistracted Communion

In an age of constant connectivity, setting "digital silence blocks"—pre-planned intervals where notifications are turned off—creates space for uninterrupted Spirit communion. Early-morning phone shutdowns allow uninterrupted breath prayers and lectio without email pings. Midday digital sabbaths—two-hour windows—invite contemplative silence, creative reflection, or unhurried prayer walks. Evening technology-free periods foster deeper family interactions around the table, integrating table liturgies and intergenerational storytelling. Retreat centers offer "digital detox" weekends, where participants surrender devices at the door and rediscover spirit-shaped awareness sparked by physical presence. Recognizing digital silence as essential discipline prevents scattered attention and allows the Spirit's still, small voice to speak clearly. These daily rhythms ground believers for the relational ecologies and vocational faithfulness that follow.

5 Relational Ecology in the Spirit

5.1 Conflict Transformation via Gentle Confrontation (Galatians 6:1)

Gentle confrontation begins by recognizing that the Spirit's presence in both parties makes each worthy of restoration rather than punishment. When conflict arises, the first step is to pray silently, inviting the Spirit to soften hardened hearts and grant wisdom (James 1:5). Approaching the other with humility—"Brothers and sisters, if someone is caught in a transgression, you who are spiritual should restore him in a spirit of gentleness"—frames the encounter as mutual healing rather than accusation. Active listening, a gift of the Spirit (1 Cor 12:8), ensures that each person feels heard before responding. By paraphrasing the other's concerns and asking the Spirit to correct misunderstandings, dialogue shifts from defensive sparring to collaborative problem–solving. Incorporating "I" statements—"I felt hurt when…"—under the Spirit's guidance prevents blaming and opens space for confession. If emotions escalate, pausing the conversation for breath prayers ("Spirit, give us peace") can de-escalate tension. Bringing Scripture into the dialogue—perhaps Ephesians 4:26 on "anger without sin"—grounds the conversation in God's truth. When both parties agree to seek reconciliation under the Spirit's umpiring, they often find new unity emerges. Practical exercises like role–reversals, guided by Spirit-prompted questions, foster empathy. Shared prayer following the confrontation invites the Spirit to knit wounded relational fibers back together. Over time, communities that practice gentle confrontation notice fewer recurring disputes, as the Spirit's transformative grace reshapes conflict patterns. Recognizing conflict as an opportunity for Spirit-led growth transitions naturally into practicing forgiveness.

5.2 Forgiveness Flow: Receiving and Releasing Debts

Forgiveness is a twofold Spirit-empowered act: receiving God's pardon and extending pardon to others, thus releasing relational debts. Romans 8:1 assures us that "there is therefore now no condemnation for those who are in Christ Jesus," enabling believers to receive forgiveness from the Father through the Spirit's witness. Internalizing this truth dissolves self-condemnation and opens hearts to forgive others. Practically, one names the offense in prayer—"Lord, I forgive X for…"—and imagines setting a ledger ablaze, symbolizing debt release (Matt 18:21–35). The Spirit often accompanies this with a surge of peace or unexpected compassion. In group settings, corporate forgiveness rituals—shared confessions followed by mutual laying on of hands—amplify the Spirit's work across individuals. Journaling acts as a secondary layer: writing a forgiveness letter (not necessarily sent) clarifies emotional steps, after which the Spirit confirms release. When bitterness resurfaces, quick forgiveness prayers harness Spirit power to maintain flow. Churches encourage periodic "forgiveness renewals," seasons when congregants revisit past hurts under Spirit guidance, ensuring no resentment remains hidden. Recognizing forgiveness as Spirit-empowered rhythm prepares communities for deeper mutual submission.

5.3 Mutual Submission and Honor across Gender and Generation

Ephesians 5:21 exhorts believers to "submit to one another out of reverence for Christ," indicating a Spirit-led mutuality that transcends hierarchical power. In practice, gatherings begin with a shared prayer of mutual submission—leaders ask for Spirit's humility before teaching, while lay members promise Spirit-enabled respect. In intergenerational panels, younger voices prophesy to elders, reflecting the Spirit's reversal of expectations (1 Sam 16:13). During decision-making, each age and gender group prays silently for insight, then shares without interruption, modeling the Spirit's equanimity. Celebrating Spirit-prompted contributions—such as a teenager's innovative ministry idea or a matriarch's seasoned counsel—affirms divine gifting across demographics. Mentoring circles rotate leadership roles, ensuring that every member experiences both giving and receiving guidance. Conflict resolution protocols specify that cross-gender disputes be addressed in mixed-gender teams under Spirit-led neutrality. Retreats include "honor rituals," where participants publicly bless those who have exemplified submission or leadership, invoking Spirit anointing on their ongoing service. Recognizing mutual submission as Spirit-generated koinōnia dissolves cliques and fosters a communal ethos of honor and shared authority. This relational ecology supports celebratory milestones that follow.

5.4 Celebrating Milestones—Spirit-Shaped Rituals of Joy

Milestones—births, baptisms, graduations, ordinations—are occasions the Spirit sanctifies for communal joy and thanksgiving. Spirit-led celebration begins with prayerful selection of Scripture passages—Psalm 118:24, "This is the day that the Lord has made"—that contextualize the milestone in God's narrative. Rituals may include anointing with oil as a tangible sign of Spirit blessing (1 Sam 16:13). Community bands together to compose spontaneous songs or poems under Spirit inspiration, reflecting unique testimonies. Gifts given often bear spiritual significance—Bibles with passages highlighted by the Spirit or handmade items infused with prayer. Sharing stories of God's faithfulness in the days leading up to the milestone reinforces the Spirit's guidance throughout the journey. Potluck meals at such events become feasts where the Spirit's abundance is tasted in diversity of dishes. Visual presentations—photo slideshows with Spirit-affirmed captions—help participants remember God's movement. Symbolic gestures, like lifting newly ordained leaders on chairs (Acts 8:17), invite Spirit-uplifted courage. Rituals conclude with communal declarations—"We celebrate you in the Spirit"—that affirm ongoing divine accompaniment. Recognizing milestone celebrations as Spirit-shaped joy embeds communal memory with testimony, flowing seamlessly into vocational faithfulness.

6 Vocational Faithfulness and Marketplace Witness

6.1 Craftsmanship Spirituality: Excellence as Worship (Colossians 3:23)

Colossians 3:23 instructs believers to work "heartily, as for the Lord and not for men," framing every task as an act of worship under the Spirit's gaze. Whether writing code, baking bread, or teaching students, practitioners invite the Spirit to refine their skills and instill a pursuit of excellence. Micro-practices—praying over the first draft of a report or the first pan of baked rolls—align technical proficiency with Spirit-led purpose. Professionals report that when they dedicate their workspace as an altar—prayer at the start of each day—projects gain creativity and integrity beyond mere job performance. In team contexts, Spirit-informed quality reviews set benchmarks not solely by profit or metrics, but by communal values of service and beauty. Celebrating small victories—a smoothly functioning program, a perfectly risen loaf—as gifts of the Spirit fosters gratitude and ongoing strive for craftsmanship. Recognizing excellence as worship shifts motivation from external validation to divine commendation, preparing individuals for ethical decision-making grids.

6.2 Ethical Decision Grids Guided by Kingdom Values

Marketplace dilemmas—pricing, labor practices, environmental impact—require Spirit-informed ethical grids. Leaders construct decision matrices where each option is measured against kingdom values: justice, stewardship, compassion, integrity. During deliberations, teams pause to pray, asking the Spirit to highlight long-term communal flourishing rather than short-term gain (Prov 16:8). For example, a manufacturing company might balance higher wages against profit margins, trusting Spirit-led creativity to sustain viability. Start-ups report that Spirit-prompted innovations—such as closed-loop production—emerge when ethical grids challenge existing models. Peer advisory boards, under Spirit guidance, review grid outcomes and request clarifications when values conflict. Recognizing these ethical tools as Spirit-directed frameworks ensures that vocational faithfulness becomes credible witness rather than marketing rhetoric. This ethical grounding supports Spirit-enabled mentoring of younger colleagues.

6.3 Mentoring Younger Colleagues—Spirit-Enabled Multiplication

Mentoring in the marketplace under the Spirit's oversight transcends hierarchical training to become partnership in co–learning. Experienced professionals invite younger colleagues into real projects, praying together at project kickoff—asking the Spirit to impart wisdom, creativity, and humility. Reflection sessions follow completion, where mentor and mentee review what the Spirit taught through successes and failures. Mentors model Spirit-led discernment by vocalizing their own prompting—"I felt uneasy about that decision, so I paused and prayed"—demonstrating transparency.

In cross–sector cohorts, Spirit-animated dialogues enable peers from different industries to share lessons, broadening mentees' horizons. Apprentices report that receiving Spirit-inspired affirmations—"I see God forming courage in you"—fosters vocational identity and resilience. Recognizing mentoring as Spirit-enabled multiplication transforms workplace dynamics into discipleship pathways, laying foundation for kingdom entrepreneurship.

6.4 Kingdom Entrepreneurship for Societal Renewal

Kingdom entrepreneurs launch ventures that integrate profit with purpose, guided by the Spirit's vision for justice and community welfare. Market research begins and ends in prayer, inviting Spirit revelation on unmet needs—affordable childcare, ethical supply chains, mental-health services. Business models adopt triple bottom line frameworks—people, planet, profit—ensuring that Spirit-led social impact remains central. Customer interactions incorporate Spirit-informed hospitality: businesses offer free services to vulnerable populations or partner with local nonprofits. Start-ups host monthly "Spirit Roundtables," where entrepreneurs share challenges and pray for breakthroughs. When setbacks arise—regulatory hurdles, funding shortfalls—kingdom entrepreneurs lean on Spirit-enabled perseverance, often discovering alternative paths or partners. Recognizing entrepreneurship as divine co-creation encourages believers to view their vocational endeavors as mission fields, seamlessly transitioning into servant leadership principles.

7 Servant Leadership in the Spirit

7.1 Authority as Foot-Washing Stewardship (John 13)

In John 13, Jesus redefines authority by washing His disciples' feet, modeling servant leadership empowered by the Spirit to humble himself. Contemporary leaders replicate this by engaging in ordinary acts—making coffee for staff, sitting with the marginalized, cleaning meeting rooms—demonstrating that no task is beneath Spirit-led authority. Boardrooms begin with a foot-washing ceremony: executives wash the shoes of front-line workers, praying for Spirit-given empathy. Leadership retreats include role-reversal exercises, where senior staff serve interns, eliciting Spirit-fostered humility. Post-leadership surveys show that teams with foot-washing rituals report higher trust and morale. Recognizing servant authority as Spirit-infused countercultural practice sets a tone of mutual care that informs transparent decision-making.

7.2 Decision Transparency and Collaborative Listening Meetings

Spirit-led servant leaders practice radical transparency, sharing decision rationales—budget allocations, hiring choices, strategic pivots—in open forums. Collaborative listening meetings invite employees or congregants to voice concerns and Spirit-given ideas before final votes. Leaders begin each session with prayer, asking the Spirit to guard hearts and illuminate blind spots. Active note-taking and public posting of meeting minutes honor the Spirit's promptings for clarity and accountability. When contentious issues arise, Spirit-led facilitators guide structured dialogues that ensure all voices are heard, reducing the temptation for covert agendas. Recognizing transparency as Spirit-shaped stewardship prevents power hoarding and enables collective ownership of vision. This collaborative ethos contributes to healthy team health rhythms.

7.3 Guarding Team Health—Empathy, Rhythms of Rest, Celebration

Servant leaders under the Spirit prioritize team well-being: they schedule regular check-ins, use pulse surveys to measure stress, and enforce "no-meeting" days for focused work and rest. Leaders model healthy boundaries by taking sabbaticals, turning off email notifications on weekends, and openly celebrating burnout recovery as wise stewardship rather than indulgence. Empathy training workshops, guided by Spirit-led case studies, teach active listening and trauma awareness. Quarterly "Spirit Retreat Days" include guided prayer, creative expression, and communal meals—moments for the team to receive Spirit renewal together. Recognizing team health as Spirit's concern cultivates environments where creativity, resilience, and loyalty flourish, leading into strategic succession planning.

7.4 Succession Planning: Raising Spirit-Anointed Next-Gen Leaders

Healthy organizations embrace Spirit-led succession, intentionally identifying and mentoring future leaders long before vacancies arise. Servant leaders pray for prophetic insight into each team member's gifting, then create development pathways—job rotations, leadership shadowing, spiritual retreats—tailored to those gifts. Annual "handover rituals" symbolically pass keys or stoles to emerging leaders, accompanied by Spirit-inspired prayers of commissioning. Feedback loops ensure that successors receive Spirit-provided correction and affirmation as they step into responsibility.

Recognizing succession planning as Spirit-ordained process secures organizational continuity and honors divine gifting. As leadership structures renew, these teams stand ready to foster stewardship of body, mind, and emotion.

8 Stewarding Body, Mind, and Emotional Health

8.1 Temple Theology Applied to Nutrition, Sleep, and Movement

Acknowledging 1 Corinthians 6:19–20's temple theology, believers view their bodies as sacred Spirit dwellings, warranting care in nutrition, rest, and exercise. Spirit-led discernment guides personal diets: one might fast from processed foods while praying for Spirit clarity, or incorporate fasting cycles that echo Jewish sabbaths over years (Leviticus 25). Sleep hygiene becomes a spiritual practice: evening breath prayers and Scripture reflections prepare the body-temple for restorative rest. Movement—walking prayer, yoga-informed postures, sports—becomes embodied worship as participants pray for the Spirit's renewal with each step or stretch. Church wellness ministries organize Spirit-filled fitness classes—praying between intervals—integrating spiritual and physical disciplines. Recognizing the body as mortal temple under the Spirit's care counters neglect and supports holistic health journeys, transitioning into distinctions between mindfulness and Spirit-fullness.

8.2 Mindfulness versus Spirit-Fullness—Similarities and Distinctions

While secular mindfulness emphasizes present-moment awareness, Spirit-fullness situates presence within the triune God's abiding fellowship. Both practices slow cognitive churn, but Spirit-full mindfulness—rooted in the Spirit's witness—discerns divine direction rather than mere detachment. Meditation on Scripture, guided by the Spirit, transforms mental focus into relational engagement, whereas secular mindfulness often lacks an external referent. Retreat guides teach participants to notice bodily sensations, name them as possible Spirit promptings, and respond with breath prayers. Workshops contrast secular breath-counting with breath prayers that invoke the Spirit, underscoring how the same techniques differ depending on ultimate object of attention. Recognizing these distinctions equips believers to borrow helpful attentional skills while preserving Christ-centered intentionality. This integrative perspective readies souls for processing anxiety with lament and gratitude.

8.3 Processing Anxiety with Lament, Gratitude, and Trusted Companions

Anxiety, the hallmark of modern life, finds remedy in Spirit-led lament and gratitude practices combined with community support. Lament psalms such as 42 and 77 provide language for expressing fears and doubts before God, inviting the Spirit's empathy and guidance. Following lament, structured gratitude lists—documenting three Spirit-given blessings daily—reorient brains toward hope (1 Thess 5:18). Trusted companions, trained in Spirit-sensitive listening, walk alongside those wrestling with chronic anxiety, offering prayer and perspective. Pastoral care teams integrate cognitive-behavioral tools—thought logs, grounding exercises—with Spirit-led prayer to address rumination. Community prayer corridors—small groups meeting midweek—offer safe spaces to voice anxieties and pray for Spirit peace. Recognizing anxiety as a pathway for deeper reliance on the Spirit reframes distress into discipleship. These holistic care networks transition into formal resourcing through therapy and medical care.

8.4 Resourcing Therapy and Medical Care as Spirit Gifts, Not Rivals

The Spirit's healing work encompasses clinical and pastoral resources in synergy rather than competition. Psychology and psychiatry offer diagnostic clarity—depression inventories, trauma assessments—that the Spirit uses to plan recovery. Pastors refer parishioners to licensed professionals when spiritual care alone is insufficient, trusting that the Spirit can operate through secular vocations. Therapy sessions begin and end with prayer, inviting Spirit oversight over cognitive restructuring and emotional healing. Medical interventions—medications for anxiety, dietary supplements—are accepted as Spirit gifts enabling individuals to participate more fully in communal life. Ethical guidelines ensure informed consent and spiritual privacy. Recognizing clinical care as complement to spiritual direction avoids false dichotomies and reflects Paul's holistic anthropology. This integrated stewardship of body, mind, and emotions ensures believers are whole-hearted participants in the Spirit's redemptive mission.

9 Technology, Attention, and Discernment

9.1 Algorithmic Liturgies—How Apps Catechize the Soul

Algorithm-driven apps curate content—daily devotionals, worship playlists, prayer prompts—based on past engagement, subtly shaping believers' spiritual diets. Users quickly discover that the "For You" feed reflects earlier selections, creating a feedback loop that reinforces existing preferences rather than challenging growth. The Spirit, however, often leads us beyond comfort; when an app repeatedly suggests only upbeat worship songs, the absence of lament psalms may signal a need for broader pneumatological input (Psalm 13). Discernment requires users to ask whether the content aligns with Scripture's full emotional range—joy, sorrow, conviction, comfort—and to occasionally override algorithmic suggestions. Developers and church leaders can work together to introduce surprise elements in digital liturgies: random Scripture verses, guest-created prayers, and community-sourced testimonies. This communal curation under Spirit guidance ensures that technology serves rather than enslaves our attention. Believers learn to evaluate "suggested content" against biblical norms—does this hymn extol God's holiness or only affirm my feelings? Over time, conscious curation trains the soul to detect the Spirit's nudges, even when they diverge from app algorithms. Families can practice together by comparing devotional recommendations and praying for Spirit-led discernment. In small groups, participants share moments when an algorithmic prompt felt discordant with the Spirit's leading, turning these into teachable "algorithm check" discussions. Recognizing algorithmic liturgies as potential catechisms of the soul prompts intentional countermeasures—manual overrides, diversified sources, periodic digital fasts—ensuring that the Spirit, not software, directs our worship.

9.2 Designing Attention Rules: "Screen–Sabbath," Notification Triage

To counter screen overload, communities establish "screen–Sabbath" periods—regular blocks of time when all devices are silent or off. During these intervals, believers practice analog fellowship: face-to-face conversations, letter writing, unstructured play, or silent contemplation. Notification triage further refines attention: color-coded categories (red for emergencies, yellow for community prayer updates, green for personal study resources) guide which alerts are allowed through. Before enabling any app's notifications, users pause to ask the Spirit if they truly need that input now, fostering disciplined dependence rather than reactive pings. Offices and homes post visual reminders—"Pause for the Spirit"—to resist the impulse to check screens reflexively. When a sudden notification breaks silence, individuals pause for a breath prayer before opening, distinguishing urgent from distracting. In pastoral settings, leaders model notification triage by only responding to urgent communications during designated hours. Over weeks, the Spirit rewires attention patterns; the mind becomes less fragmented, more capable of sustained prayer or study. Families practice collective notification silences during meals, Sabbath afternoons, and bedtime routines, deepening relational presence. Recognizing these attention rules as Spirit–inspired disciplines transforms screens from masters into servants of our spiritual life.

9.3 Holy Curiosity: Leveraging Tech for Mission and Learning

Rather than rejecting technology outright, believers cultivate "holy curiosity," exploring how digital tools can advance the gospel. Online language-learning apps enable missionaries to acquire basic greetings and Scripture verses in target languages before deployment, under Spirit guidance for cultural sensitivity. Virtual reality simulations offer safe training grounds for cross-cultural evangelism, allowing learners to practice Spirit–led conversation patterns with AI-driven interlocutors. Social media platforms become mission fields when Christians disciple small online groups, sharing Spirit-inspired devotionals and facilitating prayer chains. Webinars on theological topics, streamed globally, invite Spirit–birthed interactions across time zones—Q&A segments revealing shared burdens and prompting communal intercession. Podcasts featuring local saints tell Spirit–wrought testimonies that inspire hospitality and partnership in distant contexts. Technology incubators in churches spark Spirit–led solutions for community issues—food-waste apps, elder-care scheduling platforms—integrating faith and innovation. Recognizing tech as a mission multiplier under the Spirit's hand reframes digital fluency as a vocational calling rather than mere convenience.

9.4 Digital Reconciliation—Spirit-Led Tone in Online Discourse

Online debates often devolve into polarization, but believers can apply Spirit–led principles of koinōnia (Eph 4:3–4) to digital interactions. Before commenting on social platforms, individuals pause to pray for the Spirit's wisdom—"Lord, guide my words to build up, not tear down." Tone-check tools—private drafts reviewed by prayer partners—help detect potential harshness or sarcasm. When misunderstandings arise, Spirit–prompted conciliatory private messages restore trust before public corrections. Online forums moderated by Spirit–sensitive stewards include "peace corners," where participants commit to listening prayer and refrain from argumentation. Digital reconciliation rituals may include posting apologies and prayers for unity, modeling confession in the public square. Recognizing that screen anonymity can mask humanity, believers emphasize their shared identity in Christ to temper debates with compassion. Over time, communities that practice digital reconciliation become online beacons of the Spirit's peacemaking power.

10 Hospitality, Generosity, and Justice

10.1 Opening Homes and Tables to Strangers and Neighbors

Biblical hospitality enacts Leviticus 19:34's command to "love the stranger," and the Spirit transforms ordinary meals into sacred fellowship. Hosts who pray for Spirit guidance before inviting guests often sense needs they can meet—dietary restrictions, childcare arrangements, or prayer requests. Shared tables become forums for cross-cultural exchange: a Syrian refugee family brings traditional dishes, while hosts offer prayers inspired by Isaiah 58's call to comfort the oppressed. Regular "open-house Sundays" establish predictable rhythms for introducing newcomers to community life under the Spirit's embrace. Hospitality teams train members in Spirit-led listening, ensuring every guest's story is heard with empathy. Kids learn early to set extra places at the table, internalizing the Spirit's expansive welcome. Recognizing table fellowship as a Spirit-driven ministry dissolves barriers of class, ethnicity, and faith background, preparing hearts for budgeting generosity.

10.2 Budgeting for Benevolence—Spirit-Prompted Giving Plans

Financial generosity arises from Spirit-wrought conviction rather than guilt-driven tithing. Congregations teach members to create Spirit-prompted giving plans: regular prayer over budgets results in allocations to local charities, global missions, and community initiatives. Spreadsheet tools include columns for "Prompted Projects," where individuals record Spirit inspirations—perhaps a need for school supplies or microloans—and set reminders to follow through. Small-group "charitable discernment" sessions pray over proposed gifts, seeking Spirit validation before funds are dispersed. When economic downturns hit, Spirit-led communities pivot giving toward urgent needs—food banks, eviction prevention funds—reflecting James's emphasis on practical love (James 2:15–16). Recognizing budgeting as a spiritual discipline under Spirit guidance prevents transactional giving and fosters joyful partnership in God's economy.

10.3 Advocating for the Marginalized as Isaiah 61 People

Jesus's reading of Isaiah 61 inaugurates Spirit-empowered advocacy for the poor and captives. Under Spirit conviction, church teams lobby for policy changes—minimum-wage laws, prisoner reform, refugee support—rooted in the gospel's preferential concern. Faith-based advocacy workshops incorporate role-play to help participants articulate Spirit-inspired arguments to legislators, echoing Amos's prophetic boldness in political courts. Public testimonies from those rescued by Spirit-led ministries—homeless shelters, addiction recovery—humanize policy debates. Recognizing advocacy as Spirit-initiated mission grounds civic engagement in worship, blending prayer vigils outside government offices with Psalm 82's call to defend the weak.

10.4 Community Projects: Food Banks, Legal Aid, Environmental Stewardship

Spirit-led generosity manifests in tangible community projects: food banks that distribute groceries alongside prayer cafés where volunteers pray over each bag; legal-aid clinics staffed by Christian lawyers offering pro bono counsel under Spirit-led compassion; environmental stewardship initiatives—community gardens, river clean-ups—undertaken as embodied worship. Planning teams begin each project meeting with communal prayer for the Spirit's guidance, ensuring efforts meet real needs rather than organizational agendas. Data-driven impact assessments—measuring meals served or legal cases won—are balanced by testimonies of hope restored, under Spirit promptings. Recognizing these projects as Spirit-infused ministries transforms social service into sacramental outreach, moving naturally into resilience in suffering.

11 Resilience in Suffering and Spiritual Warfare

11.1 Naming the Battle: Flesh, World, and Powers (Ephesians 6:12)

Paul's metaphor of spiritual armor acknowledges conflicts on three fronts: the flesh's desires, the world's temptations, and the demonic powers. Spirit-awareness begins by identifying which front is most active: overeating or lust indicates fleshly assault, cultural cynicism signals worldly pressure, persistent fear or oppression hints at demonic activity. In group settings, prayer teams map these battlegrounds, laying chart paper with "Flesh, World, Powers" and inviting the Spirit to spotlight areas needing armor. Personal spiritual inventories—journaling temptations and tracking their patterns—reveal where believers must apply specific armor pieces. For instance, memory of sinful shame may require the breastplate of righteousness (Isa 59:17) and the helmet of salvation (1 Thess 5:8). Recognizing the multi-layered battle under the Spirit's teaching prevents one-dimensional approaches and fosters comprehensive resilience.

11.2 Lament Psalms as Spirit-Authorized Protest

Lament psalms—Psalm 44's cry for vindication or Psalm 94's plea for justice—provide biblical models for Spirit-authorized protest against systemic evil. Churches integrate lament liturgies into spiritual warfare gatherings, alternating confession with collective petitions for God's intervention. Worship bands lead chant-like renditions of laments, enabling communal catharsis under Spirit-guided expression. Testimonies of inner release following lament gatherings underscore the Spirit's healing of anger and grief. Recognizing lament as prophetic protest brings corporate social justice under the umbrella of Spirit-led worship, transitioning into armor practices.

11.3 Armor Practices: Truth-Telling, Righteousness Acts, Gospel Readiness

Putting on the belt of truth involves regular Scripture memorization and mutual accountability to speak honestly in challenging contexts (John 8:32). The breastplate of righteousness comes alive through acts of justice—visiting orphans, defending the oppressed—that enact sanctified living (Isa 1:17). Feet shod with readiness for the gospel (Eph 6:15) manifest in spontaneous sharing of hope to the suffering. Prayer mantles—literal or symbolic—may be draped over worshipers as they pray for cultural breakthroughs, reminding them of the Spirit's presence. Recognizing these armor practices as Spirit-enabled equips believers for both internal and external battles.

11.4 Hope Routines—Future-Oriented Imagination, Communal Intercession

Hope is nurtured by envisioning God's promised future: reading Revelation 21 passages or meditating on Isaiah 65's new heavens.

Small groups create "vision boards" with Spirit-inspired images and Scripture, revisiting them weekly in prayer. Corporate intercession shifts from problem lists to prophetic declarations—"Let the desert bloom"—anticipating Spirit-wrought revival in communities. Hope routines conclude with celebration songs and shared testimonies of recent breakthroughs. Recognizing hope routines as Spirit-energized practices sustains resilience through prolonged trials and readies communities for creative engagement with creativity and worship.

15 Lifelong Growth and Finishing Well

15.1 Spiritual Friendship Triads for Sustained Accountability

Triads—groups of three—balance intimacy with confidentiality, enabling Spirit-led accountability that resists both peer pressure and loneliness. Each member rotates in roles: the one who shares, the empathic listener, and the Spirit-led pray-er. Meetings begin with a brief examen, noting consolations and desolations, and invite the Spirit to highlight growth areas. Over months, triad members track prayer requests, answer follow-up questions, and celebrate answered prayers, fostering mutual encouragement. Spiritual friendships modeled after David and Jonathan (1 Sam 18) emphasize covenant loyalty under the Spirit's guidance. Triads also practice "iron sharpening" dialogues, gently confronting areas of unrepentance with Spirit-infused love (Prov 27:17). Recognizing triads as lifelong companions ensures that no believer journeys alone, preparing hearts for midlife reevaluations.

15.2 Midlife Reevaluation—Spirit-Guided Pruning and New Fruitfulness

Midlife is often marked by questioning prior achievements and seeking renewed purpose. The Spirit leads in pruning—letting go of worn-out roles or destructive habits—while prompting new fruitfulness in emerging seasons. Retreats for midlife reevalutions include guided solitude, where participants listen for Spirit whispers identifying what to discard and what to embrace. Group dialogues share stories of unexpected callings—second-career ministry, creative arts, mentoring—that arose in Spirit-led transitions. Spiritual directors help midlifers discern vocational pivots with three-stranded-cord frameworks, checking Scripture, community, and inner witness. Journals document old dreams laid to rest and new visions born, mapping Spirit's ongoing leading. Recognizing midlife reevaluation as

Spirit seasons of pruning and sowing fosters hopeful renewal rather than midlife crisis.

15.3 Elderhood as Blessing Reservoir: Intercession, Wisdom Letters

As believers age, the Spirit gifts them with accumulated wisdom—life lessons, answered prayers, tested character—that becomes a reservoir of blessing for younger generations. Elders are encouraged to write "wisdom letters" to mentees, recording Spirit-illuminated insights on faith, marriage, and ministry. Communities host "Elders' Circles," where seniors pray corporately for emerging leaders, invoking the Spirit's commissioning. Health permitting, elders join intergenerational mission teams, offering Spirit-led encouragement to peers on the field. Recognizing elderhood as Spirit-appointed spiritual capital reframes aging as service rather than decline, completing the arc of lifelong growth.

Conclusion The practical pathways outlined here transform the lofty call to walk by the Spirit into tangible rhythms and routines that permeate every facet of life. From heightened awareness in simple tasks to structured discernment, virtue formation, and sustainable disciplines, these practices invite the Spirit to shape habit, heart, and community. As individuals and congregations adopt rules of life, breath-based prayers, corporate fasts, and Sabbath delights, they cultivate a living environment where the Spirit's fruit and gifts flourish. This integrated discipleship ensures that the renewal we have traced through Scripture, tradition, and global movements finds expression in humble obedience, joyful service, and relentless hope—embodying what it truly means to live in step with the Spirit.

www.ingramcontent.com/pod-product-compliance
Lightning Source LLC
LaVergne TN
LVHW051540080426
835510LV00020B/2798